CHICAGO'S INDUSTRIAL DECLINE

CHICAGO'S INDUSTRIAL DECLINE

The Failure of Redevelopment, 1920–1975

Robert Lewis

CORNELL UNIVERSITY PRESS   ITHACA AND LONDON

First published 2020 by Cornell University Press
Printed in the United States of America

Library of Congress Cataloging-in-Publication Data

Names: Lewis, Robert D., 1954– author.
Title: Chicago's industrial decline : the failure of redevelopment, 1920–1975 /
    Robert Lewis.
Description: Ithaca [New York] : Cornell University Press, 2020. |
    Includes bibliographical references and index.
Identifiers: LCCN 2020012527 (print) | LCCN 2020012528 (ebook) |
    ISBN 9781501752629 (hardcover) | ISBN 9781501752643 (pdf) |
    ISBN 9781501752636 (epub)
Subjects: LCSH: Industrialization—Illinois—Chicago—History—20th century. |
    City planning—Illinois—Chicago—History—20th century. | Chicago (Ill.)—
    Economic conditions—20th century.
Classification: LCC HC108.C4 L493 2020 (print) | LCC HC108.C4 (ebook) |
    DDC 338.9773/1100904—dc23
LC record available at https://lccn.loc.gov/2020012527
LC ebook record available at https://lccn.loc.gov/2020012528

Contents

Tables

Figures

Acknowledgments

Every book has people who contributed in various ways to its making. This, my third and final book on the historical geographies of industrial Chicago, is no different. In fact, many of the same people that played a part, both large and small, in the previous two have figured in the fashioning of this one. To start at the top, I need to thank Virginia McLaren and Rick DiFrancesco, the two most recent chairs of the Department of Geography and Planning here at the University of Toronto, for the terrific institutional support they have given me over many years. I would also like to extend many thanks to department staff—most important, Kathy Geisbrecht, Maria Wowk, Jessica Finlayson, Tas Hudani, and Yvonne Kenny—for their help over the years. A bunch of department colleagues—Alana Boland, Matt Farish, Paul Hess, Debby Leslie, Scott Prudham, and Katherine Rankin—have sustained me through some difficult times and I thank them very much for their friendship.

A Social Science and Humanities Research Grant, "Industrial urban renewal and the industrial change, Chicago, 1930–1973," allowed me to visit archives in Chicago and Washington, DC. I would like to thank the staff at the Municipal Reference Collection and Special Collections departments at the Harold Washington Library Center, Chicago; the Special Collections and University Archives of the University of Illinois, Chicago; the Special Collections Research Center of the University of Chicago; the Chicago Historical Museum; and the National Archives at College Park for their assistance. I should add that the staff at the interlibrary loan office at the University of Toronto went out of their way to help me locate hard-to-find sources from a variety of locales.

I have been very lucky to have worked with Cornell University Press. The editorial staff—most notably Michael McGandy, Susan Specter, and Clare Kirkpatrick Jones—have been superb. Two of the book's readers, Dominic Pacyga and Domenic Vitiello, provided generous, incisive, and thoughtful remarks on the first draft. The book is much better because of their comments. I would like to thank Florence Grant for her copyediting skills. The book's excellent index was compiled by Celia Braves. Thank you.

I would like to extend a special thanks to Nick Lombardo, who has provided me with unrivalled research and intellectual support over the last ten years. A student and now a friend, Nick's intelligence, judgement, and enthusiasm have played a huge part in the making of this book as well as my previous one on the calculative politics of industrial property in wartime Chicago.

The writing of this book bears the weight of great personal loss. I would like to thank my children, Yonah and Lev, and their partners, Sandra and Erin, and my family friends, Mark, Julia, Nadya, Gord, Kathy, Richard, Susan, Betsy, and others who have done so much to help me work through this difficult period. I have been greatly heartened by the fact that my first grandchild was born on the day after I had completed the proofs. She is the daughter of Yonah and Sandra, who use words in quite different ways in their work than I do. My hope is that Pearl Lila will absorb all sorts of words and use them to make her part of the world a better place.

Abbreviations

AEC	Atomic Energy Commission
CACI	Chicago Association of Commerce and Industry
CARDC	Chicago Area Research and Development Council
CECD	Mayor's Committee for Economic and Cultural Development
CHA	Chicago Housing Authority
CLCC	Chicago Land Clearance Commission
CPC	Chicago Plan Commission
CREB	Chicago Real Estate Board
DUR	Department of Urban Renewal, Chicago
EDA	Economic Development Administration
EDC	Economic Development Commission
IIT	Illinois Institute of Technology
MPC	Metropolitan Planning Council
MPHC	Metropolitan Planning and Housing Council
MRC	Municipal Reference Collection, Harold Washington Library Center, Chicago
NARA-CP	National Archives at College Park, Maryland
NWSPB	Near West Side Planning Board
PHN	Proquest Historical Newspapers
R&D	research and development
SSPB	South Side Planning Board
UICSC	University of Illinois, Chicago, Special Collections and University Archives

CHICAGO'S INDUSTRIAL DECLINE

Introduction

VISIONS OF CHICAGO

The great advantages inherent in Chicago's location as a focal point of rail, truck, water, and air routes and, therefore, its accessibility to raw materials and markets will undoubtedly continue to be decisive in maintaining and enhancing Chicago's pre-eminence in manufacturing.

Chicago Plan Commission, 1951

In 1973, Chicago's leading business organization, the Chicago Association of Commerce and Industry (CACI), published a promotional booklet that outlined the city's attractions for industry.[1] *Invest in Chicago* called on financial companies, developers, and industrial firms from across the country to invest in the region's manufacturing. The writer laid out the area's locational assets: low construction and transport costs, numerous industries, a welcoming business climate, and a diverse labor force. None of these were unexpected for anybody who knew anything about plant location; these variables had been trotted out as enticements to industrial managers by urban boosters for more than a hundred years. This locational trope had shaped the rhetorical and material understanding of the industrial United States for some time. Postwar Chicago, it was believed, had been and would continue to be one of the United States' more important centers for industrial investment.

Despite framing the Chicago metropolitan region as an attractive place for industrial investment, the tone of the CACI publication is downbeat, almost somber. It appears as if the booklet's writers were resigned to the fact that Chicago was no longer the industrial dynamo it once was: "There is no such thing as a perfect metropolitan area in the light of business requirements. On balance, the Chicago Area is attractive to firms."[2] For a promotional publication, this is a remarkably candid statement: one that just a few years earlier would have been unthinkable. Since the 1830s, people and groups of all persuasions had actively pushed the city's strengths, pointing to the advantages available to manufacturers.[3] These promotional activities were one reason why Chicago, despite intense competition from Saint Louis, Pittsburgh, and New York, had managed to become one of the world's great industrial cities by the end of the nineteenth century.

A generation earlier, in 1957, the CACI had put out another promotional document. The essays assembled in *Chicago's New Horizons* had a more confident tone than *Invest in Chicago*. Alan Sturdy, the publication's editor, boasted that this was the moment to celebrate the "phenomenal growth" that had taken place since World War II. In this short time, the population had grown by 1.4 million, four hundred thousand new dwelling units had been built, and $3 billion had been invested in new factories. All this, Sturdy opined, made Chicago a "great modern metropolitan community" and "destined to continue its recent phenomenal rate of growth." Speaking in the same vein, Charles Willson of the CACI's Industrial Development Division extolled the locational "advantages" that "put Chicago far ahead of any other center." The region's steel firms were "magnets drawing countless new plants to the Chicago area."[4] The features that had made Chicago a great industrial center in the nineteenth century, such as a diversified labor force, an excellent transportation system, and a powerful industrial bourgeoisie, continued to drive the city's economic development in the 1950s.[5] The difference in tone about the status and future of the city in the two CACI publications could not have been starker.

Why the difference in tone between *Invest in Chicago* and earlier studies? It wasn't simply a chance difference, unreflective of how city leaders saw their industrial future. By the 1970s, something had taken place that forced local elites to reassess Chicago's industrial development. City leaders in the 1950s still believed that by mobilizing its manufacturing strengths, Chicago would avoid the industrial vicissitudes troubling other cities such as Detroit and Philadelphia. By the 1970s, however, factory doors had closed in unprecedented numbers, investors had fled to other regions, and manufacturing employment had fallen dramatically. These troubles forced the CACI and other civic organizations to accept industrial decline as central to the urban economy. They had to admit, albeit grudgingly, that the previously taken-for-granted dominance of the area's unrivalled locational assets no longer prevailed. The processes of capitalist cumulative causation that had driven Chicago's growth since the mid-nineteenth century were no longer operative; agglomeration economies had become diseconomies. Indeed, by the 1970s, it was obvious to most observers that the city was in a spiral of industrial decline.

The reluctance of Chicago's postwar civic and business leaders before the 1970s to accept what in hindsight is obvious is understandable. They had good reason to have as much faith in the local economy as they did in capitalism, and they had an unwavering belief in the latter. To question the former would have been difficult at the best of times, but to do so in the postwar years when the US capitalist economy was pitted against the Soviet command one would have been to question both the idea of the United States as a political entity and capitalism as an economic system. The belief that the American way of life was superior to the Soviet one was deeply embedded in the industrial power of US cities. To ask whether Chicago was in decline would have been tantamount to questioning the nation's economic and social system.[6]

But the city of Chicago's manufacturing was in decline. With the exception of the expansion that accompanied wartime industrial mobilization, the city had experienced varying degrees of relative and absolute industrial decline from the interwar years. A slow decline of manufacturing jobs is apparent during the 1930s and well under way after World War II. There were fewer manufacturing jobs in 1958 than there were in 1929. At the same time, the city's share of metropolitan industrial jobs fell from more than three-quarters in 1929 to less than half by 1972. By Lyndon Johnson's presidency, many of the industries that had made Chicago a leading economic center after 1850 had departed or were in terminal decline, leaving behind a devastated and deindustrialized landscape in the city.[7]

In the pages that follow, I examine Chicago's industrial decline and the response of the city's place-dependent bourgeoisie to its fading fortunes. The book begins by charting the history of industrial change between 1920 and 1975 and then looks at the creation of industrial redevelopment programs in the city of Chicago in the postwar years as city leaders responded to these industrial changes. I make three broad arguments.

First, I argue that the city of Chicago experienced industrial decline from the 1920s. Most studies of the rise and fall of urban manufacturing have dated decline to the 1970s. By all measures, however, the city of Chicago, and this was the case in most northern cities, experienced structural and nonreversible industrial decline after World War I. This decline was part of a broader process of capitalist investment decision-making that evaluated industrial property in terms of its profitability. One effect of this was to create two quite different sets of industrial spaces in metropolitan Chicago: the city and the suburbs. While industrial executives viewed city land as blighted, inadequate, and unprofitable, they regarded suburban space more positively; Chicago's industrial decline was inextricably linked to the industrialization of the suburbs.[8] The result of these processes of employment change and factory investment that occurred between 1920 and 1970 would reformulate the industrial geography of metropolitan Chicago.

Second, I argue that city leaders implemented several industrial renewal initiatives in the postwar period in an attempt to reverse industrial decline. Even though they might have wished to ignore the economic realities that plagued the postwar city, they had little choice but to try to staunch the inexorable bleeding of manufacturing jobs from Chicago. Two main redevelopment blocs emerged after 1940, both of which used federal funds to refashion the built environment. One, which developed around the machinations of the Metropolitan Housing and Planning Council looked to create a postindustrial city that housed a range of corporate control and command functions. The building of this postindustrial city, it was believed, required replacing old working-class, African American, and manufacturing districts with new, high-end, white residential areas, commercial and leisure centers, and modernist office towers.[9]

The other bloc consisted of place-dependent groups with strong business and political ties to the success of the city's industry. A concern of these groups was to find ways to reinvigorate the city's industrial base. In this case, the answer was industrial renewal. In the 1950s and 1960s, agencies such as the Chicago Land Clearance Commission and the Mayor's Committee for Economic and Cultural Development devised a range of programs with the dual purpose of stopping factory closings and attracting firms to the city. The strategies planned to address capital disinvestment were centered on an institutional fix that linked industrial property relations, blight, and renewal. These place-dependent interests sought to convert blighted residential and industrial properties into new modern industrial sites. This, so the argument went, would draw greater investment to the city.[10]

My final argument is that industrial renewal failed for two reasons. One was that the place-dependent coalitions of developers, financiers, politicians, small business owners, and industrial managers that worked to counter deindustrialization were fighting a losing battle. The forces of industrial decline were simply far too powerful. The pull of locations in the suburbs, the Sunbelt, and sites outside the United States was too strong to keep industry in Chicago. The widening search by corporate industrial and financial capital for more profitable locales ensured that the city's neglected industrial spaces were no longer competitive. By 1975, in spite of more than twenty-five years of industrial renewal programming, the city's industrial base remained extremely fragile. The hollowing of the city's manufacturing base had been under way for fifty years; it could not be resuscitated by the patchwork industrial renewal policies established by the city's bourgeoisie.

The other reason for the failure of industrial renewal was that it was undermined by coalitions looking to build a postindustrial city on the ruins of the industrial one.[11] From the 1950s, alliances consisting of people from real estate, health, education, finance, and government pushed a new vision for Chicago, one that Larry Bennett calls the "Third City."[12] These coalitions sought to reap profits by building corporate office and middle-class residential projects and bringing the white middle class back to the central city.[13] By the 1980s, postindustrialism was well under way, ensuring that Chicago was "transformed from a regional hub serving local companies to a global financial and logistics center."[14] These efforts were focused on the Loop and the adjacent areas north and west of the Chicago River. While these districts became home to high-end residential neighborhoods and gleaming office towers, large swathes of the city remained in extremely poor conditions. As Brian Berry had noted, these local interests created "islands of renewal in seas of decay."[15]

The result of these efforts to build a segregated and differentiated city undermined attempts by the place-dependent bourgeoisie to reverse the city's industrial fortunes. The postindustrial coalition was able to exercise more effective territorial control than the smaller and less powerful industrial one by linking the decline of manufacturing to the need for new spaces to house the new sectors of the postindustrial economy and the white middle class. This, it was argued, would be an effective means of preserving the city's place in the US urban hierarchy, creating a modern economy, and generating new avenues for profit making. While the benefits of the shift to a postindustrial place can be debated, the impact of the actions of the city's civic and business leaders on local industry cannot. The postindustrial economy was built on the ruins of the industrial one.

The Roots of Industrial Decline

Barry Bluestone and Bennett Harrison's 1982 announcement that deindustrialization began in the 1970s has profoundly shaped our understanding of industrial decline in both the United States and the industrial cities of the Manufacturing Belt.[16] They characterized the period before the 1960s as one of low unemployment, rising incomes, and declining inequality. These years were the "postwar glory days" when most Americans experienced increasing economic prosperity.[17] Others agreed. A study of Great Lakes cities argues that the 1960s was a period of "strong national economic growth," while the 1970s ushered in inexorable industrial decline.[18] One authoritative online encyclopedia entry states that deindustrialization "began in the 1970s," and is associated "with cheap industrial imports from newly industrialized countries as well as with the ongoing transformation of the maturing economy of the United States itself."[19]

From this perspective, deindustrialization replaced the glory days of US manufacturing after 1970, as industrial managers closed factory doors in northern cities and moved plants to the American South or overseas. Summarizing a generation of industrial decline studies, Bluestone states that the impact of economic change from the late 1960s was "cataclysmic," as postwar economic growth was replaced by violent and unprecedented economic restructuring.[20] Despite the cracks that appeared in urban economies after World War II, it was during the

1970s that regional and international competition led to large-scale industrial decline. A 1984 study of national industrial change notes that "the convergence of the recent recession, a secular decline in the rate of growth, and the accelerating structural reorientation" led to massive employment decline, with the loss of more than five million manufacturing jobs between 1976 and 1982.[21]

The narrative, however, tells only part of the story of the United States' urban decline. Several historians have challenged this view, arguing that deindustrialization did not emerge suddenly in the 1970s, and push the origins of decline to the postwar years. Indeed, as I show here, the industrial distress experienced in the 1970s had been in place for at least fifty years in Chicago and other northern industrial cities. Some date the decline from the early postwar years. In his study of postwar Detroit, Tom Sugrue argues that "the 1950s marked a decisive turning point in the development of the city—a systematic restructuring of the local economy from which the city never fully recovered." What was new, and what distinguished the 1950s from earlier times, was a permanent reduction in the industrial workforce and widespread plant closings. In his opinion, these years were the first "sign of long-term economic problems." This was "not just a momentary economic lull" but "the beginning of a long-term and steady decline in manufacturing employment that affected Detroit and almost all other major Northeastern and Midwestern industrial cities."[22] One of these was Chicago.

In a similar vein, Steven High argues that decline in the industrial North began after World War II, when firms undertook two primary locational practices: relocation and plant obsolescence. Both of these involved the large-scale movement of capital from one location to another.[23] Mark McColloch notes that deindustrialization was under way in the steel and electronic industries after 1945; the 1979–83 economic depression was simply an "acceleration of trends that already existed."[24] Dominic Pacyga makes the case that the decline of Chicago's "old-line industries," such as food processing, furniture, and apparel, was well under way during World War II.[25] For some scholars, permanent industrial decline started in the 1940s and 1950s, and accelerated from the late 1960s.

For others though, industrial decline can be dated back to the interwar period, if not earlier. Pittsburgh lost iron, shipbuilding, textile, and cigar industries from the 1920s. The postwar decline of its steel, glass, and aluminum industries continued prewar patterns. Some writers have pushed the story back even further, arguing that "industrial growth and industrial decline have been standard features of the American economy since the early nineteenth century." From nineteenth-century saddle making to early twentieth-century shipbuilding, industrial decline had been integral to the everyday experience of specific locales at different times.[26] In his study of Philadelphia, Philip Scranton argues that "at the regional level, the real erosion of the central city as a favored location for large firms" was clearly under way by the late 1920s.[27] As Domenic Vitiello has noted, the decline of the city's Bush Hill area after 1890 was symptomatic of the industrial restructuring that was sweeping through northern industrial cities by the early twentieth century.[28]

Other authors have made the same point. In a study of a Yonkers textile firm, the decline of the New England textile industry from the 1880s is shown to be the result of a corporate strategy of capital migration to southern states. By the early 1920s, half of all textile production was located in the South, and this movement continued after 1945. Lower wages and taxes, less productive plants, higher worker expectations, and aggressive regional boosterism combined to precipitate the shutdown of northern mills and the expansion of southern ones.[29] Elsewhere, the first signs of permanent decline were felt in the Pennsylvania anthracite coal region from the 1920s.[30] Similarly, Jefferson Cowie outlines the early origins of deindustrialization in Camden, New Jersey. In the mid-1930s, Camden accounted for almost all the manufacturing operations of RCA, one of the country's largest electrical appliance makers; ten years later, the city's share had declined to a quarter. Work was siphoned off to the company's other plants in the immediate postwar period so as to exploit lower wage rates and to exercise greater managerial control at the new plants.[31] As these studies suggest, many of the processes that devastated the Manufacturing Belt's economy after 1970 were operating much earlier in the region's central cities, industrial towns, and resource districts.

Much of the work on deindustrialization has focused on two scales. The first is regional. In this case, the industrial decline of the Manufacturing Belt in the 1970s is linked to the rise of the Sunbelt. The problem with this approach is that the region is conceptualized as a coherent entity in which economic processes have similar effects. It assumes that different regions, however defined, undergo change in the very same way. The result is that the entire Manufacturing Belt is considered to have experienced the rusting of its industrial base, while the Sunbelt uniformly felt the benefits of industrial growth. This is not what happened.

This problematic reading of the Rust Belt and Sunbelt ignores the specificity of place to make the argument about regional change. One source of this framing is that capital investment is considered to operate at the national scale and to have regional effects. It can be argued that Bluestone and Harrison set the tone and the agenda for national studies of deindustrialization. Longitudinal, statistical examinations of the United States and of regions were undertaken with an emphasis on employment and unemployment, plant openings and closings, and investment and disinvestment in order to show that the Manufacturing Belt's industrial base had been crumbling since the early 1970s.

The second scale is local. Writers have shown that undifferentiated urban regions, from single-industry cities such as Youngstown and Flint to diversified metropolitan areas such as Buffalo and Philadelphia, all experienced decline at the same time.[32] This idea engendered a series of detailed studies of distressed places that examined the effects of deindustrialization, such as high rates of unemployment and increased social problems.[33] In some cases, these studies ignored the position of suburban areas, pointing only to the changes taking place to the city's industrial base. In others, they incorporated the suburbs into the analysis but uncritically included them with the city. The result was an undifferentiated metropolitan area in which the linked processes of disinvestment and investment had similar effects across quite different spaces over an extended time period.

What is missing from this perspective is the place specificity of economic activity. Even those spaces considered economically and politically coherent, such as regions and metropolitan areas, exhibit quite different industrial patterns within their boundaries. The interconnections within a place and between places contribute to a range of spatial outcomes. The competition between different locales for industry and the exhaustion of a propulsive industry have local effects as well as regional and national ones. An important difference that writers on industrial decline have ignored is the one between the Manufacturing Belt's central cities and suburbs. Although they are part of the same metropolitan region, the city and the suburbs have quite different economic assets that are affected in quite different ways by the same processes. Cities and suburbs are subject to uneven development in the same way that regions are.

In other words, industrial decline is multiscalar. It occurs simultaneously at the national, regional, and local levels but with different effects in different places over time. In his study of Trenton, New Jersey, John Cumbler shows that the city experienced its greatest growth between the 1830s and the 1920s. He argues that the cause of the city's decline after 1900 was the business elites' inability to make the shift from civic capitalism (on which the city was built) to bureaucratic capitalism (which developed in the late nineteenth and early twentieth centuries). Nonlocal capital came to dominate, and Trenton's industrial affairs were taken over by corporate interests with little or no concern for local matters.[34] A firm in Trenton became just one of many economic units across the country placed within a corporate calculus of profits and market share. The story is the same in Philadelphia; city-based specialty firms were replaced by national corporations from the 1920s.[35] In his study of the Sellers, an important Philadelphia industrial family, Vitiello argues that "national capitalism would eclipse their mode of family capitalism." As with Trenton and elsewhere, the loss of local economic power engendered large-scale manufacturing loss and had "devastating consequences" for the city.[36]

Corporate capitalism had a twofold effect on local economies: it both undermined and strengthened them. In the cases of Trenton, Pittsburgh, Philadelphia, and Chicago, corporate scale and scope economies weakened central-city locational assets. In some cases, this led to firms' moving out of the city. In others, firms slowly disinvested, causing plants to fall into physical disrepair and productive inefficiencies. Factories closed as production was transferred to newer sites in the suburbs or other areas across the country. The more flexible and smaller staple producers that dominated sectors such as textile, clothing, furniture, and machine tools were unable to implement the strategies used by the bulk and staple firms found in other sectors. In his analysis of Philadelphia's textile industry, Scranton notes that flexible and batch producers "simply ran down their capitals, liquidating on the death of the proprietor or when insolvency threatened." These trends did not occur at the same time in all sectors. Decline was lagged and sequential within and between sectors, occurring in different ways at different times. Nevertheless, these processes contributed to the decline of central cities' industrial bases after 1920.[37]

In other words, a different picture emerges of the industrial histories of US urban districts after 1920 if we view the city and suburbs as different places with different industries. To understand the long histories of (de)industrialization forces us to explore the impact of differential place-based economic growth.[38] Several writers have noted that the suburbs became home to an increasing share of the nation's industry after 1920.[39] This work, however, has ignored the connection between industrial decline and suburbanization, and has not taken note of differential sectoral trajectories. Rather, the focus has been to describe and explain industrial decentralization, with the aim of showing how industrial clusters emerged on the metropolitan fringe. The notion that postwar suburbanization before 1945 was linked to deindustrialization has not been pursued.

A key finding of this book is that industrial decline in Chicago had a specific intrametropolitan geography from the early twentieth century. While the forces driving deindustrialization after 1970 may have swept across many of the older industrial regions of the United States, industrial decline before then operated at a different spatial scale. The closing of factories, the loss of employment, and low reinvestment in older facilities that haunted the Rust Belt after the postwar glory days had its parallels in the pre–World War II period. The suburbs become the growth engine of metropolitan development, leaving the central cities behind. As industry flocked to the Chicago suburbs from the 1920s, the story in the city of Chicago was quite different. Industrial growth in the suburbs after 1945 was paralleled by large-scale decline in most of the central city's industrial districts.

Redevelopment, Property, and Dependency

One response to the decline of a city's manufacturing was industrial renewal. In Chicago, this involved the reassessment of industrial property relations and public-private interaction. After World War II, the problems of industrial decline forced the city's place-dependent elites to create a new calculative politics of industrial property. As a growing number of the city's elites acknowledged, the fortunes of industry were inextricably linked to the availability and quality of industrial land. Business leaders, planning and city officials, and real estate developers came to realize that they had to directly intervene in ways that would enable land to be more effectively used for industrial purposes. A growing body of commentators slowly accepted in the immediate postwar years that this aim could only be realized through the development of a federally funded postwar renewal program that refashioned both the residential and industrial districts of the United States' central cities.

Since the 1960s, scholars have identified the processes that supported the building of a modern postindustrial city on the rubble of its deindustrialized ruins.[40] Key among these are the provision of postwar federal funding for slum clearance, the building of freeways to link the city with the suburbs, the creation of a language of blight as a rationale for renewal, and the power of the real estate and the financial industries to refashion the built environment.[41] Much of this work has focused on the razing of blighted areas and the building of both public and high-end housing on redeveloped land downtown.

Urban renewal clearly reinforced the racial and class geographies of the postwar metropolitan area. As Kevin Gotham has noted, a defining feature of the US city after 1900 was the racialization of urban space.[42] The real estate industry and homeowner associations worked with local government to establish a racially segregated city through restrictive covenants and other discriminatory housing practices.[43] Accompanying the building of a racially defined dual housing market was the hardening of class residential divisions.[44] One key element of the postindustrial city that emerged after 1950 was the creation of high-end residential districts in the name of urban renewal on sites that had been inhabited by both white and minority working class.[45] In these ways, three main groups—government, grassroots associations, and the real estate industry—used urban renewal programs to solidify the discriminatory residential geographies of the city that had been put in place from the end of the nineteenth century.

Most work on urban renewal focuses on housing and commercial revitalization. The dynamics of urban renewal are clearly related to the racial and class structures of urban society; the causal link between government-funded programs of renewal, discriminatory practices in the housing market, and the refashioning of urban space to the benefit of the white middle class are clear. This dynamic is not so evident in the building of industrial renewal programs, as industrial decline and the subsequent attempts at industrial redevelopment were relatively autonomous from race. The case of the United States paralleled what was taking place in western Europe and Canada, which were also experiencing industrial decline and redevelopment.[46]

While this relationship was not causal, it wasn't coincidental either. Issues of land clearance, relocation, housing markets, and so on were both racialized and classed. The main focus of real estate agents, local government, and community leaders (both white and black) was on how these issues affected housing markets, property values, and residential conditions. For Chicago's working class and minority groups of all classes, renewal was considered to be both a threat and a promise. A threat as it undermined neighborhoods through the destruction of the area; a promise in that it offered better housing in the future.[47] These issues spilled over to those interested in industrial matters and redevelopment. In this case, concern was not so much with maintaining a dual housing market and a strict color line. Rather, the focus was on assembling land for and creating the tools to undertake industrial redevelopment.

This is one reason why little of the existing work on urban redevelopment, class politics, and the racialization of urban space has considered the place of industrial redevelopment in the broader context of government-supported urban renewal programs. Federal legislation from 1937 onward greatly favored residential development and housing renewal. This changed after World War II as the Housing Acts of 1949, 1954, and 1965 increasingly opened up federal funds for nonresidential development, most of which focused on commercial and ancillary functions.[48] While industry was not as important as housing in postwar urban renewal, it was nonetheless a concern for local civic and industrial elites alarmed about the city's industrial fortunes. Reflective of this unease are the studies of industrial renewal undertaken by cities and private and public agencies after World War II.[49] The primary concern of these studies was to assess the scale of decline and to offer solutions that required intervention by public partnerships such as land clearance agencies and redevelopment committees.

Most of the important studies of Chicago's public housing, neighborhood change, the making of the second ghetto, and urban renewal have explored various elements of the racialization of urban space and the making of class and racial barriers.[50] Little has been said about industrial redevelopment. One reason for this omission is that the scale of industrial renewal in Chicago was small compared with housing and commercial redevelopment. Nevertheless, agencies had been created by the late 1940s in Chicago that used municipal powers of eminent domain, slum clearance, and redevelopment in the name of industrial revitalization.[51] This was the case for other cities such as Saint Louis, Newark, Philadelphia, and Pittsburgh, where real estate interests, financial institutions, and local governments pushed the federal government to shift funds from residential to nonresidential uses in order to reverse industrial decline and generate profit-making land development.[52] Increasingly, business interests in Chicago, Philadelphia, and other cities in the Rust Belt came to realize that federal funds could be used to revitalize their downtown industrial districts and promote central-city economic redevelopment.[53] In many ways, the processes that underpinned industrial renewal, most notably the creation of federal renewal programs, an ideology of blight, and new forms of property relations, were the same as those for housing. But industrial redevelopment has its own history, distinct from other renewal activities.

Industrial firms are place dependent. This dependency results from the fixity of real property and the nonsubstitutability of exchange relationships. All productive activity takes place in place. Industrial sites house the built environment—land, factory, and utilities—that makes production possible. These fixed spaces require heavy capital investments that have a long time horizon and are difficult to valorize in the short run. They cannot be easily moved or dismantled. At the same time that firms are fixed by locational immobility, many are dependent on a variety of exchange relations such as labor markets, supplier networks, and government policy that are unique and difficult to replace. Once in place, many industrial facilities, even those that are part of multiunit corporate entities, operate within a specific market, much of which is local or metropolitan.[54]

For these reasons, manufacturers and other place-dependent economic interests, most notably real estate, financial, and government, are forced to reproduce profitable production conditions. They have to find an institutional fix to reduce the costs of place dependency. The long-term horizons of industrial fixed capital force local interests to coalesce around the protection of those investments that are deeply embedded in place. Industrialists and others have to acquire control over land and buildings. They have to negotiate with competing interests and with local governments. They have to operate at various scales simultaneously, from the industrial site to the federal boardroom. In sum, they have to manage various networks of power within a place and between places.[55]

One institution enlisted by industrial corporations to help reduce their place dependency is government, both local and nonlocal. Government plays three roles. First, it functions as the key decision maker mediating between different pressure groups. Second, it supports the ideological conditions for private and public relationships. Third, it provides material resources such as new infrastructures and tax incentives that enable a firm to remain in place.[56] One important way that government can minimize the problems of place dependency is through industrial redevelopment. This is what happened in Chicago, Newark, Milwaukee, and other cities after 1945, as governments under pressure from real estate and other interests introduced policies, programs, and legislation that allowed local coalitions to reshape industrial property relations and the built environment in order to defend existing investments. The intention was to minimize the negative effects of dependency and to make a place more profitable.[57]

The public-private partnership was key to the efforts to minimize place dependency and to fight industrial decline. These partnerships allocate resources from
both the public and private sectors to specific activities. In each case, relatively
autonomous agents undertake calculative relationships that have a mutually
agreed-upon productive outcome. These partnerships have three common features: differentiated but linked business and state interests and structures; a private-
sector business elite that is willing and able to collaborate with the public sector;
and an ideological structure that legitimizes such partnerships. Using the powers
of eminent domain and federal funding, the public-private partnership flourished
after 1945, as local growth coalitions responded to industrial disinvestment.[58] In
these cases, the main purpose was to revitalize the downtown by assembling and
clearing blighted land. Governed by local committees of place-based corporate
and political elites, programs were established to rebuild the city's industrial base.
Compelled by the strictures of the various postwar housing acts, private developers, financiers, and industrialists were forced to work with local government to
undertake industrial redevelopment.

City leaders saw the refashioning of property relations as the most promising means to promote industrial redevelopment. This strategy required government intervention in the local land market. Property is a system that organizes
the ownership, use, and transfer of economic assets within a society. For this
reason, the state often becomes entangled in property issues. For stretches of
time, these relations remain relatively stable, structured as they are by legislation,
power relations, custom, and state policy that is difficult to change even when
the conditions for change are favorable. Property relations, however, are neither
static nor absolute, and pressures for change emerge from the social, economic,
and political demands of the day.[59] This is what happened in US cities from the
nineteenth century. As David Schultz argues, the meaning of property changed
"from a thing-ownership to a bundle of rights . . . from a natural political to a
conventional utilitarian economic commodity."[60]

By the interwar period, industrial property was seen as a "problem" that had
to be quickly solved. The most obvious means was through the public-private
partnerships. The pressing concern of most northern urban business and civic
leaders was that inadequate central-city industrial property was causing manufacturing firms to move to suburban greenfields and locales farther afield. As
they saw it, only by refashioning the city's property market to favor industrial
producers could the city combat its declining industrial base. Changes to industrial property, it was argued, would lead to the revitalization of industry, which
would in turn provide more jobs, taxes, and profits. Previously, of course, business leaders showed little interest in government intervention in property matters. The prerogatives of capital were barely disturbed, even with the increased

intervention of New Deal programs. This position only began to change in many industrial cities after 1945, with the crisis induced by relentless industrial decline. One area in which civic and business leaders welcomed government assistance was the creation of good-quality industrial land.[61]

The understanding of property as a commodity with a specific and malleable set of rights was deployed in several important ways by those looking to refashion the city. From the 1920s, both the government and the courts became heavily involved in renegotiating the relationship of industry, property, zoning, and redevelopment.[62] In the postwar years, industrial redevelopment became linked to growing government intervention in property relations. Municipal governments increasingly intervened in several ways with property relations, most notably through land-use controls, land assembly, and eminent domain. Public-private partnerships were given the right to assemble blighted property that could be sold to private developers for industrial redevelopment. Similarly, the courts used decisions, such as *NYHA v. Muller* (1936) and *Berman v. Parker* (1954) to legitimize a new meaning of property, one that would underpin residential, commercial, and industrial redevelopment of US cities.[63]

The underlying principle of increasing state and legal intervention in property relations was the public good. By the postwar period, it was understood that property was subject to the demands of the "public," not just individuals. Blighted land, which was considered to be inefficient and expensive, worked against the public good. Industrial property, however, is different from other forms of property. It requires heavy investments, and represents a large share of funds drawn from a company's working capital. The high degree of nonliquidity means that industrial property is slow to turn over and difficult to dispose of. A firm's profits are shaped by the value and use of the land and the processes that it houses. This is complicated by the fact that industrial property is typically highly customized. The land and the built environment for one firm frequently have a form and set of equipment that may not work for others. Moreover, changes to technologies and function can make industrial processes and the factory itself obsolete. Industrial firms are also highly immobile because of the high cost of stopping production processes and moving equipment, even in the face of obsolescence.[64]

These characteristics ensure that industrial real estate requires specific attention. The demand from manufacturers for customized industrial facilities makes it necessary to get specialized support from experienced brokers. At the same time, the large amount of funds tied up in the factory, machinery, and other facilities force firms to employ industrial property brokers to seek financial and leasing arrangements to mitigate these large fixed-capital expenditures. Industrial agents are required to have knowledge of the local industrial market. Even firms seeking rental property have very high search and moving costs. It is incumbent upon industrial firms seeking either new or rental facilities to make a careful analysis of the options. The industrial broker is essential to the success of this process.[65]

Lurking behind the public discourse about the character of the industrial property market for redevelopment was the desire of property developers, factory builders, and financial institutions to generate profits. The demolition of old areas and the building of new structures provided new opportunities for profit making. Federal government grants to cover the "rent gap"—the difference between the market value of the land and what developers were willing to pay for that land—subsidized private industrial redevelopment. Direct federal intervention meant that central land could be more easily and profitably converted to new and "higher" uses. At the same time, local governments in Saint Louis, Newark, and elsewhere used eminent domain laws to assemble, prepare, and sell property to developers for industrial uses.[66] In this way, place-dependent interests were able to transform state largesse into profitable ends. Coalitions of industrialists, real estate interests, and financial institutions collaborated with public agencies to defend and push their business interests.

The history of industrial redevelopment in Chicago between 1945 and 1975 is one of a calculative politics devoted to reframing the place of urban industrial property. These politics involved an ideological commitment to state support for property development by private enterprise. Ideas about the role of the markets, eminent domain, and government intervention in urban matters that were circulating among place-dependent elites shaped the growing importance of industrial renewal in the boardrooms of city hall, planning agencies, and corporations. The unifying concept that emerged from the multiscalar relations that linked industrial sites in Chicago to the legislative spaces of Springfield, Illinois, and Washington, DC, was that the reworking of property relations would help solve the city's problems of manufacturing job loss, falling property values, and obsolete factories. For many, mobilizing the city's economic advantages and new property relations under the guidance of public-private partnerships would foster an industrial renaissance.

The Plan for the Book

The emergence of industrial renewal as a strategy for dealing with industrial decline began in the 1940s. Although industrial decline can be traced back to the 1920s, if not earlier in some places, concrete action by local leaders that sought to change the course of industrial development only took place with the winding down of World War II and the search for tools to create a postwar industrial renaissance. Accordingly, the story told here focuses on the action of the post-1940 period. It is necessary, however, to trace decline back to the interwar period, when the first signs of deindustrialization began to appear. Consequently, I explore the interwar origins of decline to understand postwar redevelopment. In particular, the dissemination of the idea of blight has relevance to how contemporaries understood and worked toward both residential and industrial revitalization of inner-city districts.

My story ends in the early 1970s, when the publication of various studies marked a major break in the thinking about the city's economy. The studies signaled two things. First, they reflected a shift from a strategy that used the rebuilding of the city's physical form to renew the industrial base to one that deployed fiscal tools to stimulate economic growth. Second, the studies show that city leaders came to accept that manufacturing would no longer be central to the city's economy.[67] By the late 1960s and early 1970s, the strategy consisted of two parts. The first involved replacing old industries (farm implements, transportation equipment, and meatpacking) with new ones (plastics, biomedical engineering, and electronics). By this time, the coalition had aggressively pushed the building of a postindustrial economy centered on producer, logistic, and financial services geared to global interests and a social geography consisting of deep racial and class divides. The second required shifting attention from the demolition of blighted districts as the main stimulant for economic growth to the creation of tools, such as employment training, financial subsidies, and district revitalization.[68]

By 1970, renewal as a movement to deal with urban problems was coming under serious attack from many quarters. It received increasing negative press from the early 1960s. By the 1970s, newspapers such as the *Chicago Tribune* published articles critical of the city's renewal process. Journalists criticized the renewal program for perpetuating white flight, racial segregation, and economic stagnation. The programs, despite the hundreds of millions invested into clearing and rebuilding whole parts of the city, had had very little positive effect on most cities.

Local criticism was linked to a growing body of scholarly work that questioned the efficacy and fairness of the renewal programs. In the 1960s, several influential studies offered scathing critiques of the ideas, goals, and practices of federal programs.[69] At the same time, the federal government had started to condemn its renewal policies and program. As Victor Spallone, director of the Bureau of Housing for the Cook Department of Public Aid noted, "urban renewal has been a dismal failure."[70] Collectively, these criticisms denoted the downfall of postwar urban renewal and the shift to new strategies for dealing with the racialization of urban space, growing class divisions, and economic development. The formal ending of the programs came with the drying up of federal funding in 1974.

This examination of how place-based elites addressed urban redevelopment, industrial decline, and property relations been 1920 and 1975 has three main parts. The first consists of two chapters that explore the history of manufacturing loss in the city roughly between 1920 and 1970. Chapter 1 focuses on uneven industrial decline in metropolitan Chicago. This involved the extensive but jerky decanting of manufacturing employment from the central city from the 1920s and the wholesale exodus of industrial jobs from the city after 1945. In the following chapter, I examine the built form of deindustrialization through an examination of the metropolitan geography of factory construction after 1945. Building on the argument laid out in the previous chapter, the analysis shows that little new capital investment flowed to the city, while the suburbs became the prime location for the construction of new industrial facilities.

The second part of the book consists of two chapters that link the discourse of blight to industrial decline and the subsequent search for a viable industrial renewal program in Chicago. Chapter 3 builds on scholarship that demonstrates how the discourse of blight shaped renewal. While most of this work considers how the racialization of urban space underpinned housing markets and urban renewal, I show that Chicago political and business leaders worked to turn some of the city's blighted land into productive industrial space. Some agency officials believed that the overhaul of some of the city's "waste lands" for industrial redevelopment would reverse decline by delivering jobs, taxes, and prosperity. The new set of industrial lands and the associated set of property relations that emerged out of urban renewal were created by all three levels of government and legitimized in the courts. Chapter 4 examines the attempts by the city's public-private partnerships to fight industrial decline in the 1950s by linking blight, property, and redevelopment. Two cases are used to illustrate the point. The first is the South Side Planning Board's failed attempt to redevelop an area of the South Side as an industrial district. The second looks at the fight between residents and the Bodine Electric Company over the property rights embedded in the zoning ordinance and the way in which these rights shaped industrial redevelopment.

The final part presents a chronological narrative of institutional fixes implemented to counter industrial decline. I explore different programs and institutions that supported the city's industrial renewal program. Chapter 5 examines the Chicago Land Clearance Commission, the city's major industrial redeveloper in the 1950s. By the 1960s, as chapter 6 demonstrates, the Mayor's Committee for Economic and Cultural Development substituted the commission's strategy of using government funds to replace razed blighted space with new industrial districts with one focusing on science-led redevelopment and the revitalization of deteriorated factory districts. Chapter 7 looks at the other main industrial redevelopment strategy that emerged in the 1960s—the building of industrial parks. The building of industrial parks in the 1960s and 1970s, such as the Ashland

Industrial Center in the deindustrialized Stockyards, was a failure despite the allocation of significant funds by public-private partnerships. Like previous attempts, the institutional fix of the industrial park could not solve the city's manufacturing decline.

By the 1960s, Chicago's industrial base had been eviscerated, and its place-dependent industrial and civic leaders were fighting a losing battle to maintain the city's industrial prominence. The structural forces arrayed against it, as was true of other industrial centers across the Manufacturing Belt, were relentless. A combination of more attractive locational assets elsewhere (the suburbs, the South, and overseas), corporate strategies that sought increased market share and profits at the expense of places, the dominance of a growth coalition looking to create a postindustrial city on the ruins of the old industrial one, and limited local options to rejuvenate manufacturing led to continued and uneven disinvestment in the city's industrial base. The long-term consequence was that fewer factories and industrial jobs were to be found in Chicago at the beginning of each new industrial cycle. The slow process of decline that began in the 1920s became a tsunami of industrial loss from the second half of the 1940s. The powerful dynamics of capital investment could not be fixed by promoting visions of a new economy or by implementing initiatives by public-private partnerships seeking to recalculate the place of industrial property in the central city.

INDUSTRIAL DECLINE AND THE RISE OF THE SUBURBS

In June 1962, Nick Poulos, a reporter with the *Chicago Tribune*, argued that Chicagoland led "by a whopping margin all other regional complexes in the country in industrial development." Poulos was not alone in his reading of the trends of industrial investment and employment growth since the end of World War II. In 1957, Thomas Coulter, the chief executive officer of the Chicago Association of Commerce and Industry (CACI), wrote that there had been "unprecedented industrial expansion in the Chicago Metropolitan Area during the past five years" and that the organization expected "even more growth in the next five years in the metropolitan area."[1] Similar pronouncements on the region's postwar industrial growth vigorously promoted a rosy image of manufacturing health. In 1965, the Northeastern Illinois Planning Commission forecast that industrial employment in the Chicagoland area would reach 1.1 million by 1985.

The problem with these rosy pronouncements was that these commentators were ignoring the systematic decline of the city's manufacturing base. The US census provides the basic outline of the story. The city of Chicago lost 173,000 manufacturing jobs between 1945 and 1963 (table 1.1). The optimism of Poulos and others was misplaced. Industrial decline in the city of Chicago can be dated to the end of the 1920s, with the collapse of the growth cycle centered on the rise of the corporation as the main business organization and the rise of steel, chemicals, electrical appliances, and machinery as the period's growth industries.[2]

One result of this process was the spatial reconfiguration of manufacturing investment at both the metropolitan and regional levels as firms began to rethink their geographies of production and to search for alternate investment sites.

TABLE 1.1 Manufacturing employment in metropolitan Chicago, 1919–72

YEAR	METROPOLITAN CHICAGO	CITY OF CHICAGO	SUBURBS	CITY OF CHICAGO SHARE (%)
1919	520,133	403,942	116,191	77.7
1929	550,903	405,399	145,504	73.6
1939	486,214	347,839	138,375	71.5
1947	760,140	523,130	228,010	70.0
1954	724,436	469,010	255,426	64.7
1958	662,438	389,607	272,831	58.8
1963	667,634	350,368	317,266	52.5
1967	769,800	382,700	387,100	50.4
1972	674,700	293,100	381,600	46.5

Source: US Census of Manufacturers (Washington, DC: Government Printing Office, various years).

The interwar reconfiguration was preceded by an earlier pattern that emerged after 1880, which featured the simultaneous building up of the central city and the suburbs but was dominated by the central city.[3] The interwar changes were predicated on the relative decline of the city and the rise of the suburbs as the preeminent location for industrial production and employment. The deindustrialization that many identify as starting in the 1970s was simply the outcome of a process that dates back to the breakdown of an old system of industrial organization in the interwar period, the poorly directed affairs of wartime mobilization, and the shift of production to the suburbs in the immediate postwar period.

Industrial decline was not uniformly distributed across Chicagoland before the 1970s. From the 1920s, there are two main patterns: the relative and absolute decline of the city and the continued and rapid growth of the suburbs.[4] In whatever way it is measured—number of firms, employment growth, or factory construction—the city experienced incremental decline, while the suburbs took over as the metropolitan area's premier location of new production space, especially after the end of World War II. To suggest that industrial decline in the city of Chicago has a long history is not to argue there was absolute decline in manufacturing employment in the metropolitan area before World War II, although there were fewer industrial workers in Chicagoland in 1939 than there were in 1919 and 1929.[5] Rather, it is to argue that the roots of the devastation unleashed by the deindustrialization of the 1970s had been planted in the city before World War II.

Decentralization in Chicago

In 1942, a Chicago Plan Commission (CPC) report noted that a major problem facing the city was "the trend toward decentralization of Chicago industries to adjacent and nearby suburbs."[6] The CPC report was not the first to identify this issue. In 1915, the Chicago reformer Graham Taylor pointed out that "huge industrial plants" were "uprooting themselves. . . . With households, small stores, saloons, lodges, churches, schools clinging to them like living tendrils, they set themselves down ten miles away in the open."[7] Using more mundane language, the economist William Mitchell wrote in 1933 that "industrial displacements as have occurred in the region since 1920 have been in the direction not of increased industrial concentration within the city proper," but in the areas "immediately surrounding the urban nucleus." This change was not solely due to the expansion of noncity manufacturing units.[8] Firms were also leaving the city for the suburbs.

A similar point was made in the 1920s in several articles by Scrutator, a pseudonymous *Chicago Tribune* journalist. On the eve of the Great Depression, he wrote that firms had "been reaching towards the boundaries of the switching district" forty miles outside downtown Chicago.[9] He reported on a speech in March 1929 given by James Cunningham, the president of the Illinois Manufacturers' Association, who said that "the tendency" at that point was "to spread out," which meant that the "industrial growth of the great cities" was "retarded."[10] Scrutator added the caveat that suburbs can be inefficient compared to the "great cities," which are "markets as well as centers of productive industry." While "some industries might profit by such a removal, others might not."[11] Nevertheless, evidence from studies made by the Middle West Utilities Company showed that city growth "after a certain point of saturation creates more handicaps than facilities for productive industries."[12] As noted in 1924, "industrial decentralization" was "passing from theory to fact" as firms moved to the suburbs to escape high land values, congestion, and labor strife.[13] Scrutator and the other commentators were pointing to a shift in the balance of city and suburban employment and the associated restructuring of the region's industry that would have enormous implications for the local economy over the next fifty years.

The situation was more extreme than these writers realized. Between 1879 and 1919, more than 430,000 new manufacturing jobs were created in Chicagoland.[14] Of these, 75 percent were to be found in the city, while the remainder was located in the suburbs. Including the suburban areas annexed by the city, it is evident that the city of Chicago was the major generator of industrial employment up to World War I.[15] This changed after World War II, as the city's dominance of the region's industrial employment waned. The city's share of Chicagoland's jobs declined to only half by 1967 (table 1.1). As Scrutator and others had pointed out, the city's industrial supremacy was under attack by the 1920s, as corporate executives searched for cheaper production sites. The city lost an absolute number of industrial jobs in the interwar period and after the end of the war.

The decline during these two periods was not insignificant. In contrast to the suburbs, which gained industrial workers during the interwar years, the city lost

TABLE 1.2 Manufacturing employment change for selected years, 1919–72

YEAR	METROPOLITAN CHICAGO		CITY OF CHICAGO		SUBURBS	
	NUMBER	% CHANGE	NUMBER	% CHANGE	NUMBER	% CHANGE
1919–39	–33,919	–6.5	–56,103	–13.9	22,184	19.1
1919–72	154,567	29.7	–110,842	–27.4	265,409	228.4
1939–47	273,926	56.3	184,291	53.0	89,635	64.8
1947–72	–85,440	–11.2	–239,030	–44.9	153,590	67.4

Source: US Census of Manufacturers (Washington, DC: Government Printing Office, various years).

14 percent of its industrial base over this period (table 1.2). A 1942 CPC report showed that industrial suburbanization was sharply curtailed during the depression, but restarted after 1935. Even after the employment gains from incoming firms, the city still had a net loss of four thousand jobs in the last years of the 1930s.[16] The shifting balance of industrial work associated with the deindustrialization of the central city was a long time in the making; it did not just appear with the end of the "postwar glory days" in the 1970s.

The city of Chicago's declining share of employment was a direct result of the establishment of factories in the areas ringing the city. One *Chicago Tribune* reporter noted in 1940 that "within recent years factories [had] moved farther and farther away from the center of the city."[17] Along with a number of older satellite cities such as Elgin and Joliet, the city declined relative to the rest of Chicagoland. Industrial growth increased dramatically in an assortment of suburbs, including Cicero, East Chicago, and Gary. Much of this growth came from arrivals: "the number of industries moving outward from Chicago" was "particularly pronounced in the suburbs immediately outside the city limits."[18] Just as Scrutator had argued a decade earlier, city companies were looking for cheaper land, lower taxes, more docile labor, and the opportunity to install modern production systems in new factories. Even in those cases where central-city factories were not closed, corporations tended to invest more heavily in greenfield sites in the suburbs and other parts of the country. At the same time that firms were leaving for the greener pastures of the suburb, an insufficient number of firms were moving into the central areas to compensate for this loss.

This was the point that Irving Salomon, president of Royal Metal Manufacturing, was making in 1928 when he outlined the reasons why his furniture wire firm set up a branch plant outside the city. A few years earlier, it had started up a new product line at its South Side metal furniture factory. While this gave the company greater markets, it created problems for factory operations because of overcrowding, handling system inefficiencies, and high overhead costs. By the early 1920s, these diseconomies forced company executives to make a decision about location. As they saw it, Chicago had many advantages—transportation, labor supply, local market, and specialized services—which they did not want to give up. But small towns also had advantages, most notably lower property prices and labor costs. Royal Metal executives chose to take advantage of both, taking some of the company's Chicago workers to Michigan City, Indiana, while moving to a larger factory space on the city's Lower West Side. By staying in Chicago, the firm was able to reap the design and supply benefits that came with being in the United States' furniture capital. By hiving off the run-of-the-mill operations to a factory in Michigan City, the firm was able to reduce its freight and labor charges in a plant "designed to give us the greatest possible efficiency."[19]

As the Royal Metal case suggests, the changing geography of industrial employment was an outcome of the two aspects of the political economy of place. First, the investment patterns affecting Chicago were greatly determined by industrial decision makers who had a regional or national gaze. In the case of Royal Metal, there were distinct advantages to moving production out of Chicago. At the same time, large multiunit corporations with a national focus came to play an increasingly larger role in the Chicago's economy, as they did in Trenton, Philadelphia, and elsewhere.[20] In Chicago, the rise of oligopolies in steel, meatpacking, transportation equipment, and other sectors gave significant control over the local economy to absentee owners with little interest in Chicago's industrial, political, and social affairs.[21] Investment decisions about installing new machinery, revitalizing the factory, or building additions were subject to the machinations of a distant industrial managerial class that did not necessarily prioritize Chicago factories over those elsewhere. Economic control shifted from the local bourgeoisie to a small group of national capitalists with interests across the country.

Secondly, Chicago was subject to the politics of place dependency and property. Industrialists, developers, and other agents with long-term investment in Chicago had focused on making real property attractive to investors since its beginnings in the 1830s. Land was central to successful place-based industrial development in at least two ways: the price, location, and quality of land defined the way that places were articulated to outside interests; and it provided the material basis for local production activity and business interactions. In the case of Royal Metal, Salomon used land in a small Indiana town to siphon off employment from its Chicago works. Through actions such as these, Michigan City was one of many municipalities that contributed to Chicago's declining place in the metropolitan area from the 1920s. Closer to home, suburbs created more competitive options for industrial land, which over time worked to undermine the city's economic foundations.

Suburban place makers worked to create advantages that could not be replicated in the city. For heavy industries that required extensive amounts of land, the most obvious was the provision of large tracts of cheap land close to excellent and cheap transportation facilities where complex factory layouts and low-cost working-class housing could be built. Place entrepreneurs also created space that allowed smaller companies experiencing rapid growth and changes to product lines and production processes to substitute rented, generic inner-city spaces for plants specially designed for their new needs. In some cases, suburban place makers put a great deal of forethought into planning the appropriate conditions to attract and retain industry. In others, industrial development was a cumulative process that gathered steam as more and more firms relocated to the suburbs. A brief overview of East Chicago and Cicero illustrates just how industrial suburbs challenged Chicago's industrial supremacy.

East Chicago was planned as an industrial center from the very start. Initially, its location adjacent to railroads and Lake Michigan, along with large tracts of cheap, level land made the district well suited to industrial pursuits. The first plant opened in 1888, and by 1924, the city had twenty-five thousand workers employed in forty-five firms. The industrial base was anchored by two of the United States' largest steel corporations: Inland Steel and Youngstown Sheet and Tube. An assortment of associated metalworking and petroleum firms composed the remainder of the city's industrial base.[22] From the 1890s, several land development and infrastructure companies laid out the city for industry. Plans were put in place for the construction of an outer harbor on Lake Michigan, a ship canal from the lake to the Grand Calumet River, and a belt-line railroad to connect the city with other regional railroads. Huge tracts of land close to the railroads, the harbor, and the canal were set aside for industry. Some companies built worker housing.[23] By the 1920s, a substantial industrial town had been established by suburban place entrepreneurs. What had once been considered "'waste' land" had been become home to industrial investment and employment that might have otherwise gone to Chicago.[24]

Suburban Cicero formed around industries that had moved from Chicago. From the 1880s, each new subdivision boom introduced new land development projects and new industrial companies. Before 1930, the most important "improvements" were two anchor firms—the Grant Locomotive Works and the Western Electric Company—transportation facilities, such as suburban railroad services, and working-class housing. Driving this place-building process were organizations such as the Grant and Equitable Land Associations and the Cicero Manufacturers Association. These helped build up a viable class structure, cement the place of industry in the town, and create the basis for a distinctive industrial suburb on the city's western edge.[25] By 1950, 339 manufacturing firms employed 62,887 workers. Many of these firms had moved from Chicago, thus contributing to disinvestment in the city's manufacturing base. Most companies expanded when they moved from Chicago, investing in land, building, and equipment. This was the case with Western Electric's move from downtown Chicago to the new Hawthorne facility in Cicero. By the time of the Great Depression, the huge electrical equipment firm had made numerous additions to its Hawthorne plant, making it one of the largest in the metropolitan area.[26]

For industrial executives looking at Cicero, the actual location was incidental; they could have chosen from an array of similar places in the western suburbs. What company managers were seeking was a site on Chicago's periphery where they could take advantage of locational assets created by place-making entrepreneurs: a growing labor market, large tracts of cheap land, low taxes and fewer regulations, and private rail sidings within the metropolitan switching area. As one firm representative noted in 1949, "the government of the Town of Cicero is willing to cooperate with industry to keep the tax rates under control and to supply ample fire and police protection."[27] Suburbs such as Cicero and East Chicago were important developments that competed with Chicago for new industrial starts and for the city's own firms. By the end of the Great Depression, an array of similar suburban places dotted Chicagoland, drawing companies, investment and workers from the city.

Wartime industrial mobilization temporarily halted manufacturing decline in the city. The massive public and private investment in defense factories after June 1940 created unprecedented amounts of new production space and jobs across the metropolitan region. It was estimated that at the height of defense production in 1943, the region's factories employed more than a million workers. Investment in the area's industrial economy, however, was not evenly distributed. Much of the new employment bypassed downtown.[28] As the CPC reported in 1942, "the locational tendencies of the new war plants in the Chicago area are serving to weld together as well as greatly augment the arc of industrial development on the rim of Chicago."[29] The construction of new sprawling airplane engine and aluminum factories on the metropolitan rim and massive additions to steel and chemical mills in the southern Calumet district served to concentrate investment and work in areas outside the older central industrial districts.

In 1943, the CACI proclaimed that Chicago was experiencing "an industrial renaissance." Wartime mobilization had led to the establishment of "new types of manufacture," which, the association believed, "may prove to be the seeds" of "post-war industries of types never before known in Chicago." These industries would complement existing ones and "materially broaden and strengthen our already strong industrial base."[30] The aircraft industry, in particular, was the focus of both wartime expenditures and the anticipated postwar renaissance. During the war, the CACI argued that it would become a major postwar industry. Indeed, with the appropriate backing, Chicago would become "the nation's aviation center." To provide this encouragement, the association's Aviation Committee analyzed the city's advantages and laid out the steps needed to make Chicago the nation's leading aircraft district. The CACI also actively tried to convince corporate leaders who had opened factories in Chicago during the war to stay once the war had ended. They provided them with information about Chicago's locational advantages, such as transportation, diverse industrial base, large labor pool, and good business climate.[31]

Despite these fond hopes, wartime expansion in the metropolis was not sustained after the end of hostilities. While the city continued its long-term decline after 1945, the suburbs remained the major site for new manufacturing activity in the postwar years (see tables 1.1, 1.2). There was no sudden burst of decline as Barry Bluestone and Bennett Harrison have posited. Instead, industrial employment in the city slowly ratcheted down in the thirty years after World War II. In fact, the immediate postwar years were not good ones for the city, as manufacturing employment fell from a high of close to a million in 1943 to 469,000 by 1954. The city's industrial dominance was severely eroded as investment in new and existing factories could not counterbalance the job loss from slow-burn disinvestment, factory closings, and plants leaving for the suburbs or other regions. With the exception of a positive hiccup between 1963 and 1967, this pattern of decline continued over the next eighteen years. Meanwhile, the absolute number of jobs in the suburbs continued to increase up to the late 1960s.

The fading fortunes of the central city's industry were rooted in the decisions by business executives and place-based entrepreneurs to shift investment from Chicago. Much of the job loss that began after 1919 and accelerated after 1945 was a direct product of firms' closing their doors in the city and shifting machinery and workers to new premises in the surrounding areas in Illinois and Indiana. In some cases, as we have already seen, factories were constructed in places such as East Chicago and Cicero by large corporations with a national reach. By the late 1920s, both places had built an industrial base that siphoned off plants, investment, and employment from Chicago. This continued in the postwar period, as suburban entrepreneurs in a growing number of places dedicated themselves to anchoring industrial investment and attracting manufacturing capital from Chicago and from across the United States.

Some observers were not oblivious to suburban charms and the problems they posed for the city. Leverett Lyon, the chair of the CACI, listed the advantages of the suburbs as "more space, cheaper land, and lower taxes." For residential use, they held "the additional advantage of a more satisfactory environment for the home and family, and for industry the added attractions of increased freedom from legal controls and from labor union regulation."[32] A 1961 planning study reported that firms moved because land was not available in the city for expansion. An *Illinois Labor Bulletin* study showed three-quarters of the investments in industrial construction in Cook County over the previous five years had gone to the suburbs.[33] Numerous other postwar studies showed the same process of decline after 1945.[34] Newspapers reports made the same point. A *Chicago Tribune* study of the city's West Side and other inner-city districts found Chicago had lost four hundred firms and seventy thousand jobs between 1950 and 1965. This, not unexpectedly, had negative multiplier effects, including the closing down of other businesses and a large drop in retail sales.[35]

Chicago was not unique. Many northern industrial centers experienced central-city decline and suburban growth between 1929 and 1972 (table 1.3). In some cases—notably Detroit, Buffalo, Pittsburgh, Akron, and Philadelphia—the decline was more than 25 percent. In these cities, large automotive, chemical, steel-working, electrical appliance, and aircraft corporations, freed as they were from the central city, started building new factory complexes outside the city and disinvesting in city plants. In contrast, the suburbs of most Manufacturing Belt districts experienced industrial growth from the 1930s. In the Sunbelt metropoles of Los Angeles, Houston, and Atlanta, both city and suburbs had growing industrial employment after 1929. As executives moved capital from one place to others in search of profits and market share, Sunbelt metropoles became the locales for new industrial investment.[36] The rise of new industries in metropolitan areas such Los Angeles (aerospace and electronics), Seattle (aircraft), San Francisco

TABLE 1.3 Manufacturing employment change in thirteen metropolitan areas, 1929–72

METROPOLITAN AREA	TOTAL		CENTRAL CITY		SUBURBS	
	NUMBER	% CHANGE	NUMBER	% CHANGE	NUMBER	% CHANGE
Sunbelt cities	520,886	313	162,768	147	358,118	645
Los Angeles	434,299	380	110,085	146	323,214	240
Houston	46,637	210	33,569	206	14,068	219
Atlanta	38,850	114	18,114	98	20,836	196
Manufacturing Belt cities	374,102	13	−268,591	−14	642,693	66
New York City	215,058	25	58,559	10	156,499	52
Detroit	200,661	67	−80,141	−36	280,802	392
Chicago	116,731	21	−55,031	−14	171,762	118
Cleveland	40,976	23	−31,477	−21	72,453	242
Saint Louis	18,120	12	−20,294	−19	38,323	85
Buffalo	2,709	2	−27,771	−40	30,480	66
Youngstown	2,310	4	−4,312	−21	6,622	20
Philadelphia	−1,233	−1	−61,209	−25	59,976	59
Akron	−10,948	−16	−25,082	−42	14,144	193
Pittsburgh	−46,105	−20	−21,924	−36	−24,173	−15

Source: US Census of Manufacturers (Washington, DC: Government Printing Office, various years).

(shipbuilding and electronics), and Houston (petrochemical), accelerated after World War II. The history of industrial development in the Manufacturing Belt after 1920 was one of extensive central-city decline

Four Firms

Central to the expansion of the suburbs of metropolitan areas in the North and the Sunbelt industrial districts was the ability of place-based entrepreneurs to build a more attractive set of locational assets than those found in Chicago's older industrial districts. In the search for better work sites and production profits, an increasing number of industrial executives from the 1920s eschewed what they believed were the city's locational diseconomies. The dynamics driving the decline of the city's industrial economy and the associated negative discourse about its work sites can be understood by exploring the locational behavior of four different firms before the 1960s.

At the end of World War I, the candy manufacturer E. J. Brach made a range of products in four separate downtown plants. In 1923, Brach executives decided to build a new facility to house all of the company's operations. Ignoring suburban attractions, such as cheaper land, it built a $5 million facility on Chicago's West Side that housed all the company's activities under one roof.[37] Over the next forty years, the 1923 factory was expanded eighteen times.[38] By the 1960s, the twenty-three-acre sprawling plant with a million square feet of floor space was the country's largest candy factory. After having made the decision to remain in the city, the company was thus obliged to accommodate its ongoing expansion plans at the 1923 plant because of the extensive sunk costs that it accumulated with each addition. In the postwar years, the city's business leaders continued to view the locational assets of the city's West Side, most notably proximity to the railroad and highways, sufficient amounts of industrial land, and stable, white working-class residential districts, as important considerations, ones that reinforced the firm's earlier investment decisions.

The investment decisions of Acme Steel Goods tell an altogether different story and go some way to explaining the decline of the central city. Established in 1884, Acme moved to a plant in the city's Bridgeport area in 1904. By 1917, expansion plans forced the firm to consider building a new production facility. Unlike Brach, however, Acme purchased a 133-acre site on the Little Calumet River in suburban Riverdale. By 1929, the company had built a hoop mill, a second rolling mill, and a third hot mill at the new site in the southern suburbs. By the time of the Great Depression, the Riverdale plant had become the company's main production center. Between 1947 and 1956, the company undertook an expansion program, a good deal of which occurred outside the Chicago region. Acme acquired firms in Racine, Wisconsin, and Newport, Kentucky, and built a new factory in Scarborough, Canada. In 1957, they began a $23 million expansion of the Riverdale plant.[39]

Acme's postwar expansion involved a deliberate policy of disinvestment in its Bridgeport plant, which was shut down between 1955 and 1957. All its operations were transferred to Riverdale. Reflecting on its future plans in 1957, the company's president, Guy Avery, noted that the new round of investment in the suburb would "fulfill the vision of those who purchased the Riverdale property 40 years ago."[40] Unlike Brach, Acme executives as early as World War I saw its city site, located as it was on the deteriorated South Branch of the Chicago River and in a heavily congested area, as a liability. This corporate vision consolidated the city's already diminished character. Acme executives shifted capital to more productive and newer facilities in Riverdale in order to increase profits, expand markets, and remain nationally competitive. At the same time, Acme's building of suburban factory space contributed to the gradual disinvestment in one large city factory and to the declining fortunes of the city's industrial base.

In contrast to Brach and Acme, the Electro-Motive Corporation, a General Motors subsidiary, moved directly from Michigan to a suburban factory.[41] In 1935, the firm announced that it was looking at four different sites in the Chicago area to build locomotives. The most likely choice was a property close to the transportation equipment complex to the south of the city. Ultimately, however, the company bought a seventy-acre site from the Indiana Harbor Belt Railroad in the west side of suburban McCook, where it built an extensive locomotive production complex. By 1946, the firm had bought another 125 acres of land, built ten additions, and created hundreds of thousands of square feet of new working space. By the 1960s, it was a sprawling complex made up of hundreds of buildings located in several contiguous suburbs.[42]

Since the company was a subsidiary of one of the United States' largest industrial corporations, with huge financial assets and a large national market, Electro-Motive's siting was very much part of a corporate scanning of viable locations across the country. Given the amount of fixed capital allocated to the locomotive factory, General Motors was very careful in its site selection.[43] That the Chicago region was chosen is not unexpected, given the importance of its heavy equipment, transportation, and steel manufacturing complex. It was also not surprising that by the 1930s, suburban locations would be competitive with those in Chicago. General Motors saw suburban Chicago as an attractive site, as areas such as McCook allowed the corporation to reap the benefits of the city's extensive manufacturing complex, while providing direct access to the Belt railroad line and plentiful suburban land.

Yet another firm attracted to the suburbs was Nuclear-Chicago, a manufacturer of radioactive measuring and radioisotope equipment, founded in 1946 by three graduate students who were employed by the army's Special Engineer Detachment during World War II to work on the Manhattan Project at the University of Chicago. The company's first workshop was located in a storefront with nine hundred square feet of working space on Fifty-Fifth Street near the university. In 1947, responding to the need to increase output and its workforce, the company moved to the city's Near North Side. By 1954, it produced 241 products, employed 135 workers, and occupied the top three floors of a seven-story building. Eventually, this location proved inadequate, and five years later, the company left the city for the sylvan charms of suburban Des Plaines, where it built an $800,000 factory with fifty-five thousand square feet of floor space on nine acres of land.[44]

Just like Acme and Electro-Motive, Nuclear-Chicago assessed its locational options, didn't like what it saw in the city, and moved to the suburbs. Chicago offered few obvious attractions for firms operating in postwar, high-tech industries such as electronics and instruments. Pushed out of the teeming industrial districts north of the Loop by developers looking to turn the area into an office and high-end residential district, Nuclear-Chicago had few options in the city. Nor was the company enticed by the older industrial suburbs south and west of the city, where the old-line, heavy industry firms such as Electro-Motive and Acme Steel were concentrated. Rather, they sought the suburbs to the north, which housed manicured and modern one-story factories that catered to light and consumer product industries.

Despite the differences of scale, product, and workforce, the move of the three firms to a suburban site contributed to the decline of the city's industrial base. In some cases, slow disinvestment by corporations such as Acme Steel led to the bleeding of employment, while in others, new firms such as Nuclear-Chicago looked for facilities to match their modern image. Some companies, such as Electro-Motive, ignored the city altogether and settled in the suburbs from the outset. Working with a calculus that sought to balance the structural requirements of their industry with the specificities of the firm, all three made different locational choices than Brach, which remained in place. All three determined that a suburban location was the most profitable choice. This was a trend more representative of firm behavior in Chicagoland after World War I than that of the candy maker. While other firms made the same decision as Brach, an increasing number of others did not. The imbalance, which started in the interwar years, accelerated after 1945. The result, of course, was ongoing disinvestment from central industrial districts and the growing importance of the suburbs as centers of metropolitan Chicago's industrial employment.

At the same time that Chicago's suburbs were attracting a growing number of city firms, regional competition for old-line and new industries ate into the city's industrial base. A prime example of the declining fortunes of Chicago's industry is meatpacking. Long-term disinvestment from the 1920s by the city's Big Three packers—Armour and Co., Swift and Co., and Wilson and Co.—resulted in the dissolution of what had been the largest slaughtering complex in the world. For some companies, the shift started as early as the late nineteenth century, with the development of new production, transportation, and distribution technologies.[45] A 1933 report describes the forces affecting the industry as early as the 1920s: high wages, taxes, and transportation costs, and tighter government regulation all favored locating packing houses close to western materials and markets. Consequently, new plants were built in the western states, while the "capacity for handling hogs in Chicago [was] not being increased."[46]

With no attachment or loyalty to Chicago or its residents, the meatpackers continued these investment practices in the early postwar years. They disinvested, leaving behind what was becoming increasingly obsolete plant. The reluctance of packing executives to install modern machinery from the 1920s made Chicago's packinghouses less efficient and less productive, which only reduced their ability to compete with the modern plants being built in the West. Adding to this was the packers' concern over growing labor militancy, increasing transportation costs, and the welcoming embrace of more pliant municipalities elsewhere. These long-term processes became evident to everyone in the 1950s, when all three major meat producers permanently closed their Chicago plants.[47]

Swift spent more than $300 million on modernizing its plants across the country after 1945, but very little of this went to Chicago. New packinghouses were opened in Wilson, North Carolina, Rochelle, Illinois, and elsewhere. The company permanently closed its Chicago slaughtering facilities between 1957 and 1959. Wilson started first. Between 1952 and 1955, it shut its local cattle and hog facilities, built a modern plant in Kansas City, and laid off thousands of workers. Armour followed suit, shutting down the city's slaughtering plant in 1959. A year later, it sold all its Chicago property and built new modern factories in Houston and Oklahoma City. By 1960, all the major plants were closed, and the workforce, which had reached fifty thousand during World War I and thirty thousand in the 1920s, was reduced to a mere six thousand. By 1960, as Dominic Pacyga has so eloquently stated, Packingtown had the "appearance of an industrial ghost town."[48] Chicago was no longer "the hog butcher for the world."

As the four firms and the one industry illustrate, on balance the city had been losing industrial employment to the suburbs and locales elsewhere since the 1920s. Forty years of investment in other locales across the country had wrought an inevitable result: the establishment of firms from a range of industries in the suburbs and the permanent decline of longtime Chicago industries, such as meatpacking and heavy metal. At the same time that the industrial districts in the city such as Bridgeport and Back of the Yards were in free fall, other parts of the metropolitan area were experiencing large-scale industrial development. One such area was the northern suburbs.

The Northern Suburbs

In 1949, the journalist Harry Adams reported on a housing study of the northern suburbs by the Real Estate Research Corporation. In sharp contrast to the problems found in the city, the company painted a rosy picture of residential development. The newspaper article featured pictures of "attractive new homes" in Winnetka and Glenview that promised all the advantages of suburban life. The study did recognize that the new middle-class suburbs were not without their problems. Questions of "dead" land and disorganized planning, for example, had to be addressed if orderly residential development was to take place. And yet, despite these problems, it was assumed that the rapidly growing northern suburbs such as Skokie, Niles, Franklin Park, and Morton Grove were going to be the home of white "prestige seeking suburbanites" looking to escape the central city.[49]

The narrative of the white middle-class dweller moving to the suburbs is, of course, the typical one set out in the popular and scholarly literatures. Adams, however, presented another side of the suburbs, one that linked residential and industrial growth.[50] The caption under a photograph of a factory in Norwood Park noted that "much industrial expansion already [had] occurred in the general area and helped give rise to a housing boom."[51] Norwood Park was not alone. Residential development in many northern suburbs was driven by industrial expansion. Not only did factory building generate population growth in the suburbs, it also threatened the city's economy. The divergent paths of central-city and suburban industrial development elucidated by the Real Estate Research Corporation in 1949 would become starker over the next quarter of a century. By the early 1970s, the suburbs were the growth node of industrial metropolitan Chicago. The northern suburbs, in particular, became the primary focus of the region's manufacturing growth.

This section examines the northern suburbs in order to illustrate how postwar suburban growth contributed to the industrial decline of the city. While the following chapters provide a detailed discussion of the attempts by the city's civic and business leaders to counteract this trajectory, here I focus on the creation of locational assets that underpinned industrial development in the northern suburbs. It is impossible to comprehend the response of urban elites to central-city industrial decline without understanding the rise of the industrial suburbs. Those in the north were some of the most dynamic parts of the postwar metropolitan area. As one observer noted in 1965, "the northwest quadrant of the metropolitan area" was "one of the four fastest growing areas in the country."[52] Municipalities such as Skokie and Franklin Park became home to hundreds of factories employing close to one hundred thousand blue- and white-collar workers by the early 1960s.

Data taken from the Illinois Manufacturers' Association's *Industrial Directory* provide insights into the changing industrial geography of the northern suburbs and the impact this had on the central city's industrial base. The most notable point is the rapid rise of the suburban industrial base (table 1.4). In 1924, the suburbs had only thirty-two firms with a total of 946 workers.[53] This had risen to 1,136 and 92,743 in 1962. The area's industrial growth started slowly between 1924 and 1950. Industrial mobilization during World War II furthered the building of an industrial base in suburbs such as Evanston, Lincolnwood, and Skokie. This initial growth, however, was itself overshadowed by massive expansion between 1950 and 1962. Many suburbs participated in this growth north of the city limits, while some, most notably Skokie, Franklin Park, Morton Grove, Niles, Northlake, and Des Plaines, became home to a substantial industrial presence.

A comparison of the 1950 and 1962 directories indicates that the major increase in factory investment came from three sources.[54] The most common was fixed-capital investment made by the 811 start-ups and firms from outside the city. The fact that 625 firms had fewer than twenty-five workers suggests that many were local firms that serviced the suburban market with finished products (such as printed goods and ornamental ironwork), and provided specialized products or did contract work (such as dies and tools and heat treating) for larger corporate firms. Some investment came from outside the region altogether. A few examples

TABLE 1.4 Manufacturing in Chicago's northern suburbs, 1924–62

LOCATION	WORKERS EMPLOYED			NO. OF FIRMS		
	1924	1950	1962	1924	1950	1962
Northern suburbs (total)	946	15,442	92,743	32	175	1,136
Selected suburbs						
Skokie	0	2,099	17,439	0	25	231
Franklin Park	140	1,636	11,610	2	27	261
Morton Grove	0	1,912	10,093	0	9	39
Niles	0	1,160	8,732	0	3	44
Northlake	0	0	8,720	0	0	13
Des Plaines	165	1,198	8,038	2	11	66

Source: Industrial Directory (Chicago: Illinois Manufacturers' Association, various years).

provide a flavor of the firms attracted to the area in the 1950s: the Glendale, California, firm General Controls, Inc., built a factory to produce pressure and temperature automatic controls in Skokie; New York's Avon Products, the world's largest manufacturer of cosmetics, built a $1.3 million factory in Morton Grove; the Indianapolis firm Inland Container constructed a corrugated box plant on a Franklin Park site purchased from the Chicago and North Western Railroad.[55]

Second, firms moved from the city to the northern suburbs. These accounted for about a fifth of the area's new factory stock. The 215 firms that were located in Chicago in 1950 but had factories in the northern suburbs in 1962 employed 47,604 workers. In many cases, Chicago-based firms moved lock, stock, and barrel from their 1950 locations; in others, the new suburban plant was simply a cog in a multiunit metropolitan system of firms. One of the earliest to move to Skokie was the drug manufacturer G. D. Searle and Co., which built a large manufacturing, research, and recreational center in a landscaped setting in 1941.[56] Another was Automatic Electric Co., maker of telephone systems, which moved from a seventeen-story complex in downtown Chicago to single-story plant in Northlake in the late 1950s. The new modern plant "permitted arrangement of all storage, processing, assembly and shipping departments in orderly, straight-line sequence," which was a major organizational and design improvement on its unwieldy and congested Chicago facility.[57]

The attraction of the suburbs for Chicago firms looking to rebuild their production facilities was reiterated by Willard Brown, manager of the real estate company Arthur Rubloff and Co. in 1969, when he discussed the importance of the removal of large companies such as A. B. Dick Company, a maker of copy machines and office supplies, to suburbs such as Niles. Dick's move from downtown Chicago proved "that industry could operate successfully in the suburbs and this helped to attract other large as well as small firms to that particular area."[58]

Finally, many firms plowed profits back into their existing suburban factories, contributing to the doubling of employment in the suburbs between 1950 and 1962. Two examples illustrate the impact of this investment. Having moved to Skokie only five years earlier, Searle announced a $1.5 million expansion scheme in 1946. Once completed, the factory was double the size of the original one.[59] Similarly, Bell and Howell, the movie equipment maker, made several additions to a World War II defense plant in Lincolnwood that it had purchased for close to $2 million in March 1946. Over the next decade, the company built three additions to the original three buildings valued at more than $3 million. In 1946, for example, it built a fabricating building for optical product manufacture and research on forty-one acres that it had recently acquired adjacent to the defense plant.[60]

In all cases, investment was channeled from the city into new suburban industrial sites. A growing number of civic and industrial leaders appreciated the advantages of suburban locations. Roger Sutfin of the Central Manufacturing District, for example, noted that "industry is considered the economic base-builder" of the suburbs, as it reduces the residential tax burden, provides employment for industry and other sectors, and creates financial stability. In order to gain industrial jobs, municipalities had to consider issues such as annexing land for future use, and the provision of zoning, water, sewers, building codes, and city services. This, Sutfin averred, would be "the beginning of a planned, orderly industrial development that will be a credit to the community."[61]

One example of large-scale industrial development in the northern suburbs was the building of a massive body of factories around O'Hare International Airport, which opened in 1944.[62] The importance that this new transportation node had for postwar industrial development in the northern suburbs was noted by several interested commenters and trumpeted by the local press. In 1967, Chicago's Herman Walther, a former president of the American Institute of Real Estate Appraisers, observed that "the 'hottest' industrial zone in the Chicago metropolitan area continue[d] to be near O'Hare International Airport."[63] Two years later, another observer noted that the region's "dynamic industrial growth" was based on light industry and warehousing, and this was "most often associated with the opening of O'Hare International Airport." The author went on to say that "almost 30 industrial parks are closely packed around the periphery of the airport."[64] A few weeks earlier, another interested observer noted that business activity in the area was "stimulated by the development of the airport and major highways" and that most firms "locating in the area [had] national connections or . . . use for air transport."[65]

The activities of suburban place makers, including government officials, property developers, and industrial executives around O'Hare, reconfigured the region's industrial geography. This was patently obvious to Loren Trimble, the director of Commonwealth Edison's industrial department. By the late 1950s, he wrote, "distance to the Loop was dropped in preference to time in minutes from O'Hare as a basic determinant of an industrial site." This shift was linked to the agglomeration effects that the airport provided for manufacturers. While firms may have been looking to escape the central city's diseconomies, they were also seeking the advantages of close proximity to the airport. From the middle of the 1950s, industrial developers bought land, developed industrial sites, and then sold or leased improved property to firms seeking access to the airport's transportation and agglomeration economies. The airport also provided a symbolic role for industry, as "association with the area indicated modernity."[66] The one-story, landscaped factories built in the northern suburbs close to the airport, a symbol of modernity and unprecedented global reach, projected an aura of efficiency and orderly development that differentiated the district from central areas.[67]

Along with the decisions by industrial managers, the building of an industrial base in the northern suburbs was in the hands of a "coterie" of about one hundred industrial real estate agents who pushed the attractions of the districts to the north of the city.[68] One member of this coterie was Warren Haeger of the Indust-Realty Company, who described his trade as "a specialized business that requires knowledge in many areas, including law, engineering, architectural design."[69] Utilizing these specialized skills, the region's industrial real estate agencies, such as Bennett and Kahnweiler, and Nardi and Podolsky, determined the choices open to industrial managers and shaped the region's industrial landscape. These industrial property agents were also members of the Society of Industrial Realtors. The two main duties of these real estate developers were to provide information to their clients about potential sites (zoning, workforce, transportation, etc.) for their factories; and to negotiate between their client and the property owner once the site had been chosen.

In the thirty years following the end of World War II, these industrial real estate agencies opened up the northern suburbs to industrial development. This involved, among other things, pushing the idea of the central city's inferior locational assets. As early as 1946, they pointed to the problems of central-city industrial land. The list of problems was long and included punitive building restrictions, an outmoded zoning ordinance, and the absence of suitable sites. The city's 1942 zoning ordinance, it was believed, hampered industrial construction, as it did not allow for additions in heavy manufacturing districts, and much of the unoccupied land zoned for industry was low-lying and not suitable for modern manufacturing operations. Furthermore, rezoning of nonindustrial land was at the discretion of the local aldermen, which could make new additions difficult. In contrast, industrialists looking to set up in suburbs such as Franklin Park and Skokie faced fewer obstacles than those considering industrial districts in the city.[70]

Milton Podolsky, a leading industrial real estate agent, analyzed the problems of industrial space in the city for a 1972 committee investigating Chicago's economic base. For Podolsky, industrial suburbanization was a "natural occurrence" that involved firms being "squeezed out of space in the city, as manufacturing techniques improved and expansive one story factories became the norm, and as skilled laborers moved from decaying inner city neighborhoods to middle class homes in the suburbs." Podolsky told the committee "that 30 to 40 per cent of the city's industrial buildings [were] obsolete and subject to replacement by modern structures in the suburbs." These problems were compounded by the quality of available labor, traffic congestion, changing transportation requirements, displacement of industry by urban renewal, and proximity to customers. These problems in turn were rolled into a discourse of blight that allowed place entrepreneurs such as Podolsky to focus on the clearance and renewal of the city's built environment.[71]

According to another real estate broker, city industry moved because of the better space, transportation, and labor force found in the suburbs. Industrialists, he argued, "view the region as the most promising in the metropolitan vicinity. This area sells itself."[72] Similarly, a Society of Industrial Realtors study argued that industry moved to the area close to O'Hare because it had the region's best range of locational assets.[73] This view was reinforced by other studies by various city and metropolitan planning agencies such as the Northeastern Illinois Planning Commission.[74] Industrial property brokers such as Haeger described the suburbs as the real center of activity in the metropolitan region because they were already "saturated with industrial development," were close to highways, and, compared to Chicago, had lower-priced factory sites.[75] The coterie of real estate and ancillary agents actively framed the city's factory space as unappealing: congested, expensive, and inefficient. The suburbs were framed as the opposite.

The advantages of the suburbs were zealously defended by local industrial associations that had been established to coordinate and protect the interests of the suburb's industrial class. One of the first was the Franklin Park Manufacturers Association, established in 1949. Its purpose was "to coordinate all matters of common interest to manufacturers, and form a central organization to work toward the good of the community." It showed little interest in metropolitan issues or federal legislation, instead focusing on mundane issues essential to the smooth working of their local production facilities, such as extending city transit systems to the suburbs, ensuring access to workers, and providing a forum for local factory managers to promote their products.[76] The association's efforts to help local industrialists attracted interest, and its membership tripled in ten years. Members were invited to attend talks given by local business and civic leaders on topics that covered, among other things, the future plans for O'Hare. In some cases, talks were given by important national politicians and organizations. A representative from the National Manufacturers Association, for example, informed local industrialists about labor relations and what to do when unions came to the plant.[77] The purpose of organizations such as the Franklin Park Manufacturers Association was to protect industrialists' interests in the suburbs.

In sum, the suburban "golden corridor" experienced dramatic industrial growth in the thirty years after the end of World War II. The northern suburbs became home to over a thousand factories by the late 1950s. Anchored by large infrastructures, most notably the O'Hare Airport and the Kennedy Expressway, the area grew enormously. The early growth continued into the 1970s. Between 1968 and 1974, industrial executives invested more than $1.8 billion in residential, commercial, and industrial projects in the area, outstripping investment in the city by more than 55 percent. As the older northern suburbs reached full capacity by the 1960s, much of the new investment went to Elk Grove Village, Des Plaines, and Schaumburg.[78]

The postwar expansion of the northern suburbs was a continuation of the relentless bleeding of manufacturing employment that the city had suffered from the 1920s. At first, the decline was relative, as the suburbs simply outpaced the city, or, in the case of the 1930s, did not decline as much as the central city. The single largest recipient of Chicago's industrial jobs and investment before World War II was the outlying white suburbs. While the city lost tens of thousands of industrial jobs in the 1930s, the suburban total grew. After 1945, industrial suburbanization accelerated, as suburbs such as Skokie and Des Plaines grew enormously. For the most part, these suburbs became the home of a white population that sought the new jobs and escape from the simmering racial and class tensions of the central city. The suburbs offered good employment opportunities in a segregated residential space. At the same time, the change became absolute, as industrial employment fell dramatically from close to a million workers in 1943 to fewer than three hundred thousand by 1972. In other words, and contrary to what Bluestone and Harrison and others have argued, industrial decline of the central city started at least fifty years earlier than the 1970s. Given the uneven development of capital investment, deindustrialization was as much an intrametropolitan phenomenon as it was a regional and international one.

Driving this suburban expansion were the actions of company executives, who either disinvested in their Chicago plants while moving investment to other parts of the country or closed down local factories altogether. Searching for cheaper labor and land, fewer regulations, and more pliant and welcoming governments, corporate leaders sought more profitable sites than those offered in the city. Subject to decades of underinvestment and disinvestment, the city's old industrial districts were no longer attractive to firms seeking to install new production systems on large tracts of land. The cumulative effect of these processes was to undermine the industrial bases of some places while expanding those of others.

This is what happened to the central cities of the Manufacturing Belt between the 1920s and the early 1950s, as industrial growth lagged behind their suburban districts. With few exceptions, the older industrial cities reached their industrial employment peak in the late 1940s. This fact has two major implications. First, the cities missed out on the "glory days" of US postwar industrial expansion; growth was concentrated in the rapidly expanding suburban districts. Second, rather than a "cataclysmic" impact that devastated the industrial heartland after 1973, industrial decline was slow, cumulative, and selective. Even in those cities that suffered wholesale industrial decline, the writing had been on the wall for some time before the devastation of the 1970s and 1980s.

BUILDING THE SUBURBAN FACTORY AND INDUSTRIAL DECLINE IN POSTWAR CHICAGO

An analysis of 209 building projects in 1920 and 1928 listed in the Chicago-based weekly real estate magazine, the *Economist*, shows that the city was by far the major recipient of factory investment.[1] Only eighteen construction projects were undertaken outside the city's boundaries. Some of these involved firms leaving Chicago for the more sylvan areas of the metropolitan fringe, such as Abbott Drug's move to North Chicago. In other cases, suburban firms made additions to existing plants, such as those made by Ingalls Shepard to its Harvey plant. The suburbs also became home to starts from elsewhere. Pratt Food moved its plant from Philadelphia and opened a new animal remedy plant in Hammond. Despite this range of suburban projects, Chicago remained the prime location for most of the industrial space being built in the 1920s.

By the 1950s, the situation has been reversed, as the metropolitan suburbs became the place of choice for firms new to the area and those leaving the city. This changing geography of construction began to gather pace in the 1930s and accelerated after World War II. What had begun as a slow stream in the interwar period became a flood in the postwar years. As Leonard Yaseen, the president of the Fantus Factory Locating Service, predicted in 1962, "in the next decade, it will be the very rare exception when a manufacturer decides to build a factory in a big city area."[2] The previous chapter examined industrial decline through the lens of the changing geography of industrial employment. This chapter shows how this employment loss in the central city was rooted in site selection decisions made by the managers of industrial and financial firms about more profitable locations for fixed-capital investment. The focus on factory construction provides a different perspective on the impact that industrial change had on the built environment.

Studies of the relationship between local economic change, politics, and place dependency have demonstrated the tenuous hold that places have on productive forces and the unequal relationship that exists between place and capital.[3] This was evident in interwar Chicago as industrial executives increasingly viewed the city as an unsuitable location for new factories and sought greener pastures in the city's suburbs. By the 1930s a new economic value of space was being created across the metropolitan area, one in which central spaces were labeled as mainly black and poor, congested and blighted, and having little economic and social value. Suburban sites, to the contrary, were framed as the home of prosperous white families and modern, productive industry.

The relationship of capitalists to place is twofold. First, they use it as a site for the production of commodities, revenue, and profit.[4] Place is a repository of labor power, supplier networks, transportation facilities, and housing, all of which are essential for commodity manufacture. The profits made from circulating capital can only be realized by the immobility of capital in a place and by the successful operation of a place's economic, political, and social assets. Second, capitalists view place-based material objects as things that need to be controlled and manipulated in order to make these profits possible. In order to extract value from investments in land, machinery, and infrastructures, local groups consisting of developers, the local state, landowners, and financial institutions have to create calculative coalitions that both nurture and defend their place-based assets. These groups have to establish an appropriate set of place-based relations of production in order for firms to reap the benefits of fixed-capital investments.

In doing this, corporate managers face certain challenges. One is that the tension between the mobility and fixity of capital creates crises in place, which in turn have differential effects across metropolitan and regional landscapes. Communities are subject to interplace competition, which unless protected against by elite alliances can devalue the fixed capital that firms have stored in a locale. As the capital invested in factories and other structures cannot easily be moved, firms need to devise methods to protect their investments from the devaluation that comes as capital shifts from one location to another. A second challenge is the maintenance of social order and the existence of a viable working population. The restless dynamics of class and race can undermine a place's attractiveness to investors. A final challenge is the obdurate character of land and the value that individuals and firms attach to it. In the face of land's unique quality—most notably, its irreplaceability and nonsubstitutability—industrialists have to increase land value and the profits that they make by changing what takes place on the land.[5] All this has important effects on place-based capital investment and ultimately on a locale's industrial base.

Factory construction activity in Chicago reflects the industrial manager's calculations about the city's suitability as a manufacturing space. The large, one-time investments required to build new facilities ensure that construction is a key indicator of the executive's understanding of place-based fortunes both in the present and in the future. As several writers have noted, the pressure on local industrial relationships became increasingly fraught with the rise of corporations after 1900.[6] Freed from the dependency on one place and the obstacles inherent in old locations, the multiunit corporation was able to shift capital from one locale to another with greater ease than had previously been the case. Interplace competition allowed corporations to derive specific benefits by pitting one site against another. The broadening set of choices emerging after 1900 became generalized after 1930, as industrial corporations and financial institutions created a new metropolitan geography of factory construction, one that favored the suburbs.

I examine this new geography of factory construction in metropolitan Chicago through an analysis of 830 factories built between 1945 and 1960.[7] The analysis shows the emergence of the suburbs as the unrivaled place for industrial building. After a description of the data set, an analysis of the shifting metropolitan geography of factory construction shows that the suburbs were the most favored location of production space after 1945. Finally, I discuss two key elements that underwrote this geography of factory construction in the suburbs: the emergence of scientific site selection practices and the development of new arrangements to finance construction.

Factory Construction

Postwar business leaders were confident that wartime expansion would lead to the continuation of Chicago's position as an industrial powerhouse in the early postwar years.[8] Most place-dependent executives in planning, manufacturing, real estate, utilities, and finance believed that firms would build new premises across the city to meet growing demand and to house new production technologies. This investment, it was believed, would generate multiplier effects, creating service, retail, and construction jobs, and boosting the city's tax base. The argument pushed by groups such as the Chicago Association of Commerce and Industry was that the aircraft, electronic, and chemical industries would move to the city while additions would be made to firms in established industries such as steel, metalworking, meatpacking, and furniture.[9] The result would be the renaissance of the city's industrial sectors and its economic prowess.

In the eyes of the city's industrial boosters this is what happened. One of the earliest postwar reports noted that factory construction underpinned Chicago's position as a major industrial center. A 1955 report by Commonwealth Edison showed that Chicago was among the nation's leaders in factory construction, confirming wartime announcements that the city would continue "to hold its competitive position" in the postwar years.[10] Other reports made the same point—Chicago's continued industrial supremacy was based on sustained factory construction.[11] This misplaced optimism was voiced by William Kaplan, the president of the Chicago chapter of the Society of Industrial Realtors, a group with especial interest in the vitality of the city's industry. In 1948, Kaplan prophesied that the "soundness of values inherent in properly located factory and warehouse properties" lay in Chicago's diversity of manufactured products, position as the United States' central market, vast supply of skilled labor, and influx of new industries.[12] Chicago's industry, it was argued, would continue to dominate the country.

These announcements were misleading. An analysis of the construction of 830 factories in metropolitan Chicago presents a quite different picture than the one presented by the city's economic and civic elites. Not surprisingly, this construction activity paralleled the pattern of employment change outlined in the previous chapter. Much of the growth in construction described in the reports by Commonwealth Edison and others took place in the suburbs. At the same time, the data indicate, contrary to the generally received deindustrialization thesis, that change was incremental, not cataclysmic. The historical geography of factory construction was a drawn-out process that affected different places in dissimilar ways. Ultimately though, the end result was that the suburbs received most postwar investment and the city did not experience an industrial renaissance.

Despite the optimism of booster groups, the data show that more than three-quarters of the value of the fixed capital invested in additions to existing factories or the building of new ones in Chicagoland was made outside the city in the suburbs (table 2.1). Of the more than $1 billion, only $253 million, or less than a quarter, went into city factories; the remaining $750 million found its way to suburbs such as Skokie and Hammond (figure 2.1). This disparity was noted by

TABLE 2.1 Industrial construction activity of metropolitan Chicago, 1945–60

TYPE	CITY OF CHICAGO		SUBURBS		METROPOLITAN CHICAGO	
	NUMBER	COST ($000)	NUMBER	COST ($000)	NUMBER	COST ($000)
Addition	306	169,903	205	447,052	511	616,955
New	125	83,213	194	326,579	319	409,792
Total	431	253,116	399	773,631	830	1,026,747

Source: *Engineering News-Record*, 1945–60.

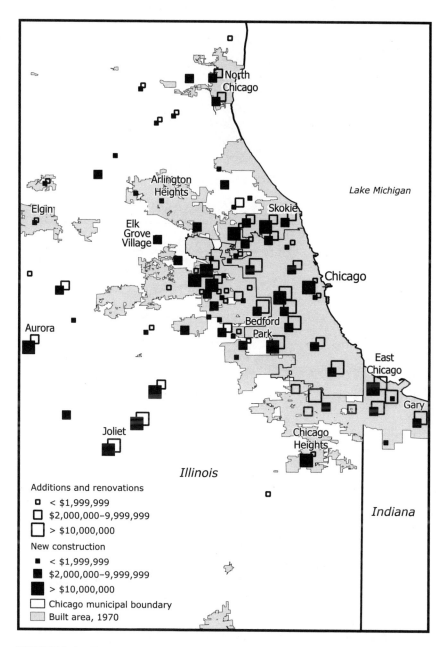

FIGURE 2.1 The geography of factory building in metropolitan Chicago, 1945–60. With a few exceptions, most factory construction in the Chicago region between 1945 and 1960 took place on the outer perimeters of the city or in the suburbs. Compiled from the *Engineering News-Record*, 1945–60.

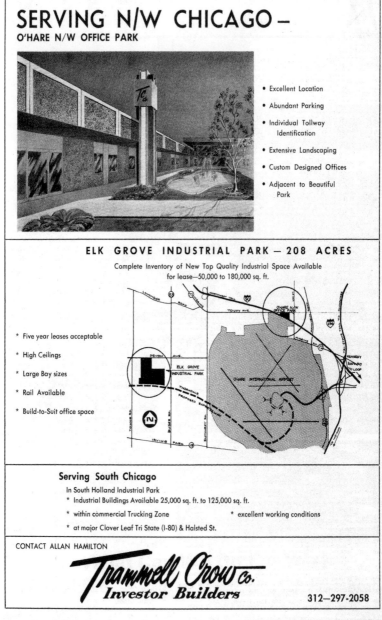

FIGURE 2.2 Elk Grove Industrial Park, 1969. Companies such as Trammell Crow worked actively to build industrial complexes in the suburbs after World War II. One of the largest was the Elk Grove Industrial Park. These districts were touted as having better and more modern industrial space than could be found in the city. *Third Annual Metropolitan Chicago Industrial Development Guide, 1969*, 29, box 225, folder 2418, Chicago Urban League records, Special Collections and University Archives, University of Illinois at Chicago.

a *Chicago Tribune* reporter in 1952 when he observed the "startling growth" of factory building in the suburbs and its relative absence in the city.[13]

The vast amount of building that occurred in the city took the form of additions to existing facilities. Three-quarters of the building that took place in the city and two-thirds of the value went to adding new space to old factories. Some were very small. In the Stockyards area, for example, F and F Laboratories made a $40,000 addition to its cough drops factory in 1945, while Acme Aluminum Foundry carried out a $68,000 nonferrous foundry addition in 1949. At the other end of the spectrum, a few national corporations invested heavily in their existing units: Ford made a $4 million addition to its Hegewisch automotive assembly plant on the city's South Side; and Republic Steel spent more than $22 million on a seamless tube mill and warehouse at its sprawling South Chicago plant.[14]

For some firms, adding new facilities to old production units was considered a viable option. The high levels of capital sunk into a plant combined with dependency on in-place assets such as a captive labor force and supplier relations meant that an addition was considered by many central-city firms as the best way to proceed. Certainly, the economic success of an industrial place is dependent upon the ability of that place to retain its manufacturing operations. Under these conditions, factory construction reflects the ongoing attractiveness of a place to industrial investors in the long term. The city's precarious position is highlighted by the fact that few companies were willing to build an entirely new factory in the city after 1945, while some firms settled for investing in small additions to old plants. In contrast to the city, a smaller number of building actions in the suburbs were additions, but they accounted for a larger value than those in the city. The cost of building the 205 suburban additions easily outpaced the amount invested in the 306 made in the city. Industrialists considered the suburbs a much safer bet over the long term and a larger part of their future plans.

In terms of new factories, 80 percent of the Chicagoland's total value was found outside the city; the suburbs were the region's major postwar construction site. Many of these new facilities would come to house plants that closed their doors in the city and set up shop in Riverdale, Melrose Park, or Elk Grove Village (figure 2.2). Factories of all sizes and shapes were built in the new industrial suburbs between 1945 and 1960, but the dominant mode was the single-story, through-flow building with parking laid out in a landscaped setting.[15]

Two new buildings in Evanston illustrate the importance of the modern factory in the changing industrial geography of the Chicago region. The Sentinel Radio Corporation constructed a new plant in the northern suburb in 1947 that "built around the straight-line production of radio sets," according to the industrial journal *Factory Management and Maintenance*. "Raw materials are received on the west end of the plant, flow via straight continuous methods through one of the four production lines, and emerge as completely finished radio sets ready for shipment." This new, through-flow factory consolidated the existing three plants, the main one being an old-style, four-story factory that was no longer considered appropriate for modern manufacturing practices. Rather than the problems associated with the awkward layout of the old premises, the new plant made it possible for Sentinel to produce radios without "any *backtracking*, any *lost motion*."[16] Time and motion are money, and suburban factories were considered the most effective means for getting it.

Ten years later, another Evanston factory made the news. Labeled the "factory of the month" by the *Chicago Tribune*, the new Orange Crush bottling plant boasted a factory surrounded by a "lawn and evergreens with plantings of flowering bushes and vines." It was different from the old one it replaced in the blighted sections of downtown Chicago. As Ernest Fuller opined, "the eyesore factory of yesterday is giving way to a new type of industrial architecture." Not only did Orange Crush's modern building reduce production costs; it also, he noted, "enhance[d] property values and beautifie[d] neighborhoods."[17] In the opinion of the Sentinel and Orange Crush executives, the modern, streamlined industrial design that was found in the suburbs far away from the city's congested streets made for better production efficiencies, lower costs, higher profits, and better worker morale. They were not alone; an increasing number of executives made the same decision after 1945.

Multiunit construction provides another perspective on the central city's declining place. A multiunit action was one in which a firm built a new plant separate from an old plant that continued to operate as a production unit. Typically, the new factory was a separate but complementary unit that fulfilled a particular niche within a company's broader operations. Even though the thirty-nine multiunits were not a particularly large share of all activity, they provide insights into how company executives viewed the locational advantages for manufacturing in different parts of the metropolis. In contrast to the previous hundred years of factory construction, three-quarters of these branch plants by number and value were built in the suburbs, and most were branch plants of central-city firms. Reflective of the declining position of the city within the metropolitan geography of industry, not one suburban firm built a branch plant in the city.

One firm to open up a branch unit in the suburbs while maintaining its city factory was Motorola, Inc. Until the early 1950s, the company, which had started from a small radio manufacturer, had its main operations on the city's northwest side. In 1952, the company announced the building of a $3 million TV assembly plant in suburban Franklin Park. Some of the operations of the company's main city facility were shifted to the new suburban site in order to escape the city's crowded conditions, to increase production efficiencies, and to reduce costs. The city's diminished role in the corporate spatial division of labor was signaled in 1960, when Motorola moved its headquarters from the city to Franklin Park.[18] Motorola was not alone; other firms made the same decision, including Rand McNally (Skokie), Burny Brothers Bakeries (Northlake), and Crown Rheostat and Supply (Elk Grove Village).

It wasn't only city firms that built suburban branch plants. Some suburban firms also opened new facilities in other parts of Chicagoland while maintaining their main plant. One case is Ceco Steel Products, which had operated its main plant in suburban Cicero since the 1920s. In 1952, Ceco brought property in Broadview, a suburb to the west of Chicago, as part of its national expansion program. Three years later it built what would become the company's steel joist and reinforcing bar fabricating operations. In 1958 it expanded its facilities and moved from being a simple fabricator of metal products to a maker of steel, when it opened a steel mill near the western suburb of Lemont. Rather than relying on other steel producers, the new mill on the Chicago Sanitary and Ship Canal made ingots for the Cicero and the Broadview plants. This was not the end of the suburban expansion. Four years later, Ceco built a fabricating plant next to the steel mill. This was one element of a three-part redevelopment program with major operational shifts among the Chicago region's plants: the Broadview bar fabricating operation was shifted to the Lemont plant; the Broadview factory was remodeled to accommodate merchant trade products; and the Cicero plant increased its production of metal windows and doors.[19]

These examples show that the suburbs attracted new construction investment from corporations with several facilities in the Chicago region. The end result of these multiunit construction programs by Motorola, Ceco, and others was to expand their productive facilities, to increase production efficiencies to give the company a competitive edge, and to create a complex spatial division of labor across the metropolitan region. One effect was to channel fixed-capital investment from the central city to the suburbs, and in the process contribute to the expansion of the suburbs and the decline of the central city.

A final indicator of the growing suburban dominance of factory construction was its share of construction activity valued at $10 million or more. There are twenty-four cases in this category (table 2.2). Once again, the suburbs dominated construction. Not surprisingly, all the large builders were corporations with a national and sometimes international reach. The construction decision would have been taken after extensive research on sites across the country. The fact that all of them had considerable capital investments in the Chicago region obviously played a significant role in the determination of the location of these investments. Even large corporations were place dependent. Nevertheless, corporations such as Caterpillar Tractor and Youngstown Sheet and Tube did have

TABLE 2.2 Industrial construction activity of $10 million or more, 1945–60

FIRM	COST ($000)	TYPE OF WORK	LOCATION	YEAR LISTED	WORK DONE
Inland Steel	100,000	Addition	East Chicago	1956	Slabbing mill
US Steel	25,000	Addition	Gary	1956	Sintering plant
Buick Motor	25,000	New	Willow Springs	1951	Jet engine plant
Ford Motor	25,000	New	Chicago Heights	1955	Stamping plant
Acme Steel	24,000	Addition	Riverdale	1957	Blast furnaces
Republic Steel	21,000	Addition	Chicago	1951	Seamless tube plant
Caterpillar Tractor	17,000	New	Aurora	1956	Factory
Automatic Electric	16,000	New	Northlake	1956	Factory
US Rubber	16,000	Rehabilitation	Joliet	1951	Ordnance plant
Chicago Sun Times	15,000	New	Chicago	1955	Publishing house
Texas Co.	15,000	New	Lockport	1945	Catalytic cracking plant
Ford Motor	14,700	Rehabilitation	Chicago	1951	Jet engine plant
Hotpoint	12,000	Addition	Cicero	1950	Refrigerator plant
Youngstown Sheet & Tube	12,000	Addition	East Chicago	1956	Coke ovens
Ceco Steel Products	11,000	New	Lemont	1958	Steel mill
International Harvester	10,000	Addition	Chicago	1956	Ammonia absorber plant
Standard Oil	10,000	Addition	Hammond	1954	Nitrogen fixation unit
Standard Oil	10,000	Addition	Whiting	1959	Hydroforming unit
Standard Oil	10,000	Addition	Whiting	1953	Crude oil distillation plant
Texas Co.	10,000	Addition	Lockport	1956	Plant
Youngstown Sheet & Tube	10,000	Addition	East Chicago	1951	Plant
Libby, McNeil, Libby	10,000	New	Chicago	1959	Canned meat plant
Amoco Chemical	10,000	New	Joliet	1957	Chemical plant
Union Carbine Chemical	10,000	New	Whiting	1958	Polyethylene plant

Source: Engineering News-Record, 1945–60.

other options in other locations. Executives did see the importance of the fixed investments already in place as well as the future promise of the Chicago suburbs. The city was no longer an important part of the locational calculus for most manufacturing managers.

Industrial executives came increasingly to the conclusion that sites in the Chicago suburbs or further afield in the American South and West were better options for fixed-capital investments than those available in the city. These sites had lower wages, cheaper land, entrenched workers, and fewer unions. Industrial executives increasingly came to believe that the problems of the city's expensive and blighted factory districts and hostile African American and white, working-class cultures could only be solved by moving to other locales. Two key elements underpinned this suburban exodus: the creation of scientific site selection methods and the development of new industrial financial practices. As two management science specialists writing in the *Harvard Business Review* stated in 1968, location had become increasingly complex and "must be analyzed within the framework of long-range corporate planning" and new financial frameworks.[20]

Scientific Industrial Site Selection

Contributing to Chicago's industrial geography was a site selection industry that promoted scientific practices as a means to produce greater economic efficiencies.[21] Beginning in the interwar period, a cadre of planning, real estate, and engineering experts built a powerful industry that captured a growing share of building opportunities and reframed the industrial location decision. The aim of these experts was to provide a controlled production space for their clients, free from the nuisances of the older factory districts found in the center of the country's metropolises. This had two important linked effects: to facilitate industrial decentralization and to contribute to the industrial decline of the central city. The scientific site selection process that emerged after 1930 helped create a differentiated industrial metropolis—one in which some areas such as central Chicago were deemed problematic, while suburbs such as Skokie were considered more suitable for modern production operations. The end result of this practice of prioritizing the suburbs as the most efficient and rational productive space was to contribute to the undermining of manufacturing in the central city.

This site selection industry emerged from the confluence of two processes. The first was the rise of the large multiunit corporation. By the early twentieth century, the widening gaze of corporate managers allowed for a larger set of sites in different regional markets and cost areas across the country to be considered as suitable production sites. Unlike the owners of single-unit and family firms with deep business and personal attachments to place, corporate executives scanned the national landscape to find the optimal location for their plants. They were no longer held captive by having to choose from a few locations in one or a limited set of localities. By the 1930s, entrepreneurs with expertise in factory location were looking to both create and fill this need. The second process was the construction of conventional locational practices as problematic by a group of experts versed in real estate issues, industrial economics, and engineering. The new locational entrepreneur framed industrial location decisions as problematic by casting the existing plant selection methods as unsystematic, inefficient, and costly. They called for a scientific approach to factory location.

The increasing complexity of the location problem as determined by the widening demand from corporations and the attempts by location entrepreneurs to create a new industry meant that the problem could not be solved by the traditional means of site selection. Rather, the answer, according to Charles Wood, an industrial engineer, was to bring experienced professionals who could steer clear of "prejudice" and bring their assorted expertise to bear in a systematic manner on the problem.[22] The basic move taken by the new site selection entrepreneurs was to repackage the long-standing "factors of location" approach (labor, raw material, markets, transportation, and utilities) in a way that made the process appear to be more complicated than it actually was. The key action that site selection experts gave to the repertoire of locational decision-making was to add a new language to the old system of locational assessment and to reconceptualize decision-making as problematic and in need of advice from a coterie of knowledge-based professionals.

By the late 1930s, these site selection professionals had established a variety of methods to push their case. This included making comparative studies about places geared to the specific needs of their clients; analyzing information gathered by experts trained in economics, real estate development, and engineering; and creating a range of "optimal" locations, most of which were outside the central city. These entrepreneurs also emphasized the importance of linking locational decisions to factory design and construction costs. Design, costs, and location became increasingly interrelated, with optimal sites increasingly equated with suburban locations. With these methods in hand, these experts sold their services to an ever larger number of firms, especially multiunit corporations working in a national market.

The plant location experts created a body of ideas and practices they labeled scientific site selection. The emergence of these methods was signaled in 1930, when George Smith of the Industrial Club of Saint Louis noted that "in the past, manufacturers, for the most part, have been guided in the selections of their locations more by prejudice than by scientific research."[23] Smith claimed that "90 percent of our industries are located without any preliminary study of the economic fitness of the location." He reiterated this in 1938, defining site selection as a cost-benefit analysis of location, arguing that "research based on an analysis of costs is essential in determining where an industry can secure the largest number of economies in production, overhead, and distribution expense." He warned against "extravagant community, state, or regional advertising campaigns, supported by nothing more than brass bands or pretty pictures" as they undermined "detailed engineering studies of the economic fitness of a locality."

In Smith's view, "success in manufacturing depends more and more on econo-mies resulting from good plant location." This in turn depended on the making and utilization of expert scientific studies.[24]

Smith was not alone. In 1937, Wood wrote that the problem of location could only be solved by "the combined experience of engineers, factory executives, and economists."[25] Twenty years later, Raymond Bartlett of the National Industrial Development Exposition, a clearinghouse for industrial land, made a similar point: "site selection for industry had become an industry and a science in its own right."[26] In 1958, a factory organization specialist noted that site selection was "rapidly changing from an art to a science" and that sites were only selected "after intensive surveys of all factors that might affect manufacturing costs and efficiency." He identified business climate, labor relations, and local government support as being particularly important.[27] All these writers refer to the emergence of an industry made up of professionals who, they claimed, possessed the exper-tise to turn old-style ad hoc location decision-making into a new, scientific one centered on the proper analysis of economic, social, and political factors.

In the 1930s, the site selection experts began to make clear links between location, design, and costs.[28] One indication of this was the 1935 creation of an annual competition for the best factories built during the year by *Factory Man-agement*.[29] The competition emphasized linking cost, design, and location in a scientific way by experts from the engineering and real estate fields. The experts' main task was to devise methods that would allow manufacturers to find the "best" location and then to build a factory designed to reduce operating costs and increasing profits. What all these experts had in common was the concern that the spatial arrangement of the old multistory plant was inadequate for modern needs. They also pointed out that older industrial centers, such as Chicago, had far too many inefficient buildings. One study found that more than a quarter of Chicago's industrial space in 1963 was housed in buildings of five or more stories, while a substantial proportion had between two and four stories. These multistory buildings were "inefficient and no longer suited to modern industrial production methods." The fact that more than two-thirds of all floor space was located in factories built before 1940 made the situation more intolerable.[30] As the argument went, new industrial space in one-story buildings was necessary because "correct layout prevents useless movement of materials, ineffective pro-cedure by employees, consumption of time to no purpose." The mantra of the site section industry was that the multistory factory was out of date, while the single story was "the building of today."[31]

This had obvious spatial implications. The old multistory factory on a con-stricted and expensive lot was concentrated in the central city, while the single-story factory required much larger tracts of land that could not easily be found downtown. The absence of large and affordable tracts of land in central cities required manufacturers to look to the suburbs and rural areas for land that could accommodate the sprawling single-story factory. By the 1930s, the idea that the city's older plants were inefficient and needed to be replaced with those on larger lots became a central tenet of modern industrial location: new building design was to be married with a new location to produce more effective factory space.

The corollary of this was that the old industrial cities were inefficient and expensive. Overcrowded with obsolete production facilities, the central districts of Chicago, Detroit, and other cities were considered dysfunctional and unprofitable locations. This idea was fueled by the growing obsession with blight and its perceived impact on the capabilities of specific parts of the metropolis to house efficient and productive industrial space. New locations had to be found. The site selection industry had to ensure, in the words of Stephen Helbrun, a member of the National Resources Planning Board, that firms did not stay in an "improper location," which increasingly became defined as those in the central city.[32] Accordingly, site selection entrepreneurs pushed their clients to build new manufacturing space in the metropolitan suburbs and adjacent small towns. They pointed to the diseconomies of the central cities of the industrial North and the attractions of suburban locations across the country.

These efforts had a direct effect on central Chicago. By the 1930s, much of the city, especially the area within a couple of miles of the Loop, had become identified as an improper location for modern industry. The site selection industry and trade journals such as *Factory Management* pushed the single-story plant in a suburban site as the most effective location for the modern factory. As one observer noted, to best take advantage of the combination of design and location required manufacturers to "build away from the congested centers of population, in order to secure sufficient land at permissible prices."[33] This, however, did not stop all firms from building new factories in the city. The radio maker Hallicrafters, for example, built a new plant "designed for the straight-line production of both technical and home radios" just after the end of the war.[34] Eschewing the sylvan charms of the suburbs, company executives realized that the city offered sufficient advantages to a concern mass-producing commodities that required access to supplier plants. They decided to stay and constructed a modern plant built around the production process suitable for radio manufacture.

The vast majority of single-story factories, however, were built in the suburbs. The Sentinel Radio plant in Evanston, as mentioned above, was designed along straight-line principles with the intent of minimizing wasted movement and time. Similarly, Automatic Electric moved from a multistory complex in downtown Chicago to a single-story plant in suburban Northlake. Unlike older factories in the central city, a suburban plant "permitted arrangement of all storage, processing, assembly and shipping departments in orderly, straight-line sequence."[35] As one observer of the Chicago factory world noted in 1962, the search was for well-designed "flexible factories" that allowed for "multi-purpose uses with little or no structural conversion necessary," as well as for future expansion. The best location for these, he stressed, was in the region's "outlying areas."[36]

The professionals who used engineering, economic, and real estate expertise to undertake site selection were found in two main venues. Some were employed in in-house real estate or engineering departments. When IBM and Nabisco built new plants in Dallas and Fair Lawn, New Jersey, a company site selection team consisting of executives, engineers, managers, and lawyers toured the country looking at options. The Willard Storage Battery Company in Cleveland employed a vice president and a mechanical engineer to oversee all the company's locational and factory construction issues. When the battery company moved its facilities after World War II, the decision-making process involved two steps: to determine the company's need for the new plant and to have company officials make a survey of potential sites. Once these steps were completed, company executives chose the location that was considered to provide the lower overall manufacturing and distribution costs.[37] Location became framed through a rational scientific lens.

Developing in-house expertise to assess factory sites at several locations was necessary if companies were to make the right choice. Firms with central-city factories were confronted with a wider set of unknown choices when they considered building new branch plants in the suburbs, rural communities, and areas outside the region itself. To trade the familiarity of a known place for the unknowns of another was fraught with the promise of economic misadventure. To ensure that this wasn't the case, firms increasingly used their own in-house experts, such as traffic managers, economists, and real estate agents, to evaluate potential sites from a range of choices to determine those that were not in an "improper location."

At the same time, many firms contracted their locational services out to engineering and management consulting firms and to more specialized industrial brokerage companies that sprung up in increasing numbers in the interwar years. The industrial engineer Charles Wood, for example, was the location specialist for Lockwood Greene Engineers, Inc., an industrial engineering company that had long been involved in factory building, in Chicago and elsewhere.[38] Lockwood Greene was not alone. After World War II, an increasing number of firms specializing in site location studies emerged to meet the growing demand for new production sites (figure 2.3). In Chicago, firms such as Harrington, Tideman, O'Leary and Company offered an array of services, including industrial brokerage, development of new facilities, and finding new sites for prospective

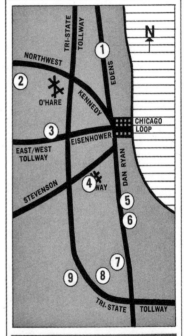
FIGURE 2.3   Industrial parks in metropolitan Chicago, 1969. One of Chicago's largest industrial real estate companies was involved in building industrial parks across the metropolitan region. As was common in the postwar period, most of those parks were built in the suburbs. *Third Annual Metropolitan Chicago Industrial Development Guide, 1969*, box 225, folder 2418, Chicago Urban League records, Special Collections and University Archives, University of Illinois at Chicago.

industrial firms. All of them favored locations on the edge of the city itself or in the suburbs.

Perhaps the single most significant company to shape Chicago's plant location choices and to make site selection a modern profession was the Fantus Factory Locating Service. Felix Fantus established a real estate company in Chicago in 1919 to help firms relocate their plants. In 1934, Fantus's son-in-law, Leonard Yaseen, broke off from his father-in-law's company to establish the Factory Locating Service in New York City. The company was so successful that Yaseen took over his father-in-law's operations at the end of World War II and brought in his brother-in-law, Maurice Fulton, to run the Chicago office's site selection operations. From these two key locales, the company came to play a leading role in the postwar industrial location industry. In 1951, Yaseen boasted that the firm had helped more than twelve hundred industrial firms find a new location. By 1965, Fantus employed fifty engineers and economists to prepare comprehensive and confidential reports for their twenty-five hundred clients. This list had grown to more than four thousand by 1977.[39]

The company's main strategy was to convince industrial executives of the problems of locating in the central city and the advantages to be gained by moving to the suburbs. In a 1939 interview, Yaseen stated that old industrial cities were plagued by high wages and tax rates. Moving out was the answer. This argument reappeared in various guises over the next three decades. In 1954, after berating government officials for using regulations to push industry out, Yaseen stated that "New York City no longer offers an opportunity to big industries, the mainstay in an economic crisis, in seeking to locate here."[40] Seven years later, Ronald Reifler of the company's Chicago office told Fred Eaton, assistant chief of the Industrial Location Division of the federal Business and Defense Services Administration, that the locational problems faced by cities were of their own making. In his opinion, a bad location was the product of an unsatisfactory local business climate and inadequate locational assets.[41]

Chicago was no different. According to Fulton, the city's land prices, congested space, mixed land uses, and unruly workers were pushing firms to the suburbs (figure 2.4). Chicago's locational assets were compromised, and its reputation as an industrial center was in disarray. Firms were looking to leave big cities such as Chicago, as they "were reluctant to move into a community dominated by some of the more aggressive union organizations." In other cases, the prevalence of antiquated factories in many inner cities meant that uneconomic practices could not "be eradicated without complete removal from the location." In his view, the result was that firms which had been located in the Great Lakes cities for a generation or more were increasingly opening up plants in "completely different areas" across the country and in small towns. Not surprisingly, he averred, cities

FIGURE 2.4   Factories and homes in the Near West Side, c. 1932–36. For an increasing number of observers, old industrial areas such as Ogden and Carroll, in the Near West Side, had become problematic spaces by the 1930s. The deteriorated factory, transportation, and residential environment was no longer considered conducive to effective manufacturing operations. Box 6, file "Municipal Reference, Buildings, Industrial, Photographs," Department of Urban Renewal Collection, Special Collections, Chicago Public Library.

such as Chicago were susceptible to the "raiders from the South, the Southeast and the Southwest."[42]

While Fulton may not have been less than sympathetic to southern raiders, he certainly made the point of advising his client firms in Chicago to move to greener pastures, both in Chicago suburbs such as Skokie and Elk Grove Village and in the more attractive locales to be found in the South and West.[43] As one reporter noted, the Chicago Fantus office had helped some of the city's leading companies define their branch plant strategy, and in the process, determine the geography of factory construction in the metropolitan area and elsewhere.[44] In the middle of the 1960s, for example, the company was behind the relocation of several significant Chicago firms: Automatic Electric to Huntsville, Alabama, Zenith Radio to Springfield, Missouri, and Advance Transformer to Monroe, Wisconsin.[45]

By the immediate postwar years the main elements of scientific site selection were firmly in place and clearly affecting the volume, type, and location of factory construction in the metropolitan area. Numerous organizations, including site selection companies and railroad industrial development departments, offered in-house and outside contractual expertise to Chicago firms looking to build new factories. Groups of experts who had specialized economic, real estate, and engineering knowledge established practices to determine the most profitable site for firms seeking to move their factory or open a branch plant. Framing central Chicago with its racial, class, environmental, and property issues as a problematic space, site selection experts pushed industry out of the city and into suburban and rural areas. Journals such as *Factory Management* and *Architectural Record* disseminated information about the best locational practices to a readership of industrial, political, real estate, and financial managers. Finally, as the sample of 830 construction actions has shown, a growing number of Chicago industries were seeking to find homes for their modern, single-story plants outside the city. In many cases, this building took place in the suburbs; in some others, it was across the rest of the country.

The efforts of these locational experts contributed to the city's industrial decline and the rise of the suburbs as the metropolitan region's major area of factory construction and manufacturing employment. Choosing a site away from the city center for a new factory was not enough. The industrial landscape that the site selection industry created with its search for optimal locations across the country had to be matched by the development of appropriate industrial financial methods. After 1940, a new set of institutions became involved in financing factory construction across the Chicago metropolitan area, ones that heavily favored the suburbs.

Financing Factory Construction

In 1920, the Yellow Cab Co. took out a mortgage to help pay for a new $1 million taxi and truck plant it was building on the city's far west side. The $600,000 first mortgage issue was underwritten by the Chicago investment banking firm S. W. Strauss and Co.[46] More than a quarter of a century later, Hallicrafters Corp. assumed a first mortgage of $382,500 at 4 percent and a second mortgage of $430,000 to pay for its new factory on West Fifth Street. Mortgages were not the only way that firms funded the building of factories in Chicago.[47] Firms also found the capital necessary for new construction by using current reserves, taking out bank loans, and issuing capital stock securities. The mortgage, however, continued to be a key instrument for companies such as Yellow Cab and Hallicrafters to build industrial space.[48]

Many industrial property transactions continued under the traditional mortgage after 1945, and for good reason. The instrument's simplicity and flexibility allowed industrial firms to build while permitting the liquidity of their existing funds. At the same time, the mortgage market was an important outlet for commercial banks and savings and loan companies looking to make safe, long-term investments. Following the line of thought pushed by the site selection industry, financial institutions put increasing stock in suburban properties. After World War II, life insurance companies became an increasingly important player in factory construction, and by 1973, the industry had plowed between 20 and 30 percent of its total investments into mortgages, making it one of the largest lenders in the country.[49]

Despite the mortgage's advantages, industrialists often had difficulty acquiring funding for factory construction. As early as the mid-1920s, the Chicago Real Estate Board and the Chicago Mortgage Brokers' Association noted the reluctance of banks to invest in industrial property, as investors favored commercial and large-scale residential projects. Factories, they averred, did not have the "elasticity" of offices and apartment buildings; it was difficult to use factories for any other purpose. Another problem was that the payments on interest and principal that came from industrial earnings were not as secure as office and apartment rents.[50] Walter Berg, a mortgage banker who was vice president of Dovenmuehle, Inc., a leading real estate company and construction loan financier, said that investors were reluctant to invest in new industrial facilities in Chicago because of the risks associated with providing loans for construction. The result was that most lending institutions did not employ staff capable of working with industry.[51]

The growing scale of factories after 1945 forced industrial executives to look for new sources of construction capital. Financing became more difficult with the growing competition for scarce funds during the postwar boom and the increasing reluctance of local banks to meet company needs. Moreover, executives were frequently unwilling to dip into their internal reserves. For many, the traditional mortgage placed undue restrictions on the use of working capital by locking it into long-term construction and repayment schedules. Capital, it was believed, could be more productively deployed in other areas of the business if funds could be diverted from construction. The result was that many manufacturers were hesitant to increase their debts or to use capital reserves to build new factory space. Industrial executives had to find a way to counter these problems. Working with the financial sector, they came up with two solutions, both of which would have a huge impact on the availability of investment for new factory construction and on the suburbanization of fixed capital. Both would contribute to the decline of industry in the central city and the industrial growth of the suburbs.

The first was the growing importance of life insurance companies as direct owners of industrial real estate and as investors in industrial construction after 1945.[52] Before the war the ability of insurance companies to invest in real estate was limited to residential and commercial mortgages.[53] By 1950, however, life insurance companies were the country's largest mortgage lenders, out-lending both commercial banks and saving and loans associations.[54] This change became increasingly visible after 1940, as insurance companies turned to construction loans and property ownership as well as mortgages. Their involvement grew dramatically over the following years, and by the end of the 1950s, insurance firms had acquired significant equity in residential, commercial, and industrial properties, and, to a lesser extent, construction loans. By the end of 1982, along with $140 billion in mortgages, the insurance companies had $20 billion in equity.[55]

One outlet of this activity was industrial property. The rise of the life insurance sector as an industrial property and mortgage holder was made possible by rewriting the legislation governing the activities of insurance companies in property ownership and development. In 1942, the Virginia state legislature allowed life insurance companies to own and develop real estate. By 1947, the number of states that permitted life insurance companies to own property through law or by default had grown to forty. According to the Institute of Life Insurance, the passing of New York state legislation in 1945 led the way for the relaxation of restrictions on insurance investment across the country.[56] This was to have an enormous effect on residential, commercial, and industrial property by broadening the investment options for the industry's "vast stores of idle funds" produced by the demographic and political changes that had been under way since the 1930s.[57]

One area where life insurance companies invested their vast store of idle funds was in the construction of middle-income apartments. In New York City, Metropolitan Life worked with the city to tear down a huge swath of the multiethnic, working-class Lower East Side and replace it with Stuyvesant Town, an apartment complex built for the white middle class. In Chicago, New York Life Insurance built Lake Meadows, a middle-class complex placed on land assembled and cleared by the city and taken from African Americans owners. These two projects were defining moments of the industry's entry into residential urban renewal. Looking for a safe investment, insurance companies such as Metropolitan Life and New York Life worked with all levels of the state to gain access to subsidized land while building middle-class homes on the cleared land. This provided the insurance companies with a steady return on the income gained through the difference between the market and real value of the acquired property. The benefit for the city government was that it brought back the white middle class to the city while eliminating blight and increasing the tax base. For African Americans and members of the working class who were dispossessed, the outcome was less satisfactory.[58]

Life insurance companies also became involved in owning new factories. In doing so, they played a significant part in the industrial geography of the post-war Chicago region. This point was made by Thomas Parkinson, president of the Equitable Life Assurance Co., when he said in 1950 that the industry had "channeled . . . great sums of money needed to keep factories and plants producing."[59] At the same time that firms were seeking to free up working capital for profit-making ends, insurance companies were looking to make long-term stable cash returns, which involved managing their capitalization rate. High rates of return involve risk, while insurance companies prefer stable cash flow over an extended period. As Parkinson pointed out, the highest return may not be the best option; rather, financing the construction of corporate factories with long-term and secure gains may be a safer strategy than working with other riskier investment options.[60]

In this calculus, and this was the one pushed by the site selection industry, the suburbs were considered the safest location for these investments. At the same time, the large corporations were considered by insurance firms to be the safest and most profitable focus for their investment activities. The result of these two trends was that a significant share of the insurance sector's industrial property investments went to underwrite the building of the corporate factory in the suburbs. Two examples illustrate this. Ceco Steel, the Cicero metal fabrication company, financed the construction of its large bar steel-making unit in suburban Lemont in 1958 with loans totaling $11 million assembled from five life insurance companies. The New York City investment banking firm Hornblower and Weeks arranged the loan from its Chicago office.[61] A few years earlier, in 1949, the Prudential Insurance Company financed the expansion of Rand McNally's printing plant in suburban Hammond. As part of its expansion plans, the company obtained a $1.5 million, fifteen-year mortgage from Prudential to buy and make additions to the old W. C. Conkey printing plant at the site.[62] In both cases, insurance companies considered the suburban sites of the two well-regarded corporations to be worthy of long-term investment.

By the 1940s, insurance companies were turning to financial instruments other than the traditional mortgage to satisfy the demand for new factories, open up the suburbs to factory building, and produce stable returns for themselves. One loan instrument they used was the corporate trust deed. The deed allowed a trustee who worked for other interests to take title to the mortgaged property, and to use a firm's credit as collateral rather than the real estate. These deeds have been used for large-scale transportation financing since the 1830s, but they became increasingly common for other purposes from the 1930s.[63] Using the trust deed and other instruments, insurance companies became more and more associated with industrial real estate matters. Industrial loans grew from $92 million in 1935 to $1 billion in 1945 and $2.7 billion in 1950. As one authority noted, the placement of industrial loans with life insurance companies and trust funds became "one of the most important methods of financing corporate enterprise."[64]

The second development that financed Chicago's postwar industrial construction was the growing popularity of the leaseback.[65] By the 1940s, financial institutions were looking to move out of mortgages and invest their funds into equity holdings. Insurance companies were leaders in doing this. They and other financial institutions looked to the leaseback, a device that enabled industrial firms to build a new plant or have one built for them, which they then sold to investors, who in turn rented it to the industrial firm on a long-term lease. In the immediate postwar years, the leaseback became an increasingly important instrument for companies looking to make stable, long-term investments and to deepen their investment portfolios by adding equity holdings to the simple mortgage.[66]

The leaseback became increasingly important as a way to finance suburban factories after 1945. The New England Mutual Life Company, for example, purchased a site and built a new factory for Rand McNally in Skokie at the end of 1951. The printer leased it back for thirty-five years at an annual rent of $5 million.[67] This trend was not lost on Chicago's real estate industry. In 1966, Stephen Nardi, a leading Chicago industrial real estate agent, noted that firms building in the suburbs preferred to use internal funds as working capital rather than to have it frozen in a factory building. Leasebacks allowed firms looking to build new factories on suburban sites to find ways of financing construction other than taking out mortgages. This way, they could approach financial institutions to fund the building and to take ownership of the property. As Nardi made clear, the long-term leasing system and property management by financial institutions provided industrial executives with both financial flexibility and new production space. These financial arrangements, which were "still growing nationally and in the Chicago area," contributed to the increasing importance of manufacturing in Chicago's suburbs.[68]

Nardi was not the first to identify the growing relationship between the insurance industry, leasebacks, and suburban construction. In the mid-1940s, the Mortgage Bankers Association of America devoted a half day at its annual convention to discuss the reasons for and the yields obtained from the increased investment by insurance companies in industrial and commercial real estate. One organizer explained that large and medium-sized institutions across the country were making these investments in the early postwar years: forty states had authorized insurance companies to invest in nonhousing property in one form or the other by 1947. He made the same point about the purpose of the leaseback. In his opinion, the acquisition of industrial properties from firms by insurance companies who then leased them back to corporations was becoming more common. The result was that "the insurance company gets an investment returning a higher yield than is otherwise available while the industrial company puts its money to work in its business on a more profitable basis if invested in real estate which it occupies."[69] It worked for everyone.

Insurance companies had an explicit policy to invest only in certain districts, most of which were located in the suburbs. Insurance companies proceeded very cautiously, as they were worried about lending to concerns that could not meet their strict guidelines and could not guarantee repayments over an extended period of time. Given the widening gap between how most observers viewed the virtues of central and suburban space, the result was the flow of industrial investment to new construction in suburban districts by national corporations with good credit ratings. As C. J. Flaherty, Prudential's executive director, told a national convention of industrial developers in 1954, "the type of plant we prefer is . . . a modern one-story building with general purpose use with a square foot area of between 25,000 and 50,000 square feet." This type of industrial building was concentrated in the new postwar industrial suburbs.[70]

High corporate taxes and unsettled securities markets were identified as the immediate causes of the growing number of Chicago industrial firms leasing rather than owning new facilities. Under these conditions, suburban sites were considered the safest location for investment. As one observer noted, "of prime importance to the plant operator is that he can acquire use of a new factory, built to his design, without impairing his working capital." Firms such as the Mutual Life Insurance Co. of New York and Metropolitan Life started to lease suburban buildings to firms because "they provide a better rate of return than is available from either private or government securities."[71] The overall result was that the leaseback had become a defining element of the financing of industrial construction in postwar suburban Chicago and the United States.

The growing prominence of this investment instrument led to the establishment of agencies specializing in organizing leaseback arrangements between financial institutions and suburban industrial concerns. In 1946, the Mortgage Corp., one of the Chicago's largest property agencies, opened an industrial construction department to offer executives the opportunity to order and lease property. The company's focus was the Chicago suburbs. According to the president, C. Robert Lazerus, the firm offered industrial facilities that could be leased for a term of several years. The company was willing to negotiate flexible rental conditions, depending on the needs of individual firms. In Lazerus's opinion, executives preferred to lease rather than own factory space for several reasons, including tax write-offs and not having to be involved in the complicated real estate and construction businesses, which were both a distraction from production activities.[72]

The growing demands for industrial mortgages, equity, and construction loans had the effect of spatially segmenting the metropolitan property market. Over the course of the postwar period, these financial practices had a twofold impact: they reduced the attraction of the central city as a construction site while elevating the suburban districts to a place of prominence. One result of the growing association between Chicago's industrial companies and financial institutions was the reconfiguration of the relative status of the two production zones. Some companies, such as North Chicago's Abbott Laboratories, which made additions valued at $4 million to its research facilities and chemical laboratory in the mid-1950s, continued to build by using internal funds. Most other firms took capital from a variety of financial institutions to fund the construction of new plants. In the case of Evanston's Sentinel Radio, a mortgage of $300,000 financed an addition. Sometimes, banks loans were taken out to build production space, make other types of improvements, and retire existing debts. American Colortype took out a $1,050,000 bank loan at 3.25 percent in 1945 from a consortium of Chicago and New York City banks to retire an existing debt of $300,000 and to make improvements to their plant.[73]

Leaseback funding typically found its way to the suburbs. As one reporter noted, investors in industrial properties looked to channel their funds to "choice property" on the metropolitan fringe.[74] Prudential was one of several firms that underwrote the building of suburban factories, which contributed to the hollowing out of the postwar city. In 1947, Fischer Company, an electrosurgical equipment maker, moved from the city to a new $500,000 plant in Franklin Park. As part of the insurance company's nationwide industrial program that was intended to create financial stability, Prudential purchased the factory and leased it back to Fischer.[75] Seven years later, Prudential participated in two leasebacks in other suburban districts. One involved the construction of a $3 million plant for Ditto, a maker of duplicating machines, on a tract sold to Prudential by Ditto, who leased the plant from the insurance company for twenty-five years. In the same year, the microphones and acoustic devices manufacturer Shure built a $760,000 plant in Evanston that was purchased by Prudential and leased back to the manufacturer.[76]

The agents involved in building new postwar production space—real estate brokers, builders, industrialists, and financiers—worked with new financial instruments to provide advantages to manufacturers searching for new suburban plants and the financial industry looking for stable, long-term profits. The new markets for industrial mortgages, equity, and construction loans allowed industrial executives to free up scarce funds for working capital while providing financial institutions, most notably life insurance companies, with a steady stream of stable income over a long period of time. Much of this capital investment went to the suburbs, which was the home of most new construction after World War II. The effect was to refashion the industrial geography of the postwar metropolis. The suburbs replaced the central city as the primary location for industry.

By whatever measure, the city lost its dominant position as the site for factory construction as companies invested in the suburbs after 1945. The attractions of the suburbs stood in sharp contrast to the industrial diseconomies of central-city districts that had been under way since the 1920s and accelerated after 1945. Even though industrial leaders may not have always acknowledged these changes, they did respond to the issues in front of them. For some, the response was to flee the Chicago region altogether, seeking profitable investment opportunities in other locations. The opening of meatpacking plants in Cedar Rapids, Iowa, and Omaha from the 1920s, for example, led inevitably to the decline of Chicago's industry, with the eventual closing of most of the meatpacking factories in the 1950s.[77] For other industrial managers, the suburbs became the focus of construction investment. In some cases, this involved opening a branch plant in a new subdivision; in others, it meant uprooting the entire factory and moving lock, stock, and barrel to the suburbs. Others, especially those in older industries with heavy fixed capital or supplier commitments in the central city, tended to stay in place. The linked processes of suburban growth and city decline were substantively aided by the rise of the site selection industry and new financial tools, both of which heavily favored the suburbs over the central city.

The next five chapters look at the solutions devised by the city's place-dependent elites to industrial decline in Chicago between 1945 and 1975. One was to build public-private partnerships and institutions that would harness local resources to fight industrial decline. Another was to rewrite the social relations of industrial property. As the anchor of locational decision, land became the locus of change and subject to actions from those interested in the city's industrial economy. What became increasingly clear after World War II was that the city's bourgeoisie would have to find solutions that would allow for long-term industrial redevelopment. In order to reformulate the place of industry in the city, it was necessary to rethink property relations. To this end, the place-dependent elites had to create a discourse that would shift the blame for industrial decline away from the industrial decision makers and to provide the rationale for their response to industrial decline. That discourse centered on the idea of blight and is the topic of the next chapter.

BLIGHT AND THE TRANSFORMATION OF INDUSTRIAL PROPERTY

In an April 1955 speech to the American Industrial Development Council in Washington, DC, James Follin, the commissioner of the federal government's Urban Renewal Administration, outlined how the federal slum clearance and industrial renewal program functioned. He told his audience of industrial and municipal managers that the first task was to identify the blighted lots that required attention. These lots were to be purchased from the owners and then worked on by a set of measures, which ranged from rehabilitation and conservation to complete clearance. Once this process was completed, the cleared property was to be sold to new owners. Follin finished his talk by noting that most of the blighted land available for industrial redevelopment happened to be downtown residential slums. He also noted that these tracts could be converted to any type of land use, including industrial, as long as redevelopment followed an approved city plan. In other words, new industrial space could be created by reworking the central city's blighted residential areas.[1]

While this notion may have seemed self-evident to Follin, it was relatively new in 1955. Since the late nineteenth century, the overriding concern of urban elites in Chicago and elsewhere had been for residential redevelopment. From the 1920s and continuing into the postwar years, the building of new housing on cleared slum land, it was believed, was the key to the city's economic and social development. This was the point made by the journalist Thomas Furlong in 1947, when he claimed that slum removal was "Chicago's No. 1 job."[2] Furling was voicing the position of the city's place-dependent leaders who wished to build a postindustrial city by using federal funds to push ahead with both public housing and high-end residential redevelopment. This effort began with the Housing Act of 1937, which permitted land clearance and slum demolition for public housing. It was continued with the Housing Act of 1949, which channeled federal funds to cities so that blighted districts could be redeveloped as predominantly residential. In city after city, the result was the same—a concerted push for residential renewal on inner-city blighted land.[3]

The idea that residential redevelopment was the only way to undertake urban renewal and revitalize the central city, however, was beginning to be questioned in the immediate postwar year. For those interested in dealing with the problems of industrial disinvestment and competition from other locales, the idea that renewal could be undertaken with government support was attractive. Learning from the residential renewal movement, some city leaders became to develop a solution based on creating public-private partnerships to turn blighted areas into factory districts. Even though industrial managers were reluctant to work with government, the desire to neutralize competition and the need to find answers to problems forced them to consider this unpalatable option. For industrial executives, the problems of blight—deteriorated buildings, vacant lots, and obsolete infrastructures—were compounded by the difficulties of land assembly, high land prices, and the location of good industrial property. At the same time, several of the city's civic and private agencies which had similar concerns about the deteriorating character of downtown industry formed a loose coalition around the provision of government-subsidized and privately owned industrial sites in the city's blighted areas. For the next two decades, as city leaders battled industrial decline, a number of attempts were made to transform blighted areas into productive factory space.

At the close of the war, the private-public partnership that brought together government officials, property developers, and industrial managers to turn blighted land into functioning industrial property was still in its early stages. By 1951, however, the Chicago Plan Commission (CPC) was already working on turning some of the city's downtown blighted areas into industrial districts.[4] West Central, the first federally funded industrial district, was still being worked on in 1955. While industrial renewal emerged as a formal program in Chicago and elsewhere in the early 1950s, its origins lie in the earlier slum clearance movement. In the case of industry, however, it was the intersection of the idea of blight and the decline of the city's economy that shaped industrial redevelopment.

Few writers have made the link between industry and blight. When they have, they usually show how blight was caused by the invasion of residential areas by factories. Typically, attention is given to the relationship between race relations, the deterioration of housing areas, the creation of a language of blight, and the rise of residential renewal.[5] A few writers, however, have shown how blight is related to urban economic development. Colin Gordon notes how the link between decline, renewal, and funding is reflected in the growing presence of nonresidential matters in the postwar federal housing acts.[6] Others have explored how city leaders in Philadelphia, New York City, Newark, and other municipalities created agencies that would devise and implement solutions to address relentless job loss, factory closings, industrial underinvestment, and blighted central-city districts.[7] This was also the case in Chicago between 1930 and 1950, as place-dependent leaders saw the redevelopment of blighted areas as factory districts as a solution to urban decline.

Investigating Blight

In May 1930, as the Great Depression wreaked havoc on US cities, a *Chicago Tribune* editorial raised the issue of Chicago's "waste lands." These numerous public and private "eyesores" with their vacant land and uninhabited buildings were "damaging to the city." The solution the editorialist proposed was to raze the structures and clean up the land in order to make it "socially productive."[8] Seven years later, another journalist referred to Chicago's blighted area, a belt of "declining population and property values" stretching up to five miles in all directions from the central business district. The writer pointed out that something had to be done to make the city's central districts "a more desirable location for factories and warehouses."[9] The same point was also made in 1938 by Oscar G. Mayer in his inaugural speech as president of the Chicago Association of Commerce and Industry (CACI). Rezoning, he opined, would lead to the "rehabilitation of the large blighted area and the rejuvenation of Chicago as an industrial and residential city."[10] In Mayer's view and that of others, the equation was straightforward: clearance of blighted districts would reverse economic decline. In a similar vein, Henry T. Heald, president of the Illinois Institute of Technology, gave a speech to three hundred civic leaders in October 1946 to drum up support for a slum clearance program on the South Side. He told his audience, "we have two choices— either to run away from the blight or to stand and fight."[11]

All four writers were concerned with the same issue. Whether it was called waste land, slums, or blighted areas, the city's leaders were pointing to what they described as the rapid deterioration of Chicago's central-city districts and the creation of what they deemed unproductive property.[12] The terrible conditions of Chicago's white working-class and African American districts worsened from the early 1930s as factories closed, unemployment rose to unprecedented levels, housing construction more or less halted, and blight spread across the city.[13]

Armed with the rhetoric of waste lands, eyesores, and other forms of urban decay, commentators argued that something had to be done about residential deterioration while increasing industrial investment.

But this was not easy. Local elites such as Mayer and Heald could operate only within the market-based parameters of property and investment strategies. Fixed capital and industrial networks cannot be easily dismantled or moved without cost.[14] Property relations are entrenched in law and custom and are difficult to change.[15] Heald's question of whether to run away or fight was more than a rhetorical device for those with place-dependent investments. While upper- and middle-class homeowners could flee the central city for the halcyon estates of the suburbs without much loss, this was not the case for many others who were trapped by income or race in the central city's blighted districts. Similarly, for central-city business property owners with large fixed investment, escaping from downtown blight was not an option. The only economically feasible response for those dependent on Chicago's property and business was to stay and fight what they saw as the invasion of blight into their residential and industrial neighborhoods.

Chicago was not alone in constructing blight and the social geographies of race and class as the problem. Urban business and political leaders across the country were concerned about the impact of blight on urban housing markets. In particular, they were worried that the growing white working-class and African American populations and the failings of the built environment were driving the white middle class out the city. Blight became a central concern for national and urban leaders who sought a means to fight the physical and economic deterioration of the central cities. By the end of the 1930s, the relatively ineffectual tenement house and slum clearance movements with their emphasis on the provision of housing for low-income Americans had been replaced by the redevelopment movement and its focus on the building of well-to-do housing. This shift in emphasis was clothed in the language of blight.[16]

By the start of World War II, a coalition of civic and business agencies had emerged with the goal of redeveloping Chicago's blighted areas.[17] It had become evident to city elites from most sides of the political and business spectrum that individual action could not turn blighted districts into productive space. What was required was an alliance of like-minded groups to take effective control over land though a combination of eminent domain and federal funding. The real estate industry needed government assistance to assemble tracts of land for redevelopment. This, in turn, required the active support of national organizations, such as the National Association of Real Estate Boards. Only by reaching across the boundaries of local territory could local elites gain control of property, eliminate blight, and undertake renewal.

This, however, required precise information about the extent and location of blight in the city. One of the earliest appraisals of the city's blighted areas was a 1930s land use survey, which the CPC undertook with the New Deal agency the Work Projects Administration. The results were published in 1942 and 1943.[18] In the 1942 report, Robert Klove estimated that nine square miles of land were blighted and another twelve were "near blighted," mostly surrounding the central business district.[19] The survey directors told T. T. McCrosky, the agency's executive director, that the work grew out of the "realization that many agencies, public and private, and many communities had a growing need for data on the use of land in the city."[20] This knowledge was important for two reasons. One was to help identify the land that had to be redeveloped in order to reinvigorate the inner city's depressed values. The second was given by Harold Smith, a columnist for the *Chicago Tribune*, who noted that the information taken from the survey could be used to build high-end housing, which would stop the middle and upper classes from leaving the city.[21]

The area that was set out by the CPC and other organizations as especially problematic was the African American neighborhoods on the city's South Side. In this view, redevelopment could only proceed if these neighborhoods, which had been constructed as problematic by the city's elite, were razed and replaced with middle-class housing. This logic was clearly understood by George Nesbitt, the racial relations officer of the Chicago and Detroit offices of the Public Housing Administration. In a 1949 report on slum clearance, he noted that the city's planning and political agencies had for some time considered razing desirable South Side neighborhoods and moving the inhabitants to districts far from the city center.[22]

But this step was heavily resisted by both the white and black populations. Nesbitt quoted a 1935 Metropolitan Housing and Planning Council (MHPC) study that reported that "in all parts of the city property owners were fearing and bitterly resenting the possibility of a widespread scattering of these Negroes." Even though the postwar situation differed in terms of a much larger black population, different sociopolitical conditions, and the resistance of blacks to rehousing proposals, the fact remained that the "determination [had] been made to redevelop the South Side without disturbing the existing racial pattern in the city." He also argued that most African Americans "suspect that, in the absence of public policy and controls to prevent it, the real masters of urban redevelopment will be the forces intent upon recapturing Negro living space for the 'right' people, while at the same time ruling Negroes the 'wrong' people to live elsewhere in the city."[23] Nesbitt made clear that most people in the city believed that the elimination of blight and the work of urban renewal should reinforce racial divides, not break them down.

A defining moment in the establishment of blight as a specific spatial problem was a tour of the "bleak belt of deteriorated communities around the central business district" in October 1941. Sponsored by the CAC, the tour gave city business and political leaders a glimpse of the blighted areas occupied by a large number of the city's African American and white working-class populations. The tour members came from the cream of Chicago's bourgeois class: managers from the city's leading industrial and retail establishments sat next to executives from the Chicago Real Estate Board (CREB), the Chicago Building Congress, the Chicago Title and Trust Co., and the Fort Dearborn Mortgage Co. The purpose of the tour was to give a "preliminary over-all picture of the potential projects in which private capital may be invested" under a slum clearance act that had recently been passed by the state legislature.[24]

The idea for the tour came from the desire to showcase the CPC's ten-step plan to deal with blight. As McCrosky pointed out, the plan identified the steps necessary for successful redevelopment. Before this could take place, the CPC had to determine the extent and location of deterioration. The CPC proposal rested on building a public-private partnership and involved two elements. First, the municipal government would use its eminent domain powers to transfer property from "inefficient" owners to productive ones. Second, public-private agencies would acquire and clear this property before selling it to private developers. In McCrosky's opinion, the CPC plan would have two positive effects. It would stimulate construction, which would make the central blighted areas competitive with outlying ones, and it would allow downtown business interests to protect their investments and mortgages.[25] Not surprisingly, given the influence the tour participants had with city politicians, this plan had been implemented by the end of 1947.

At the same time, Chicago's leading real-estate companies devised other plans to deal with the problems of blighted space. The CREB, for example, announced a plan in 1943 to give private interests control over the city's blighted areas. The board announced that Percy E. Wagner, a former federal real estate appraiser, had been appointed chairman of a new committee with a mandate to establish a slum betterment program. The committee was to make a study of Chicago's blight, propose remedies, and look at what was being done by the CPC and other agencies. Once this stage was completed, the committee was to consider existing and contemplated slum improvement legislation. According to the CREB's president, Percy Wilson, it was imperative that his organization and others got immediately to work in order to capitalize on postwar opportunities. Not surprisingly, the committee immediately turned its attention to the redevelopment of blighted areas. The task was to devise a program for private-enterprise-led slum rehabilitation to ensure that blighted areas contributed "to both the sociological and financial value of the community."[26]

Chicago leaders were aware of similar ideas percolating among civic and business leaders in other cities.[27] The National Association of Real Estate Boards, the country's most important real estate organization, had been pushing for redevelopment of blighted areas. The *Chicago Tribune* reported on the association's semiannual survey of the real estate market in 1943, which showed that 110,000 acres had to be rehabilitated in 177 cities. As the authors noted, it was only with "complete large-scale replanting and rebuilding" that the central areas of US cities such as Chicago could be "radically changed." Picking up on similar arguments made elsewhere, the association argued that "getting the land together for such projects is the key to the problem." The real estate association's ideas were identical to those laid out in the CPC proposals on blight. Both the national and local organization stressed that solving the property problem could only be achieved if the government used its appropriation powers to acquire blighted land. This, it was argued, was to be done through the actions of private-public agencies that would assemble small, independent plots into large tracts that would entice private real estate interests to invest in redevelopment.[28] For real estate and planning agencies, the key to redevelopment and blight was property.

Other Chicago organizations became involved in the debate about blight, property, and redevelopment. After 1945, the fight against blight and falling property values was heavily pushed by the MHPC. With its active and powerful leadership, broad membership, and ardent desire to refashion the city, the MHPC was the perfect vehicle for taking control of Chicago redevelopment (figure 3.1). The council's program has been clearly laid out by Arnold Hirsch, who notes that the city's business interests were "locked in a desperate struggle for survival" and that the "large institutions used their combined economic resources and political influence to produce a redevelopment and urban renewal program designed to guarantee their continued prosperity."[29] In the immediate aftermath of the war, the MHPC worked to find solutions to blight with several other local organizations with interests in real estate and planning as well as the mayor's and governor's offices.[30]

This search for solutions took several directions. One was to reduce the power of the Chicago Housing Authority and to give greater control over housing to the MHPC and city council.[31] The Chicago Committee for Housing Action, made up of people involved in the redevelopment program, was established to oversee the writing of legislation on measures to eliminate blighted property and to provide greater powers to private industry over the housing market at the expense of public housing. Led by downtown business interests, the committee was "charged with the task of developing a housing program for the city" based on elimination of slums and blighted land, the minimization of public housing construction, and the creation of a private program of redevelopment.[32] It was

FIGURE 3.1 Metropolitan Planning and Housing Council annual luncheon, 1955. It was at moments such as this that ideas about urban renewal were discussed by Chicagoans interested in the future of the city. Note the photograph above the speaker showing Lake Meadows, the first major renewal project in the city. Box 3, folder 1, Mildred Mead Photographs, Special Collections Research Center, University of Chicago Library.

successful. Legislation allowing for the creation of a land clearance commission that would purchase, condemn, and clear blighted land and then sell it back to private interests was passed in 1947.

Another solution was to rationalize downtown's racial and class geographies. In 1947, the MHPC contracted with the planner Miles Colean and the Real Estate Research Corporation to make reports on two West Side areas, downtown labor markets, and residential development. The reports argued for the building of separate black and white neighborhoods on redeveloped land. Eradicating blight would strengthen racial and class residential divisions, provide profits for the real estate industry and more municipal taxes, and lay the basis for a modern city.[33] This racialized growth ideology was predicated on the idea that eliminating blight would create jobs and housing for all classes, which in turn would increase growth and prosperity for all. As Nesbitt noted in 1949, the effect of the redevelopment program on blacks was "to both exact the sacrifices of relocation and retain the practice of residential segregation."[34] Despite this, the MHPC and other community organizations argued that by linking slum clearance with the maintenance of separate racial and class areas, the trickle-down effect would be felt across all areas of the city.

The South Side Planning Board made a similar argument. The agency argued that blight, which "attacks and destroys the industrial and commercial areas as well as residential ones," was associated was deteriorating physical structures and pathological social relations. The answer was to raze the poor and black neighborhoods and replace them with middle-class housing and other features of the postindustrial city. The board believed that it was necessary to create a new landscape that allowed for the building of a new productive social and political order. This could only be attained by the destruction of blighted areas, which were "relics of an outdated era."[35] According to Wilford Winholtz, the board's executive director, the aim of the organization was to tear down the district's blighted areas and to replace them with a modern and more productive environment.[36]

The city's place-dependent elites also looked to establish the conditions that would allow them to broaden the political space for action. By the fall of 1946, the coalition of downtown interests was working to convince the public to support their program for eliminating blight. In his 1946 speech, Heald warned that "Chicago now faces the danger of becoming a dying city" and outlined a program for dealing with the fifteen thousand acres of blighted and near-blighted land that had been identified by the CPC and other local agencies. Reiterating the points made by others, the Illinois Institute of Technology president told his audience that renewal was only possible if the city acquired slum lands through eminent domain, used public funds to write down land from its acquisition cost to the real value, and made cleared land available to private developers. Only with government-supported land assembly could the problem of blighted areas, filled as they were with "mixed ownerships, complex land titles, and tax delinquencies," be dealt with adequately.[37] Heald reiterated this view a year later in a talk at "Chicago Builds," a forum organized by the Chicago Building Congress. Once again, he made it clear that blighted areas were Chicago's "most pressing problem."[38] Only with public support, he maintained, could private interests eliminate the problem.

Government Intervention

Most Chicago leaders by the late 1940s agreed with Heald that it was necessary to use federal funds to finance local government action and to subsidize private redevelopment. In the interwar years, city elites had begun to realize that federal largesse had to be used if the city was to be defended against the economic and social losses of blight. One tool was direct federal control over the housing market through the building of public housing. Although there may have been some support for this at first, it quickly soured, and, as Brad Hunt has shown, the city's public housing agency faced insurmountable difficulties after World War II, when it came under increasing attack from many quarters. There were those who believed that public housing depressed property values and produced little overall benefit to the housing market. There were those, such as most of the city's real estate and political interests, who viewed any direct government intervention in the housing market with hostility.[39] While they may have been in favor of indirect support to drive private development, they were vehemently opposed to government-funded agencies getting directly involved in building provision, even if it was only for the city's poor.

In this view, a more productive way to use federal largesse was to allow private interests to build high-end residences on blighted land in desirable locations that had been prepared by public agencies. Not surprisingly, most of Chicago's organizations pushed this option. The CPC lead the cause. After 1945, it built on its attempts during the war to establish the ideological credentials of blight as the reason for building public-private partnerships to reframe property relations. In so doing, the CPC echoed the MHPC's position by advocating for the creation of an agency to assemble blighted land for private development and to end the Chicago Housing Authority's monopoly to acquire slum property through eminent domain. A 1946 CPC report called for the appropriation of land, federal funding of a slum clearance program, and the "adoption of a comprehensive city plan for developing land in the city to its best social and economic use."[40] In the process of calling for the elimination of blight and the creation of economically productive land, the city's planning agencies made what was to be a compelling case for building a partnership between government and business. To do this, the renewal coalition had to move from searching for blight to actually doing something about what they had found. Action had to be taken.

This was laid out by Mayor Martin Kennelly in a 1947 speech to promote the city's slum clearance program drawn up by "a committee of leading citizens." The mayor laid out the rationale for government intervention in the property market. Reiterating points made by others, he said that blight was a major problem: "Slums are not only bad business for the people who live in them—they are bad business for those who don't live in them—and bad business for our city as a whole." They drained the city's financial resources and forced people and business to leave for the suburbs. He warned his audience that "unless we find the means to reverse this process, unless we can hold or recapture for Chicago the homes and business which make a city and support it, our troubles as a municipality can be expected to multiply." He repeated the idea being pushed by the CPC and others that the only viable way to do this was to have government assemble large enough plots of property so that developers could acquire land at a reasonable cost. "It assumes that, inasmuch as reclaiming the slums is both good and necessary for the city's progress, it is the responsibility of government to exercise its power and provide funds necessary to attract private capital to this vital task." In his opinion, the elimination of blight and the renewal of the cleared areas "constitute[s] a public responsibility."[41]

The task was clear; the state had to directly intervene to eliminate blight if the successful revitalization of the city was to take place. This role could not be left to the private sector alone, as it did not have the necessary police powers and funding to undertake profitable redevelopment. To raze blighted areas, the pro-renewal group had to help government determine the best locations for redevelopment. This guidance was provided by the CPC survey, which gave the city's place-dependent elites the material basis on which to build a coalition around the blighted areas that had to be eliminated and the rationalization for government intervention in urban renewal. The composition of the technical advisory committee led the way. It comprised fifty-four people from all corners of Chicago business and civic life, including those from real estate, utilities, finance, education, planning, business, the media, and many city and county departments. Not all were equally active on the committee, and the long list does not necessarily mean that an effective coalition was in play. Nevertheless, the list of names does signal that important city decision makers had realized it was time to create a more effective organization for dealing with industrial decline, eliminating blight, and preserving property values. And that it was time for government to intervene to ensure these outcomes.[42]

The intention of the CPC survey makers was to identify where blight was located so that a public-private coalition funded by the federal and local governments could profit from building a new postwar city. The search for information to allow the coalition to both fight and profit from industrial decline, falling property values, and deteriorated buildings required placing boundaries around areas designated as problematic. Oscar Mayer of the CACI made the case in his review of the association's activities: the survey had given the city the opportunity to make an effective intervention into blighted areas.[43] The coalition of civic and private interests built in the late 1930s had shown that questions of industrial decline, overcrowding, and racialized space were intimately linked to blight and the city's future. By the end of World War II, Chicago's civic and business communities were forced to kick-start capitalist urbanization by establishing an empirical basis of the city's blighted character and to accept that their aims could only be achieved by direct government intervention.

At the same time, pressure was on the Illinois General Assembly to pass legislation to allow private interests to redevelop blighted areas with the support of government funding and police powers. The first attempt to have the state support large-scale redevelopment, the Neighborhood Development Corporation Act of 1941, was not very successful. It did, however, pave the way for the pro-redevelopment interests to create effective legislation that could be used to eliminate blight and to entice private investment into new high-end housing.[44] Not surprisingly, the city's building and real estate interests were at the center of writing up the legislation. The first attempt to get the bill passed failed in June 1939. Undaunted by this setback, the city's real estate interests went back to the drawing board. The newly created Chicago Building Congress completed a redraft in August 1940 with the aid of experts in law, planning, zoning, and municipal government.[45] Most importantly, the revisions vested the powers of eminent domain in a local board. Previously these had been under the authority of a state board. With this revision, local real estate, political, and developer interests were able to determine the pace, extent, and location of redevelopment. The resulting bill became the Neighborhood Redevelopment Corporation Act of 1941.[46]

The purpose of the act, which gave property capitalists access to blighted land, was to eradicate slums, separate different use districts, increase property taxes, and keep middle-class families in the city. Very few organizations took advantage of it, and it died a slow death, becoming irrelevant with the passing of the much more effective Blighted Areas Redevelopment Act in 1947.[47] What is significant about the 1941 act is that it showed that the city's place-dependent elites could work with each other and with state politicians to devise ways to enhance profit-making opportunities through redevelopment. A coalition interested in preserving property values and remaking the city came together to build up the structures of information gathering, legislative oversight, and administrative control to vanquish blight while creating profitable returns for property owners and investors.

With the 1947 legislation in place, the coalition had to turn its attention to a basic issue: How would redevelopment of blighted areas take place? The answer was to invest authority in a public-private agency that would acquire blighted land and prepare it for the use of private interests. Using the trope of making blighted land productive, the CPC and MHPC called for a publicly authorized land clearance committee that would transfer property from one set of private owners to others. The intent was to take property away from unproductive functions and to transfer it to those able to create productive economic and social ends by rebuilding blighted land.

Support for this position came from various quarters. Mayor Kennelly told the CAC in 1947 that he was fully behind direct government support of private redevelopment.[48] Similarly, Joseph E. Merrion, a builder, agreed with public support of private development, arguing that if land assembly created large tracts of cleared land, "private enterprise" would "be eager to absorb the blighted areas for new home construction."[49] As a result of this pressure from the growing redevelopment coalition, the city took advantage of the 1947 act to establish the Chicago Land Clearance Commission.[50] Over the next fifteen years, the agency would take the lead in eliminating the city's blighted districts. Arguing that blight was costly to the city, the commission sought to turn small parcels held by tax-delinquent owners into large tracts that could be used for productive purposes, including industrial (figure 3.2). Using the authority invested in it by Illinois legislation and funding, the clearance agency laid the basis for the redevelopment of blighted property in the 1950s.

Beginning in the 1930s, federal housing acts worked alongside state legislation to drive redevelopment. The Housing Act of 1937 gave local agencies the authority to undertake land clearance and slum demolition for public housing. Twelve years later, the Housing Act of 1949 created urban renewal as a federal agency, the Urban Renewal Administration, and laid out the rationale—"housing for all Americans"—for the elimination of blight and the building of urban renewal programs. The act's goals of replacing substandard housing with new residential neighborhoods were predicated on two conditions: local approval of the program and private sector construction. The act allowed a local agency to buy land through negotiation or by eminent domain, and permitted local government to acquire private property and to pass ownership to new people.[51]

The work of the MHPC, the CPC, the real estate industry, and others had paid off with the passing of the 1947 Blighted Areas Act. The land commission was authorized to acquire land for slum clearance that would be passed on to private enterprise for redevelopment at a cost lower than purchase value. By 1947, the planning and housing agencies had got what they wanted: a partnership with government that provided them with large tracts of land at heavily subsidized prices while giving property interests enormous scope to rewrite the urban landscape while making a profit. The passing of the 1949 Housing Act codified and solidified the building of a public partnership geared to urban redevelopment that had been laid out in the 1937 Housing Act and the Blighted Areas Act. These legislative tools shaped the extent and character of residential redevelopment for a generation. More importantly for our story here, they were also instrumental in the transformation of blighted land into industrial property in the 1950s and 1960s.

FIGURE 3.2 The cost of blight to Chicago. This illustration from an early publication of the Chicago Land Clearance Commission sets out some of the problems of blighted land. It was meant to convince the general public of the economic logic of urban renewal. Chicago Land Clearance Commission, "Redevelopment Project No. 3. A Report to the Mayor and City Council of the City of Chicago and to the Illinois State Housing Board on a Proposal to Redevelop a Blighted Area on the Near West Side" (Chicago: Chicago Land Clearance Commission, June 1, 1951).

Blight and Industry

The federal government and the military became involved in industry in new ways after 1940. While production increased greatly during the war, fixed-capital investment in new defense factories produced an unprecedented volume of munitions. Much of this capital investment came from federal coffers. This military and government ownership of industrial land, factories, machinery, and equipment temporarily resuscitated an ailing urban economy, fueled large-scale industrial growth, and reframed the operations of the property market. In Chicago, the city's industrial base was rejuvenated, as firms turned to producing goods for the war effort. At the same time, many of the large government and private industrial investments were made in the suburbs or the city's outer edge, reinforcing the worsening conditions of the inner city's factory and residential areas.[52]

By the summer of 1945, it was unknown whether these wartime investments would anchor a new cycle of investment. Some of the city's business and civic leaders believed they would. Others, however, feared that industry would revert back to the interwar pattern and desert the central city for suburban greenfields, leaving blighted districts in their wake. Most local commentators, even those discussing industrial redevelopment, understood blight as a residential matter. This was also the case in postwar studies of Philadelphia, Milwaukee, and Detroit. When these studies did discuss the deterioration of industrial districts, they typically framed the causes as being those that produced residential blight: rundown physical structures, dis-functional land uses, and technological obsolescence.[53] These studies rarely used the term "industrial blight," preferring "obsolescence." One of the few studies that did use the term was a 1957 American Society of Planning Officials report, which stated that "industrial areas become blighted when they no longer function properly as places to produce goods."[54] For all intents and purposes, this definition was no different from that of residential or commercial blight. What difference there was rested solely on the type of use that took place on the land. Regardless of the definition and the similarity between residential and industrial blight, what was becoming increasingly clear in the years immediately after World War II was that industrial blight would shape the future of the city's postwar industrial landscape one way or another.

Not surprisingly, a growing number of voices in Chicago and elsewhere after 1945 called for the need to redevelop blighted land—both residential and industrial—for industry purposes.[55] While the link between housing, race, and blight would continue to dominate the postwar process of urban redevelopment, a growing number of civic leaders argued that industrial blight and employment decentralization were ongoing problems that had to be solved. This point was emphatically made by Leverett Lyon, the CAC's chief executive officer, in the last years of the war. In a 1943 study of the city's industrial prospects, he noted that "among the most vexing problems" facing industry were "those involving obsolete, or blighted, areas and the increasing amounts of vacant land within the city limits on which taxes [were] delinquent."[56]

Lyon had made a similar point a year earlier, when he noted that blight was increasing as industrial and residential buildings were torn down and left empty or replaced with parking lots. The result was a pattern with "slums or run-down structures in the old, centrally located districts; a fringe of new subdivisions on the outskirts; and in between, various stages of obsolescence and blight." This accentuated the advantages of the suburbs which could boast of more space, cheaper land, and lower taxes than could be found in the central areas. The suburbs had the added attractions of "increased freedom from legal controls and from labor union regulation."[57] In Lyon's view, and he spoke for many of the city's place-dependent industrialists, blight spurred industrial decline, which further increased population loss and the spread of blighted districts. Blight, in their minds, was directly associated with a vicious downward spiral of industrial and population decline and the spread of crime and disease.

Lyon wasn't alone in his views on industrial blight and redevelopment. The CPC argued that something had to be done about the conditions of many of the older industrial districts. In 1942, McCrosky wrote in the commission's overview of how to plan the Chicago economy that it was necessary to create a "more ordered and more rational utilization of land throughout the city" in order to allow for the dispersal of heavy manufacturing to the outskirts and for the "near-in industrial districts [to] be rebuilt in part with modern loft buildings suitable for light manufacturing, and in part devoted to residential use."[58] In this view, blight was to be eliminated and replaced in part by "rebuilt" industrial districts. Four years later, H. Evert Kinkaid, the CPC's executive director, noted that "blighted areas call for comprehensive development—industrial, commercial, residential— in accordance with the city plan."[59] Industry was now a subject for redevelopment.

In a similar vein, the MHPC agreed that it was necessary to widen the boundaries of what could be considered blighted property in order to accommodate industrial renewal. A report of the council's December 1946 planning committee began by stating that "no greater problem faces our city than the rebuilding of the vast blighted areas." At the same time, the council, following the lead of the CPC and the CACI, broadened the scope of land that could be redeveloped to include industrial. As the report noted, the elimination of blight required determining "which portion of the blighted areas" was "suitable to and needed for housing, which for industrial, and commercial uses."[60] A year after the cessation of the war, Chicago's most powerful planning and business agencies were drawing a direct link between blight, industry, and redevelopment.

The rationale used for turning blighted land to industrial uses was similar to the one for residential redevelopment. In December 1946, the CPC and the MHPC commented on what they believed was a self-evident truth: the purchase, clearing, and sale of blighted property solely for residential purposes was "uneconomic and unfortunate."[61] Given the demand for more centrally located industrial property, it did not make economic sense for all blighted property, even land that had previously been used for residential purposes, to be developed for housing. Turning some of this land into industrial property would not only eliminate blight but also increase the city's tax base, ensure a rational use of otherwise unproductive property, increase employment in a range of sectors, and stimulate redevelopment in adjoining areas. It was clear to the city's social, planning, and business agencies that some of the central city's obsolete property should be converted to industry.

By 1949, the CPC, urged on by the MHPC, had made progress toward that end. A long letter to Elizabeth Wood, director of the Chicago Housing Authority, and Ira Bach, executive director of the Chicago Land Clearance Commission (CLCC), from the agency spoke at length about blight and industry. Wood and Bach were informed that the planning agency was still working on establishing the West Central industrial district, an area that would be the United States' first industrial site funded by the federal government as part of its urban renewal program. The agency had met with several interested industrial groups to test out ideas about the extent of industrial areas in the city.[62] The importance attached by the CPC to industrial matters can be gleaned by the fact that the agency had a senior planner, research associate, and draftsman working on the dossier in December 1949, and would launch a string of publications on industrial redevelopment in the early 1950s.[63] Industrial redevelopment was clearly on the table.

From the 1930s, the meaning of blight was redefined in several ways that allowed for redevelopment. By defining blight in the "proper" way, business and political leaders were able to rewrite property relations so as to give them better access to "unproductive" and "wasteful" land. In the 1930s, most observers considered blight to affect residential but not industrial areas. C. Louis Knight, for example, defined blighted areas as districts with residential property that had been invaded by industrial uses, and which became home to "undesirable racial elements." The result of underinvestment in housing construction was that large swathes of the central city's residential districts were subject to "economic retardation, physical deterioration, and economic decay."[64] Knight had little interest in industry other than as a cause of residential deterioration. Industry was a problem to be solved to bolster the city's residential offerings, not for itself.

Knight's thinking on blight and housing was rooted in the social-ecological thinking of the day, which argued that population succession and housing market

forces inevitably created blighted districts.[65] Most members of the city's governing classes agreed with this analysis. The inevitability of blight was portrayed as
a fact in government studies, private planning documents, business reports, and
newspaper articles. Ecological theory gave the city's growth alliance license to
approach blight as a problem without a solution other than government intervention in the wholesale destruction of slum areas and the preparation of the
cleared land for industrial as well residential renewal under private control.

After World War II, the idea that industrial redevelopment could eliminate
blight became more common. Robert Garrabrant made this point in 1955, when
he argued that industrial redevelopment of blighted areas was critical to the survival of the city and industry. In his opinion, redevelopment had to be "designed
to clear badly deteriorated areas within American cities and to restore them to
usefulness, decency, and economic solvency."[66] It was also made by Dean Swartzel
of the MHPC's Center for Neighborhood Renewal in 1958, when he remarked
that "urban is an omnibus process." What he meant by this is that city leaders
had "to overcome and prevent the deterioration in, and provide for the sound
maintenance" of the fabric of the city as it grew and changed over time. This goal
would be made possible by "the use of all public and private resources" that could
be found or "devised."[67] For Garrabrant and Swartzel, the omnibus character
of urban renewal included the incorporation of industrial property into urban
redevelopment.

As an idea molded by experts, blight proved extremely adaptable to different
changing interpretations of urban life. The social-ecological ideas of the 1930s
and 1940s gave way to economistic ideas that permeated and in some cases dominated social science thinking by the 1950s. The tenuous and hazy gradations of
blight by journalists, planners, and others during the 1930s were replaced by the
sophisticated working of detailed numeric data gathered by academics and other
experts after 1940. One of the first studies to do this was the CPC's *Residential
Chicago*, which laid out the scale and character of the city's blight on the eve of
World War II. This effort continued over the next two decades.

Some writers worked with both sets of ideas without any apparent contra-
diction. The sociologist Leo Reeder, for example, undertook a numerical analysis of the move of the city's industry to the suburbs between 1941 and 1950.
Using positivist tools of simple causation, he argued that the inner city was
home to both industrial and residential blight. The city's inner zone was "in an
advanced stage of obsolescence and deterioration—characterized by 'blight.'
It [was] the locus of the slums and disproportionate social disorganization."[68]
Reeder's work represents the replacement of ethnographic studies of ecological
succession by numeric description of locational analysis. The combination of
ecological description and simple numerical analysis favored by Reeder and his

contemporaries was replaced by the hard analytical tools of neoclassical economic theory practices by Raymond Fales, Leon Moses, and John McDonald in the 1970s and 1980s. The fact that blight could be defined by experts to suit those who needed to gain access to downtown land ensured that it reflected the economic and political pressures of the day.[69]

Regardless of their theoretical approach, writers understood industrial decline and its attendant built form, blight, as inevitable, thus allowing city leaders to divert attention away from the actual causes of physical and economic decline. The finessing of blight from a process created by investment decisions, landlord activities, and planning practices to one embedded in disembodied natural and economic processes had the effect of shifting blame from elite decision makers to the inhabitants of the blighted areas. Although often sympathetic to the plight of the poor, urban experts and city leaders frequently drew a direct relation between the occupants and the built environment. In other words, identifying blight as a problem was an extremely effective solution to the problems of economic and physical decline induced by capital disinvestment. Not only did it shift responsibility from one group to another; it also allowed city leaders to create financial and political profit while producing a new and modern world from the ruins of a busted built environment and an ailing manufacturing economy. For those interested in attracting new industrial capital to the city, blight was an extremely useful device.

Using blight for industrial renewal, however, required rewriting industrial property relations. The key change was the resituating of industrial land as a bundle of rights. This became increasingly accepted in postwar Chicago. Two elements underpinned the move of property from a thing to a bundle of rights. The first, the expansion of the meaning of public good since the nineteenth century, allowed legislatures to expand the powers of eminent domain, enabling the state to directly intervene in social and economic matters. This new power was evident during World War II, when the federal government intervened in the industrial property market in unprecedented ways and in the housing acts passed after 1937.[70] The second, the creation of property as a bundle of differentiated rights and not a unitary object, allowed for property relations to be more finely differentiated geographically. One effect of this shift was that property no longer had to be uniformly administered across space. As a result, inner-city industrial land by the late 1940s had become subject to different rules and practices than had previously been the case.

The creation of blight from the 1930s allowed property to be differentiated along the lines of public good, economic efficiency, and moral behavior. Two elements—eminent domain and selective action—affected the rewriting of the relations of industrial property after 1930. The definition of property as blighted and the growing pressure from politicians, real estate interests, social reformers, and business leaders to use public power to reassess blighted property gave government unprecedented scope to acquire residential and industrial land for resale to private interests for industrial purposes. The move to reimagine blighted land as industrial land through the dedicated intervention of public-private partnerships after 1945 and enshrined in the 1947 Blighted Areas Act relied on the precedent set by using blighted property for both private and public uses. This, in turn, was built on the support of federal, state, and municipal courts.

The Courts and Industrial Blight

The rewriting of property rights and the redevelopment of blighted land for industrial purposes as set out in the Blighted Areas Act of 1947 and its amendments would not have been possible without the support of the courts. From the early 1930s, both the federal and state legislatures became increasingly involved in property rights issues. At the same time, the courts were embroiled in expanding government authority to acquire private property to promote the public good. Public use of industrial, commercial, and residential property and the transfer of property rights from one group to another would, the courts argued, have benefits for the entire community. By the 1950s, as David Schultz notes, the courts had "come to equate the scope of a legislature's eminent domain authority to be coterminous with its police power." The result was the "expansion and politicization of legislative discretion to acquire private property."[71] The tendency for the courts to permit greater public control over urban property through eminent domain had direct long-terms implications for urban blighted areas and inner-city factory districts.

The widening definition of blighted land by the legislatures and the courts after 1930 was used to make urban property an object ripe for industrial redevelopment. This permitted land to be taken away from one set of owners, reclaimed, assembled, and transformed by local government, and sold as a package to fewer private owners. Performed in the name of the public good, this property transfer typically penalized white working-class families, African Americans and other minority groups, and small-scale property owners and industrial operations, while rewarding property developers, financial institutions, and larger industrial firms.[72]

Some property acquired under new public authority was used for industrial purposes. The CLCC used the state-authorized and court-legitimized appropriation powers to acquire land for industrial use. In the case of West Central and other developments, the CLCC expropriated industrial and residential land and replaced the blighted buildings with factories and warehouses. The US courts were central to this process. The courts' widening of what was considered appropriate public use led to the remaking of industrial property relations. By accepting the legislative move to urban renewal and the language of blight, the courts legitimatized the forced transfer of property from one private owner to another and in the process facilitated the agenda of the country's urban political and business elites. They also underpinned industrial redevelopment.

In Illinois and across the country, the courts upheld state and federal statutes that allowed blight to be used as a device for changing the social relations of industrial property. By the mid-1950s, redevelopment had become defined as state intervention in urban form and had been implemented in forty states and by the federal government. The scope of redevelopment was intimately linked to blight, which was defined by the courts as the condition of disuse or misuse of land, although this definition varied from statute to statute, and from state to state. Issues of blight, property, and urban redevelopment became staples of the courts by the late 1940s, as various interests brought their arguments both in support for and against new forms of government legislation on property relations.

Support for these changes was mixed. Title I of the 1949 Housing Act, which allowed for the use of eminent domain in renewal, faced several judicial reviews. In Florida and Georgia, the courts argued that renewal was not justifiable, and did not support the transfer of property from one owner to another. In other parts of the country, however, the courts found redevelopment to be constitutional, accepting the argument that blighted land could not be cleared without public financial aid and eminent domain. Most courts decided that the combined controls of municipal police powers and private enterprise activities were unable to do the job without new forms of public support. Agreeing with the ideas set out by experts and business leaders, the courts stated that financial institutions and industrial corporations would be unlikely to invest in factories and warehouses in the central city as long as property costs were significantly more expensive than similar land in the suburbs. A growing number of courts in the postwar period agreed that public intervention in the form of clearing blighted property and subsidizing the higher costs of central-city land was necessary before industrial redevelopment could take place.[73] It was in the public good.

Two cases with national ramifications reinforced the changing interrelationship of blight, property relations, and industry in Chicago after 1945. In 1936, in *New York Housing Authority v. Muller*, the plaintiff argued that the housing authority did not have the right to clear land for low-income public housing, as property could not be taken from one set of individuals (homeowners) and given to another (public housing residents). The New York Court of Appeals disagreed with Muller, arguing that the housing agency could take property as long as it was put to a legitimate public use, such as reducing crime and disease. The decision was upheld in the US Supreme Court. The decision in favor of using eminent domain for slum clearance set the stage for other public housing and urban renewal cases in New York City, Chicago, and elsewhere.[74]

Eighteen years later, in *Berman v. Parker*, a department store owner in Washington, DC, argued that his building could not be taken as part of a slum removal project because the building itself was not a slum. As in the Muller case, the district court disagreed. On appeal, the Supreme Court upheld the earlier decision, arguing that the federal government and the lower court had the authority to determine what was necessary for public use and that the courts had little scope to counteract the legislative meaning of public use.[75] The impact of the 1936 and 1954 decisions was to provide place-dependent elites with the authority to use government powers to refashion industrial as well as residential property rights in the making of a modern built environment.

This was the case in Illinois, where it was accepted that eminent domain could be used for public purposes. However, as with blight, the definition of public use was malleable and open to contestation. The result was that the idea of what was public was tested several times in the courts. Most judicial decisions regarding redevelopment fell on the broader meaning of public use as outlined in *New York Housing Authority v. Muller*. Several court decisions in and after 1945 confirmed that slum clearance was a necessary public use in Chicago.[76] In most cases, the decisions were based on the argument that private capital was unwilling to undertake redevelopment if blight wasn't linked to eminent domain. If unproductive land was to be made productive, so the argument went, the state had to actively intervene to help private capital make this possible. However, the right of government to designate property as blighted and to compel acquisition through police powers was not unrestricted. Even though land was subject to condemnation, the state did not have unlimited powers to condemn. The courts were very clear; governments could not expropriate property arbitrarily, but could only make a taking that was specifically designated within the categories established under legislative fiat as blighted. Within the broad ambit of these rulings and the state legislature, however, Chicago increasingly used eminent domain to acquire blighted land for redevelopment.

These court decisions legitimatized the use of expropriated property for industrial purposes. This is illustrated by the impact of the decisions made on the 1949 and 1955 amendments to the Blighted Areas Act. The 1949 amendment sought to make vacant land available to private developers by utilizing government powers of eminent domain. The original 1947 legislation had restricted the CLCC to purchasing property with buildings. The intent of the amendment was to broaden the meaning of blight and to allow the CLCC to assemble large tracts suitable for economic development from vacant and "unproductive" land and to clear title to the assembled property. The "busted" land—as one newspaper editor called it—would then be sold to private interests for redevelopment.[77]

The amendment was challenged in the circuit court by the state attorney's office and the Illinois State Housing Board as a test case. The court held that the CLCC had the right to acquire and resell property that had several owners, was tax delinquent, and housed deteriorated infrastructure. In his judgment, Judge Harry Fisher stated that the amendment was in the public interest. As the lots in question produced no taxes, were sites of juvenile delinquency, and breeding places for rats, Fisher had no qualms upholding the state's request.[78] This, however, was not the end of the matter. The Illinois Supreme Court overruled the circuit court decision on a technicality related to the financing of the CLCC. In March 1953, however, the Illinois Supreme Court reheard the case, and overturned its earlier decision.[79] The result was that the CLCC's legislated authority to use eminent domain to acquire property for redevelopment was legitimized by the courts.

The 1955 amendment widened the scope of what was considered blight once again. It laid out that nonresidential land could be acquired by eminent domain and redeveloped for private industrial use if the CLCC determined that the land could not be used for residential purposes. Opposing the 1955 change, a Chicago real estate agent argued that it allowed the taking of private property for uses other than public use. Using legislation to transfer land in order to promote private industrial interests, so the real estate agent argued, was a violation of the Illinois Constitution. The circuit court upheld the amendment, and an appeal to the Supreme Court agreed with the lower court. Both courts sided with the legislature because they considered the elimination of the blighted land was sufficient enough to justify the taking of vacant or occupied land by eminent domain for use by private industrial concerns.[80]

In this way, the legislative notion of public use of blighted land was broadened after 1940 to include both immediate purpose and ultimate use. The judicial reviews of Illinois legislation since 1940 supported the position that sufficient public purpose was an appropriate base for using eminent domain for industrial redevelopment. This support was strengthened by the 1955 amendment that allowed public appropriation of blighted areas of residential land by private manufacturing concerns. The postwar coalition of property developers, civic elites, and industrial managers used these court decisions to rationalize their desire to gain access to blighted property. City leaders argued that industrial redevelopment on expropriated land provided an array of public benefits, including the payment of back taxes on vacant or dead land, an increase to the current tax base by turning unproductive land to productive purposes, the better marketability of adjoining areas, the provision of manufacturing employment for the city's working class, and the triggering of a virtuous cycle of industrial and social redevelopment. The courts agreed.

Turning Blighted Land into Industrial Property

By the late 1940s, after twenty years of discussion, the city's place-dependent elites had established the basic framework for the elimination of blight. Chicago bourgeoisie had successfully transformed the discourse around blighted spaces from one of a problem to one of renewal. As the surveys that were undertaken from the mid-1930s suggest, this transformation required the creation of knowledge about the scale, character, and location of blight. This knowledge had to be place specific and amenable to government intervention. Information about specific city spaces was necessary if the federal government was to create policy over and provide funding for public housing and other forms of redevelopment. What was required was a move from descriptive and emotional discussions of wasted ground to an empirical and reasoned outline of the problem. Legislative and judicial authority could then be leveraged if blighted land was made into property that could be worked on by public-private partnerships.

Chicago's civic and business leaders also created the foundations for turning blighted land into industrial property. The discourse of blight started out in the 1930s as a discussion over central-city residential districts and deteriorated housing. Blight, it was argued, led to a lower city tax base, greater rates of crime, disease, and delinquency, and depressed property values. The linking of blight, property, and housing continued after World War II, as the growth coalition looked to profit by replacing the old industrial city with a postindustrial one. The ideas driving the link between blight and residential redevelopment were also taken up by those concerned with the city's declining manufacturing fortunes. The result was that Chicago's business and political worlds had been primed to accept government-led industrial redevelopment of both residential and nonresidential blighted land. As laid out in the next chapter, various groups in Chicago looked to take advantage of this in order to undertake industrial redevelopment.

INDUSTRIAL PROPERTY AND BLIGHT IN THE 1950s

In September 1953, R. W. Anderson wrote to the *Chicago Tribune*, angry at the lies he believed were being bandied around about the property owned by the Bodine Electric Company on the city's North Side. In his opinion, the arguments made by a residents' group about the impact of a new factory on noise levels and property values were "a lot of humbug." He asserted that Bodine had the legal right to build a new factory in the area, which had been zoned for industrial use since 1942. Just as important for Anderson was the city's industrial decline: "If Bodine has to move to Skokie, or some other suburb, many employees will have to get new jobs, or have to move. They would be displaced persons to suit the personal whims of a few dozen neighbors who would lose nothing by the building of a new plant." In his view, the needs of firms and their workers were pitted against the suburbs' industrial charms and the unimportant losses incurred by the area's residents. The questions of manufacturing decline, industrial suburbanization, and employment loss were deeply implicated in the contested industrial property.[1]

Cold War politics were also caught up in industrial property relations. Anderson ended his letter pushing back against the "humbug" propagated by some residents and their allies: "If it wasn't for the electric and electronic industries of the United States the good burghers of Grace and Western would be in the category of those in East Germany. It is concerns like Bodine that made Chicago the top grade industrial city it is today."[2] In the heated international conditions of the 1950s, the link between US capitalism and freedom on the one hand and the Soviet Union's draconian policies on the other was not an insignificant rhetorical flourish. For Anderson, the very qualities that made the United States a formidable industrial and political power were under attack by the desire of a few residents to dictate how Bodine's property should be used. The property rights of a private enterprise were being unfairly challenged and Chicago's place in the country's industrial hierarchy was under attack. In his view, civic leaders had to defend industries and their property rights from the unwarranted encroachments of the uninformed.

As noted in chapter 3, industrial property relations were on the agenda of Chicago's place-dependent leaders by the 1940s. Given the fortunes of the city's industry over the previous two decades, a growing number of people were looking to find ways to combat manufacturing decline, industrial blight, and a dwindling tax base. Industrial rejuvenation was necessary if decline and blight were to be defeated. A viable program of industrial redevelopment, however, involved rethinking the place of industrial property in the blight-rejuvenation equation. This required practical answers to several questions. What could be done to industrial property relations to turn the situation around? How could factories and the jobs that came with them be anchored more firmly in the city? How could industrial managers gain access to cheaper and better-quality industrial sites in Chicago?

Building on the earlier discussion about blight and renewal, I explore the ways in which a shaky coalition of planners, businesspeople, and politicians sought to regenerate the declining fortunes of the city's industrial base by reworking property relations. The organizations that were members of this coalition faced daunting and what proved to be overwhelming obstacles from residents and other city leaders. The Chicago Plan Commission (CPC) tried to turn blighted land into modern industrial districts. This effort reached its peak in the early 1950s with several publications by the CPC that linked industrial property relations and the opportunities for industrial redevelopment with blighted land.[3] The South Side Planning Board (SSPB) attempted to rejuvenate the South Side by building a model planned industrial district. It never materialized, but the rationale and the reception of the proposal spell out the postwar vision of industrial redevelopment and provide insights into why the city could not retain its manufacturing base after 1945. The failure of organizations committed to implementing plans for industrial redevelopment reflects the ability of the city's more powerful alliance to drive through its own postindustrial agenda for the central city.[4]

The Chicago Plan Commission

By the late 1940s, the concerns about industrial decline, suburbanization, and blight forced the city's leading planning agency, the CPC, to divert some of its resources to finding a solution to the city's troubling industrial situation. The answer it determined lay in industrial redevelopment. To this end, the agency undertook a survey in 1950 to ascertain the forces behind industrial decline.[5] Not surprisingly, the CPC study found that industrial decline was linked to blight and could only be eliminated by reworking property relations. This required active participation by a public-private partnership, which it believed should be the Chicago Land Clearance Commission (CLCC).[6] In the opinion of the planning agency, the most viable way forward was for the land clearance commission to use federal and Illinois regulations and funds to allow blighted property to underwrite private industrial redevelopment.

An impressive group of planning and real estate experts were deployed by the CPC to make the argument for an action plan to turn blighted space into industrial districts.[7] Four stand out.[8] Charles Blessing, a member of the CPC's executive staff, had a master's degree in city planning from MIT. After the war, he had worked as a regional planning engineer in Boston before coming to Chicago as the CPC director in 1949. He left for Detroit in 1953, where he was the director of city planning and a professor of architecture at Wayne State University. Harold Mayer, who had a PhD from the University of Chicago, worked with the CPC and the Chicago Regional Port District Board before going into academia and publishing several books on cities, planning, and transportation. The third, Frederick Aschman, was executive director of the CPC between 1950 and 1956. Before joining the agency, he had been executive director of the Cook County Housing Authority. After leaving the CPC, he established his own planning consulting firm and was a member of the Northwestern Illinois Metropolitan Planning Commission for ten years, and a lecturer in city planning at Northwestern University.[9]

Perhaps the most distinguished of the quartet was Homer Hoyt, one of the preeminent writers on housing and real estate in the country at the time. He had worked at various universities and planning agencies, as well as the Federal Housing Administration, before opening a consultancy firm in 1946. Publication of two books in the 1930s along with his extensive contract work on housing and real estate made him one of the most sought-after consultants on urban issues in the postwar United States.[10] He continued to be active in Chicago planning and housing circles for several years in a variety of consultancy positions. Among other things, he worked on the 1950 vacant land study and wrote an extremely important report on industrial development for the CLCC in 1951.[11]

These four men shaped the relationship between blight, planning, and industrial renewal in Chicago during the 1950s. All four worked with the groups that pushed local government to mobilize the legislative authority to expropriate and improve land for the public good, and to then pass on this prepared land to private industrial developers. They also worked with other city groups, such as the CPC and the Society of Industrial Realtors, to shape the direction taken by the city's business and civic leaders to create more industrial land.[12] All these individuals, agencies, and institutions with interests in property and industrial expansion formed a coalition that sought to put property and blight on the city's agenda. Two organizations were particularly active.

The Commonwealth Edison Company had shown interest in local industrial matters for some time. As a utility company, it had a deep concern for regional issues. Its industrial development department had for years worked to attract new firms to the region and to compile extensive information about industrial behavior. The company's annual reports on industrial development were a mainstay of knowledge on local developments.[13] Similarly, the Western Society of Engineers, a professional organization that had become interested in Chicago's municipal and economic affairs as early as the interwar years. In 1932, it supported a slum reconstruction bill in the Illinois legislature, and during the war it cooperated with local groups and the Chicago Ordnance District to organize wartime industrial mobilization. In 1948 it cooperated with, among others, the Illinois Institute of Technology, the First National Bank of Chicago, and the Chicago Metropolitan Home Builders Association to pass a building code to stimulate slum redevelopment.[14]

By the late 1940s, Commonwealth Edison and the Western Society were working with the CPC and other agencies to push redevelopment across central Chicago. While their attention focused on building new housing on blighted land to the south and west of the Loop, there was growing interest in industrial redevelopment. Among other places, and most importantly, this surfaced in the work undertaken by the CPC and the experts it hired to shape public and private opinion. All these groups that pushed for industrial renewal are classic examples of locally dependent institutions. The value fixed in Chicago's productive commitments ensured that the utility provider, engineering organization, planning agency, and educational institution had to protect and secure the conditions under which they could produce present and future profits, wages, clients, and services. They were not alone in seeking to turn blighted land into industrial space; other institutions—most notably, the city government, private planning organizations, and local business—worked to find ways to deal with their dependency by turning blighted land into productive property.

This was the purpose of three CPC reports on industrial renewal published between 1950 and 1952.[15] The agency knew it had to take action if the city's blighted areas were to be turned into viable industrial districts. The purpose of the knowledge supplied by Hoyt and others was to create a climate in boardrooms and courthouses to accept blight as a problem that, in turn, would allow public and private interests to refashion property relations and the built environment. The CPC and the city's other institutions saw both residential and industrial redevelopment as a means to limit the costs of local dependency. During the 1950s, these four experts along with other planners established the rationale for state intervention in industrial matters. In the calculative politics of the day, the reports mobilized information in order to persuade powerful local agents to find ways to advance the property and industrial interests of place-dependent actors.

Hoyt and the others used the three reports for three purposes: to show that blight was a big problem in Chicago; to determine the character and scale of this problem; and to propose ways of eliminating the problem. They then suggested that building a public-private partnership centered on eminent domain and turning blighted land into industrial land would be the most effective way of implementing their plans. Using their expertise acquired through university training, planning agency membership, and their hard-earned reputations, the authors of the CPC reports produced knowledge that underpinned the action that had to be undertaken by the city and the state of Illinois, and their attendant agencies. They deployed their expertise to name and put boundaries around the city's "blighted areas." In the process, they delimited both the problem and the space of dependency that should be worked on.[16]

The first report, A Study of Blighted Land, designated vacant land as blighted and established the boundaries that separated blighted and nonblighted land. The report was done on behalf of the CLCC so as to "provide a broad framework of reference and a survey of specific areas, for use in determining the best approach to the use of its powers and financial aids." The aids available to the clearance agency were the Blighted Areas Redevelopment Act of 1947 and the Housing Act of 1949. Building on this legislation and the subsequent court support for public intervention in private property matters, the report made a "technical analysis of the concept of 'blighted vacant land' as reflected in the statutory declaration that blighted vacant land tends to impair or arrest the sound growth of the community."[17] In other words, the CPC sought to widen the boundary of what constituted blighted property, and in the process to make this newly named problem subject to government-led industrial redevelopment.

The issue that distressed so many of the city's interests was that 40 percent of the city's 214 square miles was vacant and therefore unproductive. Termed as "idle," "dead," and "waste," the city's vacant land was framed as economically and socially problematic. The linguistic finessing of vacant land as idle, dead, or waste worked to move the meaning away from a simple, relatively neutral description (vacant) to a pejorative one with human characteristics. Cast as having human failings, property became established as something that had to be reformulated to escape its problematic character and to fulfill more positive ends.

The transformation of vacant land into industrially purposeful land would allow it to be revalued. It would become part of a property market that provided developers with profits, company managers with industrial land, and city officials with increased taxes.

The main conceptual move of the report that would come to underpin industrial redevelopment was the redefinition of blight. The existing boundaries, which centered on land with unsanitary buildings, were changed to include property that had no built structures. This land was relabeled and defined as being economically unproductive, socially problematic, and detrimental to the city's long-term growth. As the authors noted, "unless the State acts in the public interest to acquire title to [these properties] and then resell them to private developers, they will continue indefinitely to be 'dead.'"[18] Vacant land was invested with meaning that would permit industrial expansion and profits. For several reasons this was not easy. The 1950 study reported that the large number of private owners made it difficult to assemble property that could be effectively used for redevelopment purposes. Similarly, most of city's pre-1929 lots were considered too small for contemporary conditions. Labeling the land as obsolete, the authors framed the problem as being unsolvable without state assistance and eminent domain.

The CPC reports used these findings to focus on industrial redevelopment. According to *Redevelopment for Industry*, Chicago suffered from a "shortage of suitable industrial sites and building for certain types of industry seeking to locate or expand within the City." But all was not lost, as "in many parts of the City designated by the Chicago Plan Commission as 'blighted,'" there was land "suitable for industrial use." Some of the property consisted of deteriorated districts, while some was simply vacant. Given that the CPC had the power, tools, and funds to clear blighted districts to make large tracts, the report's preface urged "that redevelopment of blighted areas for industrial use be encouraged."[19] The problem was put very starkly: if the issues facing the city's industrial property weren't dealt with immediately, Chicago's place as an industrial center would be compromised. Rebuilding the industrial economy through the provision of new industrial property would, so the argument went, stimulate a multiplier effect, which would create jobs in other sectors, and add substantial business and residential revenues to the city's tax base. While they could not escape dependency, they could limit its negative effects.

The three reports raised four problems that had to be solved for industrial redevelopment to take place. The first was that the shortage of vacant industrial land restricted Chicago's growth. Moreover, the geographic distribution of industrial property made it very difficult for manufacturers to find viable locations. According to local real estate agents, the heaviest demand for sites was in the northwest and western parts of the city, while most of the available land was to the south.[20] This area was of little interest to most manufacturers, as it contained dirty and sprawling heavy industrial complexes, most notably steel, metalworking, and heavy transportation equipment. These sites were intermixed with blighted neighborhoods, home to ethnic and racial minorities, and tense and often fractious labor relations. This was not a good locale for new capital investment. Manufacturers looking to start a new firm in the city were unwilling to settle in such areas.

A second issue was that only a fraction of the existing space in industrial buildings was useful for modern needs. In August 1950 nearly nineteen million square feet of industrial floor space in 625 units was available for sale or lease. Of this, more than five million square feet was vacant, most of it in dilapidated buildings. At the same time, only 13 percent of the available floor space was to be found in modern one-story buildings. Many of the older multistory buildings had been left vacant after firms had moved to the suburbs in search of better facilities or has simply gone out of business. While there may have been agreement among industrial insiders that multistory buildings had their uses for light industry, the consensus was that single-story factories were better equipped to deal with modern production processes. This, of course, was a key argument of the scientific site industry. As noted in a 1959 review of industrial construction in the trade journal *Factory*, the key change since 1935 was the building of plant around the production process in single-story factories.[21] The general consensus was that the options for building these factory spaces in the city were limited.

A third problem was that blight was pushing industry out of Chicago. A CPC report noted that postwar industrial growth resulted from the expansion of existing plants, not the building of new ones. The rising number of blighted areas increased operational inefficiencies and city service costs. The CPC claimed that this was a major reason why 255 firms employing ten workers or more had moved out of the city into the suburbs between 1945 and 1950. At the same time, a much smaller number were moving into the city.[22] The city was bleeding manufacturing jobs. The CPC was not alone in linking blight to industrial flight. Carl L. Gardner, secretary of the city planning advisory board, for example, told the city council that Chicago had a "blight infected central area" and that "industries [were] moving out of this central area at an alarming rate." This problem was undermining the city's industrial supremacy.[23]

Finally, the razing of downtown industrial districts for highways caused significant industrial displacement and suburbanization. As the CPC pointed out, the tearing down of entire areas reduced the availability of land for industry (figure 4.1).[24] The MHPC was also concerned about the immediate and long-term effects of highway construction on industrial activity in the central city. According to the council's numbers, highway construction had displaced 253 firms by

FIGURE 4.1 Demolition for the Congress Expressway, 1955. As the photo shows, large swaths of houses and factories in the city were razed to make room for expressways linking the central city with the suburbs. Box 23, file "Expressways, demolition for, cleared areas and construction, 1951–1952, 1955," Department of Urban Renewal Collection, Special Collections, Chicago Public Library.

the summer of 1951. While some remained in their immediate areas, others did not, and at least 10 percent had taken the opportunity to move to the suburbs.[25]

To counter these four problems required the city to establish a situation that would allow manufacturers access to better industrial land and to undertake more favorable production conditions. By 1952 the CPC had clearly set out what needed to be done, who it was to be done by, and where it was to be done. Two years later, another report laid out the CPC's recommendations for how the city should move ahead with industrial redevelopment. Working hand in hand with the city's housing and redevelopment coordinator, the CPC pushed for the immediate start of an industrial redevelopment program based on the use of public funds and powers. The report noted that the city's renewal program was in disarray, consisting of too many agencies with too many overlapping functions. The commission recommended that "it should be the objective of the City to bring as many [as possible] of the redevelopment activities under the single policy direction of the City Council and the administrative direction of the Mayor."[26] Not surprisingly, the CPC suggested that the redevelopment program should be a formal mechanism maintained by itself in cooperation with the housing and redevelopment coordinator.

The CPC argued that even though blighted property had a specific legal meaning which had been legitimatized by the courts, it was time to rethink the categories of what could be done to blighted areas to use the resulting new classification on the ground. The organization suggested three types of areas where renewal would take place: large-scale redevelopment areas, limited redevelopment areas, and conservation areas. The CPC also set out the areas in the city that should be worked on. Unsurprisingly given the discussion over the previous ten years, the main redevelopment was to take place in the "central industrial belt," which followed the North and South Branches of the Chicago River with tentacles stretching westward between Lake, Grand, and Fifteenth-Sixteenth Streets, as well as a strip connecting these two tentacles and the South Branch that ran along Rockwell west of Western Avenue. Three other redevelopment areas were identified: the Stockyards and Central Manufacturing District; the industrial corridor along the Pennsylvania and New York Central Railroads; and the stretch along Western south to Sixty-Third. Some of these areas were home to housing, which had to be demolished to make way for the industrial expansion.

By the mid-1950s, a compelling case for industrial redevelopment had been made by the CPC with a varying degree of support from other local organizations such as the MHPC and city council. A bevy of experts had been deployed to gather data and make arguments about the need to eliminate blight through industrial redevelopment. The calculative politics that underlay the desire to reframe urban space was driven by the economic and political interests of the city's place-dependent bourgeoisie. In their minds, and those of their supporters in the government boardrooms in Springfield, Illinois, and Washington, DC, the transformation of blighted space into rejuvenated industrial space was a solution to industrial decline and a host of other problems, including falling tax revenues and obsolescent buildings. It had become generally accepted that government-led private industrial redevelopment was a solution to both the city's blighted districts and its declining manufacturing base.

The SSPB and a Model Industrial District

One organization deeply invested in eliminating central-city blight and revitalizing industry was the SSPB. It was created in 1946 as a private, nonprofit planning agency with the aims of eradicating blight, enticing investors to the nine square miles south of the Loop, and reversing the area's economic decline by promoting industrial redevelopment. Over the next ten years, the SSPB worked to redevelop a significant swath of the South Side. The intent was to replace blighted areas with new residential, institutional, and industrial facilities. The agency's aims were heavily shaped by the area's main employers: the Michael Reese Hospital and the Illinois Institute of Technology. Finding that the conditions adjacent to their South Side locations were intolerable, the medical and educational institutions had considered their options, one of which was to move out of the area entirely. After consulting with city and district leaders, they decided there were compelling reasons to stay and redevelop the area. While moving to another location had its advantages, the hospital's and the institute's leaders realized that the futures of their institutions and their investments were deeply intertwined with the economic well-being of the surrounding neighborhood.[27] Rather than escape from blight, they decided to stay and eliminate it.

From the very beginning, the board worked to turn the area's blighted territory into a modern residential, institutional, and industrial space. As Michael Carriere has shown, the SSPB, like other Chicago organizations at the time, fervently believed in ridding the area of social and physical deterioration by rebuilding the built environment and economic ties. As the wartime dust settled, it had become clear that structural change, industrial disinvestment, and racial discrimination had created a range of problems that could be solved only by a new vision of Chicago, one rooted in modernist planning principles and the transformation of the physical environment.[28] In this view, the SSPB had to create a new landscape that brought social and political order to a disorganized space. There was little to be gained from saving the South Side's blighted areas. They were outdated spaces that needed to be eliminated. Demolishing them would provide opportunities to make a more orderly, functional, and profitable world.

By the late 1940s, the South Side was a textbook example of the run-down central industrial area subject to worsening economic, social, and environmental conditions. As firms moved to the suburbs, the advantages that once had attracted them—access to railroad lines, wholesale and retail markets, raw materials, supplies and semifinished goods, and a large labor force—were being overshadowed by the area's disadvantages: old factory buildings, poor layout and off-street loading facilities, old housing and platting, dated zoning codes, inadequate railroad service, lack of joint facilities and services, and few building sites. All these combined to create a serious shortage of suitable vacant land on which to build factories for inner-city manufacturers. Moreover, the district was home to tense racial relations centered on housing. A small group of white homeowners were concerned to keep themselves separate from the much larger black population, who, in turn, were afraid of losing their housing. The way forward, both economically and socially, was to rebuild the industrial spaces of the central city.[29]

To this end, the board's leaders worked to ensure that the interests of local business and organizations were incorporated into the district's plans. Surveys were made in 1946 and 1947 to discover the occupational, racial, and business character of the area with the aim of creating a knowledge base to help redevelop the area. Building on these surveys, in March 1948, the SSPB's executive board published a series of reports and approved a community relations program with the aim of taking advantage of the population's local commitments and drawing as many people as possible into the board's activities. The program centered on establishing the credentials of the board itself and devising strategies to fight the fear held by local businesspeople, professionals, and residents about the immediate and long-term consequences of redevelopment. The reports played up the dependency of the area's population on local property values and employment, and made it clear that fundamental changes had to be made to the district if these were to be maintained. The "facts" established by the board through the community relations program were reinforced by the ideas propagated by experts such as Hoyt that eliminating blight and refashioning land use were beneficial to everyone and not just a favored few.[30] The main purpose of the board's surveys and reports was to convince Chicago's civic and business leaders that the heavily African American area was safe for redevelopment.[31]

The SSPB used several arguments to make the case for their redevelopment program. One strategy that the board deployed was to lay blame for the area's problems at the feet of the city and other citywide organizations such as the CPC. Its intention was to divert responsibility for the prevailing conditions from local businesses and property owners. This point was made by Robert Garrigan, the board's executive director, as early as 1946. He told the *Chicago Tribune*, "a slum is a result of political irresponsibility, civic lethargy, and lack of good city planning."[32] The city and the CPC were responsible for the problems in the district. Stemming from this failure was a second issue: social disorganization and blight. Wilford Winholtz, the board's acting executive director, argued that eliminating blight would positively affect individual behavior, and the social and economic basis of the South Side.[33] Deploying these arguments, SSPB leaders worked to garner popular support from local residents for their redevelopment program.

Spurred by these arguments, the board prepared a long-term vision for the area's renewal. In 1947, the resulting fifty-year "blueprint for transforming one of the city's worst eye sores of blighted property into new, attractive neighborhoods" was submitted to the CPC for approval. Among other things, the report called "for the eventual orderly redistricting of industrial and commercial establishments which now are scattered thruout [sic] the area in helter-skelter fashion." The plan called on the board to take advantage of the city's program to make large tracts available to private interests for industrial purposes.[34] The SSPB also became involved in several redevelopment activities that emerged out of the plan. The most notable was the Lake Meadows project undertaken by the CLCC and the New York Life Insurance Company. But there were others; by 1956, the board had started on the first phase of a $225 million redevelopment project, had eliminated close to seven hundred acres of what was termed blighted land, and was involved in Chicago Housing Authority projects, school building, and parks.[35] Redevelopment was under way.

As the city's elites soon found out, redevelopment was not without its problems. The attempt to rework the South Side would bring the agency into direct conflict with Holman Pettibone and Milton Mumford, the city's powerful redevelopment brokers. The SSPB's vision of industrial redevelopment did not fit in with the postindustrial one being promulgated by the Pettibone and Mumford alliance. This group, which was dominated by downtown financial and property interests, formed an interlocked place-making machine that sought to undertake central-city residential and commercial redevelopment by removing the slums surrounding the Loop, and replacing poor African American housing with middle-class apartments. Mumford, the assistant vice president at Marshall Field and Company, and Pettibone, president of the Chicago Title and Trust Company, were joined by other such as George Dovenmuehle, mortgage banker; Ferd Kramer, a leading Chicago real estate agent (figure 4.2); and Robert Merriam, past president of the MHPC and city alderman. Together, this coalition controlled the redevelopment process in Chicago after 1940. Acting as intermediaries between politicians, developers, and investors, they pushed the commercial and residential redevelopment projects that would transform the central city. Plans for turning some of the redeveloped property into industrial sites such as those put forward by the SSPB were not considered a priority by this coalition.[36]

Despite resistance from the Pettibone and Mumford alliance, the SSPB moved ahead with its plans and made some changes to the areas around the hospital and the institute. Nonetheless, the board lost the broader battle of who would direct urban renewal. This is clearly evident in the agency's early years, when the SSPB's plans for the massive grouping of railroad terminals on the area's northern section were quickly dismissed by all the other important players. The SSPB plan was to create a public authority to remove three terminals (Grand Central, La Salle, and Dearborn) and consolidate them at a cost of $300 million in one location: Union Station. In the board's view, the remaining land would be used for a mix of parks, housing, and industrial purposes. The railroad industry was quick to label the plan too expensive and too impractical, while the CPC and the city quietly went ahead with their own plans.[37]

FIGURE 4.2   Ferd Kramer. One of the city's leading real estate developers, Kramer was a key player in the coalition looking to build a postindustrial city on the ruins of the old industrial one. Box 3, folder 1, Mildred Mead Photographs, Special Collections Research Center, University of Chicago Library.

While the SSPB tried to refashion the South Side's blighted areas by building middle-class apartments and demolishing the railroad terminals, it also sought to bring industrial space into the calculation. In late 1946 and early 1947, the geographer Chauncy Harris worked with the hospital and the SSPB to make a survey of the district's industry.[38] As part of this initiative, about twenty University of Chicago graduate students asked 125 industrial firms questions about their immediate needs, plans for expansion and intention to move, labor matters, and several other issues. A year later, in the fall of 1948, Winholtz followed up by commissioning a survey to plot the district's new industrial and nonresidential construction since the end of World War II.[39] It was clear that renewal of the district's industrial base was an important issue for the SSPB.

Industrial redevelopment, however, moved slowly. A 1953 report by SSPB staff on industrial investment stated that nothing had been done as of yet to promote the industrial district. The board warned that although "Chicago's industrial future, on the surface, [looked] bright," in fact it was not. It was "urgent—and essential," it argued, that "Central Area industrial land be improved and a suitable environment provided for plants and their personnel. To insure Chicago growth and continued prosperity it must assure enough land for the overall needs of industry—and the right kind of sites for industries with specific site requirements."[40] It was the position of the SSPB that the South Side was such a location. However, the board's plans to undertake studies in order to entice firms to the area and to set up an industrial assistance service had not taken place. More needed to be done.

Despite these failings, the SSPB had made headway on plans for an organized industrial space that would "prevent sporadic site selection and harmful intrusion into residential areas." According to Spaeth and Isaacs, the SSPB should not wait for the CPC, the railroad terminal companies, or any other agency to plan and undertake industrial redevelopment on the South Side. The board should move ahead quickly: "Our problem has already been aggravated by the haphazard placement of plants and the lack of proper zoning. Not only is ordinary redevelopment endangered by the plans of the city's agencies, the institutions and the industries themselves may be impeded."[41] Spaeth and Issacs were not alone in viewing the zoning ordinance as inadequate to modern needs. According to a 1952 report by Evert Kinkaid and Associates, the existing zoning ordinance did not adequately reflect current needs. In particular, it did not account for firm mobility, new factory design, and increased production size.[42] Something had to be done if the decline of the district's industrial base was to be reversed.

To this end, Spaeth and Isaacs pushed for the building of a planned industrial district between Twenty-Second Street, the Congress Expressway, State Street, and the South Branch of the Chicago River. A 1949 report written by John Dyckman for the South Side Industrial Study Committee reiterated the argument for a planned industrial district.[43] In Dyckman's view, the district was to provide space for both large and small firms, and to create incubator space for new and expanding industries. Spaeth and Isaacs had made a similar point, noting that these modern industrial facilities would "assist in the provision of a stable labor supply and one with good morale."[44]

Sparked by these reports, the SSPB began its campaign to push ahead with building a planned industrial district. In early 1949, the board authorized its staff to prepare a program and brochure for a "properly planned industrial redevelopment." Collaborators included many of the city's most important place-making and place-dependent organizations: the CPC, the CLCC, the Commonwealth Edison Co., the Chicago Association of Commerce and Industry, the Society of Industrial Realtors, the Baltimore and Ohio Railroad, and the People's Gas, Light and Coke Co. The brochure laid out what a planned industrial district on the South Side could offer industry—well-located plant sites, local experience with industries, a cooperative community, a satisfactory tax situation, and good government. The proposal envisioned a planned industrial district with all the features that industry would need.[45]

The SSPB moved ahead with its plans. In March 1949, Winholtz sent a survey to the area's industrial executives and owners. In the accompanying letter, addressed to the "Business Manager," he told them the SSPB's aim was "to eliminate conditions which cause blight and slum areas, and guide improvements which will make this desirable section of the city a better place in which to live, work, and do business." Industrial plans, he continued, were an important part of the program: "We are now trying to analyze and solve some of the transportation, labor supply, congestion and other problems which we know plague managers of the establishments now located in the Central South Side area."[46]

The SSPB faced many obstacles in mobilizing its plans. In the first place, the CLCC, which had become the city's main industrial redevelopment agency by the late 1940s, had its own plans for where to undertake industrial renewal. Even with support from various quarters, the CLCC was finding it hard to push industrial redevelopment as a viable program.[47] It didn't help that the area chosen by the SSPB for redevelopment was an extremely contentious one, with many other interests, including the railroads, the CPC, MHPC, and the city vying for control. Industrial redevelopment was low on the agenda of the Pettibone and Mumford alliance. Moreover, a private entity such as the SSPB had little hope of building new industrial space without the government's condemnation of blighted property and channeling of public funds to industrial betterment. For those opposed to industrial redevelopment, even though public support for government-led redevelopment could be tolerated under specific circumstances, it was not acceptable for private interests to accept public funding. In the words of a *Chicago Tribune* editorial, "the use of public funds in this manner to provide industrial sites is questionable" because "the possibilities of corruption are too obvious."[48] The forces arrayed against the board's attempt to undertake industrial redevelopment were forbidding.

Despite the obstacles, the agency continued to push for the building of an industrial district. In February 1953, the SSPB completed a draft of a long report that made the case to turn the Central South Side into a modern manufacturing area.[49] The SSPB was not alone; it had the support of several city organizations, including the Chicago Housing Authority, the CLCC, and the Society of Industrial Realtors. The plans, which called for redevelopment of the area west of State and north of Cermak, was the result of a four-year study made by the SSPB and representatives from twenty Chicago organizations.[50] The report's authors argued that the South Side had the potential to become a "modern, well-planned Industrial District" that would drive industrial rejuvenation of the district and the surrounding area.[51] Working on the idea that industry was the city's lifeblood, the authors argued that renewal would provide modern facilities for firms facing intolerable environmental and economic conditions in the central city.

Building on the various reports submitted in the previous five years, the board viewed the building of a planned district as a viable solution to their industrial and social problems. The key was to build on the area's assets and to erect new factories on razed blighted areas. Among other things, this involved providing industrial sites with new buildings, room for expansion, and an efficient internal traffic system. Modernization also included using agglomeration economies and horizontal industrial integration to allow the "grouping [of] industries that are alike or complementary in their production processes" as well as the provision of services for management and workers.[52] Before this strategy could come into play, however, the SSPB had to undertake several steps.

First, the board had to get access to industrial land. Deploying the calculative politics that was coalescing around industrial property at that time, the SSPB recommended acquiring land and then delivering it "as a written-down cost to private industry." In order to do this, the board had to work with the CLCC, the only agency that had the authority to acquire property through eminent domain and then convey it to private enterprise. Second, the SSPB had to market the prepared sites. The position taken was that under no circumstances should the board try to compete with suburban areas. This could only end in failure. The aim should be to attract firms that benefited from a central location. Once again, this required the CLCC to help assemble small parcels of land into tracts of suitable size for modern industrial practices and sell the land at written-down "fair re-use value." Finally, the SSPB had to ensure that these changes would attract long-term investment capital from insurance companies and other bodies seeking long-term, stable investment opportunities in urban property.[53]

The SSPB, however, was unable to mobilize the necessary support for its planned industrial district. Despite years of consultation and the creation of a viable plan, the SSPB was unable to convince the city, the CPC, the MHPC, the CLCC, and the Chicago Central Area Committee to move ahead. In part, as Morris Hirsh, the SSPB executive director, noted in 1955, this was because the agency was unable to get local buy-in. Despite working with some industrial interests, they could not "secure greater direct participation by those who [would] gain the most from area improvement." The agency brought in out-of-town experts to try to convince local leaders to move forward. William P. Rock of the Baltimore Association of Commerce, for example, came to Chicago in 1953 to help the SSPB work through the issues facing the building of the planned industrial district.[54] Such efforts were to no avail. The CLCC was unwilling to move ahead with the land purchase. Almost two years after the plan had been formally presented, the SSPB was still applying pressure on the land clearance agency to move ahead with the project. It was unsuccessful.[55]

The main problem was that the plan was not supported by the Pettibone and Mumford growth alliance. The place-dependent alliance of financial, real estate, and political interests that controlled downtown redevelopment by the late 1940s had little time for industrial renewal. This was clearly laid out in the city's 1958 "Development Plan for the Central Area of Chicago." The plan's premise was to consolidate the downtown office and retail sectors with public and private investments by clearing 130 acres of underutilized rail yards west of the Loop to make way for a University of Illinois campus, constructing new government buildings in the north and south ends of the Loop, and constructing new privately built, middle-class housing for up to fifty thousand families. It was a plan that sought to build a postindustrial city consisting of clusters of tertiary and quaternary economic activities and distinct racial and class-based residential areas. The land for the project was to be assembled and cleared by the city under eminent domain.[56] There was little space, literally and metaphorically, for industry in these plans.

The emphasis on those postindustrial elements in the 1958 plan reflected the strong commitment by Mayor Richard J. Daley, the city planning department, and the Chicago Central Area Committee to transform the blighted industrial city into one servicing high-end residents. The result was that the SSPB's plan was rejected and the area was designated residential in the 1958 development plan. Ultimately, Chicago's powerful interests were looking to build a new bourgeois city based on high-end housing, upscale retail that catered to a metropolitan clientele, and segregated residential areas that minimized racial integration. It was left to hybrid organizations to push an alternative vision based on industrial renewal. In the end the SSPB did not have the political and economic clout to successfully fight the postindustrial alliance.

The Case of Bodine Electric Company

Zoning had played a role in the geographies of industrial land use in Chicago since the passing of the first ordinance in 1923. The placing of enforceable boundaries around what did and did not constitute manufacturing activity established opportunities and limitations on firm behavior, property values, and geographic patterns. By the 1950s, however, the problems created by arbitrary industrial categories, the distribution of zoned land, the depressive effect on land prices, and the inflexible character of the zoned areas themselves had become a burden for both public and private interests.[57] For many, the zoning of specific parcels of land as industrial was seen as detrimental to residential and community life.

The fight between residents and the Bodine Electric Company in the mid-1950s is a case in point. In many ways, as with the SSPB industrial plan, the issues raised by the conflict are reflective of the place that industry had in postwar Chicago: the contradictory role of property relations in industrial life, the fear of industry creating residential blight, and the reluctance of the city's growth coalition to impose a program of industrial redevelopment.

Many, including quite a few industrial leaders, had believed for some time that the existing zoning ordinance was oppressive. A 1938 MHPC report outlined a litany of problems that people had with it, and recommended that "immediate steps be taken to review" the onerous regulations and classifications.[58] Their advice was heeded, and major revisions were adopted in 1942.[59] These revisions to the "outmoded" regulations, however, did not eradicate the problems. The growing pressure over the next ten years to create a new zoning ordinance resulted in the striking of a committee in 1952 to make comprehensive changes to the ordinance. A report written by Evert Kinkaid and Associates presented to the council in May 1952 made the case for a new ordinance, stating that the existing one did not reflect current needs and was incapable of "rebuilding the 'old Chicago.'"[60]

These views had been held for some time. In 1947, William Clark of the *Chicago Tribune* noted that the zoning rules hampered economic expansion. Walter Blucher, the executive director of the American Society of Planning Officials, stated that the Chicago system was "vague, indefinite, virtually meaningless, and subject to political abuse."[61] Not surprisingly, Kinkaid reported that the city's zoning classification hindered redevelopment and recommended making amendments. The experts brought in to create a new system outlined several ideas, including using economic compatibility as a basis for zones, and applying performance standards to industrial zoning districts. In May 1957, the city council passed a new ordinance, one that modernized Chicago's zoning system and established the basis for renewing the "old" industrial city and for the building of the postindustrial one.[62]

Accordingly, zoning had a dual impact on industrial property in postwar Chicago. On the one hand, zoning designated areas where manufacturing activity was permitted. Not only was industrial to be separate from others uses such as residential, but different types of manufacturing were to occupy different zones. For many industrialists, politicians, and agencies in the postwar years, this was both acceptable and necessary. In their report on the SSPB industrial district in 1948, for example, Speath and Issacs wrote that "desirable industries require freedom from noxious industries, from undue concentration on the land and the encroachment of undesirable uses of properties."[63] Without zoning, industrial use of property would be disorderly, ineffective, and ultimately, unprofitable.

This was not a new idea in 1948. Indeed, this was the key idea behind the 1923 zoning ordinance, and was clearly elucidated by the urban planner Alfred Bettman in 1924. Writing in the *Harvard Law Review*, he argued that zoning was necessary to prevent uncontrolled growth and that the "stabilization of the living and working environment" was the aim of zoning.[64] Industry could not function effectively without the property controls of zoning.

On the other hand, zoning was used to inhibit the activities of industrial firms. Zoning pitted industrial, residential, and commercial uses against each other, raising the question of who had the right to determine how property could be used. As it turned out, industry was at the bottom of the hierarchy. This circumstance wasn't lost on some of the city's industrial interests. The Chicago Association of Commerce and Industry was concerned that zoning reinforced industrial decline by pushing firms out of the city and stopping new ones from moving in. The association wrote in its 1947 annual report that "there are many persons who believe that these regulations place unnecessary restrictions on the use of land for factory construction and commercial uses."[65]

As well, zoning was susceptible to the fractious calculative politics of place. Industrial needs were subject to protests from residents and from local politicians. Providing site "amendments" to the zoning code was a service that city aldermen offered to their constituencies.[66] In the minds of industrial managers, these amendments typically favored residents and restricted what industry could do on any piece of property. At the same time, residents were well aware of the impact that zoning had on their property. For many, the main concern of zoning should be to protect neighborhood property values from the intrusion of factories and other related activities. For others, the concern was with maintaining strict racial and class barriers. In particular, the largely white population living outside the South Side was very conscious how useful zoning could be for maintaining racial segregation. In their view, the city should use zoning to keep African Americans out of white areas.

The rezoning of the Bodine Electric site illustrates the complex interaction of zoning, industry, and property relations in the postwar capitalist city. In 1951, Bodine, which had made electric motors since 1905, purchased fifty acres of land occupied by the Mid-City Golf Course north of Addison Street between Western Avenue and the North Branch of the Chicago River. In the summer of 1952, the company was making plans to build a multimillion-dollar one-story factory and two-story office building. The aim was to consolidate all the company's activities and five hundred workers that were located in two factories on the city's West Side into one new modern unit on the recently purchased property.[67]

But there was a problem. Although the property was designated for industrial use, there were questions about the appropriateness of that designation.

The golf course lay on filled-in clay pits that had been operated by the Illinois Brick Co. beginning in 1901. The pits were closed in the early 1920s, and the area was zoned for apartment use in 1923. In 1924, a golf course was opened on a twenty-year lease with Illinois Brick. The property was rezoned under the 1942 zoning amendment to light manufacturing, which, it appears, was done without formal notification to the residents or golf course owner. In 1950, plans were made to turn the golf course into a $9 million rental apartment project of eight fourteen-story buildings with 1,056 family units. The project was quickly abandoned, partly because of the problems of the clay-based subsoil and its zoning designation. Unable to implement their plan, the New York City owners sold the property to Bodine for $700,000. Bodine then sold seven acres to the Victor Adding Machine Company for the construction of a three-story addition to its Rockwell Street plant.[68]

Bodine was legally within its rights to dispose of some of its land to another industrial concern and to build a new manufacturing plant on the remaining property. While it may have been used as a golf course in the past and there had been plans to turn it into an apartment district, the fact remains that the 1942 zoning amendments stipulated the area as manufacturing. The validity of this legal status, however, was questioned by some of the area's residents and their representative at city hall. In June 1953, Alderman Charles Fleck presented a fourteen-page petition to the city's Committee on Building and Zoning, arguing that the residents were unaware of the 1942 amendment until the summer of 1953. Given this, he asked the committee to rezone the area back to apartments. Bodine resisted, and a terrific battle over property rights and the place of manufacturing in the central city raged over the next eighteen months.

The hostility of the area's residents and alderman to Bodine was not unusual. In an extended discussion of the marginalization of industry, Dorothy Muncy argued that industry was seen as a burden, "operate[d] by sufferance of the community," and had "no land rights of its own." She went on to say that despite gestures to attract industry, "most communities subconsciously repel it by ill-concealed prejudice in local zoning and land policy." Industry, she continued, was open to encroachment from other uses, and was typically given the most unattractive land in the city.[69] Richard Babcock, a Chicago lawyer specializing in property law, agreed, arguing that the protection of residential rights trumped industrial ones. The intent of many of Illinois's zoning ordinances was to exclude industry from residential districts.[70] The rights of residence were paramount, and industry was considered a burden to a community.

This was the position taken by S. C. Josephsen, the president of the Artesian and Addison Improvement Association. Writing in the *Chicago Tribune*, he asked, "Does the replacement of a golf course with an industrial development in a residential area constitute a contribution to our community?" A rhetorical question, given that he already knew the answer.[71] And this was Fleck's position when he introduced an amendment to the Building and Zoning Committee to reclassify the site: the "surrounding area consists of nothing but residences and two family flats. It will become a slum because of industrial development if the zoning change is not made." The fact that this was untrue and that the area had at least three substantial factories, all built between 1947 and 1951—Atlantic Brass, Victor Adding Machine, and Bodine—did not deter Fleck from arguing that there was no industrial presence in the area. Bodine, he continued, had nothing to lose, except some of the $700,000 it had paid for the property in 1952. The community, on the other hand, had everything to lose. Concerns about the lowering of property values and spreading of blight were paramount.[72] The rhetoric of loss, value, and attachment to place are used here to prioritize protecting a structured but not all-inclusive community from the perceived distress caused by an industrial firm.

Bodine was not convinced by these arguments. It responded in three ways. First, according to the company's attorney, Vernon Welsh, rezoning the tract would be unfair, illegal, and unnecessary. Bringing in his own witnesses, he told the committee, "I have consulted with six zoning and real estate experts and have been told that the best use of the area would be light industry." Next, Welsh argued that "Chicago is in dire need of manufacturing areas." This was especially the case in that part of town where demand for industrial land was high but supply was low. He used the CPC's *Redevelopment for Industry* report of 1951 to point to the shortage of industrial land north of downtown and linked it to the city's tax base: "The city is always looking for revenue. If this site is killed for manufacturing, Bodine and others will be forced to look for manufacturing sites outside Chicago just as so many others have done. There is much talk about attracting industry to Chicago, then they turn down the first chance they get. This is the largest piece of property on the north side available to manufacturing. If it is rezoned, the city will lose tax revenue."[73] Finally, he argued that the land was unfit for residential use; that was the reason the large apartment project was canceled in 1951. Building residences would be very costly because the ground could not support high-rise structures without expensive engineering costs.[74]

Despite these legal and economic arguments, the Building and Zoning Committee found for the residents in September 1953, passing Fleck's amendment to rezone the property from manufacturing to single-family and apartment residential. A month later, the city council approved the committee's decision by a vote of forty-four to zero. This outcome was not surprising, given the feeling about industrial property and the hostility toward industry in general. While the idea of categories themselves and what constituted a particular use was not up for discussion, the flexibility of how the key players viewed property was. Against both legal statute and economic logic, the city bowed to community demands and arbitrarily reframed private property, turning land zoned for manufacturing into residential land.

Once again, the courts became a site for rewriting property rights. In December 1953, Bodine filed suit in the superior court seeking to void the recent rezoning decision. They demanded an injunction to restrain the city from enforcing the ordinance, and sued for damages of $1,250,000, arguing that the property was taken for public use without just compensation. They also told the court that in August 1953—a month before the zoning committee ruled against them—they had started building a plant using a legally issued city building permit.[75] The court case raged for two years. In July 1955, after reviewing three thousand pages of testimony, 151 court exhibits, and testimony from thirty witnesses, Judge George Fisher upheld the report's findings that it would be "arbitrary, unreasonable and confiscatory to enforce the ordinance."[76] With the decision in place, and after a twenty-seven-month interruption, Bodine resumed construction of the $1,250,000 factory in February 1956.[77]

The provision of sufficient space for industrial expansion was central to the discussion about the introduction of a zoning ordinance by those interested in Chicago's industrial property in the years before the passing of the 1923 ordinance. These industrial interests were successful in adding large amounts of zoned industrial land in the city. Indeed, they were so successful that many subsequent observers wondered whether the city had zoned too much industrial space. Nevertheless, local interests at the time believed that large tracts of property zoned for industrial use were necessary if manufacturing was to continue to be an economic force in the city. They reminded the "Commission and citizens that the life of the city depended first and foremost on its industries and manufactures." A good zoning plan would set aside enough land for industrial growth.[78]

Despite this, the place of industrial property in Chicago's hierarchy of land use was not a secure one. Not only was much of the land zoned for industry poorly located; public opinion held industrial space in low esteem, and zoning was a political calculation under the control of ward aldermen. It would take more than two years, thousands of pages of court testimony, a great deal of politicking, and huge legal fees for Bodine to gain access to its legally owned property, to build a factory on land that had been designated as industrial, and, ultimately, to protect its property rights. Bodine was obviously committed to staying in the city. Despite the clear advantages to be gained from locating in the suburbs, the company's investment and other commitments kept it tied to its location on the city's northwest side. Without an extensive financial commitment from the company, it was clear that Bodine's property rights under the law would have been taken away in the face of community and political pressure. The lesson for firms look-ing to build new manufacturing space was that they were not welcome in the city.

Moving toward Redevelopment

By the late 1940s, Chicago's industrial interests faced numerous challenges to industrial redevelopment. Planning agencies such as the SSPB came up against the power of a growth alliance that saw middle-class residential and commer-cial redevelopment as the means to profitably remake the city. Their vision of a redeveloped Chicago consisted of a new, gleaming postindustrial city, not a reinvigorated industrial one. Similarly, firms such as Bodine found obstacles to growth. From restrictive zoning to hostile residential associations, the city was no longer a hospitable place for industrial investment. As others have shown, the postindustrial city boosters led by Mumford, Pettibone, and Kramer won the battle over property rights and the future of the city. Over the next few decades, they used this vision to create a group of islands of prosperity among a sea of decline, poverty, and segregation. This vision had little time for industrial rede-velopment as practiced by agencies such as the SSPB or industrial expansion by firms such as Bodine.[79]

Despite the forces arrayed against those working for industrial redevelopment, there was some movement toward finding ways to attract industry and to rede-velop property for industrial uses. These came in different forms as agencies and corporations took steps to move industry onto the city's redevelopment agenda. The following three chapters look at three attempts at industrial redevelopment. The focus of chapter 5 is the attempt by the Chicago Land Clearance Commis-sion to redevelop blighted property as part of its program of clearing land for private interests. The methods used by the Mayor's Committee for Economic and Cultural Development to modernize the practices that induced industrial firms to invest in city property are examined in chapter 6. Finally, the strategy of creating industrial parks in the city is covered in chapter 7. Even though none of these attempts were successful, they all had an impact on the industrial fortunes of the city and the metropolitan area. The three chapters illustrate the ways that civic and business elites understood public-private relations, worked to refashion urban property relations, and played the politics of redevelopment.

INDUSTRIAL RENEWAL AND LAND CLEARANCE

In 1954, Ira Bach, the executive director of the Chicago Land Clearance Commission (CLCC) informed Nathaniel Owings of Skidmore, Owings and Merrill, an important Chicago architectural and engineering firm, that the commission would not be able to provide much support to the proposed Fort Dearborn project.[1] Owings was looking to transform the area north of the Chicago River into a massive middle-class housing complex by displacing thousands of residents and hundreds of industrial and commercial establishments. Among the problems faced by the development consortium was the assembly of a tract of land large enough to carry out the extensive project. As both Bach and Owings knew, this was only possible if a municipal agency such as the CLCC used its power of eminent domain.

In Chicago, the agency entrusted with the power of eminent domain was the CLCC. Created in September 26, 1947, it was authorized to designate blighted areas and vacant land as redevelopment projects. The agency's staff was overseen by an executive director and five commissioners appointed by the mayor with the approval of the Illinois State Housing Board. Its operations included the acquisition, relocation, demolition, and sale of buildings, all of which had to be done in accordance with a city plan. It received start-up funds of $11 million from Illinois and $25 million from the city in the form of slum clearance bonds. Federal financial assistance covered up to two-thirds of the net cost of eligible projects.[2]

Although its main purpose was residential renewal, the agency turned to industrial redevelopment in 1950. Over the next ten years, the CLCC used four industrial projects in an attempt to rebuild the city's industrial base by assembling large tracts of land for manufacturing. The CLCC believed that bringing new industrial land in better locations for industry into the city's property market would have several positive effects. At the simplest level, ridding the city of blight would create more industrial property, which would be available at lower prices than could be found on the open market. Small residential lots that riddled the central city would be assembled into larger tracts of affordable land suitable for modern industry. This in turn would have a knock-on effect of attracting new firms and providing existing ones with better opportunities for expansion. Converting tax-delinquent land to productive purposes would increase city taxes.

In the 1950s, the CLCC played a key role in the creation of new industrial property as a solution to the city's industrial decline. The agency's primary role, once it had been given the authority to undertake industrial renewal, was to assemble land for developers and industrial interests. It used state and federal legislative tools that enabled cities to appropriate federal funds for private ends, to allow the exercise of eminent domain over blighted property, and to realign ownership rights in favor of property developers. The intended consequences of these activities were to use state powers to create profits from land development, provide new jobs, and to contribute to the attempts of the place-dependent bourgeoisie to rejuvenate the city's economy.

Creating the CLCC

The CLCC was created "by a small group of interested citizens" seeking to solve the problem of urban blight by using government police and financial powers to pass on what they considered to be unproductive land to property developers.[3] By 1945 it was obvious to business and political leaders that widespread blight, falling property values, and declining retail sales were problems that would continue to undermine the city's prominence and cut into company profits. These issues were accentuated by a housing market that had suffered from years of neglect and the tensions generated by white reactions to the expansion of the African American areas on the city's South and West Sides. For some city leaders, government-led industrial redevelopment was one answer to their mounting economic and social problems.[4]

One solution, and one representing the needs of "interested citizens," was the creation of the CLCC, a quasigovernment agency with police and financial powers to refashion property relations. It emerged out of the reshuffling of the city's redevelopment politics in the immediate postwar period. The Special Committee on Redevelopment of the Metropolitan Housing and Planning Council (MHPC) was established in 1946 to devise a slum clearance program for the city. The

MHPC worked with Alderman Robert Merriam to convince the city to prioritize the renewal of slum areas by a private-public partnership: an organization
that would guarantee that the political channels for redevelopment were open to
entrepreneurial interests. Keenly aware of the city's corrupt politics, the MHPC
hoped that such a partnership would free redevelopment from city council
machinations and provide private developers with greater control over property.[5]

In 1947, the election of Martin Kennelly as mayor gave the propertied elite a
sympathetic ear at city hall. Once in power, Kennelly worked with the MHPC to
sideline the reform-based Chicago Housing Agency (CHA), the city's provider
of public housing, and to promote private housing. The council believed that
a new agency had to be created, as the available options were unable to effectively mobilize private redevelopment. The Chicago Plan Commission (CPC)
was too unorganized, and the CHA too liberal. The city required a new agency,
one that implemented a citywide strategy under the control of a new regime and
did more than the CPC's "fitful" efforts. Moreover, its mandate had to be framed
in a way that did not usurp the role of private enterprise.[6] Indeed, the aim was
to seamlessly merge government-funded urban renewal with private development. This was backed up by two reports made in 1944 and 1946 that pushed the
case for large-scale renewal by hitching private profits to state intervention.[7] To
accommodate these needs, Kennelly created the Chicago Committee for Housing
Action in 1947. Working quickly, the committee recommended the creation of a
land clearance commission and a housing and redevelopment coordinator. Both
of these proposals were implemented.

The State of Illinois also supported an agency to oversee slum clearance and
land assembly for private interest. Governor Dwight Green made this clear in
April 1947 when, following the MHPC and Kennelly, he recommended the establishment of a land clearance agency to redevelop blighted areas and the appointment of a commissioner to coordinate the city's housing program. Green joined
local civic and business interests in criticizing the CHA for the city's poor housing
record. Chicago, he believed, should consolidate all nonmarket housing activities
in one central authority. Once established, it was to work with private capital
to reclaim the city's blighted areas. To his mind, such an agency would lead to
effective redevelopment and counterbalance the CHA's social housing focus. In
other words, the solution for eliminating blight was government and business
cooperation; new private construction in slum districts was to be accomplished
by state-supported action.[8]

State enabling legislation was needed to create an agency that would remove
blight. The most important was the Blighted Areas Redevelopment Act of 1947,
which provided the legal basis for postwar renewal in Chicago and allowed for
the creation of municipal-based land clearance commissions. These were given
extensive expropriation powers allowing them to acquire property from one

set of owners, clear and make improvements to the acquired sites, and sell the improved land to private interests for redevelopment. This was to take place under the auspices of a plan. As Arnold Hirsch notes, the legislation ensured that "the profit motive would govern redevelopment, and the process itself would remain in private hands. Augmented government powers and support were necessary to aid the private sector, to enable it to accomplish that which it could not do by itself. But the priorities, goals, and implementation of the program were left to the traditional forces of privatism."[9] By the summer of 1947, Chicago's postwar growth coalition had the legislative tool at hand to implement large-scale urban renewal.

Undertaking renewal for profit was facilitated by the broad definition of blighted areas under the act. According to a 1949 amendment, these areas were defined as those "by reason of dilapidation, obsolescence, overcrowding, faculty arrangement of design, lack of ventilation, light and sanitary facilities, excessive land coverage, deleterious land use or layout or any combination of these factors, are detrimental to the public safety, health, morals or welfare."[10] Not only imprecise, it also linked the physical elements of space to social values such as morality and welfare.[11] The act was to provide "interested citizens" with the rationale for the acquisition of private property, the clearing of the land, and the sale of the improved land to developers through the use of government subsidies.

Once established, the CLCC was very much a creature of the MHPC. In 1948, the council wrote a document that used the 1944 and 1946 reports to establish the basis for the clearance agency. It laid out its administrative character, which included hiring housing and planning experts in order "to justify its recommendations unequivocally."[12] It set out the principles that were to govern decision-making, such as those that determine the location of "the most adverse living conditions," and how they can support "industry and business." The document established the criteria for selection of redevelopment sites, such as the need for rehabilitation, the elimination of contagion, and the assembly of large tracts. And, above all, it stated that all sites "should be suitable for private redevelopment." Finally, in light of the problematic industrial base, the sites chosen for redevelopment should not involve demolition of too many industrial and commercial properties.[13]

Things did not proceed easily, however, and it was not long before tensions developed between the MHPC and the CLCC. The former criticized the latter for not doing enough to forward private redevelopment. In August 1950, the council's Redevelopment Committee vented its frustration. The important real estate developer, Ferd Kramer, noted that there was an "unexpected dearth of redevelopers," which he attributed to the CLCC's inability to build a speedy administrative process. He also pointed out that the patience of the only developer interested in the agency's land, the New York Life Insurance Company, was being seriously tried by inaction. Kramer argued that it was necessary "to bring some simplicity and direction into the complications which belabor this program." To this end, the MHPC hired Coleman Woodbury, the renowned housing expert, to report on the matter. Not surprisingly, Woodbury's conclusion was that the CLCC was making it very difficult for New York Life to move ahead with their project. The situation wasn't helped, he continued, by the fact that the CPC was not providing adequate support for the CLCC.[14]

A meeting of the Redevelopment Committee, the CLCC and New York Life thrashed out these concerns. Otto Nelson, a New York Life vice president, gave an account "of the difficulties experienced by the private developer in doing business with Chicago." In the CLCC's defense, Ira Bach argued that redevelopment was bedeviled by too many interested parties and the lack of support from the CPC. The shotgun union, he continued, has proven to be "awkward and burdensome" to the CLCC. Moreover, the mayor's lack of control of city council made it difficult to get the necessary municipal support. What the city needed, according to Bach, was someone who could get things done, like Robert Moses in New York City.[15] Despite his defense of the agency, Bach agreed that the CLCC was having teething problems that hindered "sound programming."[16] Nonetheless, the CLCC was making headway. The building of Lake Meadows was the most prominent example of what a public-private partnership such as the CLCC could achieve with the appropriate eminent domain powers, federal funding, and business input. In 1950, however, the question of whether it had devised a clear strategy to pursue residential redevelopment was not settled. According to Bach, an unsupportive CPC and city council, and a critical MHPC, undermined the CLCC's ability to create effective slum clearance.

At the same time, the question of industrial redevelopment was beginning to surface. While housing had always been the CLCC's primary concern, industry had appeared on the organization's agenda by the late 1940s. In a March 1951 report, Bach stated that the CLCC was going to make a detailed study of why industrial redevelopment had to be a part of the agency's activities. Building on opinions that had been stated several times over the previous ten or more years, he argued that industrial redevelopment would facilitate the city's industrial renaissance, help with the building of industrial structures, and eliminate blight.[17] By the early 1950s, it was clear that Bach and his supporters wanted to move ahead with replacing blighted areas with industrial projects.

Beginnings of Industrial Renewal

The CLCC was not alone. In early 1950, the Western Society of Engineers approached Bach, expressing interest in redeveloping a large area on the North

West Side, stretching from Canal Street to the new Congress Expressway between Harrison Street and Roosevelt Road. Bach could not give an immediate answer, as it was unclear whether or not the CLCC had the authority to undertake industrial renewal.[18] The CLCC director turned to Washington, DC, for advice from the Slum Clearance and Urban Redevelopment division of the Housing and Home Finance Agency. The answer Bach received was a positive one, as the Urban Redevelopment division interpreted the Housing Act of 1949 as saying that financial assistance for nonresidential redevelopment could be provided if the area to be acquired was a slum and was predominantly residential in character.[19] Bach took this to the CLCC board, who agreed, and for the next decade the agency and Chicago would be foremost in the country in government-led industrial renewal.

After receiving support from the Urban Redevelopment division and the CLCC board, Bach quickly moved ahead with industrial renewal. By May 1950 the CLCC had prepared a map of the Roosevelt and Canal area, which would later become known as West Central, and received the green light to move ahead with studies of the district.[20] By the summer, the agency had devised the procedure for obtaining federal funding and completed a survey of a smaller area than had been previously laid out by the Western Society of Engineers. In September, Else Berkman, the CLCC's attorney, and Robert Gruhn, the assistant executive director, visited Washington, DC, to show the completed survey to the Housing and Home Finance Agency and to make the case for moving ahead with industrial redevelopment.[21] They received the federal government's blessing, thus publicly signaling to those interested in renewal in Chicago and elsewhere that public-private agencies such as the CLCC had the authority to use the expropriation and financial powers invested in the Blighted Areas Redevelopment Act and the federal 1949 Housing Act for industrial purposes. Industrial redevelopment was now a government concern.

While it is difficult to state categorically, the CLCC program of government-funded industrial renewal was probably the first in the United States. In 1957, an American Society of Planning Officials report looked at whether or not agencies existed "for the purpose of acquiring sites and financing construction of buildings in central areas."[22] The only example they gave of such an agency was the CLCC. Reports on industrial renewal in the 1950s from other cities such as Philadelphia give no indication that public-private industrial renewal of property was being undertaken anywhere else.[23]

Once the West Central project has been established, the CLCC looked for new blighted inner-city sites that could be redeveloped for industry. As it moved ahead, the agency was very receptive to the interests of private developers (figure 5.1). Working with organizations such as the Western Society of Engineers, the agency initiated several studies to demonstrate what was blighted and thus eligible for industrial redevelopment. The areas that were identified were considered to be

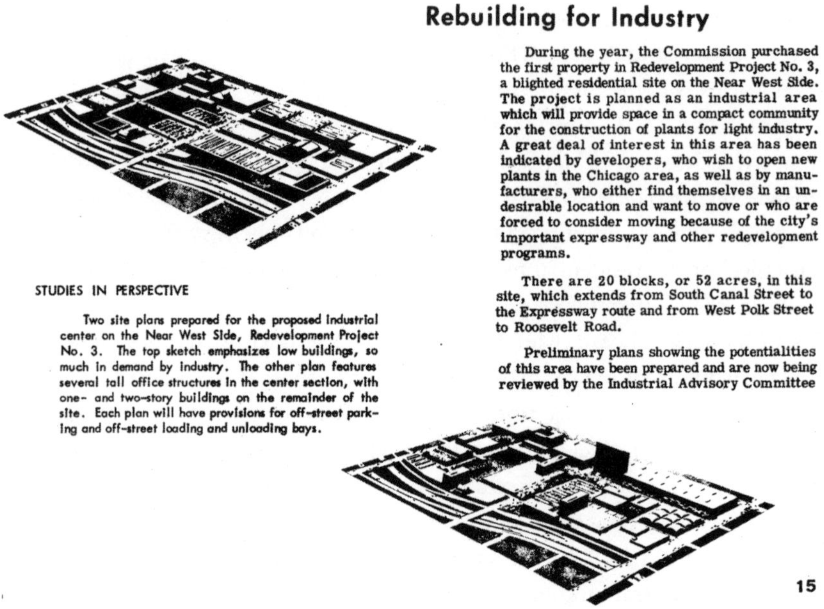

Rebuilding for Industry

During the year, the Commission purchased the first property in Redevelopment Project No. 3, a blighted residential site on the Near West Side. The project is planned as an industrial area which will provide space in a compact community for the construction of plants for light industry. A great deal of interest in this area has been indicated by developers, who wish to open new plants in the Chicago area, as well as by manufacturers, who either find themselves in an undesirable location and want to move or who are forced to consider moving because of the city's important expressway and other redevelopment programs.

There are 20 blocks, or 52 acres, in this site, which extends from South Canal Street to the Expressway route and from West Polk Street to Roosevelt Road.

Preliminary plans showing the potentialities of this area have been prepared and are now being reviewed by the Industrial Advisory Committee

STUDIES IN PERSPECTIVE

Two site plans prepared for the proposed Industrial center on the Near West Side, Redevelopment Project No. 3. The top sketch emphasizes low buildings, so much in demand by industry. The other plan features several tall office structures in the center section, with one- and two-story buildings on the remainder of the site. Each plan will have provisions for off-street parking and off-street loading and unloading bays.

15

FIGURE 5.1　Site plans for industrial redevelopment, 1953. In these site plans, the CLCC lays out some of the key elements of industrial redevelopment, such as providing space for single-story buildings, establishing the need for desirable locations, and better parking and loading facilities. CLCC, *Report to Chicagoans, 1947–1952* (Chicago: CLCC, 1953).

able to generate developer profits, stabilize industrial and residential markets, and create a "happy and healthful environment." The argument made by the CLCC about the areas it surveyed revolved around the need to turn wasted land full of "deteriorated and dangerous structures" into useful and productive property.[24] The demolition of existing blighted structures and the productive use of dead space would make for a new and modern industrial district.

To make this possible, the CLCC used the authority invested in the Blighted Areas Redevelopment Act to expropriate blighted property and turn it into its "best use"—industry. Adopting ideas from the Chicago School of social ecology, the report argued that "the *natural history* of the area [West Central] indicates a movement from residential to non-residential uses." The result of this natural movement was blighted space, inefficient use of resources, and decline. The report put this in stark terms: parts of the city were "literally rotting away." In the author's opinion, "American cities and Chicago can no longer afford the luxury of obsolescent blighted areas which are not being put to the most productive use and they particularly cannot afford the unproductive use of areas potentially suitable for highly necessary industrial uses."[25] Something had to be done if industrial blight was to be eliminated, and only government had the legal and financial power to make this happen.

Not everyone supported public financial backing for industrial renewal. A 1951 editorial in the *Chicago Tribune* opined that "the use of public funds ... to provide industrial sites is questionable" because "the possibilities of corruption are too obvious." There was no need to use public funds to subsidize industries to redevelop slums, given that industrial land created more income than residential land. Moreover, land in blighted areas was being held in purely speculative ventures. The public purchase of the land and its resale at a loss for factory building would give speculators a reward they could not get in the open market. If a public body like the CLCC was going to take land for industrial use, it should do so only with guarantees from a private developer that land would be repurchased at no loss in public funds. In other words, according to the newspaper, the provision of public subsidies for factory sites would lead to corruption and unfair profits.[26]

Despite these claims, there was swelling support for the CLCC program of industrial renewal. The First Federal Savings and Loan Association argued that Chicago was facing dire industrial conditions. Factories were leaving the city because of the absence of industrial sites large enough to accommodate one-story plants with modern off-street parking and loading facilities. The association argued that one solution was to rebuild central Chicago. The CLCC's work assembling land for West Central was a positive step forward and should be continued.[27] Similarly, Betty Savesky, a writer for the Chicago Association of Commerce and Industry, noted that the agency "has paved the way for private capital to turn four tax-delinquent, trouble-breeding sections of the city into economically sound, socially useful communities."[28] The CLCC, in her view, should be allowed to move ahead with industrial renewal.

This was reiterated by George Dovenmuehle, a powerful local real estate developer. Dovenmuehle was owner of Dovenmuehle, Inc., a company that provided construction loans for residential and income properties. He was also a leading member of the MHPC. In October 1951, he made clear his and the MHPC's support for government-led industrial renewal. He told Alderman William Murphy, chair of the city council's Planning Committee, that the MHPC had been trying for years to rid the city of blight by working with the private sector. It was the council's belief, he continued, that "the city must be flexible in its approach and seek many types of redevelopment in addition to housing." Some areas were "obviously far better" suited "from the standpoint of location, environment and nearby facilities for industry."[29]

A public-private partnership was the most appropriate means for turning blighted land into productive industrial property. Both Dovenmuehle and the

MHPC believed that the move to initiate industrial renewal would allow Chicago to compete with the suburbs for new and growing industrial firms. Dovenmuehle also explained that several other local agencies agreed with this position, including the CPC and the South Side Planning Board. He told Murphy that the CLCC had conducted numerous studies of the West Central district and had been told by private investors that they wished to move ahead with substantial investment to make it "a model industrial district."[30] Dovenmuehle was quite clear in his conviction that both the city and local business would benefit from the economic opportunities created through the refashioning of industrial property relations and the building of new industrial land.

The single most important piece of evidence that supported the CLCC's program of industrial redevelopment was a long report submitted to the agency by Homer Hoyt in June 1951.[31] He was brought in by the city's housing and redevelopment coordinator and the CLCC to report on industrial renewal in Chicago. In his report he turned his attention to the question of industrial property. Working through ideas about the relationship between Chicago's property market and declining industry, he established both the rationale for and the operating principles of the CLCC's intervention into industrial redevelopment. He then used these principles to argue for turning the blighted area west of the Loop into the West Central industrial district. Hoyt gave those looking for the economic and ideological basis for the transformation of the industrial property market what they wanted.

Hoyt's report proceeded in two ways. First, he established the principles of industrial renewal. There were seven of them, including the need to overcome the shortage of factory space and sites suitable for modern buildings, and to create effective demand for centrally located sites, the elimination of unhealthy areas, and the growth of the city's tax base. Second, he used these principles to justify the redevelopment of the West Central industrial district. Chicago was dependent on industry for its existence, he averred, "yet hundreds of factories which wanted to remain in Chicago [had] either moved to the suburbs or left the Chicago region altogether because they could not find a location in which they could operate efficiently in Chicago."[32] Something had to be done if the city was to effectively eliminate blight and compete with the suburbs for manufacturing plants.

In Hoyt's view, this something was government intervention. Large tracts of affordable land were out of the reach of industrial concerns. The solution was government expropriation of blighted property. The initial costs incurred by government in acquiring and writing down land costs would be repaid several times over by increased employment and taxes. Public-private redevelopment of the West Side district would attract and retain industry that was now moving to the suburbs because of the lack of space downtown. This in turn would create twenty-one thousand new jobs, produce a payroll of more than $84 million annually, and stimulate a multiplier effect that would produce more taxes and more retail sales. In other words, there were compelling reasons for rebuilding Chicago's industrial districts through a partnership of public and private interests. The CLCC's project was "the first step toward reclaiming and redeveloping blighted areas in Chicago, not suited to residential uses, into modern workshops and centrally-located places of employment," which would bring with them "an ever better level of living for all Chicago's citizens." He furthered argued that the city could not "fail to take advantage of this opportunity."[33]

Before action was possible, the CLCC had to ensure that industrial redevelopment had a strong legal basis. The legal status of the commission's renewal program went before the Illinois Supreme Court and US Supreme Court several times; in all cases, the final decision went in the CLCC's favor. Several decisions on eminent domain by Illinois courts also found for the agency. The Illinois Supreme Court affirmed the CLCC's right to acquire and sell land in January 1952. Two months later, the US district court dismissed a suit to halt land acquisition for the Lake Meadows project. In April 1952, the circuit court upheld the CLCC's authority to acquire blighted land. Finally, in March 1953, the Illinois Supreme Court reversed its November 1952 decision that declared a 1949 amendment to the CLCC statute unconstitutional.[34] The courts saw few legal impediments to the refashioning of property relations through urban renewal and gave the green light to public-private partnerships such as the CLCC to move ahead with building industrial districts in Chicago and elsewhere in Illinois.

As the CLCC sought to establish its credentials as a Chicago industrial redeveloper, it looked to take further advantage of a favorable court. At the behest of Ira Bach, John Gutknecht, the attorney general, filed suit in June 1956 in the Illinois Circuit Court against a 1955 amendment to the Blighted Areas Redevelopment Act. Looking to support the CLCC's ability to undertake eminent domain, Gutknecht tested the constitutionality of an amendment that allowed the agency to acquire blighted, vacant, and tax-delinquent land, and to use it for industrial purposes. Using an area at 111th and Ashland as a test case, Gutknecht stated that the CLCC had acted illegally in making studies and surveys of vacant land for future industrial use under the 1955 amendment. The CLCC had argued that most of the city's vacant land was unsuitable for residential purposes.[35]

The CLCC was not alone in thinking this. Even the *Chicago Tribune*, which had little appetite for public subsidies for private development, argued that the same principle that holds for residential purposes should hold for industrial ones. "It would be folly," an editor opined, "to condemn land that is unsuited, by its location, for residential use, and build new homes on it." The paper went on to say that industrial use of such tracts would reduce blight in the surrounding areas and create jobs.[36] A year later, in June 1957, Harry Fisher, the circuit court judge reviewing the case, agreed with the state government, the CLCC, and the newspaper, and upheld the amendment. The CLCC had the authority to acquire tax-delinquent land for resale to industrial developers.[37]

What is interesting about all these cases is that the CLCC's managers were canny enough to realize that the courts were a decisive arena for the playing out of industrial redevelopment politics. They were building on a strong foundation. As Wendell Pritchett has shown, rulings since the 1930s had made it clear that national and state courts supported the elimination of blight and had authorized urban renewal agencies to use eminent domain to transform urban land relations.[38] On this basis, the agency worked with the state attorney's office to test the waters in the circuit court before proceeding with any action.

As part of this process, the CLCC had to line up the amended Blighted Areas Redevelopment Act with the Housing Act of 1949. The success of the renewal program rested on ensuring that the two acts were constitutionally compatible, as least with regard to the land taken by eminent domain and program funding. The application of the amendments could only be assured if the friction between city, state, and federal practices was minimized. At the same time, the court cases reinforced the growing movement to restructure industrial property relations in order to attract new firms, create jobs, eliminate blight, and make profits. In this case, the pragmatism of industrial renewal trumped the principle of private property. This outcome was supported by government legislation and court decisions.

At the same time that the CLCC commissioned surveys, worked within legislation, and pursued court cases, it had to determine who was going to have access to the industrial property created through renewal. A central feature of urban renewal is the taking of property from one set of owners, making certain improvements to it, and then transferring it to another set of owners, either public or private. The CLCC used this idea in an attempt to turn inefficient, delinquent, tax-draining, mixed-use property into modern, efficient, tax-producing industrial property. By targeting the West Central area as the initial industrial project in February 1950, the Western Society of Engineers had indicated which property owners they thought should have their land and buildings taken away from them under the eminent domain powers authorized by the Blighted Areas Redevelopment Act. The question remained, however, Who were going to be the direct beneficiaries of the transformed property? There was no clear answer.

The search for an answer was triggered in March 1951, when Robert White of the Clearing Industrial District approached the CLCC with an offer to redevelop the entire West Central.[39] Clearing was a corporation that built and managed planned industrial districts. It built its first district in 1912. By 1950, its eight industrial districts in the city and the suburbs were home to hundreds of firms.[40] The corporation was looking to build another one in West Central. The CLCC did not have an immediate answer to White's question. This was uncharted territory, as all the agency's efforts up to that point had been focused on legitimatizing the idea of and creating the legal basis for industrial renewal. The practical logistics were still unclear, and the determination of who benefited from government-subsidized largesse was no simple matter. The issue was complicated by the fact that other parties were interested in working on the area as a single development. Bach met with the various parties to consider terms and options, and to determine whether the project could be done by a single developer. For legal reasons, the answer was no, although the Urban Renewal Administration in May 1952 did suggest that industrial associations such as Clearing could have a role to play under certain circumstances.[41] In Chicago though, the CLCC determined that no single developer would be allowed to develop industrial property. Government properties were only to be sold to single developers or industrial firms.[42]

Alongside West Central, the CLCC created three other industrial districts in the 1950s. The Roosevelt-Clinton district was a forty-six-acre tract located immediately south of West Central, stretching between Roosevelt Road, Canal Street, Fifteenth Street, and the new highway just east of Union Avenue (figure 5.2). The area was first subdivided in 1833, and by 1952 there were a total of 386 lots platted, 171 of which were vacant because of demolition and the exodus of industry and commerce. No new housing had been built there since before World War I.[43] Comprising a mix of residential and nonresidential uses, more than 80 percent of its structures were considered dilapidated and unfit for human habitation. Despite this, more than 1,650 people lived there, almost entirely African American. The district had been categorized as a slum and blighted area by the terms set out in the 1947 Blighted Areas Development Act. The CLCC's plan was to develop it as an area for light industry such as printing and apparel, as "the interest of possible redevelopers in the West Central Industrial District Redevelopment Project, just to the north of this project, indicates that there is a large market for this type of land in this general area of the city."[44]

The other two districts were three miles west of the Loop. The Lake-Maplewood district was a mixed neighborhood in which 56 percent of the structures were in a deteriorated state. The CLCC determined that it should be converted into an industrial district. Accordingly, the property was acquired, 2,769 people were relocated, the buildings razed, and the land sold to new industrial concerns. The Lake-California district was a twenty-three-acre tract running along the Chicago and North Western Railroad. This area was mostly residential, with 1,531 people living in 198 structures, most of which were severely deteriorated. The CLCC

FIGURE 5.2   Mixed residential and industrial district, 1957. The mixed residential and industrial district at Clinton Street and Roosevelt Road became one of the first industrial redevelopment sites in Chicago in the early 1950s. The CLCC acquired the property, razed the buildings, and sold the cleared land to new private interests. Box 20, file "MM Roosevelt-Clinton, November 1, 1957," Department of Urban Renewal Collection, Special Collections, Chicago Public Library.

determined it was blighted and eligible for redevelopment and should be turned into a light industrial district. The plan was approved by the CLCC, the city council, and the Illinois State Housing Board.[45]

With these four industrial districts, Chicago was the first city in the country to forge a public-private partnership using federal funds and government legislation to undertake industrial renewal. After 1950, private property was subjected to national, state, and municipal legislation and legal rulings, surveyed by agency and outside consultants, worked on by a range of techniques and tools administered by the agency and other institutions, and shaped by funds from federal, state, and city coffers. In the process, thousands of working-class families lost their homes and had to move to other parts of the city, numerous businesses were closed, property owners lost their land, and areas adjoining the Loop were improved to make way for industry. In other words, the CLCC cooperated with developers, industrialists, and city and noncity officials to remake the central city's industrial property market. To understand how new industrial property was created by the CLCC, the next section looks at the building of the West Central industrial district, the first and largest of the CLCC's industrial renewal projects.

Building the West Central Industrial District

In October 1949, Florsheim Shoe opened a new six- and seven-story, two-hundred-thousand-square-foot building as an addition to its existing factory at Adams and Canal Streets (figure 5.3). Florsheim, the world's largest manufacturer of men's shoes in its price and quality range, employed thousands of workers at its five factories and eighty-one retail outlets located across the United States.[46]

FIGURE 5.3 The Florsheim factory, West Central district, 1957. The Florsheim Shoe Company was one of the few large manufacturers to commit substantial resources to building new production space in the city's downtown districts. This picture shows construction work on Canal Street. Box 21, file Chicago Land Clearance Commission, Central Industrial Collection, #321, 1957–59, Department of Urban Renewal Collection, Chicago Public Library, Special Collections.

Seven years later, in December 1956, the shoemaker announced that it was going to build another addition, this time a one-hundred-thousand-square-foot warehouse and shipping center at the southwest corner of Canal and Taylor Streets, a few blocks south of its office and manufacturing plant. The company broke ground on property purchased from the CLCC in the spring of 1957 and completed the one-story facility with "modern material storage and handling equipment" a year later.[47]

The building of these two large additions in an area marked by urban decay by one of the world's largest shoe manufacturers is a testament to the enduring attraction of Chicago's older centrally located factory districts for light industry. While hundreds of firms may have left the city for single-story factories in the suburbs and other areas across the country, a few, such as Florsheim, still considered multistory factories in the Chicago's old districts to be a viable site for modern production. Florsheim still viewed the area's place-based capital and agglomeration economies as important for the success of its operations. For city and business leaders, the shoe manufacturer's commitment to the area was an encouraging sign that the city's troubled fortunes were not irreversible.

The additions consolidated the Chicago factory as the center of the Florsheim manufacturing and retail empire that stretched across the country. Despite the similarities between the building projects, the nature of their construction differed in one significant way. The 1949 building was constructed on land assembled from small lots acquired by the company's industrial property broker from twelve different owners. The acquisition process was difficult, taking several years and much protracted negotiation by the company itself. Private land assembly in postwar Chicago was time-consuming, costly, tiresome, and, for many industrial executives, a reason for uprooting their operations and moving elsewhere. The large and assembled tracts in suburban greenfields were alluring.

The conditions in 1956 were quite different. In this case, Florsheim bought a single tract of land in the West Central industrial district from the CLCC for $304,645. The company's expensive and time-consuming negotiations with individual private owners in the late 1940s were replaced by talks with the CLCC for the large tract near the manufacturing plant. Thus, the onerous negotiations with many small property owners had been shifted to a public-private organization with government-sanctioned powers of expropriation. In 1956, the shoemaker encountered quite different access to industrial land than it had seven years earlier. Along with Florsheim, the West Central district, or Project No. 3, as it was also known, became home to several firms that built factories under a set of circumstances based on government-led redevelopment.

The Florsheim additions were built in the area pointed out by the Western Society of Engineers in 1950, an area that the society, the CLCC and other interested parties considered should become the focus of the city's attempts to build a new form of space to counteract industrial decline. The CLCC noted in a 1951 report that Chicago needs "space suitable for modern and efficient convenient work places with sufficient parking, loading and unloading facilities."[48] The perceived scarcity of suitable industrial sites had led to the loss of three hundred plants to the suburbs and elsewhere since 1945. The West Side was one of the city's "deficit" areas. According to the CLCC, half the district's housing was dilapidated, half the land was vacant, and more than 40 percent was in tax arrears. Redevelopment of the area would remedy this through the building of two million square feet of factory space, the creation of twenty-one thousand jobs, and substantial additions to the tax coffers.[49]

A CLCC report sent to the mayor and the Illinois State Housing Board laid out the rationale for making West Central the city's first industrial renewal site. John McKinlay, the CLCC chair, told Mayor Kennelly and Temple McFayden, the chair of the housing board, that the area had been a slum for more than fifty years. He claimed that since the turn of the century, the district had been subject to population loss, tax delinquency and deterioration. Industrial firms had made "inroads in the area, which is currently not suitable for family living."[50] Another report asserted that West Central was an excellent example of the problematic areas undermining the city's industrial strength and its residential quality. Building on material taken from a 1950 Real Estate Research Corporation survey, a 1951 CLCC staff report stated that "the area is entirely obsolete."[51] After establishing that the district housed a poor tenant population, the authors classified 87 percent of the dwelling units as dilapidated with inadequate hot water and bathing facilities.

In the minds of the CLCC and other interests, there was little to be done other than to move the occupants out, demolish the buildings, clear the land, refashion the street layout, turn the many small lots into a few large ones, and convert it to a nonresidential district. It was cheaper to demolish and rebuild than to remodel. Converting the area would bring several benefits, including the elimination of blight, the provision of industrial space, and a higher tax base.[52] The area was positioned as contributing to the decline of an "industrial giant." To maintain "industrial leadership" and attract new industry, Chicago had to build modern facilities.[53] Shortages of vacant land, numerous obsolete buildings, and widespread blight made the older mixed-use districts such as West Central unsuitable for the building of new plants or additions to existing ones. At least 80 percent of Chicago's nineteen million square feet of industrial work space was located in old, inadequate, multistory buildings. The obstacles facing local industry were serious, and something had to be done.[54]

Furthermore, the difficulty of assembling land for residential and industrial uses made rehabilitation impossible. Land assembly was very difficult, given multiple single owners: "acquisition would be impossible for a private developer without the use of the condemnation power."[55] The poor facilities "plus the picture of the general deterioration and the excessive amounts of vacant land in this area" made it clear that the area was "in the last stages of decay and . . . particularly ripe for redevelopment."[56] Renewal would turn a problematic mixed-use area into a modern industrial one. The creation of two million square feet of factory space in one- and two-story buildings in West Central would produce jobs, check industrial dispersal, reduce traffic congestion, and increase tax revenue from $75,000 to $558,000.[57] Industrial redevelopment was a viable option according to N. S. Keith, the director of the Urban Renewal Administration, when he signed off on the project in May 1952.[58]

There were a growing number of groups in the city that supported the CLCC's plans for using West Central as a test case for industrial renewal. The CPC called for the use of public subsidy and condemnation powers at a meeting in March 1951, noting that this would be the first time an industrial project used public money to buy and clear "expensive slum property and then resell to private interests."[59] The CPC approved a general resolution calling for industrial projects. A few months later in June, a one-page document signed by the commission's secretary, Carl L. Gardner, addressed to William Murphy, chair of the city council's Committee on Housing, and the alderman Robert Merriam, made the point that West Central should "be approved for redevelopment for industrial use" as long as measures were taken to deal with the displaced population.[60]

A 1951 CPC report made a historical argument for carrying out the West Central scheme. The site had been deteriorating for several years and making the transition to an industrial area for several decades. This was signaled in the 1930s, when the Works Projects Administration demolished many of the area's buildings. A few years later, in 1943, the CPC designated the area as blighted in its *Master Plan of Residential Land Use*. The CPC followed this up in the immediate postwar years by conducting a pilot study of the area as a site for industrial redevelopment. The planning agency also made an internal planning analysis and designated the area for industrial use in the Preliminary Comprehensive City Plan. By the early 1950s, as the CPC report made clear, it was necessary for the CLCC to step in to acquire and redevelop the property.[61]

Similarly, R. J. Walters, the executive secretary of the West Central Association, wrote to John McKinlay, chair of the CLCC, in support of the development. The association, which was a business organization composed of members who were "engaged in industry or as substantial property owners on the near west side," had an interest in what happened to the area. According to Walters, his organization was in favor of property acquisition for industrial redevelopment, as the site was "ideal for light manufacturing and similar uses." Redevelopment would ensure that "a slum neighborhood" would be "removed from the Loop area" and "replaced by an orderly and highly developed tax paying industrial district." Such a development would "serve as a long overdue stimulant to a greater redevelopment of the entire section." He went on to say that factory managers concerned about expansion options would "now feel encouraged to carry out their programs." As well, those who had "been skeptical, and rightly so, about the future of the area, [might] be induced to build here."[62] Industrial redevelopment of West Central made economic sense.

Another local organization, the Near West Side Planning Board (NWSPB) supported the redevelopment. The board, which was created in 1948, sought to place industrial development as part of a broader process of area betterment. The organization had been seeking to redevelop the area since the late 1940s and had pressured the CLCC to include industrial renewal in the redevelopment program.[63] The energy behind the board was Eri Hulbert, who worked tirelessly to bring residents and businesspeople together to redevelop the area. His concern was not so much to think through better ways to undertake modern urban planning. Rather, the intent was to provide a forum for the area's residents, businesses, and institutions to protect themselves against the postwar economic and social conditions that were turning the central city's western district into a blighted area.[64]

While several agencies such as the CLCC were working to bring private and public interests together to combat blight and economic decline at various sites across the city, the NWSPB was looking to defend its own patch. The board sought to create a public-private partnership that would leverage city and federal assistance to build new and conserve existing local assets. While it is impossible to show that the board was a direct catalyst for the CLCC's decision to undertake its first industrial redevelopment project in the Near West Side, it is difficult to believe that the fulsome efforts of the NWSPB's executives operating out of their office at Hull House did not catch the attention of the city's leading renewal agencies. Indeed, Hulbert met with Dorothy Rubel, the secretary of the MHPC, in the summer to discuss mutual interests.[65] As the CLCC scanned the city to find a site to locate its first industrial redevelopment project, the NWSPB's exertions to rebuild the Near West Side would have been obvious to many working for the CLCC and other interests concerned with using renewal funds for industrial redevelopment.

Rubel's meeting with Hulbert in the summer of 1949 was indicative of the MHPC's interest in industrial renewal on the West Side. In the run-up to the council's decision about whether to proceed with the project in September 1951, the MHPC argued that a redevelopment program must reclaim industrial and commercial areas as well as residential ones. In a letter to Alderman Robert Merriam, chair of the city's Housing Committee, the MHPC noted that the city would be plagued for the foreseeable future if industrial decline wasn't dealt with. Since the war, the city had lost 255 firms employing more than ten workers each, many of which had moved to northern suburbs such as Skokie and Morton Grove. Public investments had added to the city's industrial woes, with 253 firms displaced by highway building. If industry went, so did the "life blood of the economy."[66]

Despite the obvious benefits to be gained from industrial renewal as set out in numerous reports and pushed by several public and private organizations, the CLCC plan for West Central was slow to move ahead. Along with the fight with the MHPC, the agency had a troubled history with several city departments, the CHA, city council, and, of course, those who were being displaced by renewal.[67] The politics of property was part of a heavily contested process. As the key agency handling changes to urban land in the 1950s, the CLCC became a focal point for hostility, much of which centered on fights over racial and class divides.

Nevertheless, progress was made. After the formal submission of the proposal in June 1951, it took many months for the city's Housing Committee to get around to reviewing the arguments of those for and against the proposal. Two arguments were of particular concern to the committee: the city's Democratic machine was worried that relocation would have negative voting implications for the party in the area; and some people, such as Alderman Roy Olin of the Eighth Ward believed that industrial redevelopment would pull renewal away from what he believed should be its primary focus—housing.[68] The MHPC sought to qualm councilors' fears by pointing out the plan's positive impact on the neighborhood and city.

In a 1951 letter to Murphy, Dovenmuehle wrote that "industrial redevelopment offers the first significant opportunity for Chicago to compete with outlying areas for new and expanding industry." The building of new industrial districts in the city would neutralize the allure of places such as Elk Grove Village and Lincolnwood. The committee agreed and signed off on the proposal. By the fall of 1951, the CLCC had everything ready to go: preparatory studies had been made, and "private developers" were "ready to make huge investments" in order to turn a blighted area into a productive one.[69] Industrial redevelopment, it was believed, was a win-win situation for all concerned.

In the view of the CLCC and MHPC, Project No. 3 offered an opportunity to stabilize the city's industrial base. In May 1951, a month before the committee submitted the proposal to the council for approval, Bach wrote an update of the CLCC's proceedings. In the report he noted the imminent delivery of the long-delayed CPC study on the need for industrial redevelopment in West Central. The agency intended to use it as the "foundation stone for the redevelopment of non-residential uses" and for educating the public on the need for industrial renewal.[70]

The council also made it clear that some important economic interests such as the Society of Industrial Realtors and the Chicago Association of Commerce and Industry supported the project. In a long press release, the MHPC asked "the City to stop dragging its feet on the approval of Redevelopment Project No. 3" and to let the CLCC get on with the job of restoring the city's industrial base.[71]

In September 1951, the CLCC received authority to acquire a fifty-three-acre site for resale to private developers. The letters of support from the West Central Association, the CPC, the MHPC, and others played a role in the CLCC's ability to obtain council support to move ahead with the project. With the city's backing in place, the agency could move ahead. This would involve creating a budget, opening a relocation office in the district (October 1951), obtaining approval from the Illinois State Housing Board (November 1951), and contracting out its management services (December 1951).[72]

The ability to move ahead with property acquisition hinged on federal approval of site, redevelopment, and disposition plans from the Division of Slum Clearance and Urban Redevelopment, as well as financial support from the Housing and Home Finance Agency. The former came in May 1952; the latter came a month later. A $1,754,750 federal grant allowed the CLCC to seek approval from the council to undertake acquisition, which came in September 1952. City resolution no. 52-CLCC-49 authorized the land clearance agency to send a letter to all property owners in the West Central district offering to purchase properties "at the fair market value as authorized by the Real Estate Committee of the Commission." This process continued over thirty-six months, by which time most of the property had been acquired by eminent domain and market purchase. Demolition quickly got under way.[73]

The next step was to resell the cleared property to private interests. On March 22, 1956, the city's Planning and Housing Committee approved the agency's plan for disposing of properties. The sanction of the disposal plan by the council and the state housing board allowed the CLCC to seek bids for the property.[74] This required several steps. First, the commission had to obtain appraisals of the land from two independent appraisers. Next, the CLCC commissioners used agency staff to determine the minimum value of the properties. Once this been agreed upon by the Housing and Home Finance Agency, a five-member appraisal committee of the Chicago Real Estate Board prepared estimates of the market value; this was lower than the price paid by the CLCC. Land-use controls were placed on the purchased properties. These were stringent. Redevelopers, among other things, had to observe all provisions of the redevelopment plan for forty years, submit a redevelopment progress schedule to the CLCC, and start construction no later than nine months after the contract was signed. Once everything was in order, advertisements were placed in local and national papers.[75]

The industrial district was formally dedicated with a ground-breaking ceremony in March 1957. In attendance were representatives from the West Central Association, the Central West Business Council, the NWSPB, and the Western Society of Engineers.[76] In a speech, Robert White of the Clearing District noted that the area was "envisioned as a new industrial center."[77] At the time of the dedication, the CLCC had used federal and city grants to acquire land, raze 114 buildings, sell the improved properties, and relocate residents. While the relocation task was relatively noncontentious, it did meet with resistance from the white population, which "consisted principally of Italians . . . [who] presented difficulties because of their deep-rooted attachment to the area." Despite this, ten firms, including Florsheim and Kohl and Madden (printing ink), had broken ground and started construction by March 1957 (figure 5.4).[78] Government-led industrial redevelopment was finally under way in Chicago.

FIGURE 5.4   Kohl and Madden factory, West Central district, 1958. The new printing ink factory of Kohl and Madden was completed in 1958. The single-story, modernist building was one of the first to be completed in the West Central district. Box 21, file "Chicago Land Clearance Commission, Central Industrial Construction, #s 3, 2, 1, 1957–1959," Department of Urban Renewal Collection, Special Collections, Chicago Public Library.

The End of the CLCC

The CLCC was closed in 1961, when it was absorbed along with the Community Conservation Board into the Department of Urban Renewal. Under pressure from land developers, Mayor Richard J. Daley moved to fully incorporate renewal into the municipal structure in order to create greater control over slum clearance and the sale of property to private enterprise. Civic organizations were also becoming increasingly frustrated by the slow progress being made by the land clearance agency. The arm's-length operation of the CLCC was proving unsatisfactory for a range of the city's interests. This was signaled in the late 1950s, when the council rebuffed a CLCC proposal for industrial development.[79] In order to counteract the perceived failings of the CLCC, the new Department of Urban Renewal, which was directly folded into the city's administrative structure, was given much greater powers than the agencies it replaced, including the authority to administer oaths and to subpoena witnesses and records for its hearings.[80]

Discontent with the CLCC had been brewing for some time among local business and civic leaders. Almost ten years earlier, the powerful real estate industry player George Dovenmuehle told Wilfred Sykes, an Inland Steel executive and chairman of the CHA, that he had a meeting with the mayor to discuss the city's "larger over-all planning." Two issues that came up were the businessman's disdain of public intervention in housing and the inadequacy of the CLCC. Public housing in his opinion was "evil in principle," and even though the city should intervene by clearing land, the resulting tracts should be made available for "private development." Government intervention was necessary to reorder property relations, but only if it allowed private capital full control over redevelopment. In the developer's opinion, when bodies such as the CLCC were involved in slum clearance and industrial development, they had to act more aggressively in getting land, clearing it, and offering it for sale to private developers.[81]

The most forceful critic was the MHPC, which was calling for the CLCC to be shut down by the late 1950s. This was made clear when members of its Urban Renewal Action Committee complained about the slow pace of redevelopment at an April 1958 meeting. According to Detlef Macklemann, Chicago, which was far behind New York City, "should be more aggressive in land assembly." This tardiness was compounded by the fact that too many agencies were involved in renewal. The answer was to bring land acquisition, legal activities, and project planning under the umbrella of one coordinating administration to speed up renewal. The committee discussed the options for unification, with preference given to integration of the disparate activities into a city department. Another idea was to create a Bureau of Real Estate in the comptroller office to handle all city land acquisitions. This would speed things up and provide a standardized system.[82] While the bureau wasn't created, the Department of Urban Renewal was, and the CLCC's role as the main instrument of industrial renewal was for all intents and purposes at an end.

What did the land clearance agency achieve during its fourteen-year tenure? In 1961, the CLCC had twenty-seven residential, educational, commercial, and industrial projects covering 929 acres. Only three of these were completed in the sense that the CLCC had made final settlement with the federal government. Of the rest, fifteen were in the land sale and reconstruction stage, and the remaining ones were in the land acquisition stage. For some, the agency's efforts had borne fruit. Since 1947, the agency had restored blighted tracts to usefulness, most of which had been "eyesores" and home to "various kinds of social malignancies."[83] When completed, the projects would provide space for approximately ninety-three hundred dwellings, as well as light industry plants, schools, hospitals, shopping centers, and parking lots. The net cost of the projects was $121 million, of which $81 million came from federal funds. Four of the projects, accounting for 163 acres of 929 acres operated by the agency, were for industrial and commercial purposes.[84]

From this angle, the impact of the CLCC for industrial redevelopment between 1947 and 1961 was of little significance. The four industrial projects consisted of a very small area and played a minor part of the overall operations of the clearance agency. In the case of West Central, even though properties were sold to light industry and commercial concerns, it took a long time for all the land to be sold and buildings to be constructed. The last parcel of land was approved for disposal in 1963, which was more than twelve years after the project had been approved.[85] Two years later, the West Central project was finally completed with the building of a $2.5 million federal testing laboratory. The government bought the last unsold tract at the northwest corner of Polk, Canal, Cabrini, and Clinton Streets for $258,485. In 1965, the industrial district consisted of twenty-seven new commercial and light industrial buildings housing firms that made, among other things, clothing, sheet metal products, and rubber goods.[86]

More importantly perhaps, the promise of new firm investment, employment, and taxes never came to fruition. In June 1951, the CLCC's report to the mayor claimed that industrial renewal would create twenty-one thousand new jobs and increase annual taxes from $75,000 to $558,000 in West Central. Six years later, the *Chicago Tribune* reported that only fifteen hundred jobs would be created and that the project would bring in annual taxes of $340,000. The discrepancies are large, and make a mockery of the CLCC's initial claims. The same was the case for investment in buildings. In June 1957, the agency claimed that new firms would invest $25 million in new construction. The actual amount in March 1965 was a measly $8 million. The results did not match the rhetoric, a rhetoric that had been instrumental in the getting the project approved in the first place. By most measures, industrial renewal undertaken by the CLCC in West Central and elsewhere was modest at best.

Nevertheless, to leave the issue like this would be to miss the importance of the agency for industrial urban renewal and property relations in postwar Chicago. While the on-the-ground legacy may have been minor, what the agency did do was to create significant subsidies for private property holders and reframe the city's industrial property market. In terms of subsidies, the estimated cost of Project No. 3, including acquisition, relocation, and demolition, was almost $5.8 million. However, the CLCC only received $3.1 million from the proceeds of the sale of the renewed land. The difference of more than $2.6 million was made up of payments from the federal ($1.8 million) and municipal governments ($880,000). This net cost, which accounted for almost 50 percent of the total cost, was an indirect subsidy of more than $2.6 million to a small number of private property and industrial interests.[87]

More broadly, the CLCC worked to remake the city's industrial property market. This was done by following the lead of the Western Society of Engineers in choosing the West Central area as the first site of state-led industrial redevelopment and with the support of many of the city's other organizations. Not only did it follow the market by supplying new land for industrial development; the land clearance commission also structured the character of the market in order to create new supply. At the ideological level, the CLCC legitimized state intervention in the industrial property market. At the practical level, it allowed government to transfer property from one set of owners to another. Urban renewal as practiced by the CLCC created the material, financial, legislative, and technical conditions that reshaped property in the central city, while normalizing government intervention in the market for industrial land. As Bach made clear in 1954, government-supported eminent domain was fundamental to land assembly and industrial property relations. In this way, West Central was the first industrial renewal project in the country, and as such it became a model for how to assemble small-scale private property for large-scale property development in other cities.

6

REINVENTING INDUSTRIAL PROPERTY

By the late 1950s, the loss of Chicago's industry to the suburbs and the metropolitan areas of the Sunbelt continued at an alarming rate.[1] To be generous, the efforts of the Chicago Land Clearance Committee (CLCC) to rejuvenate the city's industrial base were limited at best. The South Side Planning Board's attempt to build a model industrial district had failed in the face of more powerful forces looking to build a postindustrial city. Residents continued to use to the zoning code and highly charged local politics to fight the presence of factories in their neighborhoods. As the 1950s came to a close, the campaigns to resuscitate the old industrial economy had been shown to be wanting. Even conservative organizations whose power and authority rested on the old economy of steel, meat, and metalworking, such as the Chicago Association of Commerce and Industry (CACI), were beginning to accept that the old ways could not continue.

Something had to be done if Chicago was to maintain its position as a leading industrial economy. This was not the first time, of course, that Chicago's business and political leaders had faced the problems of economic decline. Locally dependent, they had been seeking ways to rejuvenate the industrial economy from the 1930s. After World War II, however, these attempts had become more necessary, desperate, and interventionist. Along with the promotional programs pushed by the CACI, the Commonwealth Edison Company, and the Chicago Plan Commission, agencies such as the CLCC and the South Side Planning Board looked to push government-supported industrial redevelopment. The problems of industrial decline, environmental deterioration, and falling property values, however, proved to be intractable. Chicago was losing its standing as an industrial center.

Both old and new strategies were failing. The traditional approach using an industrial booster program based on advertising the city's locational assets and the productive strengths of its older growth industries, such as steel, heavy equipment, and food processing, was no longer feasible by the 1950s. As we have already seen, Chicago's industrial base had been irrevocably damaged by this time. It became increasingly clear that the city's industrial problems could not be solved by enticing firms with the locational assets that had underpinned Chicago's growth for a hundred years. National corporations could easily find these assets in hundreds of cities across the country.

Even though industrial decline was evident to many of the city's place-dependent elites, others denied this fact. They continued to believe that Chicago's industrial fortunes could be turned around. This myopia was evident in a collection of papers published in 1957. According to *Chicago's New Horizons*, city leaders had only to publicize the city's locational strengths for industrial development to take place. Charles Willson, director of the CACI's Industrial Development Division, boasted that "Chicago, already the largest and most diversified industrial center, continue[d] to grow faster than any other, and promise[d] to keep on doing so." He also extolled the "advantages" that "put Chicago far ahead of any other center" as a choice for a new plant. Similarly, Keith Bennett, the Chicago editor of *Iron Age Magazine*, noted in a flourish of Cold War rhetoric that "the entire Chicago steel-making district can already produce half as much steel as was poured in the Soviet Union in 1956. It can produce one-third of the total output of the Communist bloc of nations."[2] In the view of these writers, Chicago was a leading industrial producer and it would stay that way as long as the city continued to build upon its traditional assets.

But this was not the case. Some business commentators realized that industries across the Manufacturing Belt such as steel were at best doing poorly and at worst facing daunting economic conditions. Plagued by poor management, stagnant demand, technological ineptitude, and overseas competition, a range of US industries, especially those concentrated in the Great Lakes and New England regions, continued to face difficult times. In Chicago, many of the city's industries that had provided the economic base for a century, such as meatpacking, were in terminal decline by the 1950s. Manufacturing employment had been falling since the end of the war, and it wouldn't be long before the steel mills, metalworking factories, and machine shops in the city and older industrial suburbs laid off tens of thousands of workers or closed their doors forever.[3] The rusting of industrial Chicago was well under way despite the rhetoric otherwise.

An alternative to reliance on past glories was to reinvent the city's industrial base and modernize its ageing factory districts. This approach required two undertakings. First, public-private partnerships had to be created that could rejuvenate industrial property.[4] Even though the work of the CLCC was a move in that direction, the fact that it was under attack by the late 1950s from some of its staunchest allies, such as the Metropolitan Housing and Planning Council, limited the inroads it could make building manufacturing space to meet the needs of the modern industrial United States. Second, several people pushed the idea that city leaders had to create industrial space that linked scientific research with practical applications. Many believed that political, military, and business leaders had to play a greater role connecting scientific research with planning and industrial outcomes.[5] This was the case in Chicago, where a number of voices sought to push local industrialists to move into new manufacturing fields, most notably science-based industrial sectors, to link these activities with civic betterment, and to reclaim the city's former dominance in the defense and electronic industries.

The CLCC, with its focus on old industries and its interest in refashioning blighted districts, showed no interest in building science-based industrial space. With the demise of the CLCC as the agency responsible for the city's physical redevelopment, civic and business leaders had to create agencies that could continue to combat industrial decline. One such organization was the Department of Urban Renewal (DUR), established in 1962 by merging the CLCC and the Community Conservation Board. However, the agency's focus was not on industrial matters. This was clearly brought out by Lewis Hill, the DUR deputy commissioner, when he stated that the agency "was primarily concerned with residential improvement." Even though the DUR recognized the importance of industrial rehabilitation, its focus remained on building new middle-class districts and commercial activities, maintaining the physical separation of residential and industrial areas, reinforcing class and racial divides, and rehabilitating selected old residential districts.[6] Its main interest was building the postindustrial city and strengthening social segregation. Industrial issues were, at best, of secondary interest.

Given the modest impact of the CLCC and the failure of the South Side Planning Board, city leaders had to find another organization to resurrect Chicago's ailing economy. The DUR was one answer, but it was limited by its structural position within the city's administration and its lack of interest in industrial matters. Something else was needed. In 1961, Mayor Richard Daley created an agency that would play a leading role in attempts to reinvent the region's industrial geographies. Despite its name, the focus of the Mayor's Committee for Economic and Cultural Development (CECD) was the promotion of industrial development.[7] Even though it was a purely consultative agency, the CECD was instrumental in shaping how city leaders viewed industrial property through the 1960s and early 1970s. Its defense of the rights of private industry over land and built environment was not a surprise for a business-backed organization. What was surprising, especially given the sclerotic attitudes of much the city's industrial leadership, was that it pushed civic and business leaders to appreciate that industrial redevelopment could only be successful by shifting the meaning of public and private use, and by linking science more forcefully with industry.

The result was that between 1961 and 1976, the CECD worked to resituate industrial property as a space for science-led industrial development and the rejuvenation of existing factory areas.[8] The committee pushed through an agenda that linked industrial redevelopment programs with the creation of new industries and the refashioning of industrial property. By forcing the city and industrial institutions to rethink how to promote industrial growth, the committee contributed to the government-led economic development policies that became increasingly common in the United States from the 1970s. With some exceptions, however, the CECD had few lasting accomplishments. It is a testament to the city's ultimately unsuccessful attempt to resuscitate an old industrial economy.[9]

The CECD and Industrial Property

In May 1961, Mayor Daley announced the creation of the CECD and the appointment of David M. Kennedy as the agency's chairman. In his announcement, Daley pointed out that Chicago was facing intense competition from other cities, and despite its stature as an industrial leader, the agency's task was to maintain existing economic activities as well as bring in new ones.[10] As the committee's executive director noted in 1964, its policy was "to work *primarily* on retaining industry in Chicago."[11] Over the next ten years, even though the CECD worked to fight industrial decline in the city by creating plans for economic growth across Chicagoland, it focus remained on the retention of industry within the city.[12]

Daley had chosen wisely. The son of a Utah rancher and politician, Kennedy received a BA in 1928 and law degree from Georgetown in 1937. Between 1930 and 1946, he was employed at the Federal Reserve in Washington, DC, working his way up to become the assistant to Marriner Eccles, the bank's chairman. He left the Reserve in 1946 for Chicago to work at the Continental Illinois National Bank, becoming president in 1951 and chairman in 1961. Between 1953 and 1954, he moved back to Washington to take a job as a special assistant to the secretary of the Treasury, Hubert Humphrey, to work on federal debt. He left Chicago, Continental, and the CECD in January 1969 to take over as President Richard Nixon's secretary of the Treasury, a position he held until February 1971.[13] Along with this background in financial and political matters, Kennedy brought another asset to the position: he was not an industrialist. As a banker, he had a deeply held interest in the financial aspect of property, industrial and otherwise, but, unlike the more moribund executives that populated the upper echelons of Chicago's industrial bourgeoisie, he was not chained to entrenched ways of thinking about industrial property and practices.

As befitting one of the country's leading bankers, Kennedy had very clear ideas about the government's role in economic matters: keep it to a minimum. This was laid out in an opinion piece published in the *Chicago Tribune* three years before he became the head of the CECD.[14] In reference to the United States' troubled economy, he noted that "this current adjustment" could "be taken in stride without resorting to massive government programs," as they would do little to solve the current troubles and would only create long-term problems. Ever a pragmatist, he changed his opinion over time. Not unsurprisingly, the attractions of various forms of government largesse were tantalizing, as he became more involved in the mundane business of working with industrialists, community organizations, and city officials to rebuild the city. The difficulties of attracting new industrial sectors, eliminating blight, and refashioning factory districts forced Kennedy to change his views.

This shift in his thinking was clearly laid out in one of his first speeches as CECD chair. After describing the challenges facing Chicago, Kennedy told his audience that the necessary changes could only be effected by the "cooperative efforts of business and our city and state officials."[15] A similar point was made a few years later in one of the CECD's first publications, the 1966 *Mid-Chicago Economic Development Study*. Despite the private character of the economy, the report noted, public incentives are required for declining districts in order to "stimulate the use and re-use of vacant land and buildings, to expand the number of employment opportunities, and to sustain the growth of private firms with attachments to Chicago." In the committee's view, it was "the coincidence of public and private interests, such as new employment on the one hand and profits on the other," which both allowed and demanded the creation of an economic development program to be a firmly established partnership between the private sectors and the public interest."[16] Kennedy, like so many other urban leaders, had come to accept that state investment, coordination, and authority were vital and acceptable elements of industrial rejuvenation.[17]

While Kennedy supported state intervention for the rebuilding of Chicago's industrial economy, he also considered the local economy to be basically sound. In his opinion, only minor modifications had to be made to get the industrial economy working properly again. This was a long-held view on his part. In 1958, he noted, "Our area has been one of the fastest growing ones in the country, and our prospects for the future are excellent."[18] This belief in the apparent rightness of Chicago's economy and the need for minor adjustments only would be a defining feature of his tenure at the CECD. His position on Chicago's economy became more nuanced as he became more involved in the CECD. By the early 1960s, he found that it had become increasingly difficult to deny the realities of Chicago's economic decline, partly because he was a spokesman on the local economy, and partly because the committee's search for federal funds relied upon the existence of an ailing economy. Without acknowledging the seriousness of the situation, the CECD and the mayor's office would have been unable to win large grants from the Ford Foundation and the federal government designed to stimulate industrial growth. In this context, decline equaled federal largesse. The CECD was very successful at acquiring such largesse.

Kennedy oversaw the successful application of several large grants. In 1963, the CECD received $125,000 from the Department of Commerce to study the exodus of jobs from central Chicago. The Economic Development Administration (EDA) gave the CECD a technical grant of $616,000 to undertake a project to find ways to reverse industrial decline in the Mid-Chicago area.[19] In 1967, the Department of Commerce furnished the committee with a $240,000 grant to begin its partnership program, which resulted in the 1970 publication *A Partnership for Action*. A year later, the EDA gave a $6.4 million grant to establish a job center in the Stockyards. In all cases, the city had to provide a minimum of 20 percent of the amount of the federal grant. With these grants, Kennedy and the CECD were able to grapple with some of the key problems facing Chicago's industry.[20]

Driven by Daley's expectations that the CECD would shake up the city's complacent industrial bourgeoisie, Kennedy forged ahead with industrial renewal using federal and local resources. To this end, he brought financial acumen, political suaveness, and a degree of creative thinking about industrial matters. To ensure that he could read the industrial tea leaves without causing too much alarm and rancor, he built an elite executive group to provide him with the support to move ahead with his plans. In 1966, the twelve-man executive was heavily stacked with industrial, financial, and utility executives who would function as "a quasi-public organization." Among other things, the executive was to use its talents to help city agencies establish a clearinghouse for information, undertake research on industrial issues, and determine future manpower needs.[21]

Kennedy made sure that the committee was well resourced. Along with an annual budget, the committee received substantial political support from the city administration. Daley was present at numerous press conferences and meetings over the years, providing political authority to the agency's sometimes controversial positions. Most important, perhaps, was the appointment of Paul N. Zimmerer, the city's planning department's director of research, as the CECD's executive director.[22] His position in the mayor's office ensured that he played a central role in transmitting ideas between Kennedy and Daley. Zimmerer took on the lion's share of the committee's day-to-day operations, working with Kennedy and the executive, and overseeing a large full-time staff. In early 1968, for example, the CECD was using the "time and energy of 23 young staff members" to build up a community-based industrial program for the Near West Side.[23] By 1976, when the CECD was merged into the new Economic Development Commission (EDC), the committee had a full-time staff of twenty-five and a budget of $243,000.[24] Like Kennedy, Zimmerer proved to be an excellent recruit for the agency.

The CECD was a peculiar organization that bounded the public-private divide. It was neither a public-private partnership nor a special-purpose district, which were the typical extramunicipal governance forms that dominated cities before the 1970s. Rather it was an ad hoc organization emerged out of a set of local needs and brought together private and public interests to work on industrial decline.[25] For Kennedy and others, the CECD and similar organizations were the best vehicle for promoting industrial redevelopment outside the restriction of existing urban governance. Public-private partnerships allowed powerful business interests to build programs at a remove from the machinations of municipal government and to create novel ways of solving problem such as industrial decline. Public-private authorities such as the CECD and the CLCC had the formal aim of renewing the blighted downtowns through authority invested in eminent domain and funds from federal coffers. The more pressing aim was to ensure that both political and business elites gained something from the exercise at the same time that blighted areas were cleared and a new built landscape created.[26] In the case of Chicago, this new landscape was a postindustrial one.

The executive committee was separate from council and the mayor's office. Kennedy and his executives could raise issues independent of city directives. The executives were businessmen who had a great deal of control over their work, both inside and outside the CECD. They were chosen because they were sympathetic to ideas set down by the mayor. It is impossible to know just how much freedom they had to devise their own plans and agendas. Nevertheless, it is hard to believe, despite the pressure that might have been imposed by Daley's machine, that these independent and powerful corporate leaders would have been content to be mere puppets of the mayor's economic development policy. At the same time, staff members including Zimmerer were government employees working directly inside municipal government. They were beholden to the strictures that came with that position. The organizational dynamics of a partnership between two separate groups with quite different degrees of responsibility and autonomy and ultimately dependent on the favor of Mayor Daley must have been difficult for Zimmerer to navigate. Nonetheless, he did, and in many ways, quite productively.

For fifteen years, the CECD sought to package industrial property in two new ways: creating science-based space, which would be linked to growth industries, both in the city and the suburbs; and rebuilding older factory spaces through partnerships with other organizations. While the CECD was first and foremost a city institution, its leaders understood that positive change to the city's industrial base required attention to the metropolitan economy. This in turn required the commission's policy makers to shake off preconceived notions of what consti-tuted proper industrial practices. The fact that Kennedy was a banker played an important part in the CECD's ability to search out new and distinctive solutions to Chicago's industrial woes. The combination of his solid corporate credentials, obvious charm and political abilities, the support of Mayor Daley and a strong executive, and his distance from existing industrial practices gave the CECD an extremely powerful basis for changing the direction of local industrial policy.

That Kennedy's committee was unable to check industrial decline says more about the obtuseness of industrial executives and the broader dynamics of indus-trial capitalism than it does about the ideas they pursued. This small group of capitalists from Motorola and others were committed to finding ways to invest capital in the city's industrial base. This required a reinvention of industrial space and the turning of blighted space into sites occupied by gleaming new research facilities and modern factories. The problem was that the CECD found it extremely difficult to convince industrial managers that its solutions to decline were worth the time and capital. However innovative the CECD may have been for the time, it was still imprisoned by the structures of a capitalist economy, one centered on privatized property relations and highly mobile capital. By the early 1970s, despite the implementation of some of the CECD's ideas, Chicago was unable to compete with the new industrial powerhouses emerging in the US Sunbelt; the CECD's few successes could not overcome the city's long-term structural decline.

Science-Based Industrial Development

In 1961, Kennedy bemoaned the loss of manufacturing firms and employment. While he was willing to accept that the meatpacking industry was gone for good, he was reluctant to do the same about the city's declining share of the country's elec-tronics industry. Something had to be done to keep the industry's older elements, such as the radio producers, in the city while devising strategies to entice high-tech forms of electronic production to set up shop. This could be achieved, the committee believed, by linking the electronic industry and other industries with research and development (R&D), federal defense contracts, and local universities.

The future of industry, so the argument went, was in R&D in new industries and products. Chicago had to promote this relationship in order to establish new technologies, create industrial employment, and expand its industrial base.[27]

One CECD concern was to strengthen Chicago's defense industry. City boosters were proud of the area's history as a defense producer, especially during World War II. They pointed out that the region was the largest recipient of wartime military construction and one of the largest recipients of wartime supply contracts between 1940 and 1945.[28] This situation was repeated during the Korean War when the armed forces looked to Chicago industries to supply necessary war materials. Despite the fillip from war in Asia, the city's business and political leaders were cognizant that Chicago's share of the country's postwar defense appropriations was declining as defense contracts flowed to areas such as California, Texas, and Massachusetts. Chicago industrialists seemed paralyzed as instrument, aircraft, and electronics manufacturers in Los Angeles, Houston, and Boston worked with military and federal officials to capture an increasingly larger share of the defense pie.[29]

The CECD wanted to reverse industrial decline by linking defense production with economic growth. This was only possible if the hard currency of defense contracts was underwritten by the soft credit of R&D in science-based studies. For the CECD and other similarly minded organizations across the country, the chain of causation ran as follows: basic research led to practical applications which led to an ever-growing share of defense appropriations; this in turn led to a virtuous cycle of growth and the reversal of industrial decline. For Kennedy and Zimmerer, the CECD's job was to find strategies that would make the city competitive with new industrial districts such as the Boston Route 128 corridor. The aim was to trigger the flow of federal funds to the region and reestablish Chicago's supremacy in defense production.

In July 1962, the CECD brought in Robert E. Steadman, economic adviser to Robert McNamara, the secretary of defense, to provide advice on how private industry could become involved in industrial research geared to defense work.[30] For Kennedy and other place-dependent agents, assistance from inside the military-industrial complex would help build a stronger R&D component, which in turn would help the city regain its industrial leadership as an electronics producer. All this was aimed at strengthening the physical and economic assets needed to build an industrial economy that prioritized federal defense needs and making producers competitive in the hunt for federal defense appropriations. Kennedy and the business-dominated committee were eager to work with local and state governments to acquire large federal appropriations to subsidize their defense, space, and science-based work and to underwrite the district's competition with other regions.

Three months later, in October, the CECD, the Illinois Board of Economic Development, and the city sponsored a conference on defense contracting and R&D. The three panels included some of the region's leading politicians (Mayor Daley and the governors Matthew Walsh of Indiana and Otto Kerner of Illinois), federal officials (navy, army, and defense officials), business executives (Motorola, CACI, Hallicrafters, Bendix, and Commonwealth Edison), and university presidents (the universities of Chicago and Wisconsin). Three themes dominated the discussion: the use of public-private partnerships for local development, the significance of R&D as growth generators, and the importance of defense contracts. As Daley noted, it was only "through a co-ordinated effort of education, industry, labor and government" that the region could "develop a cooperative program for full utilization of our capabilities and talents."[31] The CECD's task was to mobilize these capabilities and talents and to capture a larger share of US defense contracts.

The CECD quickly went about its task. Soon after the October conference, it initiated a pilot project to determine the interest of regional manufacturers in competing for federal defense contracts. The response was so positive that the mayor's office authorized the CECD to form a program to obtain federal monies. By 1965, the CECD broadened the program with the help of Chicago's financial institutions, which had joined the committee in order to help local executives acquire more defense work.[32] In early 1963, the CECD announced that it would work with two local agencies to look for ways to promote Chicago's industrial base and help local manufacturers regain national leadership in R&D and defense contracts.[33] One of these, the Chicago Area Research and Development Council (CARDC) was established in June 1962 by the CACI to promote metropolitan industrial development. In a similar vein to the CECD, the CARDC sought to coordinate and create better coordination among business, government, and science interests. The CACI was looking to move away from being a clearinghouse for information about industry to actively assisting economic development by stimulating industrial growth.

Harold Larson was appointed director of CARDC. He had worked at Commonwealth Edison's nuclear power division since the 1950s and was cognizant of both the city's declining industrial base and the increasing importance of new science-based industries. Once in place at the CACI, Larson made the case that his organization had to go after government R&D monies. The reason for this, he opined, was that the federal government and the military wanted "to marry the research and development of universities and other institutions with industry and finance." It was only by doing this successfully that Chicago could compete for government procurement contracts. This aim required close cooperation between his organization, the CECD, and the Illinois Board of

Economic Development, the other agency interested in the future of the city's R&D activities.[34]

The three organizations were to work separately, but the final results were to be coordinated. This did not happen, in part because the Illinois board was hamstrung by changing political agendas and could not commit to any long-term program. The fact that the CARDC was extremely ineffective did not help. The council's parent organization, the CACI, was moribund at best and pathologically reactive at worst. For at least a generation, it had focused on worn-out strategies of industrial promotion resting on the gospel of the city of Chicago's indisputable greatness. By the 1960s, it was still unable to free itself from its old and ineffective policies. The gap between what the CECD wanted to do and what the CACI and the CARDC were capable of doing was too wide to bridge.

Ultimately, the CARDC was unable to create a sustained industrial development program. It had disappeared from active service by 1967. Larson was unable to replace his time-worn ideas of locational promotion for newer strategies geared to linking science with industrial rejuvenation. Over the period it was active, rather than working to find ways to create a strong R&D base in the city, it undertook an insipid range of activities, including organizing seminars, publishing a glossy booklet advertising Chicago's importance as a R&D center, and producing lists of defense contractors. Not particularly exciting or innovative stuff from an organization whose object was to reverse the fortunes of a declining city operating within competitive national and global economies. Accordingly, the end result left much to be desired.

As it played out, the act of attracting defense work was to fall solely on the shoulders of the CECD. This it did by promoting Chicago as a center for nuclear research and defense materials producer. The beginnings of the committee's work are to be found in 1962 and 1963, when it brought several organizations together to push Chicago's credentials for the development of nuclear energy and the space sciences. Three events that took place in 1963 illustrate the direction that the CECD was taking and the anticipated effects this would have on industrial property in the city and the metropolitan region.

First, the Illinois Manufacturers' Association announced in December 1962 that Chicago and other Midwestern cities would hold a Space Age month in April and May 1963 to be sponsored by the National Aeronautical and Space Administration (NASA) and the CECD.[35] Zimmerer's planning staff had been building connections with other midwestern urban elites and NASA officials for a year. For all parties, the mutual benefits to be gained from active interaction were hard to deny. For the CECD the event was important in two ways. First, it was part of a larger program of mobilizing industrial assets to strengthen the region's practical application of research in space sciences. Second, it broadcast the area's R&D

strengths to the rest of the country, especially the military and NASA, and helped the region compete for a larger share of the space program's multibillion-dollar appropriations.

The second event was that the CECD worked with the University of Chicago, the state of Illinois, and the CARDC to organize a conference at the Argonne National Laboratory in September 1963. A range of talks covered the issues of Chicago's capacity for nuclear energy research and enhancing the region's visibility as a research and industrial producer.[36] In his opening address, Dr. Albert Crewe, the lab's director, told the assembled scientists, industrialists, and politicians that the region's firms should actively pool their productive and administrative expertise in order to solicit federal contracts for nuclear energy research. The resulting massive combine of forty to sixty of Chicago's largest manufacturing, financial, and utility corporations would, he believed, be highly competitive in attracting precious federal research dollars to the region. Crewe ignored the political and economic implications of such a combine to argue that it would reinvigorate the district's industrial base, trigger important industrial spin-offs across the region, and refashion industrial property relations. In his view, industrial growth had to be directly linked to corporatist nuclear and related research.

The third event was the attempt to locate a federally funded research center in the region. In 1963, a report assembled by the CECD with the support of the Illinois Board of Economic Development and the CARDC was given to NASA in support of an Electronics Research Center.[37] It consisted of documents from leading civic leaders (Kennedy of the CECD and Edward Logelin of the CACI), university leaders (William Everitt of the University of Illinois, James Brophy of the Illinois Institute of Technology), science leaders (Albert Crewe of the Argonne National Lab), business leaders (Joseph Wright of Zenith, Alton Anderson of Cook Electric, Robert Halligan of Hallicrafters, John Kennedy of James Electronics, Murray Joslin of Commonwealth Edison, and Robert Galvin of Motorola), as well the Illinois governor and the mayor. In December 1963, a delegation of thirteen led by David Kennedy visited Washington, DC, to press the city's claim to the $50 million research center. The city lost out to Boston, which was not unexpected given the scale and determination of Senator Edward Kennedy's lobbying for his home town. While disappointed by its failure, the CECD intended to make good use of the plans, knowledge, and networks that had been built in the process of preparing the application and the mounting of Space Age month, and the more general discussions coordinated by the CECD since May 1961 on the importance of science-based research for Chicago's industrial revitalization.[38]

By early 1964, then, the committee had been actively pursuing an economic strategy directly linking modern science with industrial expansion for three years. In the CECD's opinion, Chicago had to become a leader in R&D if the region was to remain competitive with Los Angeles, San Francisco, and Boston. According to Murray Joslin, vice president of Commonwealth Edison, one of the region's major economic boosters, this required building "a closer relationship between industry and the universities in the Chicago area to develop a more balanced approach to research."[39] To this end, working with other economic development groups and educational institutions, the CECD decided to bid on one of the four new research-based centers that were to be built by the federal government at a cost of $200 million.[40] The committee argued that Chicago could get ahead of its competitors and stop the bleeding of manufacturing jobs by creating new industrial sites and strengthening the city's industrial advantages. In the view of the CECD-led coalition, the new science-based industrial program was the most effective way to make this happen.

In all these scenarios, the calculative logic was that channeling federal monies into science-based research would generate multiplier effects across the region. These events would lead, so the argument went, to the building of research and production space, the capture of public and private investment, and the forging of effective state and municipal government policy. In combination, these factors would permit the mobilization of new forms of economic activity. Ultimately, the goal of the CECD's program was that practical and profitable commodities would be produced in modern factories across the metropolitan region and sold in national private and defense markets.

The single most significant event the CECD was involved in was one of the prizes of postwar physics research, the federally funded proton accelerator research center. The origins of the facility lie in increased Cold War funding for high-energy and particle physics.[41] By the early 1960s, scientists involved in nuclear research were looking to build even more powerful facilities than were already in operation in Brookhaven, New York, and Berkeley, California. In 1963, the Atomic Energy Commission (AEC) recommended that a facility be built to accommodate a significant in-house staff and to host domestic and international researchers. Washington agreed, and gave the AEC the green light to move ahead with building a $280 million, 200 billion electron volt accelerator that was twenty-four times more powerful than the Zero Gradient Synchrotron at the Argonne National Laboratory, and ten times more powerful than any other atom smasher in the world.

Winning this prize would place Chicago in the higher echelons of scientific research in the United States. It would also fit into the CECD's research-centered program for industrial revitalization, trigger industrial multipliers across the region, and strengthen the chances of winning defense contracts. While the accelerator would be good for research, it would also be good for industry and urban revitalization. Accordingly, local civic and business leaders, guided by the CECD, considered submitting a proposal. By the spring of 1965 a decision had been made. A team was assembled under the direction of the CECD and the Illinois Institute of Technology (IIT) Research Institute, in order to submit a bid.

For Kennedy and the CECD, the AEC's search for a site for a large high-energy physics facility was an opportunity not to be missed. It fit two of the commission's main strategies for reversing industrial decline in Chicago: the mobilization of federal dollars for R&D and the marriage of scientific expertise and industrial productive abilities. Kennedy was not slow to alert the general public and, by association, political and science leaders across the country to the CECD's case. In an interview with the *Chicago Tribune*, Kennedy pronounced Chicago to be the "perfect" location for such a facility. In his opinion, it fulfilled all the AEC's requirements: three thousand acres of vacant land, an appropriate amount of electricity and water, proximity to commercial, industrial, and research centers, housing for two thousand scientists and engineers, and vicinity to railroad and air transportation.[42]

Cognizant that a viable bid required the support of a range of political interests, the CECD and IIT worked closely with city and state agencies. The Illinois General Assembly prepared legislation that would allow the Illinois Board of Economic Development to condemn up to five thousand acres of land in any location in the state for the proton accelerator.[43] Several other political and business leaders supported the 240-page submission; Senator Paul Douglas, Representative Melvin Price, Governor Kerner, Mayor Daley, and the president of Commonwealth Edison backed the project. For all these, the accelerator promised the expansion of the region's basic research facilities and significant spin-off effects. For the CECD, winning the facility would be a significant contribution to the committee and Daley's attempt to produce a significant science-based industrial base in the Chicago region.

The AEC's task of choosing one location from the 126 proposals and more than two hundred sites was a highly politicized one. The site selection committee faced several difficulties. Along with the range of proposals, most of which had vociferous support from local interests, the committee had to manage interference from the White House and different costing options. Nevertheless, the AEC narrowed the field to just seven sites, two of which were in the Chicago area.[44] After several visits to Chicago and months of deliberation, the commission made its decision in December 1966. The suburb of Weston, thirty miles west of Chicago, was chosen as the site for a facility that would now cost $350 million, employ twenty-four hundred scientists, engineers, and technicians, and have an annual budget of $60 million. The National Accelerator Laboratory, as it was known before its name was changed to Fermilab in 1974, was to make Chicago one of the leading nuclear research centers in the world.[45]

With this success, the CECD had made an important start to fulfilling its mandate of making Chicago a national leader for science-based industrial development.[46] Central to this goal was resituating industrial property relations. The CECD and IIT knew that property had to be reworked in two ways to make Chicago attractive to the AEC search committee. First, industrial sites had to be created through direct government intervention that could accommodate new types of industrial work, most notably science-based industries and R&D. By allowing the Board of Economic Development to use eminent domain to create new research space, the state legislation sent a strong signal that Illinois and Chicago were open for business. Under the right conditions, property could be acquired and converted from other uses to research use at the stroke of a pen. Similarly, the participation of the IIT and other organizations in the proposal made it clear that Chicago boosters understood that a modern economy rested on attracting firms from the new industrial sectors linked to electronics, defense, and physics.

Second, the CECD had a much greater appreciation than other agencies concerned with Chicago's economy that industrial space was relational. Unlike Commonwealth Edison and the CACI, both of which promoted an individualized location model of economic development, the CECD argued that the effects of one site could have serious implications for other sites. Securing the National Accelerator Laboratory would have spin-off effects on different sites across the region. While the older industrial organizations had long been aware of the impact of multiplier effects of industrial growth, their obsession with individual property rights and their reluctance to embrace the newer links of the modern economy limited their ability to advance the city's industrial base. The CECD, on the other hand, knew very well that a private-directed and government-supported partnership that made property more amenable to modern industrial sectors was central to the success of a large metropolitan economy such as Chicago's. The ability of industrial capitalism to resuscitate itself relied on recalibrating local property relations.

Industrial Rejuvenation in the Central City

The CECD's attention to creating links across a range of institutions strung out across the Chicago region in order to create a new science-driven industrial base was paralleled by a more mundane set of activities. The committee also worked to revive some older industrial property in the central city as a way to mobilize broader economic development.[47] As Kennedy explained in 1961, economic decline could be reversed by "a workable and complete program of industrial renewal." Like many before him, he argued that too many areas needed "major changes to make them attractive to those seeking sites for expansion. Through a program for industrial renewal," he continued, they could "make land and facilities available to industry, and . . . help industries with their own planning."[48] In pursuit of this aim, the CECD did not create a systematic program geared to industrial rejuvenation of industrial property. Rather, it undertook ad hoc practices and instituted a variety of unconnected tools to redevelop blighted land and to protect existing industrial facilities. The result, of course, was that the CECD had limited success in its pursuit of economic development.

The reason why the CECD was unable to advance long-term and effective industrial rejuvenation was the same as it had been for the CLCC, the South Side Planning Board, and other postwar public-private agencies that sought to link economic development and industrial property. The entrenched mentality of Chicago's industrial leaders with respect to minimal state regulation of their industrial realm hindered innovative ways of moving ahead. The difficulties involved in changing privatized industrial property relations ensured that the economic relations of place remained fixed and intractable. The fear of racialized and blighted residential districts sent investors looking elsewhere. The search for profits in cheap labor regions and the increasing mobility of capital to other areas, both inside and outside the United States, reinforced Chicago's weakness as a location for new industrial investment in relation to the metropolitan economies of the Sunbelt and elsewhere.

By the early 1960s, as the CACI and CLCC's limited success in promoting place-based industrial redevelopment indicated, it was clear that neither private capital nor public-led renewal was able to staunch the bleeding of manufacturing investment from the city. Looking for better and cheaper locations, firms continued to move to the suburbs and beyond. Scientific site selection practices favored areas other than downtown Chicago. This conclusion was brought out by the CECD's research: the inner city lost more than twenty-six thousand industrial jobs between 1961 and 1964, while more than 450 business employing seventy thousand workers left the city between 1955 and 1964.[49] At the same time, the CLCC's ongoing attempts to undertake industrial redevelopment in West Central and elsewhere were floundering. While a few new industrial districts had been built, their impact on the city's economy was minimal at best. In the face of these daunting problems, the CECD believed that effective intervention had to be undertaken in certain areas in the city in order to rejuvenate Chicago's industrial base.

One area was the selling of the city's cultural assets. One strategy that was pursued was a promotional campaign that linked economic development and culture. The first issue of *Chicago*, a glossy magazine, was launched by the CECD in July 1964. The initial run of the hundred-page magazine comprised sixty-five thousand copies, forty thousand of which were to be sent to corporate executives and other "opinion leaders." The purpose of the magazine was to promote the city as a residential location and to revise the perception industrial executives had of Chicago as a place for business.[50] The old dated, stodgy, and individualistic promotional program that had been pushed by the CACI for more than sixty years no longer had any traction with the new industrial manager. The CECD believed that a simple recitation of old-style locational assets would not win over business leaders trained at Wharton, Stanford, or Harvard to the necessity of the building of a new industrial economy. Advertising Chicago's diverse, sophisticated, and vibrant cultural world, it was believed, would attract industrial managers searching for the intangibles of place and a modern vision of industrial properties.[51]

Running parallel with the "soft" strategy of *Chicago*, the CECD also pursued more "hard" tactics centered on making the city's production space more amenable to industrial firms. The CECD's work on rejuvenating the local industrial economy operated at two levels. The first was to create short- and long-term policies to attract private industrial investment, which would have generalized multiplier benefits across Chicago. The second was to target specific spaces for rehabilitation, renovation, or razing on the understanding that different areas in Chicago had different needs and that various tools had to be selectively applied to city subareas (figure 6.1).[52] Old, run-down areas such as Roosevelt and Clinton required different responses. Industrial rejuvenation could not be a one-size-fits-all solution to the problem of Chicago's industrial decline.

In January 1962, the CECD announced a two-year study to assemble information about the city's economic future.[53] The study was funded by a $57,500 grant from the Ford Foundation, the City of Chicago, the CACI, and various local companies. It had three objectives: identify future technological developments that might be of use to Chicago; find new industries that might wish to move to Chicago; and determine specific factors which would support local industry. The report by the management consultation firm Corplan Associates was released in July 1964.[54] Two recommendations stood out. Building on its emphasis on new technologies in new industries, the report suggested that the city had to provide programs to create expertise in electronic system design. The CECD believed that this would be important to both defense and private work. The report also emphasized the need to bring private and university research together. These recommendations moved the CECD away from a simple promotional campaign to one geared to thinking through the necessary elements of building a strong set of new industries. This, of course, underlay the work involved in the successful bid for the accelerator laboratory.

Another, more mundane, side of the CECD's program was to work with the city to find ways to keep existing companies in the city. Although it had no

FIGURE 6.1 Old mixed residential and industrial district slated for renewal, 1959. Neighborhoods such as that found just west of the Loop across the Chicago River became prime areas for industrial redevelopment after 1945. This particular area was torn down to make way for the single-story, modern factory buildings that made up the West Central industrial district. Box 20, file "Chicago Land Clearance Commission, Central Industrial Construction, #s 3, 2, 1, 1957–1959," Department of Urban Renewal Collection, Special Collections, Chicago Public Library.

executive authority, the CECD under Kennedy's leadership mediated between firms and the city bureaucracy and tried to find ways to minimize "red tape" in order to make it easier for firms to remain in the city. The CECD also sought to create on-the-ground strategies that would make Chicago competitive with other locations across the country. In the absence of any archival or published records, it is impossible to determine how successful these negotiations were. Two successes reported in the city newspapers, however, do attest to some limited action.

In 1963, Seeburg Co., a coin-operated machine maker, was looking to consolidate its city facilities into a single plant. Years of incremental expansion had resulted in a sprawling and inefficient complex of buildings. According to William Clark, the vice president of operations, the firm had several reasons for wishing to stay in the city. Along with its significant fixed capital in the Lincoln Park area, Seeburg was concerned about finding suitable labor and land in the suburbs. The company was looking to consolidate all its existing operations in the city, but only under certain circumstances. Clark asked the CECD to convince the city to provide the firm with concessions. The commission did, and the city agreed. Working with the CECD, Commonwealth Edison and Illinois Bell Telephone, Seeburg built a $5 million addition to its large plant at 1500 North Dayton. The city closed the Weed Street facility. By 1964, the new plant housed thirty-five hundred employees in a factory with one million square feet of working space.[55]

The other success was Joanna Western Mills, a producer of plastic-coated fabrics for window shades and related products. Like Seeburg, it occupied a large industrial property on the South Side made up of a sprawling set of buildings with ever-increasing operational inefficiencies that was cut up by several streets and alleys. The company no longer considered it a functional production space. After negotiating with the CECD and the mayor's office, the company agreed to build a multimillion-dollar industrial and residential complex between Cermak Road and Canal Street.[56] The plan involved spending more than $8 million to replace fourteen of the twenty-five buildings housing the company's production facilities. One hundred housing units were built on the remaining land. In return for remaining in the city, the Daley administration agreed to provide new water and sewer lines, and to revise the street layout. Happy with the outcome, Zimmerer informed the press that the retention of the textile manufacturer was the result of "a partnership for improvements among the company, the neighborhood, and the city."[57]

As these two cases illustrate, the CECD worked with individual companies and the city to strengthen the operational life of the city's older industrial properties. The CECD was able to establish a functional public-private partnership. This achievement was mentioned by Harold Mayer, professor of geography at the University of Chicago, in his report on the South Branch industrial area in 1965. He noted that the committee had been "successful in mobilizing and coordinating the efforts of city agencies in persuading existing industries, faced with locational decision, to remain and expand in Chicago."[58] While Daley's comment that the retention of Seeburg was a "milestone in the rebuilding of the city" erred on the side of hyperbole, the fact remains that the CECD was able to convince the city to provide resources in order to keep two large manufacturers from moving to the suburbs.[59]

For city leaders such as Daley and Kennedy, who believed in the importance of manufacturing to the city's economic well-being, stopping Seeburg and Western Mills from fleeing to the suburbs was a positive first step in rebuilding the city's industrial base. However, despite their best efforts, these sorts of strategies could not stem the tide of job loss and factory closures that had been happening since the 1930s. The relentless pursuit of profits, the growing mobility of industrial capital, and the increasingly uncompetitive character of Chicago's economic and physical conditions compared to the suburbs and the Sunbelt ensured that preserving a few companies, even large ones such as Seeburg and Western Mills, did very little to stop the city's industrial decline.

The CECD also looked beyond individual industrial property by working with local industrial associations and community groups. One example emerged out of the part it played in the Mid-Chicago project, which the CECD had started in the summer of 1967 under the auspices of a Department of Commerce grant. Its purpose was to allow the city, business, and community organizations, in the words of Paul Zimmerer, to "halt industry's exodus to the suburbs and reduce pockets of poverty in the inner city," and in the process create more income and a better environment.[60] To this end, the CECD worked with several groups, including the Northwest Community Industrial Council, the Pilsen Neighbors Community Council, the West Central Association, and the Back of the Yards Neighborhood Council, to kick-start the improvement program. Once in place, the CECD believed, the program would become self-sustaining and reduce the need for government intervention.

The Pilsen and Northwest cases illustrate the committee's strategy. In April 1968, a meeting took place between officials from the CECD, Urban Planning Consultants, Inc., the city, the Pilsen Industrial Council and the Pilsen Neighbors Community Council. The discussion covered several issues, including the survey of industrial trends and future development plans for the area heavily populated by Mexican Americans that ran along the Chicago River. The committee had interviewed business officials in the area about their job training problems, expansion plans, and physical conditions and were looking to introduce some programs into the neighborhood.[61] Similarly, a year earlier, the CECD worked with the Northwest Community Industrial Council to make a survey of 350 firms in the Near Northwest Side.[62] The council was formed in 1966 to combat industrial and residential deterioration and to keep companies in the area. The aim of the survey was to find the issues that mattered to industrialists and to try to devise ways to entice them to remain in the area.

Little came of the CECD plans with the Pilsen and Northwest groups. Even with the support of local agencies and the city, the mayor's committee was unable to find the appropriate tools that would trigger industrial development at the community level. The corporate search for profits in lower-cost areas of the region and across the nation was ultimately more powerful than the workings of city public-private partnerships and neighborhood grassroots industrial organizations. What the CECD's actions do show is that the committee pushed a strategy that moved away from individualized location decisions to more modern ideas of community and planned participation. The CECD believed that industrial success was rooted in the relationship between an area's industrial land and its social features. These modern ideas were inextricably linked to a variety of economic concepts that were in vogue in economic planning and policy work at the time, such as comparative advantage, factors of production, and multiplier effects.

These and other concepts provide the analysis for a growing body of economic development studies from the 1950s. The CECD deployed these ideas in their main policy documents, such as *Mid-Chicago Economic Development: Volume 1*, which laid the basis for ideas about community participation and industrial parks emerging after 1966. Another version of this idea was the planned industrial district. These had been around for more than fifty years and are the subject of the following chapter. As well as incorporating neighborhood councils into the revitalization of blighted areas, the CECD also worked with developers and financial institutions to create new types of planned industrial space. In both cases, the mayor's committee was moving toward district planning, which required a more sophisticated set of planning tools than were deployed to entice Seeburg and Western Mills to stay in the city.

The Demise of the CECD

There can be little doubt that the CECD had successes. Over the course of its fifteen-year existence, it was responsible for bringing science to the attention of the city's place-dependent elites and for making Chicago an important nuclear research and electronic center. Its crowning glory was winning the AEC's multimillion-dollar proton accelerator. Fermilab continues to be an important research center for high-level particle physics. The CECD also published a number of reports on a range of issues, such as technological and employment change, the city's manpower needs, and industrial redevelopment. The commission, especially in its earlier years under the control of Kennedy and Zimmerer, was an intrinsic part of the city's attempt to reinvent industrial space in order to eliminate urban blight and to revitalize the city's declining industrial base.

Its work in three areas was particularly important in shaping the city and the region's industrial redevelopment. First, the committee's emphasis on science-based industrial development and industrial R&D was a move away from the older model of economic development in which company labs were seen as ancillary and subordinate to production output. Second, the agency understood the necessity of shifting from older mass-production industries to new ones based on electronics and science-based research. Finally, the CECD promoted greater participation between private and public institutions (universities, neighborhood organizations, quasipublic organizations, and the city) to boost industrial development. Despite these advances, the committee was unable to stem the relentless process of industrial decline.

What the CECD did do through its existence was shift the thinking about the city's economic development. The committee's 1970 EDA-funded report, *A Partnership for Action*, signaled the end of industrial urban renewal in the city and start of a new approach to the problems of industrial disinvestment and declining districts. By 1965, the EDA had more or less taken control of industrial redevelopment from the agencies that had been responsible for it since the late 1940s. The long CECD report was centered on economic development, not industrial renewal, and focused on a range of practices that went beyond the rehabilitation of space for industrial production. It replaced the earlier model of industrial redevelopment practiced by the CLCC which revolved around the assembling of larger swathes of property by public agencies for sale to private interests. There was a relatively clear separation of public and private interaction. The EDA model that the CECD clearly represented was based on stronger links between public and private interests, much closer working relations with community organizations, and the creation of new financial tools, such as business loans to small business and the building of employment programs.

In some ways, the CLCC and CECD models were similar, most particularly in their concern with using public-private partnerships as a tool for economic redevelopment. The emphasis in the two models, however, was quite different, as is noted in the CECD 1970 report's title: *A Partnership for Action*. The idea that the partnership was active differed from the earlier one where government worked separately from capital to assemble and raze property that would eventually be given to industrial interests to work as they saw fit. While the earlier model was predicated on public-private interaction, it was of a different quality and intensity than that associated with the mandate of the EDA.

The EDA development program was centered on deploying public resources rather than undertaking land redevelopment. Urban renewal was based on purchasing, razing, redeveloping, and selling off private property. This approach was eschewed and replaced by one emphasizing direct public and private connections and the importance of private initiative.[63] The report defined economic development and framed the project as one seeking to maximize aggregate income and to increase personal incomes. The program was geared to mobilizing public and private resources that would make these gains possible. This was a significantly different approach than the remaking of industrial property in order to further industrial development.

Having said this, the project's two highest-priority programs were related to property. The conservation program brought industry, community, and the government together to work on the physical redesign of the area, while the industrial development program looked to convert vacant and dead land into productive land. The CECD could not escape the philosophical logics of its program; it could not escape the traditions established by the earlier attempts to deal with industrial decline; and it could not escape the centrality of property relations to industrial (re)development. Finally, it could not escape the relentless logic of capital mobility and one of its attendant outcomes, industrial decline. Chicago's blighted factory districts could not compete with new ones across the country and elsewhere. Despite its efforts, the CECD was unable to make any serious inroads into Chicago's declining industrial position.

The CECD came to an end with the creation of the EDC in the fall of 1975. Without a hint of irony or acknowledgment that these sentiments had been repeated many times before, Mayor Daley informed the city council that the purpose of the new agency was to encourage economic development and reverse economic decline.[64] There was nothing new here; this was the same rationale for the local state's intervention in industrial matters since the end of World War II. It had also been the CECD's mandate since 1961. What was new was that the EDC had the power to undertake activities not available to the CECD, or any preceding redevelopment agencies. Most importantly for industrial relations, the commission could issue industrial revenue bonds and use them to acquire land, buildings, and other facilities to assist with industrial development.[65] The agency was empowered to improve or repair existing industrial buildings and to sell or lease other sites to private corporations and public institutions. Thomas G. Ayers, chairman of Commonwealth Edison, and Harry F. Chaddick, a Chicago real estate developer, were named cochairmen of the EDC. It also consisted of the commissioner of planning, the director of the mayor's office of manpower, the executive director of the CECD, and a board of thirteen members from the financial and business world.

The new agency took over the CECD programs by the end of 1976, when Zimmerer resigned and moved on to teaching at Roosevelt University. Along with continuing the work on industrial development that the CECD had undertaken for many years, the EDC also had the authority to acquire and clear property, construct or remodel facilities, and recommend the issuing of industrial bonds. As Zimmerer noted, the EDC had "tremendous power, especially in the financial realm," since it would "be able to develop land . . . vacated by industry in Chicago and possibly construct facilities or attract industrial tenants on a rental basis."[66] The city was attempting to find new ways of dealing with the fact that the CECD was unable to reverse industrial unemployment and decline.

INDUSTRIAL PARKS AS
INDUSTRIAL RENEWAL

In 1969, Charles Willson, director of area and industrial development at the Continental Illinois National Bank of Chicago, asked whether industrial parks would "become the main determinant of location in the future."[1] It was a rhetorical question; he already knew the answer, which was yes. He argued that industrial parks—or as they were otherwise known, planned industrial districts and organized districts—had become the major locational choice for firms. For Willson and other Chicago observers, land use controls and other governance mechanisms imposed on industrial parks were the most effective means to build a substantial and productive industrial base. This was certainly the case in the suburbs, where they had become "a way of life" and which were home to some of the largest industrial parks in the United States.[2] By the time that Willson was writing, most of metropolitan Chicago's industrial parks were to be found in the suburbs.

The most successful suburban project was the Centex Industrial Park, built in the late 1950s in an unincorporated area west of Des Plaines, which became known as Elk Grove Village.[3] It was developed by the Texas-based Centex Construction Company, which had used community-builder practices to construct more than twenty-five thousand homes in the southern states since 1950. Some of the reasons for locating in the suburban area to the north of Chicago were to be part of the area's growing industrial cluster, to have access to an expressway, and to reap the benefits of close proximity to the O'Hare airport. In 1957 they incorporated the six thousand acres as Elk Grove Village and began building one of the largest planned industrial districts in the country on two thousand acres of prairie land. Development of the industrial park was undertaken by the prominent Chicago industrial property management company Bennett and Kahnweiler.[4]

The project proceeded quickly, housing 149 firms with seventy-five hundred workers by 1963. As one observer noted, "land that was meadows and cornfield six years ago is now covered by more than 100 industrial plants and thousands of homes." Firms had to follow zoning regulations, including setbacks, architectural design, and landscaping. For firms looking to settle in Elk Park Village, the developers offered access to various financing systems, such as purchasing sites with cash or sales contract, buying with an option to buy adjacent land for expansion, or through a leaseback arrangement. Regardless of the advantages found in the district or the financial arrangements they made with the Centex Company, firms were attracted by a suburban location in close proximity to O'Hare.[5]

As Willson's question suggests, the increasing popularity of suburban industrial districts such as Centex became a growing concern for the city's place-dependent elites in the 1950s and 1960s. Worried by the economic and locational attractions created by suburban industrial park developers, city leaders such as Willson were looking for answers to the problem. In 1969, Paul Zimmerer, the executive director of the Mayor's Committee for Economic and Cultural Development (CECD), noted that suburban industrial parks had been contributing to the city's industrial decline for some time. Other than some small additions to the Clearing and Central Manufacturing industrial districts, the city had missed out on the postwar expansion of industrial park development that had swept the suburbs. Not unexpectedly, Zimmerer believed that industrial parks could be built in the city and could rejuvenate its industrial base. But, and this was the position taken by Zimmerer and many other place-dependent elites, it was incumbent upon the municipality, industrial developers, financial institutions, and manufacturers to work together in public-private partnerships if successful industrial parks were to be built in the city.[6]

By the 1960s, industrial parks were considered a more productive means to counter industrial decline than earlier approaches, most of which had had little impact on industrial job loss and firm out-migration. For Zimmerer, the reliance on eminent domain as the means to revitalize manufacturing by the Chicago Land Clearance Commission (CLCC), South Side Planning Board, and the Department of Urban Renewal (DUR) undermined private initiative and required extensive and costly public-private interaction. Refashioning industrial property relations by direct appropriation of private land alone would not solve the city's industrial problems. Another approach had to be found. Zimmerer, Willson, and others came to accept that industrial parks, such as those that were being developed by public-private partnerships in the Stockyards, the Northwestern Center, and along the Chicago River, could provide the city with much-needed jobs, profits, and taxes. The creation of government-subsidized industrial parks, so the argument went, would be a viable alternative to the previous attempts to revitalize industry. Industrial parks, in this view, would provide the base for industrial regeneration in the city.

The Industrial Park

The industrial parks that were built in postwar metropolitan Chicago differed from other forms of industrial space. Unlike the factory districts developed by real estate and industrial firms that were sold as individual units on separate lots with no coordinated planning or common elements, industrial parks were a product of a coalition of interests involved in manufacturing, transportation, land development, and finance, which sought profits through coordinated and ongoing control over industrial space.[7] Among other things, the district furnished firms with a regulated built environment, financial support, construction assistance, and a comprehensive plan. Building on the principles of scientific site selection, district promoters devised an extensive set of locational techniques that provided industrialists with a safe, modern environment that supplied packages of benefits unavailable in most areas of the metropolis.[8] In combination, these factors formed a unique example of metropolitan infrastructure, institutions, and firm behavior.

The industrial park has been known by several names, including the planned district and organized district. While there are similarities, these terms cover different situations. According to Robert Boley, an industrial park differs from a planned and organized district in that it gives special attention to managerial oversight, land-use controls, aesthetics, and community compatibility. In practice, however, the name "industrial park" was used very loosely and referred to "any industrial district or vacant tracts of land that the owner or developer [chose] to call by that name." The term, he continued, was more often than not "nothing more than a semantic gimmick used to gain community acceptance on the one hand and to promote a piece of real estate on the other." For the most part, industrial districts differed from planned or organized industrial districts, which had deliberate land-use restrictions with proprietary control on a tract of land, were promoted by an institution that oversaw the area's planning and development, and provided infrastructures and services.[9] In the name of consistency, I will use "planned industrial districts" or "industrial parks" throughout this chapter to refer to all industrial areas consisting of many lots managed on a long-term basis by industrial and nonindustrial promoters.

Two principles shaped the development of the industrial park in postwar Chicago. The first was modern planning ideas that emerged after 1890.[10] Early planned industrial district promoters sought ways to escape blighted factory districts by building on the notion that urban areas could be designed around the orderly provision of public services and community functions. In this way, the ideas behind the Clearing and Central Manufacturing planned districts that emerged in early twentieth-century Chicago were very similar to those espoused by Clarence Stein and other planners looking to create planned residential districts. By the 1920s, planners and developers had come to accept that both industrial and residential neighborhoods could function most effectively if they were planned as an internally coherent space separate from other uses. Although the functions of industrial and residential districts were different, the underlying logic of producing ordered space inside the industrial city was the same.

The promoters of industrial parks took seriously the ideas promulgated in planning circles about the need for land-use segregation. For planners and civic-minded elites, the invasion of residential and commercial areas by manufacturing and related functions, such as railroads and warehouses, was unacceptable in a modern metropolis. The commingling of dissimilar land uses undermined the sound and necessary relationship between factory districts and the wider urban community, and led to falling property values. The separation of dissimilar uses through zoning was one solution to this problem.[11]

Second, the search for ordered space was paralleled by the search for property profits. The ideas behind planned industrial districts were not derived from the sociocultural ideals that underpinned the thinking of social planners such as Stein. Residential developers and planners sought to rethink the role and form of the neighborhoods by addressing the relationship between site development and overall metropolitan growth. Promoters of industrial districts on the other hand, while they may have made rhetorical claims about the inclusive character of their developments, were driven by other aims. Unlike Stein and other planning and urban reformers with their search for an ordered social solution to the contradictions of the capitalist city, the operating principle of planned industrial districts was the search for profit. This was to be obtained from increased traffic volume for railroad companies, greater income from higher land values, and the service fees derived from managing the industrial park. For park promoters, managed control of industrial space promised long-term stable profits through property leasing and management fees of land that was otherwise unproductive.

These two principles underpinned the development of the postwar industrial park. In a forward to Robert Boley's classic 1961 statement on industrial parks, the planner Max Wehrly described them as "self-contained" communities that facilitated and protected economic development. He made it clear that these organized districts were a segregated, bounded, and comprehensive space that could be built either through private actions alone or through public-private partnerships. In his opinion, the idea of a postwar industrial renewal project was in essence a "land development innovation" that emerged to accommodate growth and "correct blighted conditions." In other words, the postwar idea of creating improved industrial sites in West Central and elsewhere was not new. They were a more up-to-date, simplified, and diluted version of the industrial park.[12]

The zoning, planning regulations, and managerial supervision to control bounded space that characterized the industrial park were being used by those pushing industrial renewal. As with the CLCC, the South Side Planning Board, and other organizations, the interests advocating the development of the industrial park concept after 1945 were looking to govern urban space knowing that their investments were secure from blight and invasion by undesirable residential uses. Industrialists could be confident that they could make long-term investments in an environment protected by a coordinated organization.

Those seeking to build a postindustrial city considered industrial parks a necessary ingredient for the building of a modern corporate space on the ruins of the old industrial one. The deteriorated buildings, congested spaces, and aging transportation facilities of Chicago's old factory district were to be replaced by a set of managed locational assets. The planned district featured landscaped single-story factories, efficient transportation systems, and a clear separation from unwanted land uses. The provision of architectural offices, banks, and clubhouses offered firms the engineering and social networks necessary to build and maintain industrial relations. The creation of codified rules that structured district practices, most notably land use covenants, traffic planning, and financial services, ensured that companies could focus on their production activities. Once in place, these assets offered industrial managers access to a rich milieu of workers, firms, institutions, and infrastructures. For smaller firms, industrial parks supplied many of the benefits found across the central city. They reduced the transaction costs by linking customers and suppliers within a closely demarcated space. The district also allowed companies to overview competition through close proximity of firms operating in the same industry.[13]

By the 1950s, the industrial park had become a key institution of modern plant location practices. Across the United States, promoters leased property to firms that invested freed-up capital elsewhere and placed the risks of property ownership on the district rather than the firm. The managed character of the industrial park provided a range of locational assets that would have been difficult to find in the older unplanned districts. For many firms, the location in an ordered industrial environment regulated by economic actors sympathetic to their needs allowed them to create a set of interfirm relations that could not be replicated elsewhere.[14] They became a major element of suburban industrial development after 1945. They would also become a tool considered by the city of Chicago's place-dependent elites in their fight against industrial decline.[15]

Industrial Parks and Industrial Redevelopment

The industrial park has a long history in Chicago.[16] Two of the United States' first planned industrial districts, the Clearing and the Central Manufacturing districts, opened in Chicago at the turn of the century. They were planned factory areas in which the railroad companies offered manufacturers various forms of direct assistance (financial, design, and construction) and a package of locational assets (from water and street layout to zoning and security) that could not be found elsewhere in Chicago at that time. These promoters were very successful. As one contemporary noted, they turned "barren waste" into a "great industrial center" by developing "tonnage-producing industries."[17] Railroad executives were able to turn underused space alongside their railroad tracks into industrial sites for factories that would provide revenue-generating traffic for their companies. With almost thirty thousand manufacturing employees working in 160 factories by World War II, the two districts were important planned nodes on the metropolitan landscape.[18]

Other than the expansion by the Clearing and Central Manufacturing companies on disused railroad lands across the city, there were few attempts to develop industrial parks in the city immediately after World War II.[19] The only significant effort to build a new planned industrial park in the city was the failed attempt by the South Side Planning Board on blighted property just south of the Loop that was examined in chapter 4. The city's industrial real estate activity before the 1950s—whether private or public—was focused on developing industrial property that could accommodate single firms. Firms new to the city were either moving to vacant factories or looking for a single tract that would house a modern factory. For the most part, new industrial activity took place on stand-alone tracts zoned for manufacturing.

This began to change once the existing solutions to industrial decline and falling property values devised by the CLCC, CPC, and South Side Planning Board were seen as having little impact on the outflow of firms to the suburbs, the revitalization of deteriorated environments, and the maintenance of industrial land prices. Civic and business leaders began to search for other ways to solve the city's industrial problems. The industrial park increasingly became one of these solutions. By the 1950s, the industrial park was slowly becoming part of the discourse around Chicago's urban decline, the rebuilding of the local industrial base, and the promotion of a postindustrial city.

Four economic ideas shaped the promotion of the industrial park as a solution to Chicago's industrial decline in the 1950s and 1960s. One was the need to compete with planned districts that were being built in suburban areas such as Elk Grove Village and industrial areas in the southern and western regions of the United States. District promoters believed it was necessary to transfer the park concept that was being so successfully used in the suburbs to the city. This, so the argument went, would inhibit the outmigration of existing firms from the city and attract new ones. Second, industrial parks should be promoted as sites for new firms in growth sectors and science-based industries. Third, these managed and regulated industrial spaces, which were set up to cater to specific growth industries, should be directly linked to the city's urban renewal programs. In this view, federal policies, tools, and funding aimed at eliminating blight and revitalizing the city could be used by public-private agencies to underpin the building of industrial parks that would in turn drive industrial redevelopment. Finally, the city's voracious real estate industry saw the building of industrial parks as an opportunity to prop up property values, create more real estate transactions, and generate profits within a declining property market.

These economic ideas were directly linked to the racial politics of urban renewal and industrial redevelopment in Chicago. This point was made clear by the CLCC in several reports during the 1950s as they looked for ways to rationalize the usurpation of residential land from central-city residents. An increasing amount of downtown space, much of it home to African Americans, was considered to be best suited for nonresidential use, as the "the *natural* tendencies" of districts across the central city suggested that they should become planned industrial districts. In the view of the CLCC and other organizations, the fact that these districts were marked as blighted also pointed to the fact that they were not being used effectively as they could if there were used for manufacturing purposes. Reflecting the opinions of the city's business and political leaders, one report argued that "the deleterious character of the land use" arose "from sheer wastage of land, and from the mis-use of the land when compared to the purposes it could best serve."[20] By the end of the 1950s, many local observers were arguing that industrial parks could make the best use of African American land that was considered blighted and inefficiently used.

At the same time, ironically, several observers pointed to the importance of having minority groups live close to industrial parks. Even though it was proposed that industrial parks were to be built on land taken from these groups, and this was most notably the case with the areas to the south and west of the Loop occupied by African Americans, the success of park firms rested on a low-wage labor force that was considered disposable by industrial managers. Manufacturers surveyed by the Urban Associates of Chicago group in 1965 stated that having factories close to a "Negro" labor force in the inner city was one reason why firms wanted to stay in the older industrial districts; they could pay African American workers much less than their white counterparts.[21] Even though some firms may have left these districts to escape the racial tensions of the central city, for others the opposite was the case. Indeed, manufacturers noted that it was necessary to ensure the existence of an appropriate labor force if industrial activity was going to be successful downtown. The same was the case for industrial parks. This would involve creating a balance between expropriating African American properties for industry while maintaining adjacent residential neighborhoods for the population required to work in the factories.[22]

The most definitive statement about the need for industrial parks in Chicago was set out in a 1962 report written for the Department of City Planning.[23] Monroe Bowman, an architect-planner consultant, wrote an extremely strong report in favor of turning the entire six hundred acres of the Stockyards into an industrial park. His analysis started by asserting the three things that had to be done to create a "more desirable environment for Industry" in Chicago: eliminate blight, assemble sites of suitable size, and build industrial parks. He defined industrial parks as comprehensively planned developments that insured industrial compatibility, offered appropriate infrastructure, landscaping, and land use regulation, and allowed for "harmonious integration into the community." A group of industrial developers were to provide permanent managerial control over the district in order to preserve good relations between the park and the surrounding area, protect the investments of the developers and tenants, maintain high standards within the districts, and ensure the implementation of appropriate land-use zoning.

Bowman argued that this model could be implemented in the Stockyards as long as "Government and Private Enterprise sincerely work[ed] together." Various business and neighborhood groups agreed with Bowman's call for a public-private partnership to encourage industrial revitalization. His report ends with letters of support from the Back of the Yards Neighborhood Council, the New York Central System, and the Near South Side Development Association for turning the Stockyards into an industrial park. By the early 1960s, Bowman's report had spurred the acceptance of parks as the solution to the city's decline. Booster institutions such as the *Chicago Tribune* were pushing the need to move from unplanned, uncoordinated, individualized site selection to a model based on the building of managed and comprehensively planned industrial parks.

Chicago's leaders, however, were slow to accept that industrial parks could be a solution to industrial decline. The Chicago Association of Commerce and Industry (CACI), for example, resisted the idea for some time. Until the mid-1960s, its postwar industrial policy was predicated on two features: offering inducements to firms to settle on sites in favorable locations, and the inherent soundness of the city's industrial base. Perhaps more than any other organization in Chicago, the CACI believed in the innate ability of the city's industry to weather the changing industrial climate sweeping the United States. Much of this confidence came from a rabid belief in market forces and an abhorrence of government intervention in economic affairs. The association did of course welcome state action in various ways, including the defense contracts, research and development funds, and infrastructure building. But, for the most part, the CACI believed, the less government the better. Otherwise, it was asserted, the freedom of industrial managers to guide and shape market forces would be undermined, which would in turn weaken the ability of firms to remain competitive and to expand their productive capacity.

Not unsurprisingly, these ideas about the role of the state in economic affairs shaped the association's postwar industrial redevelopment program. Before 1960, the CACI's industrial policy rested on the provision of information to firms interested in moving to Chicago, and assistance to firms for the construction of new factories.[24] Charles Willson, the director of the association's Industrial Development Division, made this point in *Chicago's New Horizons*, a promotional book put out by the CACI in 1957. After making the typical hyperbolic comments about the scale of the city's industrial expansion, he argued that the investment of billions of dollars in new plants was made possible by the fact that "the selection of a site involves wide freedom of choice for most management."[25] Even with the success of Clearing and Central Manufacturing, the CACI showed little interest in supporting managerial governance over space. The association was extremely reluctant to move away from an industrial location program based on individualized action on separate industrial sites. The CACI was unable to reconcile an individualistic, market-based policy of industrial expansion with the needs of a modern planned economy.

This had changed by the 1960s, as the CACI began to rethink its industrial location strategy. The failure of the old industrial promotional tactics geared to attracting firms to individual sites in the face of systematic industrial decline forced the CACI to reassess the strategy it had used for sixty years. In 1962, the CACI started an annual report on industrial parks, and the first mention of support by the association for industrial parks appeared in the *Chicago Tribune*.[26] The following year, Edward Logelin, the CACI's president, proposed using industrial parks to make "Chicago a city in a garden." Using ideas that would be championed by the CECD during the 1960s, Logelin recommended building a ring of research and industrial parks around the Loop in order to strengthen the link between industry and research and to attract new types of industry to the city.[27] The industrial park as a means to rebuild the city's industrial base was now on the CACI's agenda.

The association looked to the suburbs as a model for industrial park development. This thinking was set out by Alvin Thomas, the information and service manager of the CACI's Industrial Development Division, and George Lamp, a research associate at the organization. After the obligatory trumpeting of Chicago's industrial strength—"the city of Chicago remains an awesome titan of industrial power"—they outlined a program of industrial park development. Thomas and Lamp argued that a partnership between industrial developers and public-private agencies would allow the city to better regulate space, provide more effective managerial control over industrial property, and cater to a complementary set of industries. This would give firms "a distinct advantage over the random location methods of the past." The "package deal" would appeal to the industrial manager, they continued, because it would take over the organization of location issues—most notably land purchase, title, service of facilities, zoning, and construction—which were expensive and difficult to implement.

But, as they pointed out, this wasn't happening in Chicago. In 1969 there were 257 industrial districts in the eight-county metropolitan area, of which only thirty-two were in the city. If the city was to survive as an industrial titan, its leaders had to redress this imbalance in the distribution of industrial parks across in the metropolitan region.[28] One way to do this was through public-private partnerships. There was a history to this approach. One of the earliest statements about the need for public-private efforts on making industrial parks the focus of the city's industrial redevelopment program was made by the Chicago Plan Commission (CPC). In a 1952 report, the commission argued that industrial parks were critical to sustained industrial development. One thing that could be done was to move factories from residential areas to industrial districts and create a modern landscape consisting of truck routes, thoroughfares, mass transit facilities, and off-street parking. This, according to the CPC, should be the responsibility of the CLCC.[29]

The CPC also linked rezoning and site selection with the building of industrial parks. In the agency's view, some of the best vacant land for future industrial use in the city was unavailable because of zoning. Rezoning for industry would have several benefits, including the provision of land, ensuring greater investment, and the elimination of blight. The CPC proposed that a dozen sites occupying more than thirteen hundred acres, mostly south of the Congress Expressway and surrounding the Loop, be rezoned. Once in place, these sites should be coordinated by a profit-motivated management company which would ensure that "industrial efficiency . . . combined with landscaping and modern architecture, creating a harmonious neighbor for other types of land use." These districts would also create higher tax revenues and employment. The CPC estimated it would increase tax revenue by about $4 million and create fifty thousand jobs.[30] Despite the attractions, implementation of these ideas remained stalled until the 1960s.

The DUR was not much more effective than the CPC. The redevelopment agency's focus on residential redevelopment ensured that any work toward building industrial parks would remain limited at best. Despite its claim in 1967 that it had given high priority to the provision of sites for planned industrial districts, the reality on the ground was that the DUR did little else but take over responsibility for the districts that had already been established in the 1950s by the CLCC. The provision of conveniently located sites for planned industrial districts was, for all intents and purposes, ignored for the next ten years.[31] According to a 1975 report written by the Urban Associates of Chicago on industrial centers located on urban renewal sites, only two districts had been added to those established by the CLCC. In both cases, the districts were unplanned, single-tract developments. This is not to say that the DUR did not understand the benefits of planned districts. What it does say, however, is that the agency did not move ahead with any programs to create public or private planned districts.[32]

Nevertheless, industrial parks were built despite the apparent reluctance of most of the city's institutions to become heavily involved in using them as part of an industrial renewal program. In the same month that Bowman submitted his report on the Stockyards, the journalist Nick Poulos noted that industrial parks had grown significantly in the Chicago region over the previous five years. Most of these, however, were found in the suburbs. Another journalist, Joseph Ator, made the same point. Not only was Chicago losing industry to the suburbs, but most of the new suburban sites were located in industrial parks such as Elk Grove Village. Poulos and Ator argued that vacant sites in older areas were available for redevelopment and could be turned into industrial parks. Public-private partnerships, they suggested, should build industrial parks, which would, in turn, allow the city to revitalize its industrial base.[33] This course of action clearly would depend on extensive government support.

The building of industrial parks such as Northwestern, Riverview, and the Stockyards was heavily supported by direct government intervention. From the 1900s, most industrial parks were built by capital assembled by private interests. This was the origin of the Central Manufacturing and Clearing districts.[34] After World War II, however, the picture changed, as municipal and federal governments across the country entered into relationships with private developers. By the mid-1950s, agencies such as the Charleston Development Board in South Carolina, which were looking to attract external investment and build up their tax base, were working hand-in-hand with railroad companies, real estate developers, and insurance firms to build industrial parks.[35]

From the 1950s, several federal agencies became involved in building industrial parks. The most important was the Economic Development Administration (EDA) of the Department of Commerce. Before 1966, the EDA had focused on the development of the country's poor rural districts. This changed after 1966, as the agency turned its attention to redeveloping deindustrialized urban areas.[36] The plans put forward by the public and private investors to build industrial parks in Chicago did not always work out as they hoped, even with the funding from agencies such as the EDA. Industrial property developers interested in building an industrial park faced a range of obstacles, most notably the competition for well-situated property from other sectors and the difficulty of attracting firms to the park. Even with significant government support, the ability of private developers to build a successful industrial park was seriously tested.

The Riverview Amusement Park abutting the North Branch of the Chicago River in one of the city's largest industrial zones north of the Loop illustrates the pressures that the city and real estate developers faced in turning nonindustrial property into industrial parks. The amusement park, which had been established in 1904, was facing difficult times by the mid-1960s, as falling attendance and growing rowdiness led to lower profits. The property was sold to the Arvey Corporation at the end of 1967. The paper products manufacturer planned to turn the land into an industrial park. The project, however, quickly became mired in controversy. The CPC and the beleaguered Chicago Housing Agency were looking to get the land for low-income housing. Other users, including a college and the police department, wished to take the land for their own purposes. Title to the land became compromised by competing claims for public and private interests. Little happened for several years, and even as late as 1972, the property was still being considered as the future home of what was to be called the Riverview Industrial Park.[37]

This changed, however, when the new owners, Draper and Kramer, one of Chicago's largest real estate companies, considered the land too valuable to be used for industry. In line with the commonly accepted ideas about the differential rent of different land uses, the property developer believed that revenues derived from industrial use were going to be much lower than those that could be obtained from commercial and office uses. Accordingly, the company took advantage of this large tract of land in the affluent district of northern Chicago by seeking commercial and other more lucrative possibilities than those that could be gained from industrial ones. They acted quickly, and by the late 1970s, the idea of an industrial park had been dropped and the Riverview Plaza shopping center had been planned and the land sold off to what would become DeVry University.[38] The plans to develop a large tract of land into an industrial park had failed in the face of pressures of the land market, fights between public and private interests, and competition from other more profitable uses.

By the 1960s, insurance companies became involved in the building of Chicago's industrial parks, as they turned their attention to widening their portfolio of industrial assets by investing in the building of selected industrial sites across the city. One favored place for these investments was the industrial park. By the early 1950s, insurance companies were looking to take advantage of the safer returns to capital offered by industrial parks. At the Bohannon Industrial Park in San Mateo, California, the developer owned the land, built factories to a company's specification, and leased the property, while working with an insurance company to build the plant. The developer Webb and Knapp, Inc., financed plant construction in Roosevelt Field, Long Island, through the cooperation of insurance companies such as Metropolitan Life. Similarly, the New England developer Cabot, Cabot and Forbes focused on building industrial parks in the Boston area by using leasebacks in partnership with the New England Life Insurance Company.[39]

The same was true in Chicago. Working with real estate developers and railroad companies, life insurance companies such as Northwestern Mutual Life of Milwaukee and New England Mutual Life of Boston financed land acquisition and factory building. Northwestern, for example, purchased the seventy-acre repair shops site on the city's West Side in October 1968 from the Chicago and North Western Railway. The plan was to build at least two speculative factories on some of the land while selling or leasing the rest to private companies. The insurance company hired Cornes and Nelson as the leasing agent for the park and immediately started demolition of the railroad's repair shops in preparation for the construction of the industrial park.[40]

Development was slow. More than four years after the purchase, little had been achieved despite extensive life insurance and EDA funding totaling more than $15 million. These funds were used to build new infrastructure such as roads, sewers, and water mains on cleared property in preparation for industrial development and to help promoters attract firms. Little development took place, and the insurance company was forced to build seven speculative buildings as a way to entice firms to the park.[41] Things progressed very slowly over the rest of the 1970s. The situation was so dire that the city was compelled to provide aid to Northwestern Mutual under the Chicago 21 Plan. This program gave assistance to industrial developers in the form of tax advantages and land write-downs for new factory construction. Using these city subsidies, the new plan was that the industrial park would be completed within five years. It never was.[42]

The lack of success in building industrial parks by the early 1970s did not dampen the enthusiasm of some of the city's industrial boosters. One of the city's most strident advocates, despite the failure of many of the parks, was Van C. Argiris, the president of the Van C. Argiris and Company.[43] Formed in 1955 to specialize in industrial property, the company brokered property for several large industrial firms, both in the city and the suburbs, over the next twenty years. He also became involved in brokering deals for manufacturers with industrial parks, such as between Midland Screw and the Morgan Industrial District on the city's South Side, and the transfer of land for new industrial parks, such as the Riverview. This experience led Argiris to become their champion. This was clearly laid out in 1971 when he pushed the idea of using government appropriation powers to create industrial parks across the city. The idea was very similar to that used by the CLCC and DUR when they pushed for the appropriation of private property.[44] Like previous boosters, Argiris argued this strategy would provide much-needed industrial land, rejuvenate Chicago's economic and tax base, and create profits for real estate brokers.

From the perspective of an industrial property broker such as Argiris, a program of industrial park construction across the city was a winning proposition for everyone involved: industrial executives, the city, and the real estate industry. However, while Argiris may have made a good living from brokering land in industrial parks, few others in the city benefited. The industrial park offered little to the manufacturer and the city administrator, despite the massive marketing campaign and the substantial funds that were deployed to build them. This was most clearly evident in the deindustrialized space of the Stockyards.

The CECD and the Stockyards

Not surprisingly, the most important booster of industrial parks in the city in the 1960s was the CECD. It was an active supporter of using government monies to build private industrial parks. From the spring of 1964, it had searched for ways to tap "the potential for industrial development inherent in vacant industrial land and buildings" and to create an "economic development action program" that would mobilize the property and buildings of the deindustrialized area on the South Side.[45] In 1966, the CECD decided to establish "a mutually supporting program through conservation, expansion of existing industry, and the creation and attraction of new industry"[46] and took steps to plan a public-private partnership that would stimulate investment in the city's deindustrialized spaces. It is clear that the CECD wanted to mobilize federal funds in order to eliminate blight and generate economic redevelopment. Public programing, it argued, would "serve as an important lever to induce new investment" and shape the mutual interests of public and private institutions. Public action would protect private investment while providing support to the city through a bigger tax base.[47] One of these recommendations was the creation of industrial districts.

The CECD, however, did not suggest that the city should own an industrial park. Rather, the committee recommended that the city financially underwrite one, arguing that it should not offer direct support to a developer to assemble land, offer financial and architectural assistance to potential manufacturers, or provide managerial oversight of the district. Instead, the city should provide support for new industrial parks through the use of federal and city funds to modernize infrastructure in order to attract private investment to existing buildings and property across the city. Using the Stockyards and Northwestern as examples, the CECD pushed for public support of industrial park construction as part of the city's broader economic redevelopment program.[48]

By 1966, the CECD had come to accept that successful industrial redevelopment relied on private interests working alongside state intervention to protect property values. The rationale for this was clearly set out in the report. In a rapidly changing economic world, it was necessary to improve property in order to "*appreciate* the value of capital stock." As the CECD saw it, investment decisions by manufacturers centered on two concerns: the potential of the "internal rate of return" on the investment, and the market value's effect on the surrounding property. In areas of declining property values, such as in central Chicago, firms would only make investment decisions where risk was minimized. Industrialists would move to other locales when the risk was too high. It was the responsibility of the CECD to find solutions to this reluctance to invest in the city's older industrial districts. Not only would the city lose the original company, but as the value of one piece of property was inextricably tied to the value of other property in the vicinity, the city could lose many others. Some form of collective action was needed to stem this out-migration.[49]

While it never directly mentioned industrial parks in its *Mid-Chicago* report, the CECD did raise the issue of an incubator park, which it considered as the "lumping of public capital" in industrial areas. This capital improvement, it was believed, would stimulate industrial investment and reduce the risk to private capital. Public monies would encourage reuse of older buildings and make city space competitive with the suburbs. Competing with the suburbs was uppermost on the minds of the CECD: the redevelopment of the central city "should match suburban developments."[50] This required establishing the conditions for incubator industries by renovating the multistory buildings that dominated the city's older industrial districts. These actions would not lead to the building of planned industrial parks, but they do indicate that the CECD was beginning to understand that a viable industrial redevelopment program had to be centered on the planning of industrial space, stronger property values, and greater overall control by public and private interests. The CECD was also well aware that protecting property values was a key to the thinking of any developer or industrialist looking to invest in the central city.

By 1970, the CECD's hesitancy about the need for planned industrial space was gone. In a report titled *A Partnership of Action*, the committee stated very clearly that industrial parks had a place in the city's industrial redevelopment program.[51] Spurred by the city's gloomy economic conditions and the continued availability of federal largesse, Zimmerer and his staff at the CECD understood that providing economic support for individual firms was not an effective means to undertake redevelopment and had turned their attention to building planned industrial districts. In *A Partnership for Action*, they established four priorities to guide ongoing redevelopment. One of these priorities was the creation of industrial parks.[52] The report argued that the first task was to stabilize existing industrial areas. This was to be followed by the building of industrial parks. The CECD was a creature of the city's business and political classes, and its new position was a clear signal that something had changed in the city's thinking about industrial development.

The task of convincing other place-dependent leaders to support the building of industrial parks in the city was not easy. Most were against the idea of using resources and expending political capital on industrial parks, as they saw too many obstacles to their successful completion. The most important obstacle for many was the question of profits. The CECD found it difficult to convince industrial managers that investing in central-city facilities would generate greater profits than in the suburbs. Accordingly, the committee worked to demonstrate that "private redevelopment of one tract was feasible and profitable" and that "industry and developers could make adequate profits in new inner-city facilities."[53] This task involved the development of an "action package," which inevitably focused on industrial property. This package consisted, among other things, of taking an inventory of sites, gaining access to funds for training programs, making market and location studies, and compiling a list of clients looking for new locations.

A Partnership for Action signified the end of industrial urban renewal as practiced from the late 1940s and the beginning of economic development programs as the dominant policy for dealing with Chicago's industrial decline. A major reason for this was the EDA's new way of approaching the problems of industrial disinvestment in industrial areas. Established in 1965, the EDA took control of urban industrial redevelopment from the agencies that had been responsible for it since the late 1940s. The CECD quickly took advantage of the opportunity to obtain federal funds to redevelop some of the city's distressed districts. The first funding that the CECD received was a technical grant of $616,000 to undertake a project to reverse industrial decline in the Mid-Chicago area.[54]

The long 1970 report focused on practices that went beyond the traditional policy of supporting individual firms. The earlier model of industrial redevelopment revolved around assembling large swathes of property, which, once the buildings had been razed, were sold to new owners. There was a relatively clear separation of public and private interests. Working with the EDA, the CECD created a model based on policies that provided a stronger link between public and private interests, closer working relations with community organizations, the provision of loans to small business, and the creation of employment and training programs. In some ways the two models were similar; this was particularly the case for the shared concern with public-private partnerships. The emphasis in the two models, however, was quite different, as is noted in the report's title. The idea that the partnership was an active one was quite different from the situation where government worked separately from capital to assemble property that would eventually be given over to industrial interests. While the earlier model was predicated on public-private interaction, it was of a different quality than the one mandated by the EDA.

The EDA-based program favored a particular type of direct public and private connections. As the report noted, "the program did not envision major public acquisition of land for development. Rather, public resources were conceived as a tool to stimulate private actions."[55] The report defined economic development as a process to maximize aggregate income and to increase personal incomes. The program that the CECD developed was geared to mobilizing the public and private resources to these ends. This was a different approach than providing locational support for firms. The two priority programs were related to property: a conservation program that brought actors (industry, community, and the government) to work on an area's physical design, and an industrial development program which looked to convert blighted property into productive land.

Perhaps more than any project, the Ashland Industrial Center in the old Stockyards reflects the complicated relationship between industrial parks, economic decline, industrial redevelopment, and public-private partnerships. This small seventy-acre site bounded by Ashland Avenue, Racine Avenue, Forty-Third Street, and Forty-Fifth Street on the city's South Side clearly illustrates the importance that industrial parks came to hold for the city's place-dependent elites from the mid-1960s. The area became the focus of activities undertaken in concert by municipal government, the CECD, insurance companies, property developers, and the federal government. It also became the site in which political and business elites attempted to move away from the old locational strategies pushed by the CACI and to implement new forms of industrial development programs, such as job training and industrial parks.

The CECD worked hard to create a partnership that could turn this deindustrialized space into a productive one. Zimmerer told a federal subcommittee on small business problems in 1968 that it was necessary to use municipal and federal funds to devise new programs to resuscitate redundant industrial space. It was also, he pointed out, necessary to recognize that "the essential goal of the private sector is profit."[56] No plan moving forward could be successful unless this truth was recognized and addressed. As Zimmerer and others knew, it was the search for profits elsewhere that underlay the making of this deindustrialized space in the first place. While place-dependent leaders may have resigned themselves to the disappearance of the city's leading industries, not all of them, including those in the CECD, accepted that Chicago could not be a home to new ones.

The Stockyards became the test case for the CECD's move to deploy the industrial park as an industrial redevelopment strategy. According to Zimmerer, the building of an industrial park in the Stockyards would create "an in-town industrial renaissance" that would lead to more jobs, more taxes, higher incomes, and a better quality of life.[57] In many ways, the Stockyards district was emblematic of the city's industrial future. It had once been the home of the city's massive and sprawling meatpacking plants. As the Big Three packers increasingly invested in new locations in Iowa, North Carolina, Kansas, and elsewhere, they also underinvested in and disinvested from the Chicago facilities (figure 7.1). By the late 1940s, this dual process of under- and disinvestment laid the foundation for the demise of one of the city's defining industries and the eventual closing of the Stockyards by the late 1950s.[58]

The idea touted by the CECD was that a public-private partnership could transform the "dismal" Stockyards into an industrial park. With proper attention, this revitalized space could become an asset for the city and for the residents living in the adjacent neighborhoods. The EDA designated the district as a redevelopment area in November 1967. This made it eligible for federal funds, which the CECD argued would allow investors to take advantage of the assets that remained at the Stockyards—its trained labor pool, large tracts of industrial land, and excellent transportation connections. These, under the correct conditions, could be turned into an industrial park. Not only would this project resuscitate the Stockyards district but it could also become a model for future industrial development in other parts of the city and show that public-private partnerships could underwrite profitable private-led economic revitalization. The EDA agreed with this thinking, and made $4,865,000 available for public improvement projects (arterial streets and utilities) with the proviso that the city find another million or so dollars to cover other costs.[59]

Mayor Daley announced the EDA funding for the Stockyards industrial park at a luncheon at the Sheraton on June 5, 1968. He told his audience of business and political leaders that $20 million would be invested in the area, which was now to be known as the Ashland Industrial Center. He noted that the area's infrastructure was currently being improved by EDA and city funding. Development

FIGURE 7.1 Child on rubble in the Chicago Stockyards, 1950. The photo shows the rubble left over from the demolition of an industrial building in the Stockyards area. From the 1950s, this district became the focus of urban and industrial revitalization for various agencies. The city would try to build an industrial park on the ruins in the 1960s. Box 3, folder 2, Mildred Mead Photographs, Special Collections Research Center, University of Chicago Library.

was to be carried out by the Campbell Development Company of Detroit, a private industrial real estate firm specializing in industrial park development and construction. It had bought the land for $2 million with the intention of creating lots to lease to industrial companies. Most of the financing was to come from New England Mutual Life, which had committed itself to making steady profits by investing one billion dollars to rebuild central cities across the country. The CECD and the city's Department of Development and Planning estimated that the Stockyards would be the home to one hundred new factories and fifteen thousand new jobs by 1980. The park was expected to open in 1970.[60]

The announcement was met with strong support from many quarters. Civic leaders, politicians, and industrialists believed that it would rejuvenate the area and the city's economy. This point was made in a *Chicago Tribune* editorial which intoned in June 1968 that the building of the center was "extraordinarily good news." Picking up on what the CECD and many other industrial commentators had observed for several years, the editorial said that the jobs that left with the meatpackers would "be regained as the new industrial park [was] developed." The park would stop the out-migration of firms to the suburbs, and allow the city, which had been plagued by unemployment, loss of tax capacity, and a variety of social problems, to rebuild its industrial base. In the newspaper's opinion, the new park "should be a big asset to the city."[61]

Despite the enthusiasm of the city's place-dependent elites, the building of the Ashland district faced at least three obstacles. One was that residential groups were hostile to the reindustrialization of the Stockyards, just as had been the case with the Bodine factory on the city's West Side. They did not want industry close to their homes. As Zimmerer told a House subcommittee hearing on small business problems in 1968, the CECD had to tread carefully. At the same time, park promoters had to recognize that it was necessary to balance the search for profits with the needs of the local population. Residential groups had to be and were to be consulted. Despite this, the CECD encountered residents who resisted the building of new industrial space in their neighborhood. While the industrial park promoters may have been able to overcome this resistance with various inducements, the fact remained that the very idea of building new factory space on the city's industrial South Side was in question.[62]

A more difficult obstacle to overcome was that industry wasn't that interested in setting up shop on Chicago's South Side in the late 1960s and early 1970s. Despite the vast amount of resources allocated to the park by the city, the EDA, and private interests, few firms were attracted to the area. The modernization of the site's infrastructures by federal funds and the extensive marketing effort by the Campbell Development Company were not enough to entice firms back to the South Side. The old industrial districts of the city, even after modernization, were not considered safe investment sites. By 1970, when the development was expected to have been ready for occupancy, only one-third of the lots had been taken up. The developer said it would take several more years before the park was completed. The demand for the district's space was so low that Campbell was considering the construction of an inventory building with spaces for several for firms which were to be leased rather than owned.[63] The suburbs continued to be an allure to many industrial companies. The attractions of suburban industrial parks such as Centex in Elk Village Grove simply outweighed those found in the Stockyards.

Perhaps just as important was that Campbell did not build a full-fledged industrial park. It was a half measure. With ample federal and city funding, the developer assembled the land, built new infrastructure, and marketed the properties. New England Mutual provided the financial backing. But there was no overall planning of industrial space. There was little attempt to allow similar industries to create synergies through proximity. Even with well-situated land and a nearby labor force, the Stockyards could not compete with the suburbs in terms of location and social stability. Without a significant competitive edge, as in the building of proximate industrial relations in an industrial park setting, the city would always end up losing to the charms of suburban spaces.

Campbell quickly deserted the park, and the lots were handled by different industrial real estate companies. William Philos of Pain Wetzel, a firm active in the park, stated in 1979 that there was "a problem selling vacant land on the south side of Chicago."[64] Philos also noted that potential investors were scared of "gangsters and race problems." While this may have been a factor in the investment decision, the fact is that the simple political economy of factory location which had been under way for fifty years worked against old central factory districts. The industrial future was to be found in the greenfields of the suburbs and the US South and West. Despite the best efforts of the CECD, the industrial park in the Stockyards was an industrial failure. The structural forces of national and global capital mobility ensured that the half-hearted attempts by public-private partnerships would not be successful.[65]

The Failure of the Industrial Park

The city's place-dependent elites turned to industrial parks such as the Ashland Industrial Center in the 1960s as one solution to the problems of industrial decline. The modernization of brownfield sites, so the argument went, would attract industry back to deindustrialized areas such as the Stockyards. The parks would offer firms a dense network of assets that yielded new interfirm dependencies centered on transportation, infrastructure, and labor, which would induce industrial revitalization. As they provided a planned, ordered, and regulated space with the benefits of geographic proximity and shared institutions, industrial parks, it was believed, were a viable alternative to suburban industrial parks.

By the early 1970s, however, the city's industrial situation was as bad as it had ever been. The reality did not match the discourse. Reports from Commonwealth Edison, the Society of Industrial Realtors, the CECD, and other industrial observers continued to document the deindustrialization of the city and the growing industrial strength of the suburbs. In 1974, William Cowley, the president of the Chicago chapter of the Society of Industrial Realtors, told Gary Washburn of the *Chicago Tribune* that the numbers of firms leaving the city, closing factory doors, and new starts were "bad" for Chicago. The problems of deteriorating neighborhoods, outdated buildings, little room for expansion, and the absence of attractive industrial sites continued to drive industrial out-migration to the suburbs. For Cowley and others, this outflow would last until the city came up with a scheme for planned industrial parks that could compete with the amenities offered in suburban areas.[66] While some industrial parks had been created since the early 1960s, the overall conclusion has to be that they had a negligible effect on the city's industrial base.

Given the dismal performance of industrial parks, business and civic leaders sought other means to revitalize the city's industry. In the 1970s, several tools were used by Chicago's economic development officials, including "tax abatements, low-interest loans, industrial revenue bonds, and a variety of other financial incentives," to promote industrial growth.[67] One was the industrial revenue bond, a device used to promote development by subsidizing industrial firms. Local governments provided tax-exempt yields, with the savings being passed on to the firms involved. The purpose was "to retain firms which are considering a relocation to another municipality, to assist firms in providing more employment located inside the municipality, and to attract new firms to the municipality."[68] After 1977, the city's Economic Development Commission used the revenue bond as a means to stimulate industrial development and compete with more favorable locations.[69] The city would sell the bonds at low municipal interest rates and then lend the money to an industrial company at the same rate. This company would then use the money to expand its business and pay the loan off in ten or fifteen years.[70]

The office park was another solution proposed to deal with the failure of industrial parks to revitalize the city's industrial base. In 1969, a Society of Industrial Realtors report noted that industrial parks in the future would change from managed spaces housing one-story factories and warehouses to regulated spaces accommodating offices and apartment buildings that would be built in the "unexploited air rights that now exist over single story roofs."[71] In 1970, the *Chicago Tribune* called the office park a "growing concept."[72] Many of the city's leading industrial real estate agencies, such as Bennett and Kahnweiler, were looking to diversify their interests out of industrial to office property. The Society of Industrial Realtors report also suggested that industrial parks might further diversify with the emergence of planning concepts that stressed self-contained communities where people could live and work. The combining of fabrication, distribution and offices of a major firm with apartments in a single building would "greatly increase the economic utilization of the land area," according to the report.[73]

The industrial park had little positive impact in Chicago. Despite the undisputed success of the early twentieth-century industrial parks, few new ones were built in the city after World War II. And those that were built typically were not very successful. This was not the case in the suburbs, where the postwar industrial park became a key to industrial development and contributed to industrial decline in the central city. City leaders believed that Chicago had to learn from the suburbs. The lessons of suburban development, however, were not easily transferred to the city. The gap between the discourse and the reality could not be bridged. Industrial parks were unable to stop industry from leaving the city for more salubrious locations in the suburbs and in the Sunbelt. Ultimately, the place-dependent coalition advocating industrial revitalization was unable to compete with the growth machine pushing for the building of a post-industrial city replete with significant amounts of middle-class housing, commercial developments, and leisure facilities. The tools of urban renewal were used to build this new city and to create new and reinforce existing social and economic ghettos. Much of the downtown land was turned into commercial and residential uses by the postindustrial city coalition.

Conclusion

IT'S ALL OVER NOW

Is Chicago slowly being stripped of its possessions? Is it becoming an economic vacuum and a city with only a past?

Loren Trimble, 1969

In 1969, Loren Trimble, the director of Industrial Development at the Commonwealth Edison Company, considered the state of Chicago's economy. Like so many other observers in the late 1960s, he raised questions about the impact of economic forces on the city's great industrial base. He asked his readers to think about what the future held for the city's great manufacturing industries.[1] Trimble, who knew more about the practicalities of industrial location in postwar Chicago than perhaps any other person, was posing rhetorical questions. He already knew the answer: Many years of deindustrialization had transformed the city. The industrial economy was vanishing by the day. The disappearance of the city's manufacturing operations existed alongside the emergence of tertiary and quaternary industries at the center of the local economy. Apartment buildings, office towers, and conference centers had replaced factories, warehouses, and working-class houses. For a quarter of a century, the city's place-dependent elites had assiduously worked to build a postindustrial economy, one centered on knowledge, services, and research. The construction of modern residential and office complexes such as Lake Meadows, the Lake Shore Apartments, the Chicago Federal Center, and McCormick Place was a material and vivid illustration of the new city that had been created since the end of World War II.[2]

Despite the attention they had given to the building of a new postindustrial city, Chicago's place-dependent elites such as Trimble were still anxious about the decline of the city's industrial base. For more than a hundred years, Chicago had been one of the United States' great industrial powerhouses and was home to some of the country's leading industries, such as steel, machinery, electrical equipment, and food processing. For generations, the city's locational assets had been unrivaled; its large and diverse labor force, massive transportation system, and extensive tracts of industrial property had been the envy of city boosters in most other industrial cities. But Chicago's position as an industrial leader was under attack from the 1920s, as the impact of the long and steady process of industrial decline undermined the city's ability to retain and attract investment.

For experienced observers of the industrial United States, the signs of decline were daunting. Shuttered factories, empty lots, high manufacturing unemployment, and broken infrastructures were evidence that Chicago's "glory years" of industrial dominance were on the wane.[3] The precarious status of Chicago's manufacturing was evident in report and after report and newspaper column after column. Many postwar commentators were aware of the city's worsening industrial position. Even though it was apparent to Trimble and other place-dependent elites by the late 1960s that a new postindustrial economy was being built on the ruins of the old industrial one, there was growing anxiety about the state of Chicago's industry and what the future held. City builders, industrial executives, and local politicians were desperate to identify the practices that would ensure that the city's economy remained healthy and resilient. All transitions to a future create anxiety about what is to replace the past. Chicago's economic and political leaders were no different in their fear of the consequences of what would replace the old industrial economy.

Following in the footsteps of other city leaders, Trimble sought information on the local economy that would give him and his peers some sense of how to move forward. What he found in his study of factory expansions in metropolitan Chicago for 1959–68 would not have surprised other members of the city's political and business leadership. It certainly would not have allayed their fears. The suburbs had received twice as many firms and expansions as the city. The prime location for new industrial investment was the northwestern suburbs, with the area around O'Hare International Airport the main focus of new factory construction. Not surprisingly, Trimble found that property and labor underpinned the changes to the region's industrial geography. The price of land in the city was double the price of comparative land in the suburbs. When firms moved to the suburbs, they doubled their floor space, which for many companies would be a far too expensive option in the city. Similarly, firms claimed they had difficulty finding suitable labor, as the city's labor market featured high wage costs, union activity, and low skills. For firms looking to expand their workforce, the city's locational assets were not competitive.[4]

Trimble was not the only one anxious about the city's problems. Milton Podolsky, a leading industrial property broker, told a city committee on Chicago's economy in 1972 that if the city's manufacturing difficulties weren't solved, then large parts of the city would become "blighted, nocturnal wastelands." He told the committee that a third of the city's industrial buildings were obsolete and subject to replacement by modern structures in the suburbs. The old, multistory buildings, which had housed Chicago's industrial firms in the past and which continued to dominate the city's industrial districts, were plagued by low ceilings, inadequate unloading facilities, and little room for expansion. These old factories, he explained, were not suitable for the late twentieth-century industrial economy. These problems were compounded by the unruly workers, traffic congestion, and residential deterioration. Podolsky's solutions were simple and unsurprising given his business interests. First, the city had to find ways to compete more effectively for industrial investment. Second, city leaders had to make this possible by using public and private funds to create industrial redevelopment programs.[5]

Both Podolsky and Trimble were part of a relatively small coalition of place-dependent interests fearful of the state of Chicago's industrial economy who were desperate to gain a modicum of control over the city's industrial assets. Both, of course, were selling their own version of Chicago's industrial situation to suit their own interests. Podolsky pushed the idea of wastelands in order to create the conditions for public intervention in the property market and to boost real estate profits. For Podolsky, this required active public-private partnerships. Ironically, as he well knew, different levels of government had been involved in industrial property matters for close to twenty-five years, without having a major or lasting effect on local land values, factory construction, and employment. Podolsky's negative view of Chicago's industrial situation ran contrary to Trimble's more positive approach. While Trimble could acknowledge the problems that the city faced, he could not openly accept that the city was experiencing systematic decline. As an employee of the region's main utility, he used data to spin a positive view of the city's industrial fortunes. The "projection for the future," he argued, "would indicate a leveling of total plants moving out in contrast with an upward trend of new industries moving in." The growing positive conditions for industry in the city, he claimed, allowed industrial executives to believe they could and would "make money in Chicago."[6]

The anxieties that Trimble and Podolsky faced were not new. In one way or another, the city's place-dependent elites had grappled with the same troubling issues for forty years. Questions about industrial decline, devalued property, blight, and their impact on Chicago had been raised since the interwar period. Trimble and Podolsky were just the latest in a long line of Chicago's moneyed class who were deeply concerned about the city's industrial fortunes and the ramifications these had for their own interests. In this book I have examined the source of these anxieties—the slow but relentless rusting of Chicago's industrial base between 1920 and 1975—and I have made three major claims. First, I have argued that Chicago experienced a long history of industrial decline that was related to the structural forces of corporate capitalism. Second, I have shown that the city's bourgeoisie looked to industrial redevelopment as an institutional fix to the problems that economic decline created, such as blighted neighborhoods and devalued property. Third, I show that the industrial redevelopment programs created after 1945 had little effect on the hemorrhaging of industrial jobs or the revitalization of the industrial economy. The problems of industrial property, factory closings, obsolete buildings, and rundown neighborhoods that Trimble and Podolsky fretted about had been a long time in the making.

Deindustrialization

Trimble's projection about Chicago's rosy future was off the mark. Chicago never recovered from the slow drip of industrial decline that had been taking place since the 1920s. The attempts by the city's politicians, planners, reformers, and businesspeople to rebuild Chicago's industrial base failed, as factories shut down and industrial jobs deserted the city in large numbers. The drip was slow but relentless before the 1940s. It became a torrent over the next quarter of a century. By 1969, when Trimble asked about Chicago's economic "possessions," the city's manufacturing structure was a shadow of its former self. Many of the industrial sectors that had been the mainstay of Chicago's economy had fled the city. Others were hanging by a thread. Most noticeably, large multiunit corporations had moved to the suburbs in significant numbers, leaving behind a few factories with massive investments in situ and a declining number of small, locally owned firms.[7]

The story of industrial growth and decline is usually couched in terms of the secular rise and fall of firms, employment, and output. In this story, to use Barry Bluestone's phrase, the "postwar glory years" of economic growth between the end of World War II and the early 1970s were followed by deindustrialization and the devastation of the Manufacturing Belt's economic landscape.[8] City after city across the New England, mid-Atlantic and Great Lakes regions felt the full brunt of the shift of capital investment to other parts of the United States and the world. In some cities, such as Chicago and New York, powerful place-dependent groups were able to resist the powerful force of capitalist change to create the conditions for a painful transition from an industrial to a postindustrial economy.[9] In most other cities, including Philadelphia, Detroit, and Buffalo, this transformation did not take place. In these cases, local groups were unable to create the institutional resources that could be used to turn the empty factory spaces into new consumption, working, and living spaces. While there may have been a short period of overlap between the glory and deindustrialized years, most writers have treated the two periods as analytically separate.

The Chicago story suggests otherwise. Industrial growth and decline coexisted in the city of Chicago from the 1920s. The city's economy exhibited a dual process that involved both the growth and decline of industrial employment, output, and the number of manufacturing firms. While some industries continued to maintain some form of stability over the years, others experienced loss. New growth industries, such as electrical equipment, developed as older industries, such as steel and meatpacking, declined. Overall though, the picture is one of inexorable decline. As early as the 1950s, despite attempts to reverse the situation, the city's industrial economy was in a free fall characterized by declining manufacturing employment, the proliferation of redundant industrial spaces, and a serious imbalance of incoming and outgoing capital investment.

To view growth and decline as separate processes, both chronologically and analytically, is to paint a false picture of the urban economy. At any one time, cities are home to a range of industries that are undergoing various degrees of change. In a rapidly expanding urban economy, such as Chicago's between 1850 and 1920, the processes leading to decline are outweighed by those producing growth. When this trend is reversed over a long period of time, as took place in Chicago and all other industrial cities in the Manufacturing Belt, the outcome is deindustrialization.

The tipping point was the emergence of corporate capitalism. The rise of the multiunit corporation as the dominant organizational form of twentieth-century industrial capitalism realigned the spatial coordinates of industrial location and created the conditions for the revaluing of industrial land.[10] Corporate executives were increasingly freed from a location in any one place and were able to take advantage of place-based assets in other locales to move their facilities out of the older factory districts. Whether it was Trenton, Detroit, Philadelphia, or Chicago, all the US cities that emerged as industrial centers between 1850 and 1920 felt the devastating effects of the rise of the corporation. The large industrial corporation was increasingly able to use the modern site selection industry and new financial tools, both of which were developed in the interwar years, to pitch locale against locale, creating a new set of winners and losers in the search for investment, employment, and growth. The city of Chicago from the 1920s was just one of the losers in the new corporate calculus of industrial location.

Industrial executives in northern cities such as Chicago faced two choices with respect to the location of their manufacturing facilities: keep their investment in situ or move capital to another locale. From the 1920s, a declining number chose the former. The factory districts of the central city were no longer attractive to a growing number of executives. Many, and this number increased greatly after

1945, opted for the latter. In doing so, they could choose from several options. Those leaving the old industrial districts of central cities could move out of the region altogether, most notably to the newly industrializing districts in the South and West. By the late 1940s, important industrial districts that were home to corporate branch plants from firms located in the Manufacturing Belt, new starts associated with the branch plants, and entirely new industries such as aerospace and petroleum had emerged in Los Angeles, Houston, and other areas. In other cases, large corporations such as Ford and General Electric channeled investment to branch plants overseas, mostly in Europe and Canada.

Most importantly, in the fifty years after 1920, industrial executives could also move their corporate investments from the central city to the adjoining suburbs. As I have shown here for Chicago, much of the industrial decline that afflicted the core centers of the great Manufacturing Belt before the end of the 1960s resulted from this shift of industrial investment from the central cities to the suburbs. Regardless of the type of factory they built, executives from most industrial sectors increasingly sought out suburban greenfields. They no longer considered the city's blighted inner districts to be a hospitable place for profit-seeking industries. From the 1930s at the latest, and through the first thirty years after World War II, Chicago's suburbs were seen as the more attractive and profitable production spaces for industry.

The movement of factories to the suburbs is nothing new. It had been a feature of the US industrial landscape since the mid-nineteenth century, with the emergence of suburbs such as East Chicago, Pullman, and Cicero.[11] Before the 1920s, the suburban exodus was relatively small in comparison with the growth taking place in the central city. The situation changed between World War I and World War II. From as early as the 1920s, a steady stream of firms left the city of Chicago for the suburbs. This turned into a torrent after 1945. The locational assets of such districts as Skokie, Des Plaines, and McCook became more attractive for new manufacturing investment at the same time that the locational features that had attracted companies to the central city in the first place became deficits.

Driving this exodus was the search by corporate executives for more favorable locations than were offered in the central city. Attractions such as cheap and non-congested land, better transportation systems, and more favorable local markets were compelling factors in the corporate search for more profitable production spaces. They were aided in this search after 1930 by the site selection industry, which identified the most productive sites as being suburban, and by the emergence of new financial instruments that facilitated suburban factory construction. At the same time, small supplier firms settled close to the corporate factories on the metropolitan edges to take advantage of vertical and horizontal linkages. In all cases, the stigma of blighted factory and residential districts contributed to the tireless exodus of manufacturing firms from the central city from the inter-war years. By the end of the postwar glory days in the 1970s, industrial Chicago had already experienced close to fifty years of industrial decline.

Chicago was not alone. After 1920, the central cities of the Manufacturing Belt lost their preeminent industrial position as corporations working with the guidance of the site selection industry sought new greenfield sites in the suburbs and the Sunbelt.[12] Between 1850 and 1920, most industrial jobs and firms were located in the factory districts in Northern industrial cities. Cities as disparate as Detroit, Akron, Philadelphia, and Trenton were the home of the United States' industrial might. By the interwar period, however, circumstances changed. The central cities became a victim of their own success as property values, labor costs, and congestion reduced their attractiveness. The growing strength of the union movement in the central city scared industrial executives, forcing them to find new territory where they could exert greater control over the labor force. Land and tax subsidies from the suburbs, small towns, and ambitious cities in the South and West of the country attracted the growing number of footloose corporations that had come to dominate the national economy. Greater returns and higher profits could be obtained by moving from the city's deteriorated industrial districts and setting up new production processes in modern, one-story factories in suburban greenfields.

In other words, a systematic process of disinvestment in existing facilities combined with the search by industrial executives for new and more profitable sites produced a discernible uneven geography of growth and decline across the metropolitan regions of the United States as early as the 1930s. Caught between the complex forces operating to create a new corporate calculus of locational profit across space, cities such as Chicago, characterized as they were by wide-spread residential blight, deteriorated industrial districts, increasing class and racial polarization, and declining property values, found it increasingly difficult to compete with industrial developers, corporations, and financial institutions who created new industrial sites in the suburbs. This was the case in city after city in the Manufacturing Belt. With the exception of New York City, all the United States' older industrial cities had lost a substantial share of their manufacturing base by the 1950s. While the scale and speed of decline varied from city to city, rust was evident across the factory districts of every great industrial city.

Industrial decline in the cities of the Manufacturing Belt continued after 1970. In the city of Chicago, close to one hundred thousand manufacturing jobs were lost between 1978 and 1987. By 2011, the city only had 65,000 employees, a fall from 293,000 in 1972, more than half a million in 1947, and close to a million in 1943.[13] The slow, jerky, and incremental decline of the city of Chicago after 1920 differed in some significant ways from the deindustrialization taking place after 1970. At a national scale, the key changes were that the manufacturing jobs that were lost were not replaced, and that international competition was much greater and more intense than it had been seventy-five years earlier. While firms in the earlier period faced competition, mainly from Europe, this was relatively minor compared to what happened after 1970, with the rise of dynamic industrial economies in the Global South. At the same time, capital had become increasingly mobile, as large-scale multinational corporations deployed new technologies across space to seek out more profitable sites and wider markets.

These recent changes have continued to have a tremendous negative effect on localities deemed inadequate for modern industrial purposes. The growing popularity of corporate diversification, which involves moving industrial assets into a range of other industrial and nonindustrial sectors, allows companies to gain better profit rates in different industries in different areas across the world. The growing importance of defense spending for many industrial sectors since the end of World War II has favored the South and West and contributed to the rusting of industry in the Manufacturing Belt. New production, transportation, financial, and communication technologies have increased the mobility of capital movement across the globe, while varying labor and environmental legislation has led to a more uneven and differentiated production landscape.[14] As Joe Gowaskie noted in a 1991 panel discussion, there is a major difference in the "magnitude of the losses" between earlier and more recent forms of deindustrialization. One major effect of the changes since the 1970s has been to undermine "most of the basic industries that propelled the United States into world economic leadership."[15]

Another way that the post-1970s decline differed from the earlier period is the loss of manufacturing employment in the suburbs, even though they were the motor driving the expansion of the metropolitan industrial economy between 1930 and 1970. The post-1970 deindustrialization discussed by Bluestone and others affected the suburbs as well as the city. After fifty years of growth, the Chicagoland suburbs faced stiff competition from other parts of the United States, and more importantly, from low-wage countries in the Global South. By 2011, the seven-county metropolitan area had 356,759 manufacturing jobs, down from 674,000 in 1972. A substantial share of this loss took place in the suburbs. In other words, deindustrialization was not only a feature of the city of Chicago from the 1970s; rust also became a defining feature of the industrial economy of suburbs in the last quarter of the twentieth century.[16]

Institutional Fix

The industrial problems that affected Chicago between 1920 and 1975 required an institutional fix. The older political and planning institutions that had overseen the city's economy before 1940 were no longer up to the task of dealing with the problems of industrial decline. The institutions that had served the city's political and business classes for a century were unable to provide viable solutions to issues such as high levels of industrial disinvestment, significant manufacturing employment loss, and the emergence of large areas of deteriorated industrial buildings that became increasingly evident in the postwar period. These older institutional forms built around an expanding industrial economy were no longer suitable.

As Joel Rast has noted, industrial renewal in Chicago required institutions that could overcome the obstacles to urban development and support large-scale reconstruction.[17] The economic realities of the postwar years could not be accommodated within existing institutional forms. In the case of urban renewal, this entailed creating more centralized and powerful agencies and departments with the authority to coordinate an array of competing political, planning, and business groups and to oversee the acquisition, razing, and redevelopment of blighted areas. The building of a modern, competitive, and profitable city required the construction of an institutional apparatus that could accommodate the pressures of the postwar period, such as the restructuring of the financial industries, the growing importance of the suburbs, the unprecedented demands of new forms of consumerism, the rise of modernist planning modes, and the search by national corporations for manufacturing sites across the country and overseas.

Most work has shown that the institutions created to oversee urban renewal have focused on residential redevelopment and set the stage for the development of the postindustrial city. There is good reason for this. These activities account for much of the renewal that took place and most of the financial resources expended by government and private institutions. Industrial redevelopment has had a minor role to play in the long and complex story of postwar urban reconstruction. Most histories have focused on the building of residences such as Peter Stuyvesant and Pruitt-Igoe or resplendent downtown office towers. Urban renewal was linked to modernist understandings of architecture, planning, space, and government intervention in the name of making the postindustrial city. The triumphalism of large-scale clearance, the dislocation of low-income and minority residents, the building of modern, streamlined buildings on superblocks, and the active orchestration of these matters by coalitions consisting of various levels of government as well as private and public-private agencies have dominated this discussion.[18]

In Chicago, these redevelopment agencies used their power of eminent domain and government funding to refashion the social geography of the city while maintaining many older aspects of this geography. Refashioning took the form of putting new functions in areas they labeled as blighted. Old African

American and white working-class districts that were occupied by thousands of small owners and renters were remade as either high-end residential and commercial areas or as public housing. In the process, these agencies established the basis for the emergence of the postindustrial city. Renewal agencies also worked to ensure that the class and racial divides that characterized the older city were kept in place by the discriminatory practices of the housing market. Working with developers, politicians, and residential associations, Chicago agencies involved in renewal, such as the Metropolitan Housing and Planning Council, the Chicago Land Clearance Commission, and the Chicago Plan Commission, ensured that the very strict social divisions that had characterized Chicago's social geography for generations remained in place.[19]

Although work on urban renewal has focused on housing redevelopment, the same problems confronted those looking to stimulate industrial growth. To ensure industrial revitalization after World War II, two things had to be put in place. First, new local institutions had to be created that allowed place-dependent elites to impose new policies, programs, and practices that would counteract the ill effects of the changing dynamics of US and international industry. Before the end of the 1930s, the most active agent of economic development in the city was the Chicago Association of Commerce and Industry, which focused it actions on regulating land use, industrial promotion, and labor relations. It also had a clear position on government's role in business affairs, which was to be as little as possible. The local state played a supportive role at best before the 1940s. Its institutional capacity focused on mediating the relations between the city's business and political classes and ensuring that urban governance supported economic growth.[20]

This role, however, had to change. The expansion of the suburban industrial economy and the declining position of the central city forced the city of Chicago's civic and business leaders to reassess the structure and function of the institutions that oversaw the urban economy, local infrastructures, the housing market, and the built environment. Realizing that neither industry nor local government could revitalize the city's industrial base or rebuild the run-down districts by themselves, the city's leadership began to seek changes to the relationship between local municipal authority, federal policy, and business needs. They had to devise new ways to enhance Chicago's position as an economic center. New institutions had to be created to allow for urban redevelopment.

The second thing that had to be undertaken to make revitalization possible was to allow for greater government intervention in economic matters. This started to take a clear shape with growing federal activity in local issues and the rebuilding of the institutional order in the 1930s. In this period, the groundwork was laid for an array of policies and programs that would incorporate cities into the broader ambit of US federalism. That these funded policies and programs were typically uncoordinated and heavily favored profit-seeking development by the urban bourgeoisie does not detract from the fact that they represented a fundamental transformation in federal and local relations.[21]

As this study has shown, there was a great deal at stake. Local booster groups in Chicago looked to take advantage of growing federal intervention in urban and business matters. The Chicago Plan Commission used federal funds to bankroll an important study of blight in the 1930s. The Chicago Land Clearance Commission and the Mayor's Committee for Economic and Cultural Development made extensive use of federal, state, and municipal monies to undertake their residential, commercial, and industrial redevelopment projects. As it played out, some of the new institutions that were created to undertake renewal could accommodate industrial redevelopment. Chicago's place-dependent elites took advantage of this to implement policies that would revitalize their city's industrial base.[22] In the process, these alliances were able to orchestrate government legislative, fiscal, and political resources to further economic revitalization. In Chicago, the result was that all levels of the state were firmly ensconced in the rebuilding of the postwar city.

The ability to move ahead with industrial redevelopment was based on the use of the public-private partnership as a vehicle for government intervention in the urban economy. Relatively independent redevelopment agencies such as the Chicago Land Clearance Committee that had the power of eminent domain and the Mayor's Committee on Economic and Cultural Development that had license to mediate between individual firms and municipal government came to shape urban renewal in general and industrial redevelopment specifically. The members of these "new instruments of urban governance," as Mark Levine calls them, were both independent and dependent on formal city administrative structures. They were independent in that they allowed civic and business leaders to proceed with redevelopment with little formal control. They were dependent in that they required financial, political, and legislative support from municipal, state, and federal officials. The main task of these local groupings was to clear blighted land, reorganize the downtown area, and remake property relations, all in the name of creating a new city.

In Chicago, an array of redevelopment agencies with slightly different mandates, and composed of government, planning organizations, and business groups, used the public-private partnership to refashion real estate in the name of industrial revitalization.[23] This was clearly brought out in a 1977 Department of Development and Planning report.[24] As they saw it, the key element of industrial renewal in postwar Chicago was the building of a viable partnership between the private and the public sectors. This idea in itself was not new. The success of Chicago as an industrial center from the nineteenth century until the 1930s relied on public-private partnerships that allowed industry to develop, a political machine that worked with business booster groups, and infrastructure agencies that enabled the building of a water- and rail-based economy. While public-private agencies had played some part in city governance before World War II, few dealt with economic or industrial planning. The few that did were typically ad hoc, site specific, and short-lived. They had more to do with establishing the conditions for industrial growth than dealing with the difficult issues of industrial decline.

This changed after 1945. The viability of these entities was being increasingly questioned by the end of the early 1930s. The rise of a new set of government-business relationships that emerged with the New Deal and wartime industrial mobilization along with the growing number of problems associated with accelerated industrial decline after World War II produced both the demand and opportunities for creating new institutional forms and the playing out of place-based industrial politics. After 1945, pushed by the relentless decline of the city's manufacturing activity, Chicago's industrial coalition worked with a new set of public-private institutions that were given the task of rejuvenating the city's industry base and devising solutions to Chicago's industrial problems.

One form that Chicago's institutional change took in the postwar years was a growing commitment by local government to establishing formal policies to foster economic development. As I have shown in this study, these new rules and policies were based on a refashioning of the built environment and urban property relations.[25] A coalition of public and private interests argued in the years following the end of World War II that the repositioning of Chicago as a viable manufacturing center could only take place by replacing blighted land with new industrial spaces. It became increasingly clear after the war that the old hands-off model centered on the Chicago Association of Commerce and Industry's dated booster strategy and city government's reluctance to intervene in industrial affairs was no longer viable. The new institutions were built in response to the failure to deal not only with deteriorating urban issues in general but with industrial ones more specifically. While the informal approach taken by the Chicago Plan Commission and city council may have worked during a period of sustained growth before 1920, this was no longer appropriate in a period of relative and absolute decline. The city's place-dependent elites had to find a new way of governing industrial change. To that end, they worked to implement programs to resuscitate the city's ailing industrial economy.

Several industrial programs were put in place. The most active agencies, which included the reconstituted Chicago Plan Commission and other private and public-private agencies such as the Mayor's Committee for Economic and

Cultural Development, the South Side Planning Board, and the Chicago Land Clearance Committee, centered their attentions on refashioning property relations.[26] It was believed by nearly everyone involved that an industrial fix could only be accomplished by creating more industrial land in more attractive locations. This required repositioning industrial property with eminent domain. As Wendell Pritchett has made clear, urban redevelopment in all its different forms, including industrial renewal, was "controlled by a small number of real estate interests and politicians who used the power of eminent domain to reorganize urban land."[27]

The result was a set of fragmented, contested, and changing industrial programs between 1945 and 1975, all of which were ultimately geared to property issues. These included the building of industrial districts and planned industrial parks, rewriting the zoning ordinance, converting "blighted, nocturnal wastelands" to more modern and productive uses, supporting science-based industrial development, and rejuvenating factory space. In all cases, as the 1977 Department of Development and Planning report noted, the goal of renewal was to use government authority over urban land to "maintain and expand conditions for industrial growth, conservation, and stability."[28] Ultimately, of course, the goal was to promote urban redevelopment that generated profits for the city's place-dependent elites. The realignment of industrial property relations was possible only if the inadequacies of the existing ones were eliminated.[29] Both federal and state legislation and funds underpinned the increasing control that local authorities had over industrial land.

The multiscalar government intervention in the local land market revolved around these changes to property relations. The view of land shifted from one where it was a separate entity subject to individual needs to one based on the idea of land as part of a larger grouping rooted in the public good. Land became subject to a broader set of planning and design controls that facilitated large-scale reconstruction. Replacing "dead" land, congested streets, and ineffective multistory buildings with new shiny factory space and modern street layouts, so the argument went, would allow for industrial growth and entice capital investment back to the city. The assembly of large tracts of downtown property through the auspices of government-sanctioned eminent domain would allow large-scale development and would make Chicago more attractive to industrial investors. This could be successfully done, however, only by the concerted efforts of private and public interests—utilities, government, financial institutions, and real estate—to reframe the social relations of industrial land. A new institutional fix centered on property had to be put in place if the physical redevelopment of the city for industry was to be successful.

Failure

Despite the extensive efforts of an assortment of powerful city political, business, and planning elites, the practices put in place between 1945 and 1975 failed to build an effective industrial renewal program in Chicago. This was not for want of trying. Ira Bach, David Kennedy, and other place-dependent elites created and then deployed a range of solutions to the city's industrial problems in the post-war period. Despite their efforts, however, they were unable to reverse industrial decline. The new institutional fix based on eminent domain and the reshaping of property relations may have worked to turn Chicago into a gleaming postin-dustrial city, but it did not provide the basis for industrial regeneration. Through a long, drawn-out process of negotiation, contestation, and consensus, the city's various booster agencies were able to build what some writers have called the "New Chicago" and the "Third City."[30]

For more than sixty years, a city-building coalition composed of place-dependent financial institutions, developers, and local government worked to rebuild the old city. This effort involved the construction of a built environment that fea-tured private development of corporate and speculative offices in the Loop to accommodate new tertiary and quaternary industries, the private development of residential and commercial space to attract a middle- and upper-class popula-tion, and the building of public infrastructures. At the same time, it strengthened already high levels of racial and income discrimination and segregation through its control over the housing market and the built environment. The result of this large-scale transformation since the end of World War II has been, as Larry Bennet and his colleagues have stated, the "mobilization of a powerful Chicago business consensus regarding the overall shape of city development, and particu-lar participants in this consensus have done much to implement its vision." This vision did not include industry.[31]

In other words, the chances of revitalizing the city's manufacturing economy in the face of the longtime process of building the postindustrial city by a ded-icated place-dependent coalition were minimal at best. There was, however, a small window of opportunity when industrial redevelopment could have been more successful than it was. The twenty years between the end of the war and the creation of Lyndon Johnson's Great Society was the time in which indus-trial redevelopment programs had a chance to make some inroads on industrial decline. As I show here, this did not take place in Chicago, though. Chicago was not alone in its inability to revitalize the industrial economy through the elimina-tion of blight and the rejuvenation of worn-out districts. Studies of other cities, most notably Philadelphia, Saint Louis, and New York City, have also shown that place-dependent leaders missed the moment after World War II to implement policies that could simultaneously work on the physical, social, and economic aspects of the local industrial economy.[32]

By the 1970s, the need to revitalize the urban economy and the built landscape was obvious to informed commentators of Chicago's redevelopment programs. Contrary to much that was written at the time, a 1975 report on urban renewal concluded that the various programs implemented to tackle urban decline since 1945 had not done enough to deal with shuttered factories, increasing employment, and deteriorating industrial districts. Despite some success, the authors felt that "a much broader program [was] needed, to reverse an economic trend that began many years ago—a trend for locating large industry away from the densely populated cities and in the more sparsely populated suburbs where enormous tracts of vacant land were available." The report continued by stating that the industrial redevelopment programs had not had "any practical effect in stemming or reversing the trend of large employers of labor to locate in the suburbs, often vacating their city plants in the process."[33] While urban redevelopment between 1945 and 1975 laid the groundwork for the building of a postindustrial city, the attempts to attack manufacturing decline and to resuscitate the industrial economy in a modern form had failed.

The dismantling of the city's manufacturing base beginning in the 1920s and accelerating after World War II could not be halted by the ineffective policies put in place by the array of public, private, and quasipublic agencies that was created after 1930. The structural forces of industrial capitalism were not to be held back by the feeble and underresourced attempts by the city's business and political leaders committed to industrial renewal. The city's industrial renewal programs were unable to stop the industrial decline that was dismantling the city's manufacturing. Despite the grandiose claims of the city's most powerful boosters, the impact of the industrial renewal program on halting the deindustrialization of the city was "miniscule."[34] There were two major reasons why the program put in place to combat industrial decline ultimately failed.

First, the fact that public and private interests focused on rewriting property relations and refashioning the built environment undermined any realistic hopes of finding solutions to the problem of industrial decline. All the key agencies involved in assessing the state of the city's industry and devising measures to reverse the structural decline framed property relations as the solution. The elimination of blight and the repositioning of property relations would, it was believed, provide the basis for industrial revitalization. As long as city leaders pushed real property to the top of their agenda and denied the importance of larger structural forces that were affecting industry in Chicago, and elsewhere for that matter, the major economic issues facing the city could not be effectively addressed. Focusing on industrial land as both the problem and the solution could not deal with the geographic dynamics of price variations of land and wages across the metropolis, the absence of significant reinvestment in land and plant by industrial executives, and the sclerotic response to the changing metropolitan and regional dynamics by city planners, politicians, and officials.

Second, the coalition behind industrial redevelopment had little power to create effective programs and policies. By the late 1940s, urban redevelopment was in the hands of a growth alliance committed to transforming the industrial city into a postindustrial one. To a large extent, that had to do with the control of the redevelopment agenda by the postindustrial coalition led by Holman Pettibone and Milton Mumford. While this coalition was willing to countenance modern industry safely tucked away in self-contained industrial parks far from the main lines of redevelopment, they were unwilling to allow industrial revitalization to get in the way of middle-class residential, high-end commercial, and service-based development. While several attempts were made to revitalize the city's industrial base, power over the reins of redevelopment remained in the hands of a largely nonindustrial bourgeoisie working through organizations such as the Metropolitan Housing and Planning Council and the Central Area Committee, who sought to create a built environment that would be home to functions other than manufacturing.

Given the failure of industrial redevelopment by the 1970s, the fight to halt industrial decline took a different direction. Rather than attempting to create industrial property that was more amenable to the development of modern production and social needs, business and political leaders turned to new programs in which property took a secondary role. Most importantly, the city turned to ways to fight what was termed technological unemployment. This involved the city's use of federal government manpower programs to help build a central-city labor force and started in the mid-1960s under the direction of the Mayor's Committee for Economic and Cultural Development. It wasn't until the 1970s, however, that manpower programs became the central plank for building an industrial renaissance.[35] Manpower programs were followed by the use of revenue bonds to support industrial investment. Industrial bonds, which provide tax-exempt yields, are exempt from federal taxes and are a federal subsidy. They were first used in Mississippi in the 1930s. They became a technique to deal with industrial decline in industrial cities in the 1960s. Chicago started using revenue bonds in 1977. By the end of 1981, the city council had approved eighty-five. But they had little effect.[36]

If urban redevelopment, as Joseph Heathcott suggests, is an "intense deliberation over the city's future," then Chicago's postwar power brokers did not envisage much of a role for industry in that future.[37] For close to thirty years after 1945, the city elites concerned with building a modern landscape that would be able to attract and retain manufacturing firm and jobs faced insurmountable obstacles. The ramshackle coalitions of developers, politicians, financiers, and business executives dedicated to eliminating blight, attracting science-based industry, and building industrial parks pushed an agenda that used government powers, policies, and funding to rewrite how land could be used. Eminent domain was central to this agenda.

Industrial redevelopment, in other words, was a distinctive but minor part of the broader urban renewal process in Chicago. The authority invested in the state to redefine property in the name of capitalist development became the keystone of the revitalization of the industrial environment in the thirty years following the end of World War II. That it failed is not to detract from the power of new government institutions to raze neighborhoods, to displace thousands of people, and to rework property relations in the name of revitalizing the industrial economy. As illustrated by the neighborhoods that have experienced the bulldozer and undergone renewal over the last sixty years, the government's ability to refashion US cities in the guise of postindustrial modernity through its control over property relations has been dramatic and unprecedented. Industrial revitalization failed because the coalition seeking to use government powers could not use them effectively against the broader spatial logic of industrial capitalism and a more powerful place-based elite looking to building a postindustrial city on the ruins of the deindustrialized one.

NOTES ON DATASETS
AND SOURCES

Postwar commentators of Chicago's industrial scene used factory construction as their main measure of the city's industrial vitality. Nick Poulos, a *Chicago Tribune* reporter, and Thomas Coulter, the chief executive of the Chicago Association of Commerce and Industry, for example, used fixed-capital investment in the postwar period to gauge the city's industrial health.[1] They were not alone. The Chicago Plan Commission used the number and value of factory construction alongside the number of establishments and production workers to assess the city's industrial growth in a series of reports it published in the early 1950s.[2] The Commonwealth Edison Company used factory construction material in its postwar annual surveys.[3] In both cases, the data were used to show Chicago's relative position with the suburbs, often writing against the evidence which showed either decline or stagnation.[4]

Assessing the industrial geographies of postwar Chicago by measuring private investment in factory construction between 1945 and 1960 is a seemingly simple task. Various published sources, including those of the Chicago Plan Commission and Commonwealth Edison, provide summaries of factory construction. However, we need to treat these reports very carefully, as they are problematic for several reasons. In the first place, it is unclear what is actually being measured: were additions to a factory or the building of warehouses and other industrial uses included? The answer: it is impossible to determine, as the authors do not describe what is included in the table's categories. In the second place, in numerous cases, projects were double counted, appearing in separate listings depending on their state of planning or completion. Finally, the listings also reported on projects that were planned but never completed. Accordingly, the accuracy of these manufacturing construction reports is shaky at best. The only viable way to determine the scale, type and location of construction of new factories and factory additions is by making an examination of the proposed projects themselves.

Data Sets

The data for my analysis of Chicago's projects in chapter 2 comes from several sources. The most important is the weekly construction listing of the *Engineering News-Record*.[5] The listing contains two sections. The Bids Asked—Low Bidders-Contracts Awarded section provides information on firms that were in the process of planning or building factories. With a few exceptions, each entry provides information for the contracts that were awarded, including firm name, construction costs, and site address. The Proposed Projects section presents information at the stage before bids were opened in order to alert the construction and industrial engineering industries that a construction job was coming along sometime in the near future.

Every entry from both these sections in *Engineering News-Record* for the sixteen years between 1945 and 1960 was put into a spreadsheet. Two major issues had to be dealt with before an analysis of the data could proceed. First, and not surprisingly, a project was listed in multiple years and sometimes in different sections in the same year. These had to be ferreted out in order to eliminate double- or triple-counting of the same project. Second, not every project listed in the magazine was completed. To verify that the jobs listed actually took place, the entries were cross-referenced to other sources. The most important were the *Chicago Tribune, Moody's Manual of Investments: Industrial Securities*, and the New Construction and Expansion of Industrial Buildings section in *Commerce*, the journal of the Chicago Association of Commerce and Industry.[6] Those projects that could not be confirmed as taking place—and these accounted for close to half the entries obtained through *News-Record*—were excluded from the analysis.[7]

There are two issues concerning the usefulness of the *Engineering News-Record* construction data that need to be discussed. First, construction plans were not always started or completed, even after land was acquired, construction contracts were signed, and engineers had the plans in their hands. In many cases, projected and planned developments never went further than the drawing board. Decisions were thwarted for several reasons, including unavailability of finance, changing business conditions, problems with zoning, and a firm's decision to shift capital to other sites.

Two examples taken from the *Engineering News-Record* illustrate this point. Peter Paul Inc., one of the United States' big five candy makers decided to open a plant in La Grange, a Chicago suburb. The Connecticut firm, which had plants in Oakland, Dallas, Philadelphia, and Naugatuck, bought a site in 1950 and planned to build a $2 million plant. For reasons I have not been able to determine, Peter Paul did not construct the factory in La Grange.[8] In another case, National Video, a television receiving tube maker, purchased an existing factory in suburban Grayslake for $512,000 from Tumble Twist Mills in 1951. The company chose this existing factory because plans to build a new factory on land bought in the northern part of the city in 1950 did not materialize. The city site was sold to Stronghold Screw, which planned to build and move there from its downtown factory. However, these plans were also abandoned. Meanwhile, National Video eschewed the Grayslake factory, and purchased and moved into a plant vacated by Barco Manufacturing, which in turn built an entirely new plant in suburban Barrington.[9] The construction of industrial facilities was not a straightforward business.

As these cases demonstrate, a company's plans did not always work out, despite all the effort that went into the selection of the site, the drawing up of plans, the search for capital, and so on. These failures to complete projects, however, were not incorporated into the summaries of Commonwealth Edison and other booster agencies.

A second issue is that the data captures only some of the industrial building undertaken in this period.[10] It is impossible to estimate the share of the total construction that actually took place that was listed in the *Engineering News-Record*. Almost all the projects in the 1946–60 data set are custom-built for a specific company. There are few speculative inventory buildings in the data set. There is no reason given in the magazine why this was the case, but it has probably to do with the fact that they were built by construction or engineering companies that did not have to advertise the job and take bids from other companies.[11] Although there is no evidence to show this, the data may have included only those projects sent in by a small number of parties, such as large construction contractors that undertook more formal bidding and awarded contracts. Small builders may have worked within more local and informal networks.

Despite these limitations, the data set created from the *Engineering News-Record* provides valuable insights into factory construction in metropolitan Chicago in the early postwar period. Certainly the material was considered robust enough for the territorial information division of Commonwealth Edison to use it for reports on industrial construction in the Chicago region. Of course, as we have seen, the utility company used the data selectively to make the case for industrial growth in Chicago. The 830 completed projects used in chapter 2 do not suffer from the same problems as material used by the utility company. Unlike Commonwealth Edison, the material I took from the *Engineering News-Record* is complemented with details about the projects culled from company histories, newspaper articles, newspapers, credit agency reports, and business journals. The intent here is to build a snapshot of factory construction within the wider constellation of local and nonlocal processes. This allows me to explore the historical geographies of investment in fixed capital and industrial property built in the postwar Chicago region. The data shows that the suburbs were the preferred location for manufacturing capital after 1945.

Sources

Unfortunately, unlike other major US or Canadian cities, there are relatively few substantial archival materials available to explore the histories of industrial redevelopment in Chicago.[12] A few records do exist. Probably, the single most important collection is that of the Metropolitan Housing and Planning Council, which provide a rich record of the city's most powerful booster agency.[13] Despite the richness of these records and a few other sets of material at the city's various university and public libraries, urban scholars have serious difficulties locating detailed primary material that enables them to explore industrial history and industrial redevelopment. The absence of appropriate corporate records that address investment decisions and site selection is bothersome, but not debilitating.

The most significant gaps in the record though are the archives of the city and the public-private agencies that undertook industrial renewal. The fact that few if any unpublished materials compiled by the city at the time—from tax assessment rolls and building permits to department meeting minutes—are extant is a severe handicap. It is impossible to reconstruct the working of critical agencies such as the city's Department of Planning or Department of Urban Renewal. This is also the case with respect to material that provides insights into the day-to-day workings of the Chicago Land Clearance Commission, the Chicago Planning Commission, the South Side Planning Board, and the Committee for Economic and Cultural Development, all of which are main protagonists in this story.[14]

Fortunately, the material for this study comes from several sources that have been cobbled together to lay out both the industrial and institutional histories of manufacturing decline between 1920 and 1975. Other than the material used to measure industrial change and chart factory construction, four sets of records have proven to be particularly important. First, the extensive Metropolitan Housing and Planning Council records document the views of urban elites about planning, housing, transportation, urban renewal, and industry. Along with the council's own records, this collection holds an assortment of material from other city-based organizations, such as the American Society of Planning Officials. Second, much smaller but equally important is the Municipal Reference Collection at the Harold Washington Library Center. This is the largest published collection of material for the key agencies driving postwar industrial redevelopment: the Chicago Land Clearance Commission, the Mayor's Commission for Economic and Cultural Development, and the Chicago Plan Commission. Third, the federal records relating to urban renewal held at the National Archives in College Park, Maryland, while meager, provided an important federal perspective on the local situation in Chicago. Finally, like an increasing number of scholars, I have taken advantage of the growing number of local and national newspapers that are digitally searchable. I have used one newspaper in particular—the *Chicago Tribune*—to garner material about Chicago's industry, planning, redevelopment, real estate, and an assortment of other key issues that would have been otherwise been unattainable.

Notes

INTRODUCTION

1. Formed in 1904, the CACI was the city's leading booster organization, providing the manufacturing, commercial, and construction sectors with business information and promoting the city to outside interests. It was concerned with city matters until the late 1950s, when it began to take an interest in metropolitan issues. CACI, *Invest in Chicago* (Chicago: CACI, 1973), 1.

2. CACI.

3. Robert Lewis, *Chicago Made: Factory Networks in the Industrial Metropolis* (Chicago: University of Chicago Press, 2008); Dominic Pacyga, *Chicago: A Biography* (Chicago: University of Chicago Press, 2009).

4. CACI, *Chicago's New Horizons* (Chicago: CACI, 1957), 3. These writers considered "Chicago" to consist of the city and the suburbs, while the writer of *Invest in Chicago* was only talking of the city. As we shall see, the growth trajectories of the city and suburbs were vastly different. To talk about "Chicago" after 1945, one needs to talk about two quite different places.

5. Other local agencies agreed. The Chicago Plan Commission (CPC) claimed that Chicago's "inherent qualities as a favorable industrial location and distribution point will continue to make it attractive to industry." Similarly, the Planning Department noted in 1963 that "there are many indications that industry can continue in the role that the city planning objective projects for it in the future." CPC, *Chicago Industrial Study: Summary Report* (Chicago: CPC, 1952), 1; City of Chicago, *City of Chicago Industrial Renewal Study: Volume I; Conditions of Industrial Facilities in Chicago—July 1962* (Chicago: Illinois Institute of Technology Research Institute, 1963), v; CPC, *Chicago Industrial Development. . . . Recent Trends* (Chicago: CPC, 1951).

6. For a discussion of the framing of the US industrial system after World War II, see Jennifer Light, *From Warfare to Welfare: Defense Intellectuals and Urban Problems in Cold War America* (Baltimore: Johns Hopkins University Press, 2003); Margaret Pugh O'Mara, *Cities of Knowledge: Cold War Science and the Search for the Next Silicon Valley* (Princeton, NJ: Princeton University Press, 2005).

7. Dominic Pacyga, *Slaughterhouse: Chicago's Union Stock Yard and the World It Made* (Chicago: University of Chicago Press, 2015); David Bensman and Roberta Lynch, *Rusted Dreams: Hard Times in a Steel Community* (New York: McGraw-Hill, 1987).

8. Robert Beauregard makes a similar argument but dates the decline of the US city to the postwar period. *When America Became Suburban* (Minneapolis: University of Minnesota Press, 2006).

9. Until 1948 the Metropolitan Planning and Housing Council was called the Metropolitan Housing Council. In 1985 it changed its name again, this time to the Metropolitan Planning Council. For the sake of simplicity, I will use Metropolitan Planning and Housing Council throughout the book to refer to the organization.

10. For place dependency, see Kevin Cox and Andrew Mair, "Locality and Community in the Politics of Local Economic Development," *Annals of the Association of American Geographers* 78 (1988): 307–25; Ray Hudson, *Producing Places* (New York: Guilford Press, 2001), 256–74; John Logan and Harvey Molotch, *Urban Fortunes: The Political Economy of*

Place (Berkeley: University of California Press, 1987); Doreen Massey, "Power-Geometry and a Progressive Sense of Place," in *Mapping the Futures: Local Cultures, Global Change*, ed. John Bird, Barry Curtis, Tim Putnam, George Robertson, and Lisa Tickner (London: Routledge, 1993), 59–69.

11. For Chicago, see Arnold Hirsch, *Making the Second Ghetto: Race and Housing in Chicago, 1940–1960* (Chicago: University of Chicago Press, 1983); Joel Rast, *Remaking Chicago: The Political Origins of Urban Industrial Change* (DeKalb: Northern Illinois University Press, 1999); Gregory Squires, Larry Bennett, Kathleen McCourt, and Philip Nyden, *Chicago: Race, Class and the Response to Urban Decline* (Philadelphia: Temple University Press, 1987). For elsewhere, see Allen Dieterich-Ward, *Beyond Rust: Metropolitan Pittsburgh and the Fate of Industrial America* (Philadelphia: University of Pennsylvania Press, 2016); Tracy Neumann, *Remaking the Rust Belt: The Postindustrial Transformation of North America* (Philadelphia: University of Pennsylvania Press, 2016).

12. Larry Bennett, *The Third City: Chicago and American Urbanism* (Chicago: University of Chicago Press, 2010).

13. The social and political geographies of race and class are not the focus of this study. For studies that cover these issues for the first seventy-five years of the twentieth century, see Allan Spear, *Black Chicago: The Making of a Negro Ghetto, 1890–1920* (Chicago: University of Chicago Press, 1967); Hirsch, *Making the Second Ghetto*; Amanda Seligman, *Block by Block: Neighborhoods and Public Policy on Chicago's West Side* (Chicago: University of Chicago Press, 2005); Jeffrey Helgeson, *Crucibles of Black Empowerment: Chicago's Neighborhood Politics from the New Deal to Harold Washington* (Chicago: University of Chicago Press, 2014); Preston Smith II, *Racial Democracy and the Black Metropolis: Housing Policy in Postwar Chicago* (Minneapolis: University of Minnesota Press, 2012); Pacyga, *Chicago*, 219–28, 290–99, 350–53; Squires et al., *Chicago*, 93–151.

14. Rachel Weber, *From Boom to Bubble: How Finance Built the New Chicago* (Chicago: University of Chicago Press, 2015), 101. Also see Pacyga, *Chicago*, 359–409.

15. Brian Berry, "Islands of Renewal in Seas of Decay," in *The New Urban Reality*, ed. Paul E. Peterson (Washington, DC: Brookings Institution, 1985), 69–96.

16. Barry Bluestone and Bennett Harrison, *The Deindustrialization of America: Plant Closings, Community Abandonment, and the Dismantling of Basic Industries* (New York: Basic Books, 1982).

17. Barry Bluestone, foreword to *Beyond the Ruins: The Meanings of Deindustrialization*, ed. Jefferson Cowie and Joseph Heathcott (Ithaca, NY: Cornell University Press, 2003), viii.

18. Richard Child Hill and Cynthia Negrey, "Deindustrialization in the Great Lakes," *Urban Affairs Quarterly* 22 (1987): 589.

19. "De-Industrialization," *Gale Encyclopedia of U.S. Economic History*, ed. Thomas Carson and Mary Bonk (Gale, 1999); *Gale In Context: Biography*, https://link-gale -com.myaccess.library.utoronto.ca/apps/doc/EJ1667500171/BIC?u=utoronto_main&sid= BIC&xid=3d3bfe2a.

20. Bluestone, foreword, ix.

21. Candee Harris, "The Magnitude of Job Loss from Plant Closings and the Generation of Replacement Jobs: Some Recent Evidence," *Annals of the American Academy of Political and Social Science* 45 (1984): 15; David Perry and Beverley McLean, "The Aftermath of Deindustrialization: The Meaning of 'Economic Restructuring' in Buffalo, New York," *Buffalo Law Review* 39 (1991): 345–85.

22. Tom Sugrue, *The Origins of the Urban Crisis: Race and Inequality in Postwar Detroit* (Princeton, NJ: Princeton University Press, 1996), 126.

23. Steven High, *Industrial Sunset: The Making of North America's Rust Belt, 1969–1984* (Toronto: University of Toronto Press, 2003), 92–109.

24. Paul Clark, Irwin Marcus, Carl Meyerhuber, Charles McCollester, Mark McColloch, James Toth, Joe Gowaskie, and David Bensman, "Deindustrialization: A Panel Discussion," *Pennsylvania History* 16 (1991): 183.

25. Pacyga, *Chicago*, 319–21. He shows that meatpacking started to decline in the 1920s. See also Bensman and Lynch, *Rusted Dreams*; Rast, *Remaking Chicago*, 87–90.

26. Clark et al., "Deindustrialization," 185, 207. See also Dieterich-Ward, *Beyond Rust.*

27. Philip Scranton, "Large Firms and Industrial Restructuring: The Philadelphia Region, 1900–1980," *Pennsylvania Magazine of History and Biography* 116 (1992): 444.

28. Domenic Vitiello, "Machine Building and City Building: Urban Planning and Industrial Restructuring in Philadelphia, 1894–1928," *Journal of Urban History* 34 (2008): 399–434.

29. Tami Friedman "'A Trail of Ghost Towns across Our Land': The Decline of Manufacturing in Yonkers, New York," in Cowie and Heathcott, *Beyond the Ruins*, 20–21. Also see David Koistinen, *Confronting Decline: The Political Economy of Deindustrialization in Twentieth-Century New England* (Gainesville: University Press of Florida, 2013).

30. Thomas Dublin and Walter Licht, *The Face of Decline: The Pennsylvania Anthracite Region in the Twentieth Century* (Ithaca, NY: Cornell University Press, 2005).

31. Jefferson Cowie, *Capital Moves: RCA's 70-Year Quest for Cheap Labor* (Ithaca, NY: Cornell University Press, 1999), 33–40; Howard Gillette Jr., "The Wages of Disinvestment: How Money and Politics Aided the Decline of Camden, New Jersey," in Cowie and Heathcott, *Beyond the Ruins*, 139–58.

32. Steven Dandaneau, *A Town Abandoned: Flint, Michigan Confronts Deindustrialization* (Albany: State University of New York Press, 1996); Irwin Marcus, "The Deindustrialization of America: Homestead, a Case Study, 1959–1984," *Pennsylvania History* 52 (1985): 169–82; Guian McKee, *The Problem of Jobs: Liberalism, Race and Deindustrialization in Philadelphia* (Chicago: University of Chicago Press, 2008).

33. See, for example, David Brady and Michael Wallace, "Deindustrialization and Poverty: Manufacturing Decline and AFDC Recipiency in Lake County, Indiana 1964–93," *Sociological Forum* 16 (2001): 321–58.

34. John Cumbler, *A Social History of Economic Decline: Business, Politics and Work in Trenton* (New Brunswick, NJ: Rutgers University Press, 1989).

35. Scranton, "Large Firms and Industrial Restructuring."

36. Domenic Vitiello, *Engineering Philadelphia: The Sellers Family and the Industrial Metropolis* (Ithaca, NY: Cornell University Press, 2013), 293.

37. Philip Scranton, *Figured Tapestry: Production, Markets and Power in Philadelphia Textiles, 1885–1941* (New York: Cambridge University Press, 1989), 324–25.

38. While the discussion about industrial decline has become more historically sensitive, there are still those who write that Chicago experienced "the onset of deindustrialization in the early 1980s." Mark Doussard, Jamie Peck, and Nik Theodore, "After Deindustrialization: Uneven Growth and Economic Inequality in 'Postindustrial' Chicago," *Economic Geography* 85 (2009): 183. They make a passing comment that there had been "warning signs" from 1947, but quickly drop the point.

39. See, for example, Robert Lewis, "Running Rings around the City: North American Industrial Suburbs, 1850–1950," in *Changing Suburbs*, ed. Richard Harris and Peter Larkham (London: E. & F. N. Spon, 1999), 146–67; and the city-based essays in Robert Lewis, ed., *Manufacturing Suburbs: Building Work and Home on the Metropolitan Fringe* (Philadelphia: Temple University Press, 2004).

40. John Baumann, *Public Housing, Race and Renewal* (Philadelphia: Temple University Press, 1987); Hirsch, *Making the Second Ghetto*; Joel Schwartz, *The New York Approach: Robert Moses, Urban Liberals, and Redevelopment of the Inner City* (Columbus: Ohio University Press, 1993); Marc A. Weiss, "The Origins and Legacy of Urban Renewal," in *Urban*

and *Regional Planning in an Age of Austerity*, ed. Pierre Clavel, John Forester, and William Goldsmith (New York: Pergamon, 1980), 53–80; Samuel Zipp, *Manhattan Projects: The Rise and Fall of Urban Renewal in Cold War New York* (New York: Oxford University Press, 2010). For a recent overview, see Samuel Zipp and Michael Carriere, "Introduction: Thinking through Urban Renewal," *Journal of Urban History* 39 (2013): 359–65.

41. Historians have demonstrated that slum clearance predated the postwar renewal of the city. Robert Fogelson, *Downtown: Its Rise and Fall, 1880–1950* (New Haven, CT: Yale University Press, 2001); Max Page, *The Creative Destruction of New York City, 1900–1940* (Chicago: University of Chicago Press, 2001); Wendell Pritchett, "The 'Public Menace' of Blight: Urban Renewal and the Private Uses of Eminent Domain," *Yale Law and Policy Review* 21 (2003): 1–52.

42. Kevin Gotham, "Urban Space, Restrictive Covenants and the Origins of Racial Residential Segregation in a US City, 1900–1950," *International Journal of Urban and Regional Research* 24 (2004): 616–33; Kevin Gotham, "A City without Slums: Urban Renewal, Public Housing and Downtown Revitalization in Kansas City, Missouri," *American Journal of Economics and Sociology* 60 (2001): 285–316. Also see Eric Avila and Mark Rose, "Race, Culture, Politics, and Urban Renewal," *Journal of Urban History* 35 (2009): 335–47; George Lipsitz, "The Racialization of Space and the Spatialization of Race: Theorizing the Hidden Architecture of Landscape," *Landscape Journal* 26 (2007): 10–23; Jon Teaford, "Urban Renewal and Its Aftermath," *Housing Policy Debate* 11 (2000): 443–65.

43. For Chicago, see Helgeson, *Crucibles of Black Empowerment*; Hirsch, *Making the Second Ghetto*; Smith, *Racial Democracy and the Black Metropolis*.

44. For Chicago, see Seligman, *Block by Block*; Squires et al., *Chicago*.

45. For Chicago, see Robert Lewis, "Divided Space: Racial Transition Areas and Relocation, Chicago 1947–1960," in *Sharing Spaces: Essays in Honour of Sherry Olson*, ed. Robert C. H. Sweeny (Ottawa: Presses de l'Université d'Ottawa and the Museum of Canadian History, 2020), 17–39; Jack Meltzer, "Relocation of Families Displaced in Urban Redevelopment: Experience in Chicago," in *Urban Redevelopment: Problems and Prospects*, ed. Coleman Woodbury (Chicago: University of Chicago Press, 1953), 409–13.

46. For Canada, see High, *Industrial Sunset*; for the United Kingdom, see Ron Martin and Bob Rowthorn, eds., *The Geography of De-Industrialisation* (London: Macmillan, 1986).

47. D. Bradford Hunt, *Blueprint for Disaster: The Unraveling of Chicago Public Housing* (Chicago: University of Chicago Press, 2009); Seligman, *Block by Block*; Hirsch, *Making the Second Ghetto*; Helgeson, *Crucibles of Black Empowerment*; Smith, *Racial Democracy and the Black Metropolis*.

48. Colin Gordon, "Blighting the Way: Urban Renewal, Economic Development, and the Elusive Definition of Blight," *Fordham Urban Law Journal* 31 (2004): 305–34; Harold Kaplan, *Urban Renewal Politics: Slum Clearance in Newark* (New York: Columbia University Press, 1963), 20–23, 96–102, 190; Pritchett, "'Public Menace' of Blight"; Scott Greer, *Urban Renewal and American Cities* (Indianapolis: Bobbs-Merrill, 1965), 18–19, 27–29.

49. For cities, see Bureau of Municipal Research and Pennsylvania Economy League, *An Approach to Philadelphia's Industrial Renewal Problem* (Philadelphia: Bureau of Municipal Research and Pennsylvania Economy League, 1956); Detroit City Plan Commission, *Industrial Renewal: A Comparative Study of the Tendency toward Obsolescence and Deterioration in Major Industrial Areas in the City of Detroit* (Detroit: Detroit City Plan Commission, March 1956); Arthur D. Little, Inc., *The Usefulness of Philadelphia's Industrial Plant: An Approach to Industrial Renewal* (Cambridge, MA: A. D. Little, 1960); Milwaukee Redevelopment Coordinating Committee, *Blight Elimination and Urban Redevelopment in Milwaukee* (Milwaukee: Redevelopment Coordinating Committee, 1948). For organizations, see American Society of Planning Officials, *Industrial Renewal Research*, Information Report 104 (Chicago, November 1957); Robert Garrabrant, *Redevelopment for*

Industrial Use, Technical Bulletin 25 (Washington, DC: Urban Land Institute, May 1955); Society of Industrial Realtors, Urban Renewal Advisory Committee, *Urban Renewal and the Real Estate Market* (Washington, DC: Society of Industrial Realtors, 1964).

50. Hunt, *Blueprint for Disaster*; Seligman, *Block by Block*; Hirsch, *Making the Second Ghetto.* This is also the case with other studies of redevelopment in postwar Chicago. Larry Bennett, "Postwar Redevelopment in Chicago: The Declining Politics of a Party and the Rise of Neighborhood Politics," in *Unequal Partnerships: The Political Economy of Urban Redevelopment in Postwar America,* ed. Gregory D. Squires (New Brunswick, NJ: Rutgers University Press, 1989), 161–77; Marc Weiss and John Metzger, "Planning for Chicago: The Changing Politics of Metropolitan Growth and Neighborhood Development," in *Atop the Urban Hierarchy,* ed. Robert Beauregard (Totowa, NJ: Rowman & Littlefield, 1989), 126–27.

51. Joel Rast's important studies of postwar industrial change rarely reference the organizations looking for a solution to the city's industrial decline. *Remaking Chicago*; "Regime Building, Institution Building: Urban Renewal Policy in Chicago, 1946–1962," *Journal of Urban Affairs* 31 (2009): 173–94; "Critical Junctures, Long-Term Processes: Urban Redevelopment in Chicago and Milwaukee, 1945–1980," *Social Science History* 33 (2009): 393–426.

52. Joseph Heathcott and Máire Agnes Murphy, "Corridors of Flight, Zones of Renewal: Industry, Planning and Policy in the Making of Metropolitan St. Louis, 1940–1980," *Journal of Urban History* 31 (2005): 151–89; Kaplan, *Urban Renewal Politics*; Neumann, *Remaking the Rust Belt.* For the UK situation, see Alistair Kefford, "Disruption, Destruction, and the Creation of the 'Inner Cities': The Impact of Urban Renewal of Industry, 1945–1980," *Urban History* 44 (2017): 492–515.

53. This is most clearly laid out for Philadelphia in McKee, *Problem of Jobs.*

54. Kevin Cox, "Spaces of Dependence, Spaces of Engagement and the Politics of Scale, or: Looking for Local Politics," *Political Geography* 17 (1998): 1–23; Cox and Mair, "Locality and Community"; David Harvey, *Justice, Nature and the Geography of Difference* (Oxford: Blackwell, 1996), 291–326; Hudson, *Producing Places,* 256–74; Logan and Molotch, *Urban Fortunes*; Michael Storper and Richard Walker, *The Capitalist Imperative: Territory, Technology and Industrial Growth* (New York: Blackwell, 1989).

55. Massey, "Power-Geometry and Progressive Sense of Place"; Doreen Massey, "Places and Their Pasts," *History Workshop Journal* 39 (1995): 182–92; Cox and Mair, "Locality and Community"; Harvey, *Justice, Nature and the Geography of Difference*; Hudson, *Producing Places.*

56. Cox and Mair, "Locality and Community"; Harvey, *Justice, Nature and the Geography of Difference*; Hudson, *Producing Places.*

57. Gordon, "Blighting the Way"; Kaplan, *Urban Renewal Politics*; John M. McCarthy, *Making Milwaukee Mightier: Planning and the Politics of Growth, 1901–1960* (DeKalb: Northern Illinois University Press, 2009), 133–35.

58. Robert A. Beauregard, "Public-Private Partnerships as Historical Chameleons: The Case of the United States," in *Partnerships in Urban Governance: European and American Experience,* ed. Jon Pierre (Basingstoke: Macmillan, 1998), 61–64; Mark Levine, "The Politics of Partnership: Urban Redevelopment since 1945," in Squires, *Unequal Partnerships,* 19–21; Gail Radford, *The Rise of the Public Authority: Statebuilding and Economic Development in Twentieth-Century America* (Chicago: University of Chicago Press 2013), 71–87, 135–53; Mariana Valverde, "Ad Hoc Governance: Public Authorities and North American Local Infrastructure in Historical Perspective," in *Governing Practices: Neoliberalism, Governmentality, and the Ethnographic Imaginary,* ed. Michelle Brady and Randy Lippert (Toronto: University of Toronto Press, 2016), 199–217.

59. Nicholas Blomley, "Law, Property, and the Geography of Violence: The Frontier, the Survey and the Grid," *Annals of the Association of American Geographers* 93 (2003): 86–107; Pritchett, "'Public Menace' of Blight"; David A. Schultz, *Property, Power, and American*

Democracy (New Brunswick, NJ: Transaction, 1992); Joseph William Singer, "Re-Reading Property," *New England Law Review* 711 (1991–92): 711–29; Lynn Staeheli and Don Mitchell, *The People's Property? Power, Politics and the Public* (New York: Routledge, 2008); Franz von Benda-Beckmann, Keebet von Benda-Beckmann, and Melanie Wiber, "The Properties of Property," in *Changing Properties of Property*, ed. Franz von Benda-Beckmann, Keebet von Benda-Beckmann, and Melanie Wiber (New York: Berghahn Books, 2006), 1–39.

60. Schultz, *Property, Power*, 65–66.

61. Heathcott and Murphy, "Corridors of Flight"; McCarthy, *Making Milwaukee Mightier.*

62. Pritchett, "'Public Menace' of Blight"; Robert Lewis, "Modern Industrial Policy and Zoning: Chicago, 1910–1930," *Urban History* 40 (2013): 92–113.

63. Nicholas Blomley, "Landscapes of Property," *Law and Society Review* 32 (1998): 567–612; Blomley, "Law, Property, and the Geography of Violence"; Pritchett, "'Public Menace' of Blight"; Radford, *Rise of the Public Authority*; Schultz, *Property, Power.*

64. William Kinnard Jr., Stephen Messner, and Byrl Boyce, *Industrial Real Estate* (Washington, DC: Society of Industrial Realtors, 1979), 17–18. The Society of Industrial Realtors was created out of the Industrial Property division of the National Association of Real Estate Boards in 1941. It specializes in the marketing of industrial properties.

65. Kinnard et al., *Industrial Real Estate*, 19–20.

66. Gordon, "Blighting the Way"; Kaplan, *Urban Renewal Politics*, 20–23, 96–102; Pritchett, "'Public Menace' of Blight"; Scott Greer, *Urban Renewal and American Cities* (Indianapolis: Bobbs-Merrill, 1965), 18–19, 27–29.

67. Rast, *Remaking Chicago*; Squires et al., *Chicago.*

68. For an example of this, see Mayor's Committee for Economic and Cultural Development, *Mid-Chicago Economic Development Study*, vol. 2, *Technical Analysis and Findings: Economic Development of Mid-Chicago* (Chicago: Mayor's Committee for Economic and Cultural Development, 1966), 88–89.

69. Herbert Gans, *The Urban Villagers: Group and Class in the Life of Italian-Americans* (New York: Free Press, 1962); Martin Anderson, *The Federal Bulldozer: A Critical Analysis of Urban Renewal, 1949–1962* (Cambridge: MIT Press, 1964); James Q. Wilson, ed., *Urban Renewal: The Record and the Controversy* (Cambridge: MIT Press, 1966).

70. Quoted in Cornelia Honchar, "Accountants Discover DUR Slum Clearances Are Flops," *Chicago Tribune*, November 5, 1970, S1, Proquest Historical Newspapers.

1. INDUSTRIAL DECLINE AND THE RISE OF THE SUBURBS

1. Nick Poulos, "Chicago Area Far in U.S. Lead on Industry Contracts," *Chicago Tribune*, June 17, 1962, A1, Proquest Historical Newspapers (hereafter PHN); CACI, *Manpower Survey, 1956, Metropolitan Area* (Chicago: CACI, 1957); Robert Nolte, "Report Forecast Industrial Growth," *Chicago Tribune*, October 24, 1965, N1, PHN. The report referred to was *Industrial Development: Metropolitan Planning Guidelines; Phase One, Background Documents* (Chicago: Northeastern Illinois Planning Commission, 1965). The CACI was established as the Chicago Association of Commerce in 1904. It changed its name to CACI in 1947. In 1992 it changed its name once again, to Chicagoland Chamber of Commerce.

2. Glenn Porter, *The Rise of Big Business, 1860–1920*, 2nd ed. (Arlington Heights, IL: Harlan Davidson, 1977).

3. For the history of the first phase of industrial suburbanization, see Robert Lewis, "Running Rings around the City: North American Industrial Suburbs, 1850–1950," in *Changing Suburbs*, ed. Richard Harris and Peter Larkham (London: E. & F. N. Spon, 1999), 146–67. Also see the collected essays on Baltimore, San Francisco, Pittsburgh, Los Angeles, and other cities in Robert Lewis, ed., *Manufacturing Suburbs: Building Work and Home on*

the Metropolitan Fringe (Philadelphia: Temple University Press, 2004). For Philadelphia, see Philip Scranton, *Figured Tapestry: Production, Markets and Power in Philadelphia Textiles, 1885–1941* (New York: Cambridge University Press, 1989). For Chicago, see Robert Lewis, *Chicago Made: Factory Networks in the Industrial Metropolis* (Chicago: University of Chicago Press, 2008); Mary Beth Pudup, "Model City? Industry and Urban Structure in Chicago" in Lewis, *Manufacturing Suburbs*, 53–75.

4. The metropolitan area for this study consists of seven counties: Cook, DuPage, Kane, Will, McHenry, Lake (Illinois), and Lake (Indiana).

5. We should be careful not to see the 1930s as an exceptional period in industrial history. The 1930s featured the culling of companies, restructuring of industries, and consolidation of a new set of industrial relations, none of which is unusual in the long-term course of industrial history. Depressions are part of capitalist social relations, and as such must be seen as a "normal," even though an exceedingly difficult, part of the cyclical character of industrial capitalism.

6. CPC, *Industrial and Commercial Background for Planning Chicago* (Chicago: CPC, 1942), 5.

7. Graham Taylor, *Satellite Cities: A Study of Industrial Suburbs* (New York: Appleton, 1915), 1.

8. William Mitchell, *Trends in Industrial Location in the Chicago Region since 1920* (Chicago: University of Chicago Press, 1933), 51, 54, 63.

9. Scrutator, "Cites Trends in Removal of City Plants," *Chicago Tribune*, April 7, 1929, B7, PHN.

10. Scrutator, "Cities Trends in Removal of Factories," *Chicago Tribune*, March 19, 1929, 33, PHN.

11. Scrutator, "Small Town Not Factory Utopia, Scrutator Says," *Chicago Tribune*, April 25, 1925, 31, PHN.

12. Scrutator, "Electric Power Gives Little Towns New Industrial Pep," *Chicago Tribune*, July 15, 1929, 25, PHN.

13. Scrutator, "Industry Begins to Make Its Way to Open Spaces," *Chicago Tribune*, October 31, 1924, 23, PHN; Scrutator, "Outlying Banks Report Nearly Billion Assets," *Chicago Tribune*, January 27, 1925, 31, PHN.

14. Employment and construction investment are the best indicators of industrial change. Here I use employment to explore the district's manufacturing economy. The next chapter uses investment in factory space to examine another aspect of differentiated industrial decline in the region.

15. Many Chicago jobs in 1919 had been created in the suburbs. The city's annexation of industrial suburbs added significantly to Chicago's industrial base. In other words, the scale of the city's manufacturing base was heavily shaped by factories originally in the suburbs. Some significant industrial areas annexed before World War I include South Chicago and Pullman. Lewis, "Running Rings around the City."

16. CPC, *Industrial and Commercial Background*, 46–47.

17. Al Chase, "Chicago Offers Outstanding Inducements to Manufacturers," *Chicago Tribune*, September 15, 1940, B12, PHN.

18. Mitchell, *Trends in Industrial Location*, 62, 51–63; Edward V. Miller, "Industrialization on Chicago's Periphery: Examining Industrial Decentralization, 1893–1936," *Journal of Urban History* 43 (2017): 720–43.

19. Irving Salomon, "Why We Moved to a Smaller Town," *Factory and Industrial Management* 76 (November 1928): 912. For Chicago's position as a furniture center, see Lewis, *Chicago Made*, 216–35; Sharon Darling, *Chicago Furniture, Art, Craft, and Industry, 1833–1983* (New York: Norton, 1984).

20. John Cumbler, *A Social History of Economic Decline: Business, Politics and Work in Trenton* (New Brunswick, NJ: Rutgers University Press, 1989); Scranton, *Figured Tapestry*; Domenic Vitiello, "Machine Building and City Building: Urban Planning and Industrial Restructuring in Philadelphia, 1894–1928," *Journal of Urban History* 34 (2008): 399–434.

21. Lewis, *Chicago Made*, 23–31; Dominic Pacyga, *Slaughterhouse: Chicago's Union Stock Yard and the World It Made* (Chicago: University of Chicago Press, 2015).

22. James Walker, "Planning for the Future of East Chicago, Indiana: General Survey of Its Social and Economic Problems," Chamber of Commerce of East Chicago, 1926, file 1, box 1, East Chicago Collection, Calumet Regional Archives, Indiana University, Gary, Indiana (hereafter East Chicago Collection); Powell A. Moore, *The Calumet Region: Indiana's Last Frontier* (Indianapolis: Indiana Historical Bureau, 1959), 226–30.

23. Moore, *Calumet Region*, 220–26, 236–41; "Activity in Factory Sites at Indiana Harbor," *Iron Age* 83 (April 18, 1909): 1141; Nathan Weinhouse, "Final Report, East Chicago Real Property Inventory and Occupancy Survey," May 20, 1935, file 17, box 3, East Chicago Collection; Moore, *Calumet Region*, 251–55.

24. Alfred Meyer and Diane Heidtmann Paetz, "Manufactural Geography of East Chicago-Whiting, Indiana: A Study in Geographic Rehabilitation," *Proceedings of the Indiana Academy of Science* 71 (1961): 171. For the Calumet region, see Robert Lewis, "Networks and the Industrial Metropolis: Chicago's Calumet District, 1870–1940," in *Industrial Cities, History and Future*, ed. Clemens Zimmerman (Chicago: University of Chicago Press, 2013), 89–114.

25. Frank Findlay, *A Survey of the Town of Cicero, Illinois* (Chicago: Council of Social Agencies of Chicago, 1937), 1–9; Helen Monchow, *Seventy Years of Real Estate Subdividing in the Region of Chicago* (Evanston, IL: Northwestern University Press, 1939), 113–15; Robert Eli Cramer, *Manufacturing Structure of the Cicero District, Metropolitan Chicago*, Geography Research Paper 27 (Chicago: University of Chicago, 1952), 21–26.

26. Cramer, *Manufacturing Structure*, 3–12, 145–48; "The Western Electric Company's Improvements," *Iron Age* 80 (July 2, 1908): 7. Other firms followed Western Electric, including Barrett Varnish, Storkline, Danly Machine Specialties, and American Phenolic Corp.

27. Quoted in Cramer, *Manufacturing Structure*, 146.

28. Robert Lewis, *Calculating Property Relations: Chicago's Wartime Industrial Mobilization, 1940–1950* (Athens: University of Georgia Press, 2016), 76–105; Perry Duis and Scott La France, *We've Got a Job to Do: Chicagoans and World War II* (Chicago: Chicago Historical Society, 1992); Coleman Woodbury with Frank Cliffe, "Industrial Location and Urban Redevelopment," in *The Future of Cities and Urban Redevelopment*, ed. Coleman Woodbury (Chicago: University of Chicago Press, 1953), 259–74.

29. CPC, *Industrial and Commercial Background*, 49.

30. CACI, *The Chicago Association of Commerce Report for 1942* (Chicago: CACI, 1943), 8.

31. CACI, *The Chicago Association of Commerce Report for 1943* (Chicago: CACI, 1944), 24, 21.

32. Leverett Lyon, "Economic Problems of American Cities," 1942, 5, folder 1, box 51, Chicago Association of Commerce and Industry collection, Chicago History Museum, Chicago.

33. The report is referred to in "Attracting Industry to Chicago," *Chicago Tribune*, May 29, 1961, 12, PHN. The relationship between industrial decline and factory building is covered in chapter 3.

34. Leo Reeder, "The Central Area of Chicago—a Re-Examination of the Process of Decentralization," *Land Economics* 28 (1952): 369–73; Leo Reeder, "Industrial Location Trends in Chicago in Comparison to Population Growth," *Land Economics* 30 (1954): 177–82; Leo Reeder, "Industrial Deconcentration as Factor in Rural-Urban Fringe Development," *Land Economics* 31 (1955): 275–80; Martin Reinemann, "The Pattern and Distribution of Manufacturing in the Chicago Area," *Economic Geography* 36 (1960): 139–44.

35. "Industrial Urban Renewal," *Chicago Tribune*, May 18, 1972, 16, PHN.

36. David Perry and Alfred J. Watkins, eds., *The Rise of the Sunbelt Cities* (Beverley Hills, CA: Sage, 1977); James C. Cobb, *Industrialization and Southern Society, 1877–1984* (Lexington: University of Kentucky Press, 1984); Dewey Grantham, *The South in Modern America: A Region at Odds* (New York: Harper Collins, 1994), 259–80.

37. *International Directory of Company Histories* (Saint James, MO: St. James Press, 1996), vol. 15; FundingUniverse (website), accessed December 27, 2012, http://www.fundinguniverse.com/company-histories/brach-and-brock-confections-inc-history.

38. In 1935, for example, a $250,000 addition was made to the warehouse to facilitate speedier handling of truck and railroad shipments. More than twenty years later, the sixteenth addition cost $1,200,000. Al Chase, "Brach Builds Big Addition to Candy Plant," *Chicago Tribune*, April 17, 1935, C16, PHN; "Brach Candy Builds New Addition," *Chicago Tribune*, November 26, 1953, H5, PHN.

39. Acme Steel Company, untitled manuscript, c. 1955, stored in the Pullman factory, Chicago (copy in the author's possession), 22–23, 30–31, 41–43, 48, 81, 92–94; Encyclopedia.com, accessed March 20, 2020, https://www.encyclopedia.com/books/politics-and-business-magazines/interlake-corporation; "Acme Steel Plant Started," *Chicago Tribune*, July 23, 1957, B7, PHN; "Calumet Region Today," special issue, *Calumet Record*, December 24, 1925, 18; file 18, box 4, Special Collections, Calumet Region Community Collection, Chicago Public Library; Gilbert Lacher, "Acme Steel Expands Cold Strip Capacity," *Iron Age* 113 (January 31, 1924): 353–58.

40. Quoted in "Acme Steel Co. to Build a New Office Unit," *Chicago Tribune*, January 19, 1957, D9, PHN; Encyclopedia.com, accessed March 20, 2020, https://www.encyclopedia.com/books/politics-and-business-magazines/interlake-corporation.

41. Electro-Motive began in 1922 in Cleveland to build gasoline-powered railcars. In 1930, it was purchased by General Motors, which had decided to move into the gasoline railcar market.

42. Hal Foust, "General Motors to Build Diesel Engines Here," *Chicago Tribune*, February 14, 1935, 23, PHN; Philip Hampson, "G.M. Diesel Division Adds 125 Acre Site," *Chicago Tribune*, January 31, 1946, 21, PHN. The McCook plant was closed in 1989, after having made fifty-four thousand locomotives.

43. The issue of whether or not General Motors, and for that matter any other company, made the "best" location choice (whatever that may mean) is moot. The important point is that they believed they were choosing the best, given what constituted best site selection practice and the particularities of their situations. See chapter 3 for a discussion of the rise of scientific site selection practices.

44. William Clark, "Firm Pioneers in Industry's Newest Field," *Chicago Tribune*, April 11, 1954, A9, PHN; "Nuclear Firm Builds Plant in Des Plaines," *Chicago Tribune*, February 18, 1959, C7, PHN; National Radiation Instrument Catalogue: 1920–1960, updated February 7, 2014, s.v. "Nuclear-Chicago," http://national-radiation-instrument-catalog.com/new_page_42.htm.

45. Keith McClellan, "A History of Chicago's Industrial Development," in *Mid-Chicago Economic Development Study: Volume III; Technical Supplement, Economic Development of Mid-Chicago*, by the Mayor's Committee for Economic and Cultural Development (Chicago: Mayor's Committee for Economic and Cultural Development of Chicago, 1966), 39–40, 47–49.

46. Paul Potter, "Meat Industry Is Experiencing Basic Change," *Chicago Tribune*, November 17, 1933, 33, PHN. On the national spread of Swift operations from the nineteenth century, see Gary Fields, *Territories of Profit: Communications, Capitalist Development, and the Innovative Enterprises of G. F. Swift and Dell Computer* (Stanford, CA: Stanford University Press, 2004), 91–135.

47. Pacyga, *Slaughterhouse*, 94, 158–66; Dominic Pacyga, *Chicago: A Biography* (Chicago: University of Chicago Press 2009), 316–21.

48. Pacyga, *Slaughterhouse*, 165. Also see McClellan, "History," 47–48.

49. Harry Adams, "Survey Sees North Shore Building Boom," *Chicago Tribune*, October 16, 1949, N1, PHN. The northern suburbs consist of municipalities running from Lake Michigan through to the area just west of O'Hare airport, and include Arlington Heights, Bensenville, Des Plaines, Elk Grove Village, Elmwood Park, Evanston, Franklin Park, Glenview, Harwood Heights, Itasca, Lincolnwood, Morton Grove, Mount Prospect, Niles, Norridge, Northlake, Northfield, Park Ridge, River Grove, Rosemont, Schiller Park, Skokie, Wilmette, and Wood Dale.

50. There is a body of work that sets out a more complex history of the postwar suburbs. See, for example, Becky Nicolaides, *My Blue Heaven: Life and Politics in the Working-Class Suburbs of Los Angeles, 1920–1965* (Chicago: University of Chicago Press, 2002).

51. Adams, "Survey Sees North Shore Building Boom."

52. "Centex Proves Magnet to Industry," *Chicago Tribune*, September 26, 1965, E1, PHN. The other three were Orange County, California, San Jose, California, and Suffolk County, New York.

53. Before the 1920s, central-city annexation of industrial suburbs greatly reduced the amount of manufacturing found in the "suburbs." In Chicago, for example, the annexation that took place in the second half of the nineteenth century shifted the municipal jurisdiction of a number of steel, transportation equipment, metalworking, and chemical industries from independent suburbs such as Pullman and South Chicago to the city. Lewis, "Running Rings around the City."

54. This involved comparing northern suburban firms found in the 1962 *Industrial Directory* against metropolitan area firms listed in the 1950 directory. While it does not capture the origins of firms locating in the suburbs, it does provide some clues about where they came from.

55. "General Controls Co. Dedicates a Plant and Warehouse in Skokie," *Chicago Tribune*, September 30, 1952, C6, PHN; Ernest Fuller, "Avon Facility to Be Built in Morton Grove," *Chicago Tribune*, June 5, 1955, B9, PHN; "Container Firms to Build West Suburb Plant," *Chicago Tribune*, June 14, 1957, C8, PHN.

56. Richard Whittingham, *Skokie: A Centennial History* (Skokie: Village of Skokie, 1988), 134–38; "Work Will Start Tomorrow on Million Dollar Drug Manufacturing Plant in Skokie," *Chicago Tribune*, June 1, 1941, B10, PHN.

57. "Automatic Electric Co.," *Factory Management and Maintenance* 116 (May 1958): A6–11.

58. "Ten Authorities View Industry Trends," in *Third Annual Metropolitan Chicago Industrial Development Guide*, by CACI (Chicago: CACI, 1969), 48.

59. "Searle Building 4 More Units at 1½ Million Cost," *Chicago Tribune*, June 23, 1946, SWC, PHN.

60. "R. G. Rhett to the Reconstruction Finance Corporation," September 22, 1947; "Prospectus Plancor No. 711," October 1, 1943. Both documents are to be found in box 26, Real Property Disposal Case Files for Illinois, Indiana, Michigan, Minnesota, Ohio and Wisconsin, Records of the War Assets Administration, NARA—Great Lakes Region, Chicago. "Lincolnwood Plant Sold to Bell and Howell," *Chicago Tribune*, March 10, 1946, A5, PHN. For a discussion of what happened to defense plants after World War II, see Lewis, *Calculating Property Relations*, 198–214.

61. Roger Sufkin, "Industry—Economic Base-Builder of Suburban Growth," in *Third Annual Metropolitan Chicago Industrial Development Guide*, ed. CACI (Chicago: CACI, 1969), 39, 83.

62. O'Hare was established as the runway for airplanes built at the adjacent Douglas Aircraft Co. defense plant. With the end of the war, the company left, and the field was slowly turned into a commercial and passenger facility.

63. Quoted in "Study Reveals Why Industries Change Sites," *Chicago Tribune*, April 9, 1967, D1, PHN; Roger Biles, *Richard J. Daley: Politics, Race and the Governing of Chicago* (DeKalb: Northern Illinois University Press, 1995), 52–53.

64. "Industry Marches North, Northwest," *Chicago Tribune*, May 25, 1969, E1, PHN. For an extended discussion of industrial parks, see chapter 7.

65. "O'Hare Area Booms with Building of Industrial Parks, Offices, Homes," *Chicago Tribune*, May 8, 1969, N3, PHN.

66. Loren Trimble, "Forecasting Locations for New Industries," *Realty and Building*, January 27, 1968, PHN. Also see Ernest Fuller, "Make Acreage Near O'Hare for Industry," *Chicago Tribune*, November 9, 1958, B11, PHN; "Firms to Drive for Industry in O'Hare Area," *Chicago Tribune*, August 14, 1960, NW1, PHN; "Industry Eats Up Land Here," *Chicago Tribune*, December 29, 1968, D1, PHN; S. N. Tideman Jr., "Industrial Real Estate Market Will Continue Strong in 1968," *Realty and Builder Annual Review of 1967* 159 (January 27, 1968): 24.

67. Lindy Biggs, *The Rational Factory: Architecture, Technology, and Works in America's Age of Mass Production* (Baltimore: Johns Hopkins University Press, 1996).

68. Nick Poulos, "Supplying Home for Industry Is Specialty of These Realtors," *Chicago Tribune*, May 15, 1958, F7, PHN.

69. Quoted in "Broadview Called Center of Industry Real Estate," *Chicago Tribune*, January 14, 1968, D2, PHN.

70. William Clark, "Big Industrial Construction Expected Soon," *Chicago Tribune*, July 14, 1946, A7, 8, PHN. The functioning of the city property market was unfavorably contrasted to that in the suburbs by city agencies. CPC, *Redevelopment for Industry. Statement on the Clearance of Blighted Areas for Industrial Use* (Chicago: CPC, 1951); Chicago, Department of City Planning, Research Division, *Locational Patterns of Major Manufacturing Industries in the City of Chicago* (Chicago: Department of City Planning, 1960); City of Chicago, *City of Chicago Industrial Renewal Study: Volume I; Conditions of Industrial Facilities in Chicago—July 1962* (Chicago: IIT Research Institute, 1963); City of Chicago, *City of Chicago Industrial Renewal Study: Volume II; Analysis of Fifteen Selected Industrial Districts* (Chicago: IIT Research Institute, 1963).

71. Dan Egler, "Expert Hits Industry Shift to Suburbia," *Chicago Tribune*, October 5, 1972, N3, PHN.

72. Hal Barger, "Suburbs Court New Industry as Tax Friend," *Chicago Tribune*, September 2, 1962, N1, PHN.

73. "Study Reveals Why Industry Change Sites."

74. Northeastern Illinois Planning Commission, *Industrial Development*, 65–66.

75. "Broadview Called Center of Industry Real Estate."

76. "Franklin Park Business Group Names New Aid," *Chicago Tribune*, November 5, 1950, NW7, PHN. It changed its name to the Northwestern Suburban Manufacturers Association in 1959.

77. Other organizations such as the Skokie Valley Industrial Association had a social function. Even though executives from some of the area's leading firms were members, the association was not engaged in public duties. Rather, the focus was to provide industrial leaders with a venue where they could meet to discuss common business concerns. "Training on Jobs Accredited at Leyden High," *Chicago Tribune*, April 21, 1955, W1, PHN. "Bus Routes Sought for 2 Suburbs," *Chicago Tribune*, February 13, 1966, D3, PHN; "Industry Unit Picks Preston," *Chicago Tribune*, October 25, 1960, N3, PHN.

78. William Gorton, "Northwest Cook County Pacesetter of Development in Metropolitan Chicago," *Chicagoland Development* 5 (1975): 2. Also see Owen Pollard, "Industrial Growth and Expansion in Northwest Cook County," *Chicagoland Development* 5 (1975): 8–9. The journal was put out by the CACI and was touted on the front page of every issue as a "guide to industrial, commercial and community planning and development."

2. BUILDING THE SUBURBAN FACTORY AND INDUSTRIAL
DECLINE IN POSTWAR CHICAGO

1. Known as the *Economist* between 1866 and 1946, it changed its name to *Realty and Building* in 1947. The review section provided, among other things, information on city and Cook County building permits (address, function, dimensions, owner, and cost) and "construction projects and plans." It is difficult to know how complete or biased the coverage was, but the listing does provide us with a view into the construction history of manufacturing in Chicago and the surrounding area.

2. Quoted in Greg Le Roy, *The Great American Job Scam: Corporate Tax Dodging and the Myth of Job Creation* (San Francisco: Berrett-Koehler, 2005), 77.

3. Kevin Cox and Andrew Mair, "Locality and Community in the Politics of Local Economic Development," *Annals of the Association of American Geographers* 78 (1988): 307–25; Kevin Cox, "Spaces of Dependence, Spaces of Engagement and the Politics of Scale, or: Looking for Local Politics," *Political Geography* 1 (1998): 1–23; David Harvey, *Justice, Nature and the Geography of Difference* (Oxford: Blackwell, 1996), 291–326; Ray Hudson, *Producing Places* (New York: Guilford, 2001), 256–74; John Logan and Harvey Molotch, *Urban Fortunes: The Political Economy of Place* (Berkeley: University of California Press, 1987); Doreen Massey, "Power-Geometry and a Progressive Sense of Place," in *Mapping the Futures: Local Cultures, Global Change*, ed. Jon Bird, Barry Curtis, Tim Putnam, George Robertson and Lisa Tickner (London: Routledge, 1993), 59–69.

4. While capitalists may have emotional attachment to place, it is typically "much weaker overall" that that of residents. Logan and Molotch, *Urban Fortunes*, 22.

5. While workers can be a serious problem for capitalists, the fact that there is a high degree of substitutability among them and they have a strong attachment to place means that they offer less of a locational constraint than land, which is hard to replicate.

6. John Cumbler, *A Social History of Economic Decline: Business, Politics and Work in Trenton* (New Brunswick, NJ: Rutgers University Press, 1989); Domenic Vitiello, *Engineering Philadelphia: The Sellers Family and the Industrial Metropolis* (Ithaca, NY: Cornell University Press, 2013), 192–215; Domenic Vitiello, "Machine Building and City Building: Urban Planning and Industrial Restructuring in Philadelphia, 1894–1928," *Journal of Urban History* 34 (2008): 399–434.

7. The material is taken from the *Engineering News-Record*, an engineering magazine concerned with large construction projects. For a discussion of the data set, see the appendix.

8. Robert Lewis, *Calculating Property Relations: Chicago's Wartime Industrial Mobilization, 1940–1950* (Athens: University of Georgia Press, 2016), 209–14.

9. CACI, *The Chicago Association of Commerce Report for 1942* (Chicago: CACI, 1943), 8.

10. Commonwealth Edison, *Survey of Industrial Development 1946* (Chicago: Commonwealth Edison Company, 1947), 1, 3–4.

11. Commonwealth Edison Company, *Industrial Expansion, 1945–1955* (Chicago: Commonwealth Edison Company, 1955); Commonwealth Edison Company, *Industrial Expansion, 1951–1956* (Chicago: Commonwealth Edison Company, September 1956); Commonwealth Edison Company, *Industrial Development during 1963* (Chicago: Commonwealth Edison Company, September 1964).

12. William Kaplan, "Industrial Real Estate in 1947," *Realty and Builder Annual Review 1947* 119 (January 31, 1948): 18

13. Joseph Egelhof, "Post-War Era Brings Boom to Chicago Area," *Chicago Tribune*, November 12, 1952, B7, Proquest Historical Newspapers (hereafter PHN). As was common, Egelhof exaggerates construction activity, stating that twenty-five hundred firms had spent more than $1.5 billion in the six-county region since the end of the war.

14. The vast majority (296 of the 306) were additions made by companies to their own plants; the rest were made by companies after they had bought an existing building.

15. Lindy Biggs, *The Rational Factory: Architecture, Technology, and Works in America's Age of Mass Production* (Baltimore: Johns Hopkins University Press, 1996); Rayner Banham, *A Concrete Atlantis: U.S. Industrial Building and European Modern Architecture* (Cambridge: MIT Press, 1986); Robert Lewis, "Redesigning the Workplace: The North American Factory in the Interwar Period," *Technology and Culture* 42 (2001): 665–84.

16. "Sentinel Radio Corporation," *Factory Management and Maintenance* 105 (April 1947): B46. The emphasis is in the original. Also see *Moody's Manual of Investments: Industrial Securities 1945* (New York: Moody's Investors Service, 1945), 1135; *Moody's Manual of Investments: Industrial Securities 1947* (New York: Moody's Investors Service, 1947), 1180.

17. Ernest Fuller, "New Bottling Plant Blends with Suburb," *Chicago Tribune*, May 27, 1956, B9, 11, PHN.

18. "Motorola, Inc., to Build Plant for 3 Millions," *Chicago Tribune*, December 29, 1952, B7, PHN; Timothy Gilfoyle, "Motorola Inc.," *Encyclopedia of Chicago*, accessed June 16, 2019, http://www.encyclopedia.chicagohistory.org/pages/847.html; *1962 Directory of Illinois Manufacturers* (Chicago: Illinois Manufacturers' Association, 1962).

19. "Plant Begun in Broadway by Ceco Steel," *Chicago Tribune*, January 13, 1955, D7, PHN; "Ceco to Build Steel Plant Near Lemont," *Chicago Tribune*, May 6, 1958, C7, PHN; "Ceco Plans Fabricating Plant Near Lemont," *Chicago Tribune*, February 6, 1962, C5, PHN; "Ceco to Spend $3,675,000; Plans Shift of Operations," *Chicago Tribune*, May 19, 1963, B6, PHN; Mark Wilson, "Ceco Corp.," *Encyclopedia of Chicago*, accessed November, 26, 2017, http://www.encyclopedia.chicagohistory.org/pages/2589.html.

20. Robert Atkins and Richard Shriver, "New Approach to Facilities Location," *Harvard Business Review* 46 (1968): 70.

21. This parallels the rise of the community builder who gained unprecedented control over the building of suburban subdivisions. Marc Weiss, *The Rise of the Community Builders: The American Real Estate Industry and Urban Land Planning* (New York: Columbia University Press, 1987); Greg Hise, *Magnetic Los Angeles: Planning the Twentieth-Century Metropolis* (Baltimore: Johns Hopkins University Press, 1997).

22. Charles P. Wood, "Where to Locate the Plant," *Factory Management and Maintenance* 95 (April 1937): 46.

23. Quoted in "Good Location Aids Industrial Success," *New York Times*, July 20, 1930, RE8, PHN.

24. George C. Smith, "Where Shall We Build?," *Factory Management and Maintenance* 96 (April 1938): B39.

25. Wood, "Where to Locate the Plant," 46.

26. Quoted in Walter Stern, "Top-Level Aides Pick Plant Sites," *New York Times*, February 18, 1957, 46, PHN.

27. Quoted in "The Top Ten—and Today's Trends," *Factory Management and Maintenance* 116 (May 1958): 35.

28. Biggs, *Rational Factory*; Banham, *Concrete Atlantis*; Lewis, "Redesigning the Workplace."

29. The results of the competition and a detailed examination of each of the winning factories were included in a special addition to either the April or May issue.

30. City of Chicago, *City of Chicago Industrial Renewal Study: Volume IV; Summary Report* (Chicago: ITT Research Institute, 1963), 8.

31. "Build the Plant around the Process," *Factory Management and Maintenance* 97 (April 1939): B35.

32. Stephen Helbrun, "Location of Industry," *Journal of Land and Public Utility Economics* 19 (1943): 253.

33. "Build the Plant around the Process," B35.

34. "The Hallicrafters Company," *Factory Management and Maintenance* 105 (April 1948): B74.

35. "Sentinel Radio Corporation"; "Automatic Electric Co.," *Factory Management and Maintenance* 116 (May 1958): A6.

36. Fred Prather, "Industry Will Seek Well-Designed, Flexible Plants in Out-Lying Areas," *Realty and Builder Annual Review of 1960* 145 (January 26, 1962): 38.

37. B. H. Shaffer and H. W. Lormer, "Preplanning for Plant Location," *Factory Management and Maintenance* 105 (October 1948): 95–102.

38. For an overview of the changing role of industrial engineering companies in building industrial plant, see Lewis, *Calculating Property Relations*, 109–11.

39. Leonard Yaseen, "You May Be Wise to Pick a New Plant Site in 1951," *Factory Management and Maintenance* 109 (April 1951): B66–68; "Busy, Quiet Firm Finds Plant Sites," *Chicago Tribune*, October 17, 1965, E1, PHN; Le Roy, *Great American Job Scam*, 68–91.

40. Prince Carlisle, "Plant Moves Go on Despite Wage Law," *New York Times*, March 26, 1939, 89, PHN; "PHN; "Plant Relocation Seen in 1951 Trend," *New York Times*, January 21, 1951, 119, PHN; "Policy Is Assailed on Tax Write-Off," *New York Times*, December 15, 1953, 69, PHN; Yaseen, "You May Be Wise"; quoted in "State Gets Plea to Woo Industry, *New York Times*, January 19, 1954. 37, PHN.

41. Ronald Reifler to Fred Eaton, March 3, 1961, Illinois, Area Redevelopment Administration, Planning Files Relating to the Assistant Administrator for Planning and Research, 1961–61, box 15, Records of the Economic Development Administration, record group 378, National Archives at College Park, Maryland.

42. Maurice Fulton, "Some Facts of Life the Great Lakes Area Faces," in *Keeping the Continent's Greatest Industrial Area Ahead: Proceedings of the Second Annual Meeting*, ed. Great Lakes Industrial Development Council (Lansing, MI: Great Lakes Industrial Development Council, 1954), 20, 21, 22.

43. Alvin Nagelberg, "Chicago Area Labor Supply Critical," *Chicago Tribune*, December 24, 1967, B7, PHN.

44. James Gavin, "Industrial Outlays in 1960 Rated to Exceed 37 Billion," *Chicago Tribune*, February 25, 1960, D6, PHN.

45. Nagelberg, "Chicago Area Labor Supply Critical."

46. Al Chase, "Taxis Boost Chicago All around World," *Chicago Tribune*, April 18, 1920, 29, PHN.

47. *Moody's Manual of Investments: Industrial Securities 1948* (New York: Moody's Investors Service, 1948), 148.

48. John McPherson, "Some Economic and Legal Aspects of the Purchase and Lease of Real Estate by Life Insurance Companies," *University of Pennsylvania Law Review* 97 (1949): 485–87. Most small firms rented space, of course, while large ones tended to own their space, either by constructing a factory or by taking ownership of an existing building.

49. Thomas Fegan, "Tools of Real Estate Financing," *University of Illinois Law Forum* 1957 (1957): 335–37; Thomas R. Robinson, "Life Insurance Companies and the Commercial Mortgage Market, 1960–1973," *American Real Estate and Land Economics Association Journal* 3 (1975): 49; James R. Webb, "Real Estate Investment Acquisition Rules for Life Insurance Companies and Pension Funds: A Survey." *American Real Estate and Land Economics Association Journal* 12 (1984): 495–520.

50. "Unite to Help Industry Get Factory Loans," *Chicago Tribune*, July 25, 1926, B3, PHN.

51. Walter Berg, "Construction Loans," in *Mortgage Banking*, ed. Robert H. Pease and Homer V. Cherrington (New York: McGraw-Hill, 1953), 239. Also see Glenn McHugh and Robert H. Pease, "Industrial Mortgages—Debentures—Notes," in Pease and Cherrington, *Mortgage Banking*, 211–12.

52. Thomas W. Hanchett, "Financing Suburbia: Prudential Insurance and the Post–World War II Transformation of the American City," *Journal of Urban History* 26 (2000): 313–28.

53. Marquis James, *The Metropolitan Life: A Study in Business Growth* (New York: Viking Press, 1947), 127–28, 245–46.

54. Norman H. Nelson, "Life Insurance Companies," in Pease and Cherrington, *Mortgage Banking*, 256.

55. Webb, "Real Estate Investment Acquisition Rules."

56. "Mortgage Unit to Study Trend in Investments, *Chicago Tribune*, September 14, 1947, SWA, PHN; "Life Firms Put 10 Millions in Realty Parcels," *Chicago Tribune*, March 30, 1947, WA, PHN.

57. "Life Firms' Real Estate Buying Heavy," *Chicago Tribune*, February 29, 1948, A7, PHN; Hanchett, "Financing Suburbia," 313–15; McPherson, "Some Economic and Legal Aspects," 482; McHugh and Pease, "Industrial Mortgages," 211–14.

58. Samuel Zipp, *Manhattan Projects: The Rise and Fall of Urban Renewal in Cold War New York* (New York: Oxford University Press, 2010), 73–113; Arnold Hirsch, *Making the Second Ghetto: Race and Housing in Chicago, 1940–1960* (Chicago: University of Chicago Press, 1983), 115–20.

59. Quoted in "Life Company Investment Keeps Industry at High Rate," *Chicago Tribune*, July 22, 1950, B7, PHN.

60. Arthur M. Weimer and Homer Hoyt, *Real Estate* (New York: Ronald Press, 1966), 450–51.

61. "Ceco Steel Products Plans 11 Million Mill," *New York Times*, May 11, 1958, F7, PHN.

62. Rand, McNally and Company, *Moody's Manual of Investment: Industrial Securities 1950* (New York: Moody's Investors Service, 1950), 294.

63. Fegan, "Tools of Real Estate Financing," 340–42; Weimer and Hoyt, *Real Estate*, 443.

64. McHugh and Pease, "Industrial Mortgages," 211.

65. While it is impossible to state with any certainty just how important the leaseback was, there can be no doubt that it became increasingly more important in the building of new factories after 1945, especially in suburban areas.

66. The origins of the leaseback can be traced back earlier. One of the first was when Safeway Stores started building, selling, and leasing back their properties in the 1930s. "Investors' Guide," *Chicago Tribune*, May 28, 1950, PHN; Hanchett, Financing Suburbia," 328. Insurance companies were the not only institutional investor in real estate. By the 1950s, company pension plans and universities provided industrial leasebacks in Chicago. "G.E. Trust Buys Continental Can Building," *Chicago Tribune*, December 29, 1955, B7; "N.U. Acquires Bottling Unit Being Erected," *Chicago Tribune*, March 27, 1956, B5, PHN. The rise of industrial property lease arrangements began to undermine the role of the investment banker. William Clark, "Firms Gain Tax Advantage by Renting Plant," *Chicago Tribune*, February 2, 1947, B7, PHN.

67. Al Chase, "Plant of Map Firm Is Being Built to Order," *Chicago Tribune*, December 15, 1951, B5, PHN. Insurance companies did become involved in the city as well. New England Mutual Life, for example, financed the industrial redevelopment of part of the old stockyards. Stephen Crews, "Industrial Park in Stock Yards to Increase Jobs," *Chicago Tribune*, June 9, 1968, SCL1, PHN.

68. "Leaseback Is Way to Expansion," *Chicago Tribune*, April 3, 1966, E1, PHN.

69. "Mortgage Unit to Study Trend."

70. Quoted in Hanchett, "Financing Suburbia," 322.

71. "Firms Gain Tax Advantage," B7.

72. Al Chase, "Mortgage Corp. Will Construct Plants for Rent," *Chicago Tribune*, August 11, 1946, NWA, PHN; Clark, "Firms Gain Tax Advantage." Chicago industrial executives were not alone in the use of leasebacks to build their suburban plants after 1945. Hanchett, "Financing Suburbia."

73. Abbott Laboratories, *Moody's Manual of Investment: Industrial Securities 1956* (New York: Moody's Investors Service, 1956), 1085–87; Sentinel Radio Corporation, *Moody's*

Manual of Investment: Industrial Securities 1947, 1180; American Colortype Company, *Moody's Manual of Investment: Industrial Securities 1945*, 213–14.

74. Thomas Buck, "Life Firms' Holdings of Realty Gain," *Chicago Tribune*, February 8, 1948, S9, PHN. Insurance companies were very cautious about investing significant amounts in central-city property. The examples that I have been able to find suggest that the leaseback was mostly a suburban phenomenon. As I show in the next two chapters, the fear of the effects of blighted property on land values greatly inhibited long-term investments in the central city.

75. "Insurance Firm Will Purchase Suburb Plant," *Chicago Tribune*, October 12, 1947, NA, PHN.

76. "Insurance Firm to Build New Ditto Plant," *Chicago Tribune*, April 1, 1954, D9, PHN; "New Factory to Be Built by Shure Company," *Chicago Tribune*, October 30, 1954, B5, PHN.

77. Dominic Pacyga, *Slaughterhouse: Chicago's Union Stock Yard and the World It Made* (Chicago: University of Chicago Press, 2015), 137–74.

3. BLIGHT AND THE TRANSFORMATION OF INDUSTRIAL PROPERTY

1. James W. Follin, "Slum Clearance and Urban Renewal for Industrial Sites" (address given to the American Industrial Development Council, Washington, DC, April 6, 1955), 2–5, box 291, General Records of the Department of Housing and Urban Development, 1931–2003, record group 207, National Archives at College Park, Maryland.

2. Thomas Furlong, "Chicago Declares War on Blight," *Chicago Tribune*, November 24, 1947, B8, Proquest Historical Newspapers (hereafter PHN).

3. For Chicago, see Arnold Hirsch, *Making the Second Ghetto: Race and Housing in Chicago, 1940–1960* (Chicago: University of Chicago Press, 1983); D. Bradford Hunt, *Blueprint for Disaster: The Unraveling of Chicago Public Housing* (Chicago: University of Chicago Press, 2009); Amanda Seligman, *Block by Block: Neighborhoods and Public Policy on Chicago's West Side* (Chicago: University of Chicago Press, 2005). For some other northern cities, see Scott Greer, *Urban Renewal and American Cities* (Indianapolis: Bobbs-Merrill, 1965); Harold Kaplan, *Urban Renewal Politics: Slum Clearance in Newark* (New York: Columbia University Press, 1963); John M. McCarthy, *Making Milwaukee Mightier: Planning and the Politics of Growth, 1901–1960* (De Kalb: Northern Illinois University Press, 2009); Joel Schwartz, *The New York Approach: Robert Moses, Urban Liberals, and Redevelopment of the Inner City* (Columbus: Ohio University Press, 1993); Samuel Zipp, *Manhattan Projects: The Rise and Fall of Urban Renewal in Cold War New York* (New York: Oxford University Press, 2010).

4. CPC, *A Study of Residential Densities in Chicago* (Chicago: CPC, 1951), 73.

5. Hirsch, *Making the Second Ghetto*; Seligman, *Block by Block*, chapters 2, 3; Michael Carriere, "Chicago, the South Side Planning Board and the Search for (Further) Order: Toward an Intellectual Lineage of Urban Renewal in Postwar America," *Journal of Urban History* 39 (2012): 411–32; Wendell Pritchett, "The 'Public Menace' of Blight: Urban Renewal and the Private Uses of Eminent Domain," *Yale Law and Policy Review* 21 (2003): 1–52; Zipp, *Manhattan Projects*. One exception to this tendency is Joel Rast, who doesn't pay much attention to blight. *Remaking Chicago: The Political Origins of Urban Industrial Change* (DeKalb: Northern Illinois University Press, 1999).

6. Colin Gordon, "Blighting the Way: Urban Renewal, Economic Development, and the Elusive Definition of Blight," *Fordham Urban Law Journal* 31 (2004): 315–20.

7. Greer, *Urban Renewal and American Cities*, 29–31; Kaplan, *Urban Renewal Politics*, 20–23, 96–102, 190; Schwartz, *New York Approach*, 229–60; Guian McKee, *The Problem of Jobs: Liberalism, Race and Deindustrialization in Philadelphia* (Chicago: University of Chicago Press, 2008).

8. "Waste Lands in Town," *Chicago Tribune*, May 29, 1930, 12, PHN.

9. "Redeeming the Blighted Area," *Chicago Tribune*, November 1, 1937, 14, PHN.

10. Quoted in Philip Hampson, "Mayer Seeks New Industries for Chicago," *Chicago Tribune*, January 27, 1938, 21, PHN. Mayer was president of Oscar Mayer and Company, meatpackers.

11. Quoted in Thomas Buck, "Heald Proposes 4 Steps to End Chicago Slums," *Chicago Tribune*, October 18, 1946, 7, PHN. This was a heavily racialized comment, as the South Side was almost entirely African American. Hirsch, *Making the Second Ghetto*; Jeffrey Helgeson, *Crucibles of Black Empowerment: Chicago's Neighborhood Politics from the New Deal to Harold Washington* (Chicago: University of Chicago Press, 2014); Preston Smith II, *Racial Democracy and the Black Metropolis: Housing Policy in Postwar Chicago* (Minneapolis: University of Minnesota Press, 2012).

12. For studies that explore the question of blight in general, see Ernest Fisher, "Economic Aspects of Zoning, Blighted Areas, and Rehabilitation Laws," *American Economic Review* 32 (1942): 331–40; C. Louis Knight, "Blighted Areas and Their Effects upon Urban Land Utilization," *American Academy of Political and Social Science* 148 (1930): 133–38.

13. Roger Biles, *Big City Boss in Depression and War: Mayor Edward J. Kelly of Chicago* (DeKalb: Northern Illinois University Press, 1984); Hunt, *Blueprint for Disaster*, 15–66.

14. Kevin Cox, "Spaces of Dependence, Spaces of Engagement and the Politics of Scale, or: Looking for Local Politics," *Political Geography* 17 (1997): 1–23; Kevin Cox and Andrew Mair, "Locality and Community in the Politics of Local Economic Development," *Annals of the Association of American Geographers* 78 (1988): 307–25; Doreen Massey, "Power-Geometry and Progressive Sense of Place," in *Mapping the Futures: Local Cultures, Global Change*, ed. John Bird, Barry Curtis, Tim Putnam, George Robertson, and Lisa Tickner (London: Routledge, 1993), 59–69.

15. David Harvey, *Justice, Nature and the Geography of Difference* (Oxford: Blackwell, 1996), 320–24; Ray Hudson, *Producing Places* (New York: Guilford Press, 2001), 260–62.

16. John F. Bauman, "Introduction: The Eternal War on the Slums," in *From Tenements to the Taylor Homes: In Search of an Urban Housing Policy in Twentieth-Century America*, ed. John F. Bauman, Roger Biles, and Kristin Szylvian (University Park: Pennsylvania State University Press, 2000), 1–17; Robert Fogelson, *Downtown: Its Rise and Fall* (New Haven, CT: Yale University Press, 2001), 317–80; Pritchett, "'Public Menace' of Blight."

17. Hirsch, *Making the Second Ghetto*; Carriere, "Chicago, the South Side Planning Board"; Rast, *Remaking Chicago*.

18. CPC, *Residential Chicago: Volume One of the Report of the Chicago Land Use Survey* (Chicago: CPC, 1942); CPC, *Land Use in Chicago: Volume Two of the Report of the Chicago Land Use Survey* (Chicago: CPC, 1943).

19. "9 Square Miles of City Found to Be Blighted," *Chicago Tribune*, January 16, 1942, 16, PHN. The survey team worked hard to create the necessary knowledge base. McCrosky and George Horton, the commission's chair, informed Mayor Edward Kelly in a letter attached to the 1942 report that the "collection, coding, tabulating and mapping of the survey information required nearly 3,000 persons during the peak period" and involved the publication of twenty-one thousand residential block and census tabulations. The results would be used to "designate broad areas for redevelopment and rehabilitation" and "facilitate the study of postwar improvement progress." CPC, *Residential Chicago*, n.p.

20. CPC, *Residential Chicago*.

21. Harold Smith, "Study Rebirth of Blighted Areas," *Chicago Tribune*, November 27, 1938, SW1, PHN.

22. George Nesbitt, "Relocating Negroes from Urban Slum Clearance Sites," *Land Economics* 25 (1949): 275–88.

23. Nesbitt, 278, 284, 285–86. Also see Hirsch, *Making the Second Ghetto*; Helgeson, *Crucibles of Black Empowerment*; Robert Lewis, "Divided Space: Racial Transition Areas and Relocation, Chicago 1947–1960," in *Sharing Spaces: Essays in Honour of Sherry Olson*, ed. Robert C. H. Sweeny (Ottawa: Presses de l'Université d'Ottawa and the Museum of Canadian History, 2020), 17–39; Smith, *Racial Democracy and the Black Metropolis*.

24. "Study Blighted Districts That May Be Rebuilt," *Chicago Tribune*, October 4, 1941, 23, PHN.

25. "Propose Fitting Slum Areas for Modern Building," *Chicago Tribune*, July 3, 1941, 14, PHN.

26. Al Chase, "City's Blight Problem to Be Investigated," *Chicago Tribune*, August 29, 1943, 18, PHN.

27. Hirsch, *Making the Second Ghetto*; Carriere, "Chicago, the South Side Planning Board"; Shirley Werthamer, "Private Planning for Urban Redevelopment: An Analysis of the South Side Planning Board of Chicago, 1947" (MA thesis, University of Chicago, 1947).

28. Al Chase, "Blight Areas Pose Problem in Rebuilding," *Chicago Tribune*, October 2, 1943, 23, PHN. For a discussion of national organizations, see Marc A. Weiss, "The Origins and Legacy of Urban Renewal," in *Urban and Regional Planning in an Age of Austerity*, ed. Pierre Clavel, John Forester, and William Goldsmith (New York: Pergamon, 1980), 53–80.

29. Hirsch, *Making the Second Ghetto*, 100. A similar process took place in Saint Louis. Joseph Heathcott, "A City Quietly Remade: National Programs and Local Agendas in the Movement to Clear the Slums, 1942–1952," *Journal of Urban History* 34 (2008): 221–42.

30. Carriere, "Chicago, the South Side Planning Board"; Werthamer, "Private Planning for Urban Redevelopment"; Smith, *Racial Democracy and the Black Metropolis*.

31. Hunt, *Blueprint for Disaster*, 38–93; Smith, *Racial Democracy and the Black Metropolis*; Hirsch, *Making the Second Ghetto*, 103–12; Carriere, "Chicago, the South Side Planning Board"; Werthamer, "Private Planning for Urban Redevelopment."

32. Hirsch, *Making the Second Ghetto*, 108, 114–15.

33. Hirsch, 106.

34. Nesbitt, "Relocating Negroes," 287.

35. Carriere, "Chicago, the South Side Planning Board," 415, 425.

36. "Letter from Wilford Winholtz to Business Manager," March 30, 1949, folder 4132, box 497, Metropolitan Planning Council records, Special Collections and University Archives, University of Illinois at Chicago (hereafter MPC records).

37. Buck, "Heald Proposes 4 Steps," 7.

38. Quoted in "Blighted Areas Held Chicago's Major Problem," *Chicago Tribune*, September 19, 1947, 41, PHN.

39. Hunt, *Blueprint for Disaster*; Smith, *Racial Democracy and the Black Metropolis*; Hirsch, *Making the Second Ghetto*.

40. "All-Developing Body for Blight Area Is Urged," *Chicago Tribune*, December 1, 1946, 27, PHN. CPC, *Housing Goals for Chicago* (Chicago: CPC, 1946), 189.

41. Martin Kennelly, "For Slum Clearance," *Commerce* (October 1947): 26, 28.

42. Some of the committee's members, most notably the CREB's Ferd Kramer, and the MHPC's Detlef Mackelmann, would become key players in the coalition that planned and redeveloped the city's blighted districts after 1945.

43. "Mayer Reports Civic Progress in Full Stride," *Chicago Tribune*, January 23, 1941, 21, PHN.

44. Werthamer, "Private Planning for Urban Redevelopment," 87–90.

45. Leland Forrester, "Spur New Move for Rebuilding of Slum Areas," *Chicago Tribune*, December 8, 1940, 1, PHN. The congress was created in 1938 by the city's building companies. At its organizational meeting in December, Elmer Jensen reminded the audience

that "large areas of our city . . . have been and are being blighted. Out of this blight, slums have been created. This city cannot continue to properly grow and develop until practical methods have been found to correct this situation." Chicago Building Congress, *Diamond Jubilee Book, 1938–2013* (Chicago, 2013), 13.

46. New York was the first state to pass urban renewal legislation in 1941, followed by several others, including Illinois. By 1948, twenty-five had similar laws. Although they varied from state to state, the laws "authorized the creation of locally chartered organizations with the authority to condemn and clear blighted areas that would then be privately redeveloped." Pritchett, "'Public Menace' of Blight," 31.

47. Illinois was not alone in creating a redevelopment act. In 1945, Wisconsin passed the Blighted Area Act (Wisc. Stat. § 66.406). As in Illinois, the act linked blight and urban renewal and established public-private partnerships to coordinate redevelopment. Milwaukee Redevelopment Coordinating Committee, *Blight Elimination and Urban Redevelopment in Milwaukee* (Milwaukee: Redevelopment Coordinating Committee, 1948). Wisconsin's act was very similar to the Illinois one of 1947.

48. Kennelly, "For Slum Clearance."

49. Quoted in "All-Developing Body for Blight Area," 27.

50. For a detailed discussion of the role of the CLCC in industrial redevelopment, see chapter 5. For an overview of the 1947 act, see CPC, *Study of Blighted Vacant Land* (Chicago: CPC, 1950), 7–10.

51. Greer, *Urban Renewal and American Cities*, 3–34.

52. Robert Lewis, *Calculating Property Relations: Chicago's Wartime Industrial Mobilization, 1940–1950* (Athens: University of Georgia Press, 2016).

53. Robert Garrabrant, *Redevelopment for Industrial Use*, Technical Bulletin 25 (Washington, DC: Urban Land Institute, May 1955). For other similar reports, see Bureau of Municipal Research and Pennsylvania Economy League, *An Approach to Philadelphia's Industrial Renewal Problem* (Philadelphia: Bureau of Municipal Research and Pennsylvania Economy League, 1956); Detroit City Plan Commission, *Industrial Renewal: A Comparative Study of the Tendency toward Obsolescence and Deterioration in Major Industrial Areas in the City of Detroit*, Master Plan Technical Report, 2nd Series (Detroit: Detroit City Plan Commission, March 1956); Arthur D. Little, Inc., *The Usefulness of Philadelphia's Industrial Plant: An Approach to Industrial Renewal* (Cambridge, MA: A. D. Little, 1960); Milwaukee Redevelopment Coordinating Committee, *Blight Elimination and Urban Redevelopment*.

54. American Society of Planning Officials, *Industrial Renewal Research*, Information Report 104 (Chicago: American Society of Planning Officials, November 1957), 21.

55. In the quarter of a century after World War II, most commenters focused on the need to build modern industrial space on blighted residential or mixed-use areas in the central city. The suburbs were not mentioned. It would only be in the late 1960s that some of the older industrial suburbs turned their attention to industrial redevelopment.

56. "Lyon Tells Problem Facing Cities: Rates of Growth Shows Decline in the Recent Years," *Chicago Tribune*, March 28, 1943, 20, PHN.

57. Leverett Lyon, "Economic Problems of American Cities," typescript, 1942, 5, folder 1, box 51, Chicago Association of Commerce and Industry collection, Chicago History Museum.

58. CPC, *Industrial and Commercial Background for Planning Chicago* (Chicago: CPC, 1942), 2.

59. "All-Developing Body for Blight Area," 27.

60. Metropolitan Housing Council, "Critique of the Preliminary Comprehensive City Plan of Chicago," typescript, December 23, 1946, 6, MPC records. The committee included, among others, Howard E. Green (chair), Milton Mumford, and Louis Wirth.

61. "All-Developing Body for Blight Area," 27.

62. CPC to Elizabeth Wood and Ira Bach, December 2, 1949, file 4612, box 545, MPC records. The West Central industrial district will be discussed in detail in chapter 6.

63. These early 1950s publications are discussed in some length in chapter 5.

64. Knight, "Blighted Areas and Their Effects."

65. Martin Bulmer, *The Chicago School of Sociology: Institutionalization, Diversity and the Rise of Sociological Research* (Chicago: University of Chicago Press, 1984).

66. Garrabrant, *Redevelopment for Industrial Use*, 3.

67. Dean Swartzel, "Memorandum on Urban Renewal," typescript, March 13, 1958, 1, file 4609, box 545, MPC records.

68. Leo Reeder, "The Central Area of Chicago—a Re-Examination of the Process of Decentralization," *Land Economics* 28 (1952): 370.

69. Raymond Fales and Leon Moses, "Land-Use Theory and the Spatial Structure of the Nineteenth-Century City," *Papers of the Regional Science Association* 28 (1972): 49–80; John McDonald, *Employment Location and Industrial Land Use in Metropolitan Chicago* (Champaign, IL: Stipes, 1984). For a discussion of paradigms in location theory, see Trevor Barnes, "The Rise (and Decline) of an American Regional Science: Lessons for the New Economic Geography," *Journal of Economic Geography* 4 (2004): 107–29. Ernest Burgess was not opposed to numerical compilation. Indeed, he took advantage of data gathered by the Census Bureau to examine city neighborhoods. Overall, though, Burgess's scholarly propensity tended to textual description rather than numerical analysis. For more on the intersection of postwar expertise and blight, see Carriere, "Chicago, the South Side Planning Board"; Joseph Heathcott, "'The Whole City Is Our Laboratory': Harland Bartholomew and the Production of Urban Knowledge," *Journal of Planning History* 4 (2005): 332–35.

70. Lewis, *Calculating Property Relations*.

71. David A. Schultz, *Property, Power, and American Democracy* (New Brunswick, NJ: Transaction, 1992), 2.

72. Pritchett, "'Public Menace' of Blight." For a discussion of the social and racial impact of this type of property transfer in Chicago, see Hirsch, *Making the Second Ghetto*.

73. Eugene Jacobs and Jack Levine, "Redevelopment: Making Misused and Disused Land Available and Usable," *Hastings Law Journal* 8 (1957): 241–59; Daniel Mandelker, "Public Purpose in Urban Redevelopment," *Tulane Law Review* 28 (1953–54): 96–117.

74. Schultz, *Property, Power*, 81.

75. Schultz, 81–82; Pritchett, "'Public Menace' of Blight," 34–37.

76. Some decisions are *Zurn v. City of Chicago*, 1945; *People ex rel. Tuohy v. City of Chicago*, 1946; *Chicago Land Clearance Commission v. White*, 1952; *People ex rel. Gutknecht v. City of Chicago*, 1953; *People ex rel. Adamowski v. Chicago Land Clearance Commission*, 1958; *City of Chicago v. Barnes*, 1964. James Costello, "Challenging the Right to Condemn," *University of Illinois Law Forum* 1966 (1966): 52–68.

77. Vacant land was "an undeveloped urban area of more than one acre, in which the ownership of lots is divided among two or more persons, and on which unpaid taxes and special assessment exceed the fair cash value of the land." "A Law to Redeem Busted Subdivisions," *Chicago Tribune*, April 2, 1949, 16, PHN.

78. "Law Is Upheld to Buy Vacant Land," *Chicago Tribune*, May 8, 1952, 2, PHN.

79. "It's Pulaski Rd., Not Crawford, Court Decision," *Chicago Tribune*, November 21, 1952, B8, PHN; "Supreme Court Denies Plea of Brinks' Slayer," *Chicago Tribune*, March 24, 1953, 15, PHN.

80. Anthony Pauletto, "Eminent Domain," *University of Illinois Law Forum* 1958 (1958): 477–80; "Land Clearing Unit Accused of Illegality," *Chicago Tribune*, June 7, 1956, A6, PHN.

4. INDUSTRIAL PROPERTY AND BLIGHT IN THE 1950S

1. R. W. Anderson, "Driving an Industry Out of Chicago," *Chicago Tribune*, September 30, 1953, 20, Proquest Historical Newspapers (hereafter PHN). Anderson's affiliation is unknown.

2. Anderson.

3. CPC, *A Study of Blighted Vacant Land* (Chicago: CPC, 1950); CPC, *Redevelopment for Industry: Statement on the Clearance of Blighted Areas for Industrial Use* (Chicago: CPC, 1951); CPC, *Chicago Industrial Study: Summary Report* (Chicago: CPC, 1952).

4. As noted in an earlier chapter, the calculative politics of redevelopment was imbued with race and class. The postindustrial vision that sought to bring middle-class whites back to the city excluded industry. Arnold Hirsch, *Making the Second Ghetto: Race and Housing in Chicago, 1940–1960* (Chicago: University of Chicago Press, 1983); Joel Rast, "Creating a Unified Business Elite: The Origins of the Chicago Central Area Committee," *Journal of Urban History* 37 (2011): 583–605; Gregory Squires, Larry Bennett, Kathleen McCourt, and Philip Nyden, *Chicago: Race, Class and the Response to Urban Decline* (Philadelphia: Temple University Press, 1987), 153–65; Marc Weiss and John Metzger, "Planning for Chicago: The Changing Politics of Metropolitan Growth and Neighborhood Development," in *Atop the Urban Hierarchy*, ed. Robert Beauregard (Totowa, NJ: Rowman & Littlefield, 1989), 126–27.

5. CPC, "Reasons for a Chicago Metropolitan Area Industrial Land Use Survey," typescript, April 13, 1950, 1, 2, file 4094, box 493, Metropolitan Planning Council records, Special Collections and University Archives, University of Illinois at Chicago (hereafter MPC records).

6. The strongest statement of this can be found in CPC, *Redevelopment for Industry*, 7–8. Chapter 5 provides a detailed discussion of the CLCC's role in industrial redevelopment in the 1950s.

7. For an examination of the "expertise" of one of the United States' leading twentieth-century planners, see Joseph Heathcott, "'The Whole City Is Our Laboratory': Harland Bartholomew and the Production of Urban Knowledge," *Journal of Planning History* 4 (2005): 332–35.

8. Other more junior researchers would also play a role in the making of the reports. One was Albert Ballert, who worked for the CPC for several years after receiving his PhD from the University of Chicago and before going to work for the Great Lakes Commission in 1956. Another was Jack Meltzer, who worked with several Chicago planning organizations in the 1950s and 1960s.

9. Aschman also worked on some important Chicago projects, such as the Central Area Committee plan, and published a coauthored book with Richard Nelson, *Real Estate and City Planning* (Englewood Cliffs, NJ: Prentice-Hall, 1957).

10. Robert Beauregard, "More than Sector Theory: Homer Hoyt's Contributions to Planning Knowledge," *Journal of Planning History* 6 (2007): 248–71; Homer Hoyt, *One Hundred Years of Land Values in Chicago: The Relationship of the Growth of Chicago to the Rise of Its Land Values, 1830–1933* (Chicago: University of Chicago, 1933); Homer Hoyt, *The Structure and Growth of Residential Areas in American Cities* (Washington, DC: Federal Housing Administration, 1939). In the early 1950s, Hoyt made economic surveys for Arlington and Fairfax Counties, both in Virginia, the Passaic-Bergen district, New Jersey, and the state of New Jersey.

11. Homer Hoyt, *Industrial Redevelopment for Chicago* (report prepared for the housing and redevelopment coordinator and the CLCC, Chicago, June 1951, Municipal Reference Collection, Harold Washington Library Center, Chicago). The report's content and its impact on industrial redevelopment in Chicago are discussed in chapter 5.

12. The Society of Industrial Realtors specializes in the marketing of industrial proper-ties and is part of the National Association of Real Estate Boards. It was organized in 1941.

13. The 1946 issue was called *Survey of Industrial Development*. The name of this pub-lication changed several times after 1946 and continued through into the 1960s.

14. "Engineers' Society Votes Approval of State Housing Bill," *Chicago Tribune*, Octo-ber 11, 1932, 6, PHN; "Factory Chiefs to Hear Army's Plan for War," *Chicago Tribune*, November 5, 1939, B8, PHN; "Form Citizens Group on New Building Code," *Chicago Tribune*, June 25, 1948, 20, PHN.

15. CPC, *Study of Blighted Vacant Land*; CPC, *Redevelopment for Industry*; CPC, *Chi-cago Industrial Study*.

16. For a useful discussion of bounding and naming on a quite different topic, see Garth Myers, "Naming and Placing the Other: Power and the Urban Landscape in Zanzi-bar," *Tijdschrift voor Economische en Sociale Geografie* 87 (1996): 237–46.

17. CPC, *Study of Blighted Vacant Land*, iii.

18. CPC, 1.

19. CPC, *Redevelopment for Industry*, n.p.

20. Only 207 acres of vacant land was north of Madison Street, and another 1,276 acres was between Madison and Ninety-Fifth Street. The vast majority—3,740 acres—was located south of Ninety-Fifth Street, mostly in the Lake Calumet area.

21. CPC, *Redevelopment for Industry*, 3–5; "A Quarter-Century of Progress in Plant Buildings," *Factory* 117 (May 1959): 66–68; Loren Trimble, "Pacesetter to the Nation: Greater Chicago's Industry Surges in the Post-War Era," *Realty and Building*, January 26, 1957, 13–18.

22. CPC, *Study of Blighted Vacant Land*, 11–22; CPC, *Redevelopment for Industry*, 6.

23. Quoted in "Show How City Can Turn Slum into a Utopia," *Chicago Tribune*, May 29, 1951, B10, PHN.

24. CPC, *Redevelopment for Industry*, 7.

25. MHPC, "For Release," typescript, September 16, 1951, file 4414, box 524, series III, subseries B, MPC records.

26. CPC, *Recommended Policies for Redevelopment in Chicago* (Chicago: CPC, 1954), 8.

27. "Group Tackles Clearing Slums of South Side," *Chicago Tribune*, September 8, 1946, S2, PHN; Shirley Werthamer, "Private Planning for Urban Redevelopment: An Analysis of the South Side Planning Board of Chicago, 1947" (MA thesis, University of Chicago, 1947), 2–7; Michael Carriere, "Chicago, the South Side Planning Board and the Search for (Further) Order: Toward an Intellectual Lineage of Urban Renewal in Postwar America," *Journal of Urban History* 39 (2012): 411–32.

28. Carriere, "Chicago, the South Side Planning Board," 425.

29. SSPB, "An Opportunity for Industrial Investment in Rebuilding Chicago, Prelimi-nary Draft," typescript, January 27, 1949, 3–5, folder 4132, box 497, MPC records.

30. William E. Hill, "An Effective Community Relations Program for the South Side Planning Board," typescript, March 4, 1948, folder 4132, box 497, MPC records.

31. Carriere, "Chicago, the South Side Planning Board."

32. Quoted in "Group Tackles Clearing Slums."

33. Carriere, "Chicago, the South Side Planning Board."

34. Thomas Buck, "Plan Revealed for Rebuilding S. Central Area," *Chicago Tribune*, November 9, 1947, S1, PHN.

35. Rudolph Unger, "Buildings Rise in Near South Area of Blight," *Chicago Tribune*, August 2, 1956, S1, PHN.

36. For more, see Hirsch, *Making the Second Ghetto*, 100–134; Larry Bennett, Kathleen McCourt, Philip Nyden, and Gregory Squires, "Chicago North Loop Redevelopment Proj-ect: A Growth Machine on Hold," in *Business Elites and Urban Redevelopment*, ed. Scott

Cummings (Albany: State University of New York Press, 1988), 183–202; Squires et al., *Chicago*, 102–9, 157–69; Henry A. Neil, "Chicago Land Clearance Commission" (MA thesis, University of Chicago, 1952), 22–24; Joel Rast, "Regime Building, Institution Building: Urban Renewal Policy in Chicago, 1946–1962," *Journal of Urban Affairs* 31 (2009): 173–94; Rast, "Creating a Unified Business Elite."

37. Rast, "Creating a Unified Business Elite," 588–93; "Rebuilding Plan for South Side Area Submitted," *Chicago Tribune*, October 27, 1947, 6, PHN; Robert Howard, "Favor New Body to Consolidate Rail Terminals," *Chicago Tribune*, November 3, 1949, 4, PHN.

38. Raymond Spaeth and Reginald Isaacs, "SSPB Industrial Study," typescript, December 1948, folder 22, box 3, American Society of Planning Officials, Chicago records, Special Collections and University Archives, University of Illinois at Chicago (hereafter ASPO records).

39. Wilford Winholtz to Council of the South Side Planning Board, typescript, September 27 1948, folder 22, box 3, ASPO records.

40. SSPB, "Opportunity for Industrial Investment," 6.

41. Spaeth and Isaacs, "SSPB Industrial Study," 2, 3.

42. Evert Kinkaid and Associates, *A Program for the Rezoning of Chicago* (Chicago, May 1952), 3–4, box 7, file 5, subject files, Harry F. Chaddick Papers, DePaul University Special Collections and Archives.

43. John Dyckman, *Planned Industrial Development for Chicago* (Chicago: South Side Industrial Study Committee, 1949), 19–62.

44. Spaeth and Isaacs, "SSPB Industrial Study," 2.

45. SSPB, "Opportunity for Industrial Investment."

46. Wilford Winholtz to Business Manager, March 30, 1949, folder 4132, box 497, MPC records.

47. For a detailed discussion of the CLCC's industrial program, see the following chapter.

48. "Subsidies for Factory Builders," *Chicago Tribune*, April 13, 1951, 18, PHN.

49. SSPB, "An Opportunity for Industrial Investment in Rebuilding Chicago," typescript, February 1953, folder 28, box 3, ASPO records. This draft was the basis for the formal report published three months later. *An Opportunity to Rebuild Chicago through Industrial Development on the Central South Side* (Chicago: SSPB, May 1953).

50. "Air Lab Today on South Side Industry Boost" *Chicago Tribune*, May 14, 1953, S1, PHN.

51. SSPB, "Opportunity for Industrial Investment," February 1953, 1.

52. SSPB, 7–11.

53. SSPB, 20.

54. "Big Industrial Area Proposed on Near S. Side," *Chicago Tribune*, May 15, 1953, B17, PHN.

55. Morris Hirsh, "Report of Executive Director," typescript, January 1955, folder 28, box 3, ASPO records; SSPB, "Minutes of Meeting," typescript, January 12, 1955, folder 28, box 3, ASPO records. It is unclear why the CLCC was resistant. There is no discussion about this in the CLCC or the SSPB records.

56. Joel Rast, *Remaking Chicago: The Political Origins of Urban Industrial Change* (DeKalb: Northern Illinois University Press, 1999), 30; Rast, "Creating a Unified Business Elite," 590; Larry Bennett, *The Third City: Chicago and American Urbanism* (Chicago: University of Chicago Press, 2010), 39–41; CPC, *Development Plan for the Central Area of Chicago: A Definitive Text for Use with Graphic Presentation* (Chicago: CPC, 1958).

57. Barbara Flint, "Zoning and Residential Segregation: A Social and Physical History, 1910–1940" (PhD diss., University of Chicago, 1977); Andrew King, "Law and Land Use in Chicago: A Prehistory of Modern Zoning" (PhD diss., University of Wisconsin–Madison, 1976); Robert Lewis, "Modern Industrial Policy and Zoning: Chicago, 1910–1930," *Urban History* 40 (2013): 92–113; Joseph Schwieterman and Dana Caspall, *The Politics of Place:*

A History of Zoning in Chicago (Chicago: Lake Claremont Press, 2006). For a recent overview of US zoning, see Sonia Hirt, *Zoned in the USA: The Origins and Implications of American Land-Use Regulation* (Ithaca, NY: Cornell University Press, 2014), especially 90–177.

58. Metropolitan Housing Council, "Zoning and Zoning Administration in Chicago," typescript, Chicago, July 1, 1938, 18, MPC records.

59. Schwieterman and Caspall, *Politics of Place*, 27–34.

60. Evert Kinkaid and Associates, *Program for the Rezoning of Chicago*, 4.

61. William Clark, "Big Industrial Construction Expected Soon," *Chicago Tribune*, July 14, 1946, A7, PHN; Walter Blucher, quoted in Clayton Kirkpatrick, "Chicago Zoning Law Assailed for Obscurity," *Chicago Tribune*, August 24, 1947, 1, PHN. Also see Schwieterman and Caspall, *Politics of Place*, 38–44.

62. Robert Boylan, "History of Chicago Zoning," typescript, January 3, 1989, box 7, file 2, subject files, Harry F. Chaddick Papers, DePaul University Special Collections and Archives; Schwieterman and Caspall, *Politics of Place*, 38–44.

63. Spaeth and Isaacs, "SSPB Industrial Study," 2.

64. Alfred Bettman, "Constitutionality of Zoning," *Harvard Law Review* 37 (1924): 840.

65. Chicago Association of Commerce and Industry, *The Chicago Association of Commerce and Industry Report for 1947* (Chicago: Chicago Association of Commerce and Industry, 1948), 49. Beginning in 1947 the association worked with the city council to study and overhaul the zoning laws. This work fed into the 1957 revisions.

66. King, "Law and Land Use," 416–17.

67. Al Chase, "Mid-City Links Bought as Site for Big Plant," *Chicago Tribune*, August 8, 1952, C7, PHN.

68. Gladys Priddy, "Battle Rages over Mid-City Factory Plan," *Chicago Tribune*, June 14, 1953, N2, PHN; Chase, "Mid-City Links."

69. Dorothy Muncy, "Land for Industry—a Neglected Problem," *Harvard Business Review* 32 (1954): 52.

70. Richard Babcock, "Classification and Segregation among Zoning Areas," *University of Illinois Law Forum*, Issue 2 (Summer 1954): 186–212.

71. S. C. Josephsen, "Factory vs. Residents," *Chicago Tribune*, October 5, 1953, 24, PHN.

72. Fleck quoted in William Pilkenton, "Seek to Halt Factory Use by Rezoning," *Chicago Tribune*, September 27, 1953, N-A6, PHN.

73. Welsh quoted in Pilkenton.

74. Priddy, "Battle Rages over Mid-City Factory Plan."

75. Gladys Priddy, "Bodine Suit Hits Mid-City Rezoning Act," *Chicago Tribune*, December 10, 1953, N-A1, PHN.

76. "Judge Strikes Family Zoning of Bodine Site," *Chicago Tribune*, July 7, 1955, N1, PHN; "Bodine Wins; City Can't Buy Street Back," *Chicago Tribune*, July 26, 1955, N1, PHN.

77. "Electric Firm Builds a New Disputed Plant," *Chicago Tribune*, February 2, 1956, N1, PHN. The company planned to retain about ten acres of the thirty-two rezoned and sell the remainder to other industries, which it did in 1958 (to a packaged soup maker) and 1959 (to WGN radio and television station). "Wyler Obtains Big Tract for New Building," *Chicago Tribune*, June 12, 1958, D7, PHN; "WGN, Inc. Seeks 12 Acre Tracts for Expansion," *Chicago Tribune*, December 19, 1959, C7, PHN.

78. Flint, "Zoning and Residential Segregation," 142–43.

79. Hirsch, *Making the Second Ghetto*; Rast, "Creating a Unified Business Elite."

5. INDUSTRIAL RENEWAL AND LAND CLEARANCE

1. Ira Bach to N. A. Owings, March 11, 1954, 1, file 4, box 31, Fort Dearborn Project records, Special Collections and University Archives, University of Illinois at Chicago (hereafter UICSC).

2. CLCC, "Report to the Mayor of the City of Chicago by the Land Clearance Commission on Its Consolidation into the Department of Urban Renewal" (Chicago, CLCC, 1961), Municipal Reference Collection, Harold Washington Library Center, Chicago (hereafter MRC), 1–2; Henry A. Neil, "The Chicago Land Clearance Commission" (MA thesis, University of Chicago, 1952), 1–16.

3. Neil, "Chicago Land Clearance Commission," 17.

4. Arnold Hirsch, *Making the Second Ghetto: Race and Housing in Chicago, 1940–1960* (Chicago: University of Chicago Press, 1983), 100–134; Amanda Seligman, *Block by Block: Neighborhoods and Public Policy on Chicago's West Side* (Chicago: University of Chicago Press, 2005); Gregory Squires, Larry Bennett, Kathleen McCourt, and Philip Nyden, *Chicago: Race, Class and the Response to Urban Decline* (Philadelphia: Temple University Press, 1987), 102–9, 158–59; Neil, "Chicago Land Clearance Commission," 22–24; Joel Rast, "Regime Building, Institution Building: Urban Renewal Policy in Chicago, 1946–1962," *Journal of Urban Affairs* 31 (2009): 173–94.

5. D. Bradford Hunt, *Blueprint for Disaster: The Unraveling of Chicago Public Housing* (Chicago: University of Chicago Press, 2009), 67–82; Hirsch, *Making the Second Ghetto*, 100–134; Squires et al., *Chicago*, 102–9; Roger Biles, *Big City Boss in Depression and War: Mayor Edward J. Kelly of Chicago* (DeKalb: Northern Illinois University Press, 1984); Neil, "Chicago Land Clearance Commission," 17–31.

6. Squires et al., *Chicago*, 155; Joel Rast, "Creating a Unified Business Elite: The Origins of the Chicago Central Area Committee," *Journal of Urban History* 37 (2011): 585–86; Neil, "Chicago Land Clearance Commission," 17–31.

7. The two reports that recommended government intervention are "Interim Report on Post War Planning and Housing," typescript, February 2, 1944, file 4349, box 518, series III, subseries B, Metropolitan Planning Council Records, Special Collections and University Archives, University of Illinois at Chicago (hereafter MPC), and Henry Heald, *Reclaiming Chicago's Blighted Areas* (Chicago: Metropolitan Housing Council, October 17, 1946). Heald set out the four-point program for the operation of the land clearance agencies that was taken up by the CLCC. Neil, "Chicago Land Clearance Commission," 21–24.

8. Neil, "Chicago Land Clearance Commission," 24–27; Thomas Buck, "Green Proposes New Program in Housing Crisis," *Chicago Tribune*, April 8, 1947, 7, PHN.

9. Hirsch, *Making the Second Ghetto*, 112.

10. Neil, "Chicago Land Clearance Commission," 7.

11. This is a point made by Michael Carriere in "Chicago, the South Side Planning Board and the Search for (Further) Order: Toward an Intellectual Lineage of Urban Renewal in Postwar America," *Journal of Urban History* 39 (2012): 411–32. The act took over renewal from the CHA, which until then had been the city's main redeveloper. Hunt, *Blueprint for Disaster*, 82.

12. MHPC, "Recommendation to the Land Clearance Commission," January 23, 1948, file 4617, box 546, series III, subseries B, MPC.

13. MHPC.

14. MHPC, "Minutes of the Meeting of the Redevelopment Committee," August 9, 1950, file 4, box 530A, series III, subseries B, MPC.

15. "Resume of the Meeting of the Redevelopment Committee," October 11, 1950, box 4, file 530A, series III, subseries B, MPC.

16. Ira Bach, "Present Status and Recommendations on the Commission Program," typescript, March 3, 1951, box 1, file 3, Chicago Land Clearance Commission Series, Robert S. Gruhn Papers, DePaul University Special Collections and Archives.

17. Bach, 8.

18. CLCC, "Minutes of a Special Meeting of the Chicago Land Clearance Commission," February 22, 1950, MRC. The Western Society of Engineers was established in Chicago

in 1869 and was an extremely active professional organization that worked assiduously to further Chicago's industrial matters.

19. Housing and Home Finance Agency, "A Guide to Slum Clearance and Urban Redevelopment Under Title I of the Housing Act of 1949," July 1950, box 258, General Subject Files, 1949–1960, Urban Renewal Administration, General Records of the Department of Housing and Urban Development, 1931–2003, record group 207, National Archives at College Park, Maryland (hereafter NARA-CP).

20. CLCC, "Minutes of a Regular Meeting of the Chicago Land Clearance Commission," May 24, 1950, MRC.

21. CLCC, "Minutes of a Regular Meeting of the Chicago Land Clearance Commission," August 9, 1950, MRC.

22. American Society of Planning Officials, *Industrial Renewal Research*, Information Report 104 (Chicago: American Society of Planning Officials, November 1957), 27.

23. Robert Garrabrant, *Redevelopment for Industrial Use* (Washington, DC: Urban Land Institute, 1955), 25; Arthur D. Little Inc., *The Usefulness of Philadelphia's Industrial Plant: An Approach to Industrial Renewal* (Cambridge, MA: A. D. Little, 1960); Society of Industrial Realtors, Urban Advisory Committee, *Urban Renewal and the Real Estate Market* (Washington, DC: Society of Industrial Realtors, 1964). A search through the Urban Renewal Administration records unearthed very little other than reference to an industrialist who showed interest in Akron's first renewal project in 1958. "Industrial Firm Shows Interest in Renewal Land," *URC Newsgram* 1, no. 5 (July 1958), box 322, General Subject Files, 1949–1960, Urban Renewal Administration, General Records of the Department of Housing and Urban Development, 1931–2003, record group 207, NARA-CP.

24. CLCC, *Report for 1950* (Chicago, CLCC, 1951), n.p., MRC.

25. CLCC, "Analysis and Recommendations on the Blighted Areas Bounded by Polk Street, Roosevelt Road, Canal Street and the Proposed South Route of the Expressway System, Proposed Redevelopment Project No. 3," typescript, February 19, 1951, 27, 28, my emphasis, MRC. Also see Carriere, "Chicago, the South Side Planning Board," for a similar case.

26. "Subsidies for Factory Builders," *Chicago Tribune*, April 13, 1951, 18, Proquest Historical Newspapers (hereafter PHN).

27. "Push Chicago Improvements, Industry Urged," *Chicago Tribune*, December 2, 1951, A6, PHN.

28. Betty Savesky, *Chicago: New Life for a Sick Heart* (Chicago: Chicago Association of Commerce and Industry, 1952), n.p.

29. George Dovenmuehle to William Murphy, October 1, 1951, file 4414, box 524, series III, subseries B, MPC.

30. Dovenmuehle to Murphy.

31. Homer Hoyt, "Industrial Redevelopment for Chicago" (report prepared for the Housing and Redevelopment Coordinator and the CLCC, June 1951), MRC.

32. Hoyt, 3.

33. Hoyt, 11.

34. CLCC, *Report to Chicagoans, 1947–1952* (Chicago: CLCC, 1953), 12.

35. "Land Clearing Unit Accused of Illegality," *Chicago Tribune*, June 7, 1956, A6, PHN; Anthony Pauletto, "Eminent Domain," *University of Illinois Law Forum* 1958 (1958): 477–80; James Costello, "Challenging the Right to Condemn," *University of Illinois Law Forum* 1966 (1966): 52–68.

36. Redeeming Blighted Vacant Land," *Chicago Tribune*, June 11, 1956, 24, PHN.

37. "Court Upholds Land Tax Sale '55 Amendment," *Chicago Tribune*, June 28, 1957, 2, PHN.

38. Wendell Pritchett, "The 'Public Menace' of Blight: Urban Renewal and the Private Uses of Eminent Domain," *Yale Law and Policy Review* 21 (2003): 22–47.

39. CLCC, "Minutes of a Regular Meeting of the Chicago Land Clearance Commission," March 28, 1951, MRC.

40. Al Chase, "Clearing Buys 148 Acres for Factory Sites," *Chicago Tribune*, December 17, 1950, A7, PHN. For an examination of the Clearing district before 1940, see Robert Lewis, "Planned Industrial Districts in Chicago: Firms, Networks and Boundaries," *Journal of Planning History* 3 (2004): 29–49.

41. "Summary of Program Review Committee Meeting," May 14, 1952, folder: Program Review, January–June 1952, box 273, General Subject Files, 1949–1960, Urban Renewal Administration, General Records of the Department of Housing and Urban Development, 1931–2003, record group 207, NARA-CP.

42. CLCC, "Minutes of a Regular Meeting of the Chicago Land Clearance Commission," June 9, 1954, MRC.

43. "Group to Begin Work to Clear Blighted Area: District Near Loop to be Affected," *Chicago Tribune*, August 3, 1952, W1, PHN.

44. CLCC, "Site Designation Report for Slum and Blighted Area Redevelopment Project Roosevelt-Clinton," December 12, 1955, 3, MRC.

45. CLCC, "Site Designation Report for Slum and Blighted Area Redevelopment Project Lake-Maplewood," September 12, 1956; CLCC, "Site Designation Report for Slum and Blighted Area Redevelopment Project Lake-California," September 12, 1956, MRC.

46. "Florsheim Shoe Will Construct 7 Story Plant," *Chicago Tribune*, October 12, 1947, W3, PHN; "This Company Stayed in the City," *Factory Management and Maintenance* 108 (April 1950): B78–79. The company had made shoes at this site since the turn of the century. Established in 1892 in Chicago, Florsheim had been bought by the International Shoe Company in 1953. "Florsheim Shoe Company," *International Directory of Company Histories* (Farmington Hills, MI: Thomson Gale, 2006), Encyclopedia.com, http://www.encyclopedia.com/doc/1G2-2841300084.html.

47. "Work to Start on Florsheim Warehouse," *Chicago Tribune*, April 17, 1957, B7, PHN. See also "O. K. Sale of Three Plots in Industrial District," *Chicago Tribune*, December 6, 1956, W2, PHN; Erwin Bach, "Dedicate Industrial Site Developed on West Side," *Chicago Tribune*, June 6, 1957, W3, PHN; "City Cleans Up Near West Side for Modern Industry: Builders to Spend 10 Million on Factories," *Chicago Tribune*, January 2, 1958, W2, PHN.

48. CLCC, *Report for 1951*, 14 (Chicago: CLCC, 1952), MRC.

49. CLCC, "Redevelopment Project No. 3. A Report to the Mayor and City Council of the City of Chicago and to the Illinois State Housing Board on a Proposal to Redevelop a Blighted Area on the Near West Side," June 1, 1951, MRC.

50. CLCC.

51. CLCC, "Analysis and Recommendations on the Blighted Areas," 16.

52. CLCC, "Redevelopment Project No. 3."

53. CLCC.

54. CLCC.

55. CLCC, n.p.

56. CLCC, "Analysis and Recommendations on the Blighted Areas," 12, 13.

57. CLCC, "Redevelopment Project No. 3."

58. N. S. Keith to Gordon Howard, "Preliminary Planning Documents in Support of Capital Grant Applications, UR Ill. 19–0–3(c) Chicago, Project No. 3," May 19, 1952, folder: Program Review, January–June 1952, box 273, General Subject Files, 1949–1960, Urban Renewal Administration, General Records of the Department of Housing and Urban Development, 1931–2003, record group 207; NARA-CP.

59. "Slum Clearing for Industry Use Proposed: Subsidy Plan Would Be Invoked," *Chicago Tribune*, March 23, 1951, B5, PHN.

60. CPC, "Recommendation Concerning Redevelopment Project No. 3 of the Chicago Land Clearance Commission," June 21, 1951, file 4414, box 524, series III, subseries B, MPC.

61. CPC, "Redevelopment Project No. 3 of the Chicago Land Clearance Commission," June 21, 1951, file 4414, box 524, series III, subseries B, MPC.

62. R. J. Walters to John McKinlay, June 29, 1951, file 4414, box 524, series III, subseries B, MPC.

63. Ernest Giovangelo, "Interim Report, October, 1955, through March, 1956, on Near West Side Planning Board Administration of Wieboldt Foundation Grant for Citizen Participation in Community Planning Program," typescript, April 5, 1956, folder 574, box 42; Near West Side Community Committee records, UICSC.

64. Eri Hulbert, "Draft Report for Discussion," typescript, February 21, 1951, folder 568, box 42, Near West Side Community Committee records, UICSC. Neighborhood action is not the focus of this book. For a study of this on Chicago's West Side, see Seligman, *Block by Block.*

65. Eri Hulbert to Dorothy Rubel, c. June 1949, file 4135, box 497, series III, subseries A, MPC.

66. Howard Green to Robert Merriam, September 14, 1951, 2, file 4414, box 524, series III, subseries B, MPC.

67. Neil, "Chicago Land Clearance Commission," 48–57.

68. "Housing Group O.K.'s Project for West Side: Area to Be Cleared for Industries," *Chicago Tribune*, September 18, 1951, A8, PHN.

69. George Dovenmuehle to William Murphy, October 1, 1954, file 4414, box 524, series III, subseries B, MPC.

70. Ira Bach, "Present Status and Recommendations on the Commission Program," revised May 1, 1951, 3, file 5, box 530A, series III, subseries B, MPC.

71. MHPC, "For Release," September 16, 1951, 3, file 4414, box 524, series III, subseries B, MPC.

72. This information was compiled from CLCC minutes of October–December 1951, MRC.

73. CLCC, "Minutes of a Regular Meeting of the Chicago Land Clearance Commission," September 10, 1952, MRC. This was not without its problems, though. "Report of Operations, Region IV, for Period Ending December 15, 1955," folder: Reports, box 297, General Subject Files, 1949–1960, Urban Renewal Administration, General Records of the Department of Housing and Urban Development, 1931–2003, record group 207, NARA-CP.

74. "Land Clearing Plan Approved by City Urged," *Chicago Tribune*, March 23, 1956, 9, PHN.

75. CLCC, "Land Disposition Plan for Slum and Blighted Area Redevelopment Project No. 3," February 8, 1956, 3–6; CLCC, "Redevelopment Plan for Slum and Blighted Area Redevelopment Project No. 3. West Central Industrial Districts," December 12, MRC, 1955.

76. Bach, "Dedicate Industrial Site," W3.

77. Quoted in Erwin Bach, "Clear Slums for 10 Million Industrial Redevelopment: Site of 'Great Fire' to Rise from Rubble Second Time," *Chicago Tribune*, March 7, 1957, W1, PHN.

78. CLCC, "Final Relocation Report Project No. UR ILL. 6–3 (West Central Industrial District)," April 15, 1958, 2, MRC. According to the report, African Americans, Mexicans, and Puerto Ricans were considered by the authors as not being a problem to relocate.

79. "City Council Unit Indorses Merged Renewal Agency," *Chicago Tribune*, May 19, 1961, A4, PHN.

80. "Powerful New Dept. of Urban Renewal Set," *Chicago Tribune*, September 26, 1961, B2, PHN.

81. George Dovenmuehle to Wilfred Sykes, January 30, 1952, folder 4, box 9, Ira Bach Papers, Chicago Historical Museum. Sykes was chairman of the finance committee of

Inland Steel and past president (1941–49) of Inland Steel. As well as his role as chair of the CHA, and had been the president of the Chicago Association of Commerce and Industry (1948–49) and vice president of the National Association of Manufacturers.

82. MHPC, "Memorandum of Meeting," April 15, 1958, file 4609, box 545, MPCs.

83. CLCC, "Report to the Mayor of the City of Chicago," 2; "Model Commission," *Chicago Tribune*, September 30, 1957, 24, PHN.

84. CLCC, "Report to the Mayor," 1–2.

85. "Last Segment of Industrial Area for Sale," *Chicago Tribune*, November 3, 1963, W6, PHN.

86. Sylvia Shepherd, "Government Testing Facilities Set for Urban Renewal Site," *Chicago Tribune*, March 21, 1965, W1, PHN.

87. CLCC, "Progress Report of the Chicago Land Clearance Commission for the Quarter Ended March 31, 1956," folder 31, box 4, Fort Dearborn Project records, UICSC. The subsidy was reduced, as a couple of government institutions (the Chicago Fire Academy and a federal testing laboratory) were built in the district.

6. REINVENTING INDUSTRIAL PROPERTY

1. David Bensman and Roberta Lynch, *Rusted Dreams: Hard Times in a Steel Community* (New York: McGraw-Hill, 1987); Anne Markusen with Joshua Lerner, Wendy Patton, Jean Ross and Judy Schneider, *Steel and Southeast Chicago: Reasons and Opportunities for Industrial Renewal* (Evanston, IL: Northwestern University, 1985); Dominic Pacyga, *Slaughterhouse: Chicago's Union Stock Yard and the World It Made* (Chicago: University of Chicago Press, 2015); Joel Rast, *Remaking Chicago: The Political Origins of Urban Industrial Change* (DeKalb: North Illinois University Press, 1999); Gregory Squires, Larry Bennett, Kathleen McCourt, and Philip Nyden, *Chicago: Race, Class and the Response to Urban Decline* (Philadelphia: Temple University Press, 1987).

2. CACI, *Chicago's New Horizons* (Chicago: CACI, 1957), 52, 78.

3. Jefferson Cowie and Joseph Heathcott, eds., *Beyond the Ruins: The Meanings of Deindustrialization* (Ithaca, NY: Cornell University Press, 2003); Steven High, *Industrial Sunset: The Making of North America's Rust Belt, 1969–1984* (Toronto: University of Toronto Press, 2003); Dewey Grantham, *The South in Modern America: A Region at Odds* (New York: Harper Collins, 1994), 259–80. For Chicago, see chapter 2; Bensman and Lynch, *Rusted Dreams*; Dominic Pacyga, *Chicago: A Biography* (Chicago: University of Chicago Press, 2009), 316–21.

4. CECD, *Mid-Chicago Economic Development Study: Volume I; Policies and Programs Prepared for the Economic Development of Mid-Chicago* (Chicago: CECD, 1966), 4.

5. For a discussion of the relationship between science, defense, and cities see Jennifer Light, *From Warfare to Welfare: Defense Intellectuals and Urban Problems in Cold War America* (Baltimore: Johns Hopkins University Press, 2003); Margaret Pugh O'Mara, *Cities of Knowledge: Cold War Science and the Search for the Next Silicon Valley* (Princeton, NJ: Princeton University Press, 2005).

6. Lewis Hill, in "Report to the Conservation Community Council on the Conference on Industrial Renewal in Lincoln Park—Near Northside," May 14, 1964, 1, folder 6, box 4, Lincoln Park Community Conservation Council records, DePaul University, Special Collections and Archives. The joining of the two agencies was a product of the State of Illinois Urban Renewal Consolidation Act of 1961, which required municipalities to create departments of urban renewal to oversee renewal and to land clearance.

7. Although the CECD was in many ways a successor to the CLCC, the new organization's focus was more clearly trained on economic development and technological innovation than on land clearance and residential redevelopment.

8. Unfortunately, the records of the CECD do not appear to exist. Accordingly, its history rests on assembling material from various other sources.

9. The chapter focuses on the CECD's attempts to protect the industrial property market and to reinvent the industrial landscape. Another feature of the CECD's work, only touched on here, was job creation and training.

10. "Daley Moves to Expand the City Economy," *Chicago Tribune*, May 12, 1961, A1, Proquest Historical Newspapers (hereafter PHN).

11. Paul Zimmerer, in "Report to the Conservation Community Council."

12. CECD, *A Partnership for Action: Mid-Chicago Economic Development Project* (Chicago: CECD, 1970), 4.

13. Kennedy remained head of the CECD until he was appointed secretary of the Treasury. He was replaced by Donald M. Graham, chairman of the Continental Illinois National Bank and Trust Co.

14. David M. Kennedy, "A Sound Position," *Chicago Tribune*, May 25, 1958, G30, PHN. The David M. Kennedy records at Brigham Young University are extensive. Unfortunately, there is little of interest on his work with the CECD; much of the material covers his years as secretary of the Treasury and ambassador to NATO (1972–73).

15. David Kennedy, "Chicago's Contribution to the Nation" in *The Future of Northeastern Illinois* (Chicago: University of Chicago Press, 1962), 92.

16. CECD, *Mid-Chicago Economic Development Study: Volume I*, 4.

17. Gail Radford, *The Rise of the Public Authority: Statebuilding and Economic Development in Twentieth-Century America* (Chicago: University of Chicago Press, 2013).

18. Kennedy, "Sound Position."

19. It resulted in the *Mid-Chicago Economic Development Study*. Also see CECD, *Partnership for Action*.

20. There was no material on the CECD in the relevant departmental records at the National Archives and Records Administration archives in College Park for these grants.

21. "Daley Moves to Expand the City Economy." The initial committee consisted of executives from Hallicrafters, Chicago and North Western Railroad, Standard Oil, US Steel, Illinois Bell, First National Bank of Chicago, Commonwealth Edison, American Telephone and Telegraph, and the Flat Janitors Union.

22. Zimmerer had an economics degree from the London School of Economics. After his resignation in 1976, he taught business management and urban planning at Roosevelt University, and worked in the Cook County Department of Planning and Development.

23. Patricia Walker, "Units Get New Plan Voice," *Chicago Tribune*, February 11, 1968, NW1, PHN.

24. "City Industry Development Unit Enlarged, Gets Rolling," *Chicago Tribune*, May 28, 1976, C9, PHN. The number of people working for the CECD would have been higher when the committee was heavily involved with the federally funded research grants.

25. In some ways, the CECD was a more arm's-length organization than the CLCC, while in others it wasn't. The latter was more typical of public-private partnerships found in the United States' urban districts.

26. See Robert A. Beauregard, "Public-Private Partnerships as Historical Chameleons: The Case of the United States," in *Partnerships in Urban Governance: European and American Experience*, ed. Jon Pierre (Basingstoke: Macmillan, 1998), 60–62; Mark Levine, "The Politics of Partnership: Urban Redevelopment since 1945," in *Unequal Partnerships: The Political Economy of Urban Redevelopment in Postwar America*, ed. Gregory D. Squires (New Brunswick, NJ: Rutgers University Press, 1989), 19–21; Radford, *Rise of the Public Authority*; Mariana Valverde, "Ad Hoc Governance: Public Authorities and North American Local Infrastructure in Historical Perspective" in *Governing Practices: Neoliberalism,*

Governmentality, and the Ethnographic Imaginary, ed. Michelle Brady and Randy Lippert (Toronto: University of Toronto Press, 2016), 199–217.

27. Kennedy, "Chicago's Contribution to the Nation," 88–89.

28. For Chicago's role in the World War II industrial mobilization program, see Robert Lewis, *Calculating Property Relations: Chicago's Wartime Industrial Mobilization, 1940–1950* (Athens: University of Georgia Press, 2016).

29. Anne Markusen, Peter Hall, Scott Campbell, and Sabrina Dietrick, *The Rise of the Gunbelt: The Military Remapping of Industrial America* (New York: Oxford University Press, 1999); Martin Schiesl, "Airplanes to Aerospace: Defense Spending and Economic Growth in the Los Angeles Region, 1945–1960," in *The Martial Metropolis: U.S. Cites in War and Peace*, ed. Roger Lotchin (New York: Praeger, 1984), 135–49; Allen Scott and Doreen Mattingly, "The Aircraft and Parts Industry in Southern California: Continuity and Change From the Inter-War Years to the 1990s," *Economic Geography* 65 (1989): 48–71; Grantham, *The South in Modern America*.

30. "Midwest Told Why It Loses Defense Jobs," *Chicago Tribune*, July 24, 1962, A2, PHN; Thomas Buck, "Chicago Area Renews Efforts to Regain Defense Contract Leadership," *Chicago Tribune*, July 29, 1962, A3, PHN.

31. Richard, J. Daley, "Remarks," in *History, Program, and Proceedings of the Lake Michigan Area Research and Development Defense Contracting Conference*, ed. CECD (Chicago: CECD, October 1962), 8.

32. CECD, *Federal Procurement Assistance Program: A Proposal* (Chicago: CECD, 1965).

33. "Chicago Seeks More Prime Defense Work," *Chicago Tribune*, January 2, 1963, C3, PHN.

34. "Daley Bill Would Spur Industry," *Chicago Tribune*, November 27, 1975, E9, PHN.

35. Roy Gibbons, "Reveal Plans for Space Age Month in City," *Chicago Tribune*, December 19, 1962, A1, PHN.

36. "Firm Urged to Combine in Atomic Bids," *Chicago Tribune*, September 27, 1963, A4, PHN.

37. CECD, *NASA Electronics Research Center in the Chicago Area* (Chicago: CECD, 1963).

38. Nick Poulos, "Plot Chicago Bids for U.S. Science Lab," *Chicago Tribune*, February 27, 1964, D7, PHN.

39. Joslin quote in Buck, "Chicago Area Renews Efforts."

40. The four centers were environment, nuclear propulsion, national data processing and information, and national communications control.

41. Lillian Hoddeson, Adrienne Kolb, and Catherine Westfall, *Fermilab: Physics, the Frontier, and Megascience* (Chicago: University of Chicago Press, 2008), 70–91. See also Catherine Westfall and Lillian Hoddeson, "Thinking Small in Big Science: The Founding of Fermilab, 1960–1972," *Technology and Culture* 37 (1996): 458–66.

42. Ronald Kotulak, "Group Bids for Construction of Gigantic A-Smasher Here," *Chicago Tribune*, May 26, 1965, 12, PHN; "Chicago Bid for 280 Million AEC Project," *Chicago Tribune*, June 16, 1965, C4, PHN. For a discussion of the national site selection process, see Hoddeson, Kolb, and Westfall, *Fermilab*, 71–84. While Hoddeson presents an excellent overview of the national politics, she ignores the CECD's role in the creation of the winning proposal.

43. Ronald Kotulak, "Await State Action on Big Atom Facility," *Chicago Tribune*, June 27, 1965, 12, PHN.

44. Hoddeson, Kolb, and Westfall, *Fermilab*. Besides Weston, the other six were South Barrington just outside of Chicago, Madison, Ann Arbor, Brookhaven National Laboratory, Denver, and Sacramento. The Barrington site was dropped after protests from its well-off population.

45. Ronald Kotulak, "How We Got an A-Smasher," *Chicago Tribune*, December 17, 1966, 1, PHN. There is disagreement about the politics of the locational decision. Catherine

Westfall argues that even if it had been highly politically charged, which she doesn't believe was the case, the choice of Weston was nevertheless made on its merits. In her opinion, the Chicago suburb was an excellent location for the new facility. "The Site Contest of the Fermilab," *Physics Today* 42 (1989): 44–52. For a brief discussion of the lab as a public institution, see Radford, *Rise of the Public Authority*, 136–37.

46. Hoddeson, Kolb, and Westfall, *Fermilab*.

47. See Guian McKee, *The Problem of Jobs: Liberalism, Race, and Deindustrialization in Philadelphia* (Chicago: University of Chicago Press, 2008), for a study of the Philadelphia case.

48. Kennedy, "Chicago's Contribution to the Nation," 8.

49. Walker, "Units Get New Plan Voice."

50. "New Magazine *Chicago* Has Debut Monday," *Chicago Tribune*, July 2, 1964, 12, PHN.

51. It is impossible to know whether *Chicago* was successful or not. Its publication run came to an end in April 1973 without any apparent or at least measurable effects on the local economy.

52. CECD, *Mid-Chicago Economic Development Study: Volume I*, 21–41.

53. "$115,000 Study Planned to Aid City's Growth," *Chicago Tribune*, January 3, 1962, 22, PHN.

54. CECD, *Technological Change, Its Impact on Industry in Metropolitan Chicago: Summary of Need, Opportunity, Recommended Action* (Chicago: Corplan Associates of IIT Research Institute, 1964); "Report Job Training Vital Need of Chicago, *Chicago Tribune*, July 23, 1964, 67, PHN.

55. William Clark, in "Report to the Conservation Community Council," 3; "Seeburg Discards Plan to Move from Chicago," *Chicago Tribune*, November 6, 1963, C7, PHN.

56. "Factory to Rebuild and Add Housing on Near North Side," *Chicago Tribune*, June 9, 1967, 3, PHN.

57. It was claimed that other firms stayed because of the CECD's negotiations with the city on the firm's behalf. Some include Chicago Wheel and Foundry (1101 West Monroe); Gazzolo Drug and Chemical (123 South Green); Chicago Candle (141 West Sixty-Second); and Amco Wire Products (2300 West Carroll). Zimmerer quoted in Walker, "Units Get New Plan Voice."

58. Harold Mayer, *The South Branch Industrial Development District* (Chicago: CECD, August 1965), 19.

59. Quoted in "Seeburg Discards Plan to Move from Chicago."

60. Zimmerer quoted in Walker, "Units Get New Plan Voice." The CECD received Department of Commerce grants in 1963 and 1967 to develop solutions to industrial decline in the Mid-Chicago area.

61. James Coates, "Lower West Side Residents to Seek Industry, Stability," *Chicago Tribune*, April 25, 1968, W1, PHN.

62. Barbara Leahy, "Industries to Be Surveyed," *Chicago Tribune*, April 23, 1967, N3, PHN.

63. CECD, *Partnership for Action*, 5.

64. "Daley Bill Would Spur Industry."

65. This may have been the first time that a Chicago public-private partnership had the authority to use nongovernment financial instruments to rework industrial property.

66. Quoted in "City Industry Development Unit Enlarged." Chaddick created one of the country's largest trucking companies before World War II. He became Chicago's director of zoning in the 1950s and then moved on to land development and the building of regional shopping malls. In the early 1960s, Chaddick purchased an old Ford plant near Midway Airport and converted it into Chicago's first major shopping mall, known as Ford City.

7. INDUSTRIAL PARKS AS INDUSTRIAL RENEWAL

1. Willson is quoted in CACI, "Ten Authorities View Industry Trends," *Third Annual Metropolitan Chicago Industrial Development Guide* (Chicago: CACI, 1969), 48.

2. CACI, 49. An element of the CECD's mission during the 1960s was the building of industrial parks.

3. Robert Boley, *Industrial Districts Restudied: An Analysis of Characteristics* (Washington, DC: Urban Land Institute, 1961), 10–11, 29. Harold Mayer, "Centex Industrial Park: An Organized Industrial District," in *Focus of Geographic Activity: A Collection of Original Studies*, ed. Richard Toman and Donald Patton (New York: McGraw-Hill, 1964), 135–37.

4. Mayer, "Centex Industrial Park," 140–45; "Centex Proves Magnet to Industry," *Chicago Tribune*, September 26, 1965, E1, Proquest Historical Newspapers (hereafter PHN).

5. Hal Barger, "Suburbs Court New Industry as Tax Friend," *Chicago Tribune*, September 2, 1962, N1, PHN; Mayer, "Centex Industrial Park"; "Centex Proves Magnet to Industry."

6. CACI, *Third Annual Metropolitan Chicago Industrial Development Guide*, 49–50.

7. In the nineteenth century, New England mill towns, such as Lowell and Manchester, and company suburbs, such as Pullman, were founded to maintain control over labor and land use. The features of these towns and suburbs were the separation of industrial and residential spaces, the laying down of a street network, and the building of worker housing. These towns and suburbs were precursors to the planned industrial park that appeared in twentieth-century US cities and suburbs.

8. For some of the early writings on the industrial park, see William Lee Baldwin, *A Report on the Dartmouth College Conference on Industrial Parks* (Hanover, NH: Dartmouth College, June 1958), 13–31; Boley, *Industrial Districts Restudied*; Robert Boley, *Industrial Districts: Principles in Practice* (Washington, DC: Land Institute, 1962); Charles Hackett, *An Analysis of Planned Industrial Districts*, Occasional Paper 4 (Seattle: College of Business Administration, University of Washington, June 1956); Michael Jucius, "Industrial Districts of the Chicago Region and Their Influence on Plant Location" (MA thesis, University of Chicago, 1932); Richard Murphy and William Lee Baldwin, "Business Moves to the Industrial Park," *Harvard Business Review* 37 (1959): 79–80; William Mitchell and Michael Jucius, "Industrial Districts of the Chicago Region and Their Influence on Plant Location," *Journal of Business* 6 (1933): 139–56; Robert Wrigley, "Organized Industrial Districts with Special Reference to the Chicago Area," *Journal of Land and Public Utility Economics* 23 (1949): 80–98.

9. Boley, *Industrial Districts Restudied*, 10–11, 29.

10. F. Alexander, "The Making of the Modern Industrial Park: A History of the Central Manufacturing District of Chicago, Illinois" (MA thesis, George Washington University, 1991); Peter Hall, *Cities of Tomorrow* (Oxford: Blackwell, 1996), 122–29; Edward Relph, *The Modern Urban Landscape* (Baltimore: Johns Hopkins University Press, 1987), 62–69.

11. The need to separate industrial and residential areas was first formally enunciated in the 1916 New York City zoning ordinance and then legitimized in the 1926 Supreme Court decision on *Euclid v. Ambler Realty*. The principle of separation between competing land uses that sustained planned industrial districts predates the first zoning ordinance. In 1905, when the first factory was built in the Central Manufacturing District, the promoters worked to separate their firms from the rest of the surrounding metropolitan area by imposing private regulations that excluded all other land uses than those for manufacturing, warehousing, and transportation. Lewis, "Planned Districts"; Hall, *Cities of Tomorrow*; Relph, *Modern Urban Landscape*.

12. Boley, *Industrial Districts Restudied*, 5.

13. Gernot Grabher, "Rediscovering the Social in the Economics of Interfirm Relations, in *The Embedded Firm*, ed. Gernot Grabher (London: Routledge, 1993), 1–31; Robert Lewis, *Manufacturing Montreal: The Making of an Industrial Landscape, 1850 to 1930* (Baltimore: Johns Hopkins University Press, 2000); Peter Maskell and Anders Malmberg, "The Competitiveness of Firms and Regions: 'Ubiquitification' and the Importance of Localized Learning," *European Urban and Regional Studies* 6 (1999): 9–25.

14. Peter Dicken and Anders Malmberg, "Firms in Territories: A Relational Perspective," *Economic Geography* 77 (2001): 345–63; Grabher, "Rediscovering the Social"; Michael Storper and Richard Walker, *The Capitalist Imperative: Territory, Technology and Industrial Growth* (Oxford: Blackwell, 1989).

15. Alexander, "Making of the Modern Industrial Park"; Jucius, "Industrial Districts of the Chicago Region"; Mitchell and Jucius, "Industrial Districts of the Chicago Region."

16. For this history, see Robert Lewis, "Planned Districts in Chicago: Firms, Networks and Boundaries, 1900–1940," *Journal of Planning History* 3 (2004): 29–49.

17. F. Stetson, "The Central Manufacturing District of Chicago," in *Manufacturing and Wholesale Industries of Chicago*, ed. J. Currey (Chicago: Thomas Poole, 1981), 3:440.

18. Illinois Manufacturers' Association, *Manufacturers in Chicago and Metropolitan Area, 1940* (Chicago: Illinois Manufacturers' Association, 1940).

19. The two districts opened up few tracts in the city after 1945. Most of their activity was in the suburbs. Central Manufacturing opened districts in Itasca and Saint Charles. Clearing was more active, opening a tract in Melrose Park (1946), two in Franklin Park (1951, 1956), and another one in Bensenville (1967).

20. CCLC, "Analysis and Recommendations on the Blighted Areas Bounded by Polk Street, Roosevelt Road, Canal Street and the Proposed South Route of the Expressway System, Proposed Redevelopment Project No. 3," Chicago: CLCC, typescript, February 19, 1951, 18, 19. For work that explores the relationship between race and renewal, see Andrew Highsmith, "Demolition Means Progress: Urban Renewal, Local Politics, and State-Sanctioned Ghetto Formation in Flint, Michigan," *Journal of Urban History* 35 (2009): 348–68; Arnold Hirsch, "Massive Resistance in the Urban North: Trumbull Park, Chicago, 1953–1966," *Journal of American History* 82 (1995): 522–50; Amanda Seligman, *Block by Block: Neighborhoods and Public Policy in Chicago's West Side* (Chicago: University of Chicago Press, 2005); Preston Smith II, *Racial Democracy and the Black Metropolis: Housing Policy in Postwar Chicago* (Minneapolis: University of Minnesota Press, 2012).

21. Institute of Urban Life, *Diagnostic Survey of Relocation Problems of Non-Residential Establishments, Roosevelt-Halsted Area* (Chicago: Institute of Urban Life, November 1965), 86–92. The Institute of Urban Life was a subcontractor to Loyola University; it prepared this report as part of a relocation study being done for the DUR.

22. Urban Associates of Chicago, *A Report to the Department of Urban Renewal, City of Chicago on an Evaluation of Industrial Centers in Urban Renewal Areas* (Chicago: Urban Associates of Chicago, 1975), 4–5.

23. Monroe Bowman, *Stockyard Study and Redevelopment Proposal* (Chicago: Department of the City Planning, June 8, 1962). The following quotes are from the report, which is unpaginated. Bowman was very liberal in his use of capitalization in the middle of sentences.

24. This was clear in the association's annual reports. For instance, see CACI, *The Chicago Association of Commerce Report for 1945* (Chicago: CACI, 1946), 53–61.

25. Charles Willson, quoted in CACI, *Chicago's New Horizons* (Chicago: CACI, 1957), 104.

26. Nick Poulos, "Chicago Area Far in US Lead on Industry Contracts," *Chicago Tribune*, June 17, 1962, A1, PHN.

27. Logelin quoted in James Galvin, "Industrial Parks to Ring Loop," *Chicago Tribune*, September 6, 1963, 5, PHN. A map showed seven industrial districts, several of which were the West Side districts created by the Chicago Land Clearance Commission.

28. Alvin Thomas and George Lamp, "A Formidable Diversified Industrial Giant," in CACI, *Third Annual Metropolitan Chicago Industrial Development Guide*, 19, 20, 21.

29. CPC, *Chicago Industrial Study: Summary Report* (Chicago: CPC, 1952).

30. CPC, 54.

31. DUR, *Annual Report, 1967* (Chicago: DUR, 1968), 36–37.

32. Urban Associates of Chicago, *Report to the Department of Urban Renewal*, 4–9.

33. Nick Poulos, "Chicago Area Far in US Lead"; Joseph Ator, "Rail Sites Can Hold Industry in Chicago," *Chicago Tribune*, September 11, 1962, B6, PHN.

34. Lewis, "Planned Districts"; Robert Wrigley, "Organized Industrial Districts with Special Reference to the Chicago Area," *Journal of Land and Public Utility Economics* 23 (1949): 180–98.

35. Norris Willatt, "Industrial Parks," *Barron's*, October 10, 1955, 13–15.

36. Fred Farrar, "Appalachia's Job Creator Invades Cities," *Chicago Tribune*, April 27, 1966, A6, PHN. The predecessor to the EDA was the Area Redevelopment Administration (1961–65). Its purpose was to create new jobs, and encourage industrial and commercial growth in economically distressed areas.

37. "Arvey Corporation to Tell Plans for Riverview," *Chicago Tribune*, December 5, 1968, G1, PHN; "Defers Action on Plan to Buy Riverview Tract," *Chicago Tribune*, December 18, 1969, N8, PHN; "New DeVry School Has Flexibility," *Chicago Tribune*, October 15, 1972, D1, PHN.

38. Michael Millenson, "Old Riverview Park Site Gets Shop Center on 2nd Try," *Chicago Tribune*, June 1980, N-B1D, PHN.

39. Willatt, "Industrial Parks."

40. CECD, *A Partnership for Action: Mid-Chicago Economic Development Project* (Chicago: CECD, 1970), 43, 57. The Northwestern Center for Industry was sometimes called the Northwest Center for Industry.

41. "Inner-City Industrial Park Doing Well," *Chicago Tribune*, February 24, 1974, B1, PHN.

42. Northwestern was one of five industrial parks that received tax and land subsidies under the Chicago 21 Plan. Natalie McKelvey, "5 Industrial Parks Attract Firms," *Chicago Tribune*, September 9, 1978, N-B1Q, PHN. For a discussion of the impacts of the Chicago 21 Plan on industry, see Joel Rast, *Remaking Chicago: The Political Origins of Urban Industrial Change* (DeKalb: Northern Illinois University Press, 1999), 3–34; Joel Rast, "Creating a Unified Business Elite: The Origins of the Chicago Central Area Committee," *Journal of Urban History* 37 (2011): 597–98.

43. Before setting up his own firm, Argiris learned the trade working with two of the city's largest real estate companies, Arthur Rubloff and Company, and Nicholas and Associates.

44. For his ideas, see "Seek City Aid for 10 Industrial Parks," *Chicago Tribune*, February 7, 1971, D, PHN; "Asks City to Raze Blight for Industry," *Chicago Tribune*, March 26, 1972, C1, PHN; David Young, "Industrial Urban Renewal: Way to Keep Jobs in the City," *Chicago Tribune*, May 10, 1972, E6, PHN.

45. CECD, *Mid-Chicago Economic Development Study: Volume I; Policies and Programs Prepared for the Economic Development of Mid-Chicago* (Chicago: CECD, 1966), i.

46. CECD.

47. CECD, 13. The study consisted of two volumes: the first was written by the CECD and the second by a team from the University of Chicago under the direction of Professor Harold Mayer. Volume 2 is a much more conservative document than the first and has little to say about public-private partnerships and industrial parks. It is mostly concerned with finding traditional locational solutions to industrial decline and blighted areas. Most of the recommendations focus on improving the physical conditions for industry in order to entice new firms to replace those moving out. It offers a traditional understanding of

industrial change. CECD, *Mid-Chicago Economic Development Study: Volume II; Technical Analysis and Findings, Economic Development of Mid-Chicago* (Chicago: CECD, 1966).

48. CECD, *Mid-Chicago Economic Development Study: Volume I*, 46.

49. CECD, 6.

50. CECD, 2.

51. CECD, *A Partnership for Action: Mid-Chicago Economic Development Project* (Chicago: CECD, 1970).

52. The other three were industrial conservation, manpower, and commercial development.

53. CECD, *Partnership for Action*, 42.

54. The project was undertaken by the staff of the CECD and financially underwritten by the EDA. Alongside the support for the project staff, the EDA contributed another $11.2 million in public funds and $3.3 million in business loans as of January 1970.

55. CECD, *Partnership for Action*, 5.

56. Zimmerer quoted in "Cities Are Urged to Welcome Development for New Industry," *Chicago Tribune*, August 25, 1968, D1, PHN.

57. Zimmerer quoted in CECD, *Stockyards 1905: Industrial Park 1970* (Chicago: CECD, February 1970), n.p. This six-page document was the CECD's major statement about the industrial park that developed after 1967.

58. Dominic Pacyga in his excellent book on the Stockyards does not discuss the redevelopment plans after the meatpackers started leaving in the 1950s and the closing of the yards themselves in 1971. His story of industrial redevelopment starts when the Stockyards area was established as a tax increment financing site in 1989. He also covers the creation of the Special Service Area tax district in 1991 and more recent attempts to revitalize the area. *Slaughterhouse: Chicago's Union Stock Yard and the World It Made* (Chicago: University of Chicago Press, 2015), 94, 158–66, 178–200. Also see Dominic Pacyga, *Chicago: A Biography* (Chicago: University of Chicago Press 2009), 316–21.

59. Ernest Fuller, "Stock Yards Industrial Park," *Chicago Tribune*, June 6, 1968, C9, PHN.

60. CECD, *Partnership for Action*, 47–51; Stephen Crews, "Industrial Park in Stock Yards to Increase Jobs," *Chicago Tribune*, June 9, 1968, SCL1, PHN; Fuller, "Stock Yards Industrial Park."

61. "New Jobs in the City," *Chicago Tribune*, June 7, 1968, 22, PHN.

62. "Cities Are Urged to Welcome."

63. "Money, Planning Needed for Industrial Park Profit," *Chicago Tribune*, February 15, 1970, D3, PHN; Alvin Nagelberg, "Report Big Industrial Park Will Replace Stock Yards," *Chicago Tribune*, March 12, 1970, D9, PHN.

64. McKelvy, "5 Industrial Parks Attract Firms."

65. By the late 1980s, the city had to throw tax increment funds at the area in another attempt to initiate industrial revitalization. Pacyga, *Slaughterhouse*, 178–200. The fact that there is only one reference in the *Chicago Tribune* to the Stockyards industrial park after 1970 supports the idea that the district did not live up to expectations.

66. Gary Washburn, "Industry Continues Flight from City to Suburbs," *Chicago Tribune*, April 7, 1974, W-B1, PHN.

67. Gregory Squires, Larry Bennett, Kathleen McCourt, and Philip Nyden, *Chicago: Race, Class and the Response to Urban Decline* (Philadelphia: Temple University Press, 1987), 16.

68. John F. McDonald, "An Economic Analysis of Industrial Revenue Bonds and the Demand for Labor," *Annals of Regional Science* 18 (1984): 40.

69. The industrial revenue bond was made possible by the Illinois Industrial Project Revenue Bond Act of 1972.

70. Illinois Advisory Committee to the US Commission on Civil Rights, *Industrial Revenue Bonds: Equal Opportunity in Chicago's Industrial Revenue Bond Program?*

(Washington, DC: Government Printing Office, 1986); Squires et al., *Chicago*, 16, 59; Mac-Donald, "Economic Analysis."

71. The report was described in "Industrial Park Design May Change Radically," *Chicago Tribune*, November 1, 1969, E1, PHN.

72. "Office Park Called a Growing Concept," *Chicago Tribune*, August 5, 1970, E3, PHN.

73. "Industrial Park Design," E1.

CONCLUSION

1. Loren Trimble, "Is Industry Fleeing the City of Chicago," in *Third Annual Metropolitan Chicago Industrial Development Guide*, by Chicago Association of Commerce and Industry (Chicago: Chicago Association of Commerce and Industry, 1969), 14.

2. Arnold Hirsch, *Making the Second Ghetto: Race and Housing in Chicago, 1940–1960* (Chicago: University of Chicago Press, 1983); Larry Bennett, Kathleen McCourt, Philip Nyden, and Gregory Squires, "Chicago North Loop Redevelopment Project: A Growth Machine on Hold," in *Business Elites and Urban Redevelopment*, ed. Scott Cummings (Albany: State University of New York Press, 1988), 183–202; Gregory Squires, Larry Bennett, Kathleen McCourt, and Philip Nyden, *Chicago: Race, Class and the Response to Urban Decline* (Philadelphia: Temple University Press, 1987); Robert Giloth and John Betancur, "Where Downtown Meets Neighborhood: Industrial Displacement in Chicago, 1978–1987," *Journal of the American Planning Association* 54 (1988): 279–90; Joel Rast, *Remaking Chicago: The Political Origins of Urban Industrial Change* (DeKalb: Northern Illinois University Press, 1999).

3. Barry Bluestone and Bennett Harrison, *The Deindustrialization of America: Plant Closings, Community Abandonment, and the Dismantling of Basic Industries* (New York: Basic Books, 1982); Jefferson Cowie and Joseph Heathcott, eds., *Beyond the Ruins: The Meanings of Deindustrialization* (Ithaca, NY: Cornell University Press, 2003); Steven High, *Industrial Sunset: The Making of North America's Rust Belt, 1969–1984* (Toronto: University of Toronto Press, 2003).

4. Trimble, "Is Industry Fleeing."

5. Dan Egler, "Expert Hits Industry Shift to Suburbia," *Chicago Tribune*, October 5, 1972, N3. Proquest Historical Newspapers.

6. Trimble, "Is Industry Fleeing," 15, 88.

7. Dominic Pacyga, *Chicago: A Biography* (Chicago: University of Chicago Press 2009); Dominic Pacyga, *Slaughterhouse: Chicago's Union Stock Yard and the World It Made* (Chicago: University of Chicago Press, 2015); David Bensman and Roberta Lynch, *Rusted Dreams: Hard Times in a Steel Community* (New York: McGraw-Hill, 1987); Rast, *Remaking Chicago*.

8. Barry Bluestone, foreword to Cowie and Heathcott, *Beyond the Ruins*, viii.

9. But even in "successful" cities such as Chicago, the impact of these changes was uneven. For an early statement about this, see Brian Berry, "Islands of Renewal in Seas of Decay," in *The New Urban Reality*, ed. Paul E. Peterson (Washington, DC: Brookings Institution, 1985), 69–96.

10. John Cumbler, *A Social History of Economic Decline: Business, Politics and Work in Trenton* (New Brunswick, NJ: Rutgers University Press, 1989); Philip Scranton, *Figured Tapestry: Production, Markets and Power in Philadelphia Textiles, 1885–1941* (New York: Cambridge University Press, 1989); Domenic Vitiello, *Engineering Philadelphia: The Sellers Family and the Industrial Metropolis* (Ithaca, NY: Cornell University Press, 2013); Domenic Vitiello, "Machine Building and City Building: Urban Planning and Industrial Restructuring in Philadelphia, 1894–1928," *Journal of Urban History* 34 (2008): 399–434.

11. See the case studies of industrial suburbanization in various US and Canadian metropolitan areas before 1950 in Robert Lewis, ed., *Manufacturing Suburbs: Building Work and Home on the Metropolitan Fringe* (Philadelphia: Temple University Press, 2004).

12. Paul Clark, Irwin Marcus, Carl Meyerhuber, Charles McCollester, Mark McColloch, James Toth, Joe Gowaskie, and David Bensman, "Deindustrialization: A Panel Discussion," *Pennsylvania History* 16 (1991): 181–211; Jefferson Cowie, *Capital Moves: RCA's 70-Year Quest for Cheap Labor* (Ithaca, NY: Cornell University Press, 1999); Cowie and Heathcott, *Beyond the Ruins*; Cumbler, *Social History of Economic Decline*; High, *Industrial Sunset*.

13. Howard Wial, *Locating Chicago Manufacturing: The Geography of Production in Metropolitan Chicago* (Chicago: University of Illinois at Chicago, Center for Urban Economic Development, 2013).

14. Anne Markusen, Peter Hall, Scott Campbell, and Sabrina Deitrick, *The Rise of the Gunbelt: The Military Remapping of Industrial America* (New York: Oxford University Press, 1991).

15. Clark et al., "Deindustrialization," 207.

16. Wial, *Locating Chicago Manufacturing*.

17. Joel Rast, "Regime Building, Institution Building: Urban Renewal Policy in Chicago, 1946–1962," *Journal of Urban Affairs* 32 (2009): 173–94.

18. For recent overviews, see Eric Avila and Mark Rose, "Race, Culture, Politics, and Urban Renewal," *Journal of Urban History* 35 (2009): 335–47; Samuel Zipp, "The Roots and Routes of Urban Renewal," *Journal of Urban History*, 39 (2013): 366–91; Samuel Zipp and Michael Carriere, "Introduction: Thinking through Urban Renewal," *Journal of Urban History* 39 (2013): 359–65.

19. Hirsch, *Making the Second Ghetto*; Bennett et al., "Chicago North Loop Redevelopment Project"; Squires et al., *Chicago*; Robert Lewis, "Divided Space: Racial Transition Areas and Relocation, Chicago 1947–1960," in *Sharing Spaces: Essays in Honour of Sherry Olson*, ed. Robert C. H. Sweeny (Ottawa: Presses de l'Université d'Ottawa and the Museum of Canadian History, 2020), 17–39; Amanda Seligman, *Block by Block: Neighborhoods and Public Policy on Chicago's West Side* (Chicago: University of Chicago Press, 2005); Jeffrey Helgeson, *Crucibles of Black Empowerment: Chicago's Neighborhood Politics from the New Deal to Harold Washington* (Chicago: University of Chicago Press, 2014); Preston Smith II, *Racial Democracy and the Black Metropolis: Housing Policy in Postwar Chicago* (Minneapolis: University of Minnesota Press, 2012). Segregation remains extremely high in Chicago today. Marisa Novara and Amy Kahare, *Two Extremes of Residential Segregation: Chicago's Separate Worlds and Policy Strategies for Integration* (Boston: Joint Center of Housing Studies for Harvard University, 2017).

20. James Barret, *Work and Community in the Jungle: Chicago's Packinghouse Workers, 1894–1922* (Urbana-Champaign: University of Illinois Press, 1987); Lizabeth Cohen, *Making a New Deal: Industrial Workers in Chicago, 1919–1939* (Cambridge: Cambridge University Press, 1990).

21. Mark Gelfand, *A Nation of Cities: The Federal Government and Urban America, 1933–1965* (New York: Oxford University Press, 1975); Gail Radford, *The Rise of the Public Authority: Statebuilding and Economic Development in Twentieth-Century America* (Chicago: University of Chicago Press, 2013), 117–38; Roger Biles, *The Fate of Cities: Urban America and the Federal Government, 1945–2000* (Lawrence: University Press of Kansas, 2011).

22. Joseph Heathcott and Máire Agnes Murphy, "Corridors of Flight, Zones of Renewal: Industry, Planning and Policy in the Making of Metropolitan St. Louis, 1940–1980," *Journal of Urban History* 31 (2005): 151–89; Guian McKee, *The Problem of Jobs: Liberalism, Race and Deindustrialization in Philadelphia* (Chicago: University of Chicago Press, 2008). A selection of contemporary reports that were looking into industrial renewal includes Douglas Jackson, *Philadelphia Waterfront Industry: Industrial Land and Its Potential on the*

Delaware River (Philadelphia, 1955); Milwaukee Redevelopment Coordinating Committee, *Blight Elimination and Urban Redevelopment in Milwaukee* (Milwaukee: Redevelopment Coordinating Committee, 1948).

23. Mark Levine, "The Politics of Partnership: Urban Redevelopment since 1945," in *Unequal Partnerships: The Political Economy of Urban Redevelopment in Postwar America*, ed. Gregory D. Squires (New Brunswick, NJ: Rutgers University Press, 1989), 20. Also see Robert A. Beauregard, "Public-Private Partnerships as Historical Chameleons: The Case of the United States," in *Partnerships in Urban Governance: European and American Experience*, ed. Jon Pierre (Basingstoke: Macmillan, 1998), 61–64. For a discussion of recent economic developments, see Karen Mossberger and Gerry Stoker, "The Evolution of Urban Regime Theory, *Urban Affairs Review* 36 (2001): 810–35.

24. City of Chicago, Department of Development and Planning, *Industrial Chicago: Elements for Growth* (Chicago: Department of Development and Planning, September 1977), 10.

25. This would change from the 1970s, as local government became much more interventionalist and created a wide set of tools and practices to encourage economic development.

26. The key documents that link industrial redevelopment with property are Chicago Plan Commission (hereafter CPC), *Redevelopment for Industry: Statement on the Clearance of Blighted Areas for Industrial Use* (Chicago: CPC, 1951); CPC, *Chicago Industrial Development. . . . Recent Trends* (Chicago: CPC, 1951); CPC, *Chicago Industrial Study: Summary Report* (Chicago: CPC, 1952); Mayor's Committee for Economic and Cultural Development (hereafter CECD), *Mid-Chicago Economic Development Study: Volume I; Policies and Programs Prepared for the Economic Development of Mid-Chicago* (Chicago: CECD, 1966); CECD, *A Partnership for Action: Mid-Chicago Economic Development Project* (Chicago: CECD, 1970); Chicago Land Clearance Commission, "Analysis and Recommendations on the Blighted Areas Bounded by Polk Street, Roosevelt Road, Canal Street and the Proposed South Route of the Expressway System, Proposed Redevelopment Project No. 3," typescript, February 19, 1951 (Chicago: Chicago Land Clearance Commission).

27. Wendell Pritchett, "The 'Public Menace' of Blight: Urban Renewal and the Private Uses of Eminent Domain," *Yale Law and Policy Review* 21 (2003): 5.

28. City of Chicago, *Industrial Chicago*, 10.

29. Colin Gordon, "Blighting the Way: Urban Renewal, Economic Development, and the Elusive Definition of Blight," *Fordham Urban Law Journal* 31 (2004): 305–34; Heathcott and Murphy, "Corridors of Flight"; Marc A. Weiss, "The Origins and Legacy of Urban Renewal" in *Urban and Regional Planning in an Age of Austerity*, ed. Pierre Clavel, John Forester, and William Goldsmith (New York: Pergamon, 1980), 53–80; Marc Weiss, *The Rise of the Community Builders: The American Real Estate Industry and Urban Land Planning* (New York: Columbia University Press, 1987).

30. Rachel Weber, *From Boom to Bubble: How Finance Built the New Chicago* (Chicago: University of Chicago Press, 2015); Larry Bennett, *The Third City: Chicago and American Urbanism* (Chicago: University of Chicago Press, 2010). Also see Rast, *Remaking Chicago*; Squires et al., *Chicago*; Pacyga, *Chicago*.

31. Bennett et al., "Chicago North Loop Redevelopment Project," 187.

32. Heathcott and Murphy, "Corridors of Flight"; McKee, *Problem of Jobs*. For the New York City case, see Urban Associates of Chicago, *A Report to the Department of Urban Renewal / City of Chicago on an Evaluation of Industrial Centers in Urban Renewal Areas* (Chicago: Urban Associates of Chicago, 1975). The same was also true for the United Kingdom. Alistair Kefford, "Disruption, Destruction and the Creation of the 'Inner Cities': The Impact of Urban Renewal on Industry, 1945–1980," *Urban History* 44 (2017): 492–515.

33. Urban Associates of Chicago, "Report to the Department of Urban Renewal," 6.

34. Urban Associates of Chicago, 5.

35. The first significant piece of legislation to deal with manpower issues focused on the training of workers in the face of technological change and automation. Gladys Kremen, "MTDA: The Origins of the Manpower and Training Development Act of 1962," US Department of Labor, accessed March 16, 2020, https://www.dol.gov/general/aboutdol /history/mono-mdtatext; CECD, *Job Accessibility for the Unemployed: An Analysis of Public Transportation in Chicago* (Chicago: CECD, 1972).

36. John F. McDonald, "An Economic Analysis of Industrial Revenue Bonds and the Demand for Labor," *Annals of Regional Science* 18 (1984): 39–50; Thomas Moore and Gregory D. Squires, "Public Policy and Private Benefits: The Case of Industrial Revenue Bonds," in *Business Elites and Urban Development: Case Studies and Critical Perspectives*, ed. Scott Cummings (Albany: State University of New York Press, 1988), 97–117; Giloth and Betancur, "Where Downtown Meets Neighborhoods," 107–8. Despite the extensive use of these bonds, the city lost almost one hundred thousand manufacturing jobs between 1978 and 1987. A 1984 study by the Chicago Department of Economic Development of the 101 projects funded between 1977 and June 1984 found that the number of jobs in the funded firms dropped by 14 percent, with almost half the firms losing jobs, and more than 80 percent of firms failing to meet their proposed targets.

37. Joseph Heathcott, "A City Quietly Remade: National Programs and Local Agendas in the Movement to Clear the Slums, 1942–1952," *Journal of Urban History* 34 (2008): 222.

APPENDIX

1. Nick Poulos, "Chicago Area Far in U.S. Lead on Industry Contracts," *Chicago Tribune*, June 17, 1962, A1, Proquest Historical Newspapers (hereafter PHN); Chicago Association of Commerce and Industry, *Manpower Survey, 1956, Metropolitan Area* (Chicago: Chicago Association of Commerce and Industry, 1957).

2. Chicago Plan Commission (hereafter CPC), *Redevelopment for Industry: Statement on the Clearance of Blighted Areas for Industrial Use* (Chicago: CPC, 1951); CPC, *Chicago Industrial Development. . . . Recent Trends* (Chicago: CPC, 1951); CPC, *Chicago Industrial Study: Summary Report* (Chicago: CPC, 1952).

3. Some examples are Commonwealth Edison Company, *Survey of Industrial Development 1946* (Chicago: Commonwealth Edison Company, 1947); Commonwealth Edison Company, *Industrial Expansion, 1945–1952* (Chicago: Commonwealth Edison Company, 1952); Commonwealth Edison Company, *Industrial Development during 1963* (Chicago: Commonwealth Edison Company, September 1964).

4. Writers also compared the city's industrial development with other cities. In their attempts to place Chicago in the best light, they frequently ignored the divergent realities of the city's decline and the rapid growth of Sunbelt metropolitan areas such as Los Angeles and Houston.

5. The *Engineering News-Record* dates from 1874. It is the leading construction magazine for large-scale projects, including factories, public and private infrastructures, highrise office and residential buildings, and sport arenas. Commonwealth Edison obtained the material for its published summaries from the magazine.

6. I undertook keyword searches of all firms collected from the *Engineering News-Record* to see whether the projects were completed.

7. The large attrition rate points to the questionable numbers posted by the Chicago Plan Commission and Commonwealth Edison. As far as I can tell, these organizations did not verify that the projects listed in the *News-Record* were actually completed. The result is an inflated number of construction projects in their summaries.

8. "Candy Firm Plans Plant in Chicago Area," *Chicago Tribune*, February 4, 1950, A5, PHN.

9. "National Video, Tube Maker, Buys a Factory in Grayslake," *Chicago Tribune*, June 5, 1951, B8, PHN; "Real Estate News," *Chicago Tribune*, November 8, 1952, PHN.

10. Many small construction projects are missing from the *News-Record*. Some projects valued at less than $100,000 were listed for the 1945–51 period. After that date, few were. Despite the presence of some small projects, it is safe to assume that most small construction projects were not included in the listing. Nick Lombardo helped me think through this problem with the data in the magazine.

11. This must have been the case with factories built by the privately owned planned industrial districts, such as the Central Manufacturing and Clearing districts. In these cases, the architectural, engineering, and construction expertise was in-house. There was little need to advertise the construction project in the *News-Record* listings. More is said about industrial districts in chapter 7.

12. For a similar situation in a different area of the city's postwar history, see the discussion of the Chicago Housing Authority records by D. Bradford Hunt in *Blueprint for Disaster: The Unraveling of Chicago Public Housing* (Chicago: University of Chicago Press, 2009), 301–2.

13. These records are held at the University of Illinois, Chicago, which is also home to other important archival collections such as those of the Chicago Urban League. The Metropolitan Housing and Planning Council records, of course, have been the basis for some of the most important urban histories of Chicago, such as Arnold Hirsch, *Making the Second Ghetto: Race and Housing in Chicago, 1940–1960* (Chicago: University of Chicago Press, 1983). The other main repositories for industrial history in Chicago are to be found at the Chicago History Museum; Special Collections, the University of Chicago; and Special Collections, the Harold Washington Library Center, although the collections are rather thin outside of a few areas.

14. All the studies of Chicago's urban history have labored under the same weightlessness of documentation. The fact that such rich industrial and planning histories have been written by Brad Hunt, Arnold Hirsch, Dominic Pacyga, and Amanda Seligman, among others, is a testament to the abilities of these scholars to wring water out of a stone.

Index

A. B. Dick Company, 34
Abbott Drug, 39
Abbott Laboratories, 63
Acme Aluminum Foundry, 45
Acme Steel Goods, 28–29, 30
Adams, Harry, 32
Advance Transformer, 56
African Americans, 49, 59, 70, 84, 100, 165; residential districts, 4, 67, 190–91; South Side population, 69, 98–99, 107, 113, 221n11; West Central population, 123, 232n78
aircraft industry, 25–26
Akron (OH), 27, 188, 230n23
American Colortype, 63
American Industrial Development Council, 65
American Institute of Real Estate Appraisers, 35
American Society of Planning Officials, 79, 106, 117, 203
Anderson, R. W., 89
annexation, 21, 211n15, 214n53
Area Redevelopment Administration, 239n36
Argiris, Van C., 171–72, 239n43
Argonne National Laboratory, 147, 148
Armour and Co., 31
Arthur Rubloff and Co., 34, 239n43
Arvey Corporation, 170
Aschman, Frederick, 91
Ashland Industrial Center, 17–18, 175, 176, 178, 179
Atlantic Brass, 109
Atomic Energy Commission (AEC), 148–50, 156, 235n44
Ator, Joseph, 169
Automatic Electric Co., 34, 52, 56
Avery, Guy, 29
Avon Products, 34
Ayers, Thomas, 158

Babcock, Richard, 108
Bach, Ira, 112, 116, 121, 135, 195; West Central redevelopment and, 81, 117, 123, 130
Back of the Yards, 32
Back of the Yards Neighborhood Council, 155, 166

Ballert, Albert, 225n8
banks, 57–59, 63, 139
Bartlett, Raymond, 51
Beauregard, Robert, 205n8
Bell and Howell, 34
Bennett, Keith, 137
Bennett, Larry, 4, 195
Bennett and Kahnweiler, 36, 160, 180
Berg, Walter, 58
Berkman, Else, 117
Berman v. Parker, 14, 86
Berry, Brian, 5
Bettman, Alfred, 107
Big Three packers. *See* meatpacking industry
black population. *See* African Americans
Blessing, Charles, 91
blight, 195, 196, 198; CLCC's views of, 113, 122, 127, 156; debates and solutions to, 70–73, 114; definitions of, 81, 85, 94, 115; government intervention, 74–77, 114, 119; impact on housing market, 68; link to industrial decline, 17, 64, 80, 95; numerical analysis of, 82–83, 224n69; problems of, 66, 70, 74, 83, 92, 95; residential *v.* industrial, 79, 81, 88; social-ecological ideas of, 81–82, 99; urban renewal and, 10, 12, 36, 66, 69, 85, 223n47. *See also* blighted land
Blighted Areas Redevelopment Act (1947), 76–77, 84, 93, 114, 117–18, 223n47; amendments to, 86–87, 115, 121–22
blighted land: arguments for redevelopment of, 17, 79–84, 165, 223n55; CLCC's expropriation of, 84–85, 117–19, 123–24; court decisions and, 84–88, 121–22; CPC's reports on, 90–97; extent and location of, 67–70, 221n19; private redevelopment of, 14, 74–77, 192–93; residential redevelopment of, 65–66, 105; SSBP's redevelopment plan, 98–105
Blucher, Walter, 106
Bluestone, Barry, 5, 7, 26, 38, 185, 189
Bodine Electric Company, 17, 89–90, 106, 107–11, 178, 228n77
Bohannon Industrial Park, 171
Boley, Robert, 161, 162